SINGING MY WAY TO SOMEWHERE LAND

Also by Alan Workman:

Singing My Way to Somewhere Land

A Journey from Shipyard Apprentice to Opera Singer

Alan Workman

UNITED WRITERS
Cornwall

UNITED WRITERS PUBLICATIONS LTD
Ailsa, Castle Gate, Penzance, Cornwall.
www.unitedwriters.co.uk

British Library Cataloguing in Publication Data:
A catalogue record for this book is
available from the British Library.

ISBN 9781852001759

Printed and bound in Great Britain by
United Writers Publications Ltd.,
Cornwall.

Author's Motto:

Your birthright is *YOU!*
Your creativity, *your* intelligence,
your energy are *YOU!*
What you *make* of that birthright
is entirely up to *YOU!*

We all have a life; a personal adventure.
This is the story of mine.

Contents

1
First Years

1929

I was born on the 20th of July at 144 Marsh Street, Barrow-in-Furness, Lancashire, the third child, and first boy, of a fairly typical working class family of the period.

My father Alexander, who'd served as a soldier through the First World War, was a shipyard worker – at least whenever work was available, which apparently wasn't all that often in those difficult years after the war. My mother, Rose Annie, was a hard-working, driving force of a housewife whose energy and determination undoubtedly kept the family going. This was no mean task in those very lean times, when all the major industries were winding down their huge wartime output and laying off most of their workforce, just as thousands of servicemen were returning to civilian life looking for largely non-existent jobs.

Barrow-in-Furness lies on the end of the Furness peninsula which juts out into the Irish Sea, and was famous for its shipbuilding, iron ore mines, and a steelworks which was renowned for developing the famous Bessemer Process, which produced the highest quality steel in the world.

Yet despite all this industry, Barrow was set in one of the most beautiful areas of England. Right on the doorstep of the Lake District, the mountains of which formed a rugged backdrop view across the Duddon Estuary, it was surrounded by rolling countryside and mature woodland. Lovely sandy beaches lay in every direction; Walney Island, Rampside and Morecambe Bay. The entry to the town itself was down a long avenue of mature trees, which usually came as a great surprise to visitors.

On the map, in those days, the Furness Peninsula was in Lancashire. However, due to later boundary changes (after I'd left, mind you) the Furness Peninsula became part of the new county of Cumbria. This being created by amalgamating the two ancient counties of Cumberland and Westmorland into one, under the new name of Cumbria; 'annexing' my Furness Peninsula in the process.

When I first heard about this change I was living in London studying singing, and thought it was a bit of a liberty; feeling somewhat like a stateless person who'd had the door slammed behind him with a stern: "And don't come back. . ." However, when I learned that there was nothing personal in it, and that they were quite happy to let me back in again – occasionally – I learned to live with it!

The year of my birth turned out to be a pretty traumatic one for the whole world as, apart from my birth, it was the year of the great 'Wall Street Crash' in America – which they could hardly blame me for – when the world stock markets collapsed, sparking off the great depression of the nineteen thirties.

OTHER FAMOUS EVENTS OF 1929 INCLUDED:
(1) Admiral Byrd made the first flight over the South Pole.
(2) The German airship Graf Zeppelin circumnavigated the Earth in 21 days and seven hours.
(3) The BBC began the world's first experimental television programmes.
(4) Segrave broke the world land speed record at 231mph.
(5) J.B. Priestley wrote *The Good Companions*.

1930 (1 year old in July)
My memory holds no images of this year (I can't think why, since I must have been there at the time). However, I do have a photograph of myself with my maternal grandmother and my older sister Jean, taken against the old whitewashed brick wall in the back yard of 144.

SOME MAJOR EVENTS OF THE YEAR:
(1) The Channel Tunnel Scheme rejected by the Government.
(2) The British airship R101 destroyed on a flight to India – Britain abandons airship manufacture.
(3) Segrave killed on Lake Windermere at 100mph.
(4) The planet Pluto discovered by Clive Tombaugh – predicted by Lowell.
(5) The BBC Symphony Orchestra & Youth Hostels were founded.

1931 (2 years old)

My sister Joyce was born on 10th June at 144 Marsh Street. Still no memory of this (my bad memory does not bode well for my future).

SOME MAJOR EVENTS OF THE YEAR:
(1) Severe earthquake tremors in London.
(2) The Empire State Building erected in New York – 1,250ft high with 20 storeys.
(3) Whipsnade Zoo opened.
(4) The first ever BBC outside broadcast – the finish of the Derby.
(5) The first appearance of Walt Disney's Mickey Mouse.
(6) The first London trolley bus ran.

1932 (3years old)

Apart from a vague recollection of my father giving me a water pistol while I was standing beside my sister Joyce's pram in the back yard, the rest of the year seems to have passed me unnoticed. However, receiving your first water pistol is undoubtedly such a momentous event that it probably blotted out everything else that occurred during 1932.

SOME MAJOR EVENTS OF THE YEAR:
(1) Great unemployed hunger marches on London.
(2) Oswald Mosley forms the British Fascist Party.
(3) The first Oxford English Dictionary published (formerly Murray's).
(4) Sydney Harbour Bridge, and new Lambeth Bridge in London, opened.
(5) Damon Runyon writes Guys & Dolls as a short story.

1933 (4 years old)

I started school at Greengate Infants. Strangely enough I actually do remember something of this – perhaps my memory store's beginning to flicker into life after all. I recall quite clearly my mother taking me to the school on that first day and handing me over. After that things seem to have got somewhat confused. Apparently about a week later my mother received a note from the headmistress asking her where I was.

"He's at school," replied my mother, somewhat bewildered.

"No he isn't," came the reply.

"Of course he is," declared my mother, "he goes off every day."

"Well, he doesn't come here," insisted the headmistress. "We haven't seen him since the first day you brought him."

Later that day, when I finally arrived home, my mother confronted me with the mystery.

11

"You didn't go to school," she accused.

"Yes I did," I declared. "I went that day with you."

"But you're supposed to go every day," she declared.

"Well, nobody told me that!" I replied.

And that was pretty well the pattern of life for me in those early years. I did go to school, of course, now I'd got the hang of it, and quite enjoyed it. I was also, apparently, a good pupil. Outside of school, however, was different. I obviously had my own view of what life was all about. The world around seemed an exciting place and needed exploring, so that's what I did.

Nobody ever knew where I was; including myself, for most of the time.

According to my mother I'd go off first thing in the morning, and turn up again around tea time, starving hungry and wacked out. I was constantly being brought back home by strangers, who'd discovered me wandering about in my unexplored wilderness miles away from Barrow. I have vague memories of scenes such as journeying back to civilisation on the crossbar of someone's bike or the occasional rattling old car trip, after questions such as: "Where the devil have you come from?" How they ever discovered the answer to this I can't imagine, since it was no use asking me such exacting questions as I hadn't a clue. On one of my expeditions I must have persuaded Tommy Arts, one of my more gullible pals, to take a trip around the world with me, because I have a vivid memory of us flagging down an old furniture van on some remote country road. Fortunately, the driver was on his way to Barrow and drove us home, having to keep stopping en route to enquire if anybody knew who the devil we were, and where we lived.

One particularly satisfying expedition I remember, was a solo trip when I ended up sitting by a blazing fire in some farm cottage eating toast and strawberry jam. For some reason they seemed to have an idea where I belonged, and after I'd been sufficiently fed, they managed to take me home – though I can't remember how.

SOME MAJOR EVENTS OF THE YEAR:

(1) Hitler was appointed Chancellor of Germany. The burning of the Reichstag in Berlin.

(2) Influenza virus was first discovered.

(3) Prohibition ended in the USA.

(4) James Hilton wrote *Lost Horizon*.

(5) Polythene discovered.

(6) Existence of the 'Neutrino' proposed by Pauli.

(7) Richard Strauss wrote *Arabella*.

1934 (5 years old in July)

Well settled into the infant school by now, and obviously enjoying it. I remember we grew some huge sunflowers outside our classroom window which always reminded me of *Jack and the Beanstalk*. Once a week the headmistress (I can't remember her name, unfortunately) would come into our classroom to tell us all a story, which she was obviously making up as she went along. It was a very simple tale about a steam train rattling along a track through the countryside, whilst at the same time a man in an aeroplane was flying along above watching it from the air. This pilot described all the smoke bellowing across the fields from the engine's chimney, and how the train kept disappearing into tunnels. I found this absolutely magic, and feel sure that this was probably the first early trigger that awakened my innate story-writing desire, something which has been with me ever since.

The only other incident that comes floating back to me from that time involves something that causes great concern in schools at the moment; bullies. Bullying, in schools and elsewhere, has undoubtedly been going on since the dawn of human history. It certainly existed in my school days, though because school children were so much younger then – the vast majority of them having to leave school at 14 years of age and go out into the real world to earn their living – the consequences were far less serious. The infant school in Greengate Street was no exception; we had our school bully. He was a lad a lot bigger than the rest of us, and used to go about pushing the other kids around. Fortunately, for some reason, he never seemed to bother me; until, one day he obviously decided it was my turn, and started pushing me. Naturally I didn't take too kindly to this, and pushed him back somewhat harder than he'd pushed me, with the result that he was sent flat on his back. This shook him so much that he scrambled up and ran off crying, much to the delight of all the other kids.The positive side of this being that he never attempted to push any other kid around again.

SOME MAJOR EVENTS OF THE YEAR:

(1) Hitler's purge on Munich, the infamous 'Night of the Long Knives'.

(2) The famous Dionne Quintuplets born in Canada.

(3) Polio vaccine discovered.

(4) W. Beebe descends half mile deep in his Ocean Bathysphere.

1935 (6 years old in July)

This was the year of the Silver Jubilee of George V, and I remember we had colourful, noisy parties in the streets and in the school. These particularly stand out as they were the first celebrations of this kind that we kids had ever experienced. One strong memory I have of this event concerns the fact that all the kids in school were given specially decorated commemorative mugs. All the kids except me, that is. When it came to my turn I was told that they'd run out, but not to worry as they'd get me one later – I'm still waiting. Perhaps mine got broken, or lost, or misappropriated by someone who decided they'd like two. However, since it was my first object lesson on the folly of always blindly trusting other people's promises, perhaps I did get something out of it. Just a thought, though, if anybody reading this comes across someone who happens to have 'two' Jubilee Mugs on their mantelpiece; just ask them how this came about. If they go a bit red in the face, then we'll all know.

Another thing that comes to mind about the infant school, was the fact that they had a music class with some sort of kids' band playing recorders, cymbals etc. I used to hear them sometimes practicing from outside the hall window. How the kids were selected for this I don't now, but the offer never came my way. I did meet one of these lucky musicians on my way home from school once. He was carrying his recorder, so I asked him to give me a go, which he did. After blowing furiously into one end of it for a couple of minutes, however, I was not too impressed with what came out of the other. So all interest in my becoming an orchestral virtuoso disappeared forever in that back street near the Greengate Infant School.

Our house in Marsh Street, like all the other houses in the street, had only one fire. This was in the living room, which 'we' called the 'kitchen', the small room where all the 'cooking' was done we called the 'back kitchen'. The fireplace was set in the middle of a big cast iron range, which had an oven on one side, a tank with a lid on the other side to give hot water, and a high mantelpiece right over the top. It was, in fact, the most dominating and impressive feature of the living room/kitchen. Its only drawback, however, was that it was a shiny black colour, and needed regular polishing with a stuff called black-lead to keep it looking as smart as the house-proud housewives of Marsh Street demanded.

This blacklead holds something of a painful memory for me, because of the day my mother sent me to the shop to get some, with the strict injunction to get back with it quickly as she was waiting for it. I remember running off to the shop obediently and setting off back home with it. It is at that point things started to take a turn for the worse. I found the mysterious little black packet rather intriguing. So I shook it a bit, then squeezed it to see what it felt like. As this was rather inconclusive, I banged it against a brick wall. This did the trick and some of the black smudgy stuff inside started to ooze out, making a great black splodge on the bricks. I found this absolutely fascinating so tried a bit more, which made an even bigger splodge on the wall. A third attempt, however, went a bit wrong, for the whole packet had split open, covering both wall and me. I tried to rub it off, but this only seemed to spread it more and more until I was all black smudge from head to foot. By this time I decided that I'd better get this horrible stuff back to Mam as quickly as I could, so ran the rest of the way, and handed over what was left of the grotty, tattered packet. I can't remember exactly what she said, but I do remember the clip on the ear that accompanied it – that is the painful bit of the memory.

In those days there was a small Methodist chapel halfway up Ramsden Street, which was just around the corner from Marsh Street. For some reason Mam used to send me there each week to Sunday School. I'm not sure why, because I don't remember her ever going to church herself. Probably, like many mothers of the time struggling to bring up kids, she was trying to make sure I at least got off to a good start with God, even if with nobody else.

I used to trot off there on my own each Sunday morning rather reluctantly, as I couldn't quite understand what it was all about. One Sunday morning, however, finally brought down the curtain on these early religious experiences of mine. This concerned a pair of old pants I had on, or I should say half on. The kids in Marsh Street were obviously never what could be called natty dressers, and I was certainly no exception. Mam had to clothe us in any old hand-me-downs she could get hold of, and modify to fit us; or almost – I remember once that I had a thick, purple overcoat which I was rather proud of, because it was 'different' and you certainly couldn't go unnoticed with that on. However, on the Sunday morning in question, I was wearing an old long, black, rubbery sort of raincoat, despite the fact that it was a blisteringly hot day. People kept approaching me with the concerned question:

"Wouldn't you like to take that heavy coat off. You look as if you're boiling away?"

To which my answer was always a definite:

"No!"

All through the Sunday School service I successfully resisted their ever more bewildered suggestions. Finally escaping at the end of the service, out into the street in my raincoat, feeling like a boiled pudding, but with my honour intact and the secret of my tattered pants with the backside hanging out (something I hadn't yet told my mother about) intact.

SOME MAJOR EVENTS OF THE YEAR:

(1) Gershwin wrote *Porgy and Bess*.
(2) Lawrence of Arabia (when known later as Aircraftman Shaw) was killed on his motorbike in England.
(3) Malcolm Campbell set a new world land speed record of 301.7mph.
(4) Sir Robert Watson-Watt invented Radio Pulse Echo Detection, which led to five Radar Stations being set up.
(5) The first Pedestrian Crossings, and the 30mph speed limit introduced.
(6) The first British 'National Park' set up – Snowdonia in Wales.

1936 (7 years old in July)

I moved up to Greengate Boys' School – which was just next door to the Infant School. Suddenly we were separated from the girls into an all male society, which somehow seemed a step towards growing up, though I doubt if most of us knew why. However, because I had four sisters by this time – my fourth sister Jill being born on 14th July this year – I probably had a bit more of an inkling than most of the other lads.

Although the Second World War was still three years in the future, I had an experience in this year which was an ominous taste of what that future had in store. I was out in our narrow back street on my own, trying to climb the towering heights of the Corporation Yard wall – this wall formed the opposite side of our narrow back street, and always seemed like a great cliff to us kids. However, because of the cracks between the bricks, it offered an endless challenge to our mountaineering skills. And on this day I was about halfway to the summit, when I suddenly became aware of an enormous silvery object floating gently by overhead. It seemed to fill half of the sky, and I was so astonished that I quickly jumped down off the wall and stood gaping up at it in amazement. I'd never seen anything like it before, and just watched in bewilderment as it slowly floated across the sky to disappear behind the houses.

I was told later that this was the German airship Hindenburg, which was supposed to be on a friendly flight over England. But when it was seen to be taking photographs of the shipyard and docks, suspicions were obviously aroused about its true mission. These suspicions were amply confirmed in 1941 when the bombing runs of German aircraft over Barrow closely followed the paths that the Hindenburg had taken.

Dad seemed to be out of work a lot during these years (like most other men), and used to spend a great deal of time going for long walks. By this time he'd started taking me with him. He always walked quickly, and I remember trotting along beside him like a tireless dog.

16

We'd go rambling off for miles through the countryside; beachcombing on Walney Island, Rampside and the Coast Road along Morecambe Bay etc. Often we'd go inland on a circular trek via the great 800 year old Cistercian ruin of Furness Abbey, set deep in the silence of its Valley of the Deadly Nightshade. Then on past the great red gash in the hillside – caused many years earlier by the collapse of the iron ore tunnels deep underneath. Then we'd follow the narrow winding country road to Yariside, onto Roose, and finally down the long Roose Road to Salthouse, and home to Marsh Street.

In those lean times street vendors trying to scratch a living were quite a common sight. These would sometimes be pushing an old cart or carrying a basket, and you could hear them shouting out their wares long before they actually appeared round the corner into Marsh Street. One particular old chap I remember, used to come clumping down the middle of the road in clogs. He wore a battered old cap and jacket and had a large wicker basket slung around his neck. This seemed to bump on one of his legs with each step, making him walk with a slight limp. As he walked he was constantly sorting out whatever it was in the basket, and shouting out some weird call which to me sounded something like:

"Post yer knee. . ! Post yer knee. . !"

As a seven year old I always found this pretty baffling, as he was selling watercress. . . And why would anyone want their knee 'posted' anyway?

At one time we had a knife grinder knocking on the door. His grinding wheel was mounted on some sort of cart, and was worked by a pedal with his foot. Mam must have felt sorry for him, as she sorted out a couple of knives for him to sharpen. Unfortunately, he was somewhat heavy handed, sending great showers of sparks hurtling in every direction. To me this was absolutely magical. Mam, however, was not too impressed, because he'd virtually ground away two of her best knives.

Street musicians also appeared in the street from time to time. I remember at least one organ grinder filling the street with romantic Italian music; though I don't think he had a monkey. Strolling vagabonds would occasionally wander through the street singing their hearts out. Some of these were actually quite good, with voices that could have rattled the slates off the roofs.

One image I have that sticks in my mind from this time is of a Lipton's Tea van with solid rubber tyres standing outside Annie Booth's shop. Another is of the corporation horse-drawn dustcarts going down the backstreets, with the dustmen literally covered in dust

17

– raking all the ash and rubbish out through the midden doors, which every house had in their backyard wall, into metal buckets, and tipping it into the dustcart.

SOME MAJOR EVENTS OF THE YEAR:
(1) The Spanish Civil War started.
(2) Germany re-occupied the Rhineland (unopposed).
(3) Margaret Mitchell wrote *Gone With the Wind*.
(4) The notorious Berlin Olympic Games took place.
(5) The Crystal Palace in London burned down.
(6) The maiden voyage of the *Queen Mary*.

1937 (8 years old in July)

Apart from my own solo wanderings, or with my mates in Marsh Street, we also went out on picnics etc., as a family. We always walked everywhere, as most people did in those days, and forever seemed to be pushing a pram with the latest addition to the family tucked up inside. Sometimes we'd trek to the Irish Sea beaches of Biggar Bank with its large, open air swimming baths and paddling pool on Walney Island, where I remember rolling our dyed boiled eggs down the grassy slopes during the Easter holidays; or further along the Island to South Shore. Occasionally we'd trek out to the beaches along the Coast Road of Morecambe Bay, but mostly we'd plod away out past the Salthouse paper mills and gasworks, then down the rough, cinder footpath that ran right alongside the railway track all the way out to our favourite beach, below the gorse-covered, sandy cliffs of Rampside.

Pushing the pram on that rutted cinder footpath was a nightmare, since it was always heavily loaded with all our food and camping provisions, as well as the baby. These would mostly be packed down in the bottom compartment which those old fashioned prams seemed to have.

Looking back now, from these days of health and safety, this regular expedition of ours always amazes me, because in those days the trains to Rampside were still running, and whenever a train came along we'd all simply scramble up the railway embankment to safety. Clinging on to the fence, and leaving the pram parked right alongside the track – minus the baby, of course – to fend for itself. This it always seemed to manage, and simply stood there fluttering and shaking in the blast of wind as the great clattering monster thundered past barely inches away from it.

On arrival at our usual spot under the sand hills, we'd pitch our home made tent – which Mam had sewn together – on a narrow strip of grass alongside the beach. And that would be our adventure base camp for the rest of the day.

We always seemed to have lots of good solid food with us to keep our healthy appetites satisfied. And the one thing I particularly remember about our Rampside expeditions, is Mam's individual home-made meat and potato pies. She'd bake them on saucers, one for each for us kids; while she and Dad would have slightly larger pies on plates. Just at the end of the beach, where the railway line and road causeway stretched out across the sands to Roa Island, there always seemed to be a man selling hot water from a little wooden hut. We'd stagger down there with all our tea cans, and he'd fill them up for a few coppers. I can't imagine him ever making a fortune, but his business enterprise was always very welcome to us.

One of the main reasons for our going to Rampside so often, I suspect, was the fact that it had exceptionally productive winkle beds. Mam, with her keen eye on augmenting our pretty strained family budget, obviously saw the winkles as a means of adding a few coppers to it – a sort of combining pleasure with survival.

Once we were all settled onto our camping patch, she and Dad would set out across the wide expanse of wet sands, with a sack, towards the winkle beds; leaving us kids to get on with the serious business of rampaging adventures among the sand dunes, and watery explorations of the rock pools along the beach.

The winkle beds must have been some distance out, because to us Mam and Dad just seemed be disappear over the horizon. Some two hours or so later they'd come staggering back, dragging the full sack of winkles behind them.

After more food and adventures, we'd eventually pack up the tent and scattered possessions, load all that we could onto the poor groaning old pram – together with the heavy bag of winkles – and set off on the long, weary trek back home down the railway line.

We kids were not only clapped out by this time, but for some reason always thirsty. I remember this particulary, because in those days there was an old farm at one point along the track with a well in a field. This was like an oasis in the desert to us. When we reached it, we kids would all scramble eagerly over the fence and run across to the well. The farmer always used to come out when he saw us coming. Then he'd draw up a shiny steel bucket of water for us on a rope. Pure nectar. No other water ever tasted quite so delicious to us kids as that did.

When we'd finally arrive back home in Marsh Street, the sack of winkles would be rattled into large pans and boiled on our old kitchen gas stove for what seemed hours; the pungent smell of boiling winkles permeating every corner of the house. It even wafted out into the street – which was probably a clever advertising ploy on Mam's part, because once cooked the winkles would be sold at the front door in small paper bags for a few coppers.

These winkle bonanzas were always memorable events in our street, partly because the winkles, being a popular delicacy with us kids, sold out very rapidly; and partly because for the next couple of days the pavements around Marsh Street would be absolutely smothered in crunchy empty winkle shells, which all the kids delighted in stamping on with their heavy boots.

SOME MAJOR EVENTS OF THE YEAR:

(1) The Duke of Windsor marries Mrs Simpson.

(2) Disney's *Snow White and the Seven Dwarfs* first screened.

(3) Boxer Joe Louis won the world heavyweight title.

(4) Billy Butlin opened his first holiday camp – Skegness.

(5) The first successful jet engine tested.

(6) The German Zeppelin 'Hindenburg' destroyed by fire in the USA.

2

Ice Cream & Bridges

1938 (9 years old in July)
My youngest sister Jacqueline was born on the 10th August this year,
bringing the final figure of our family to nine; Mam and Dad, Joan,
Jean, Alan (myself), Joyce, Colin, Jill, and Jacqueline. Which seems a
heck of a crowd, especially as 144, where we lived, was a small, three
bedroom terrace house (Coronation Street type).

What makes this even more astonishing, 'looking back', is that for
a long period of time at 144 we also had a paying lodger. His name was
Henry Dixon and he was probably in his early twenties. What he
actually did, how he came to be living with us in Barrow, or how we
all fitted into that tiny house, I've no idea. He comes across in my
memory as a sort of plodding, farm worker sort of chap, who kept
himself pretty much to himself. He must have been picking up various
odd jobs here and there, though, like all the other men had to in those
lean times. I do, however, remember that at one time he was trundling
around the streets with a donkey cart selling ice cream. To us kids this
seemed great, because he would come home for his dinner in the
middle of the day, leaving the donkey tied up at the front door where
we could stuff him up with all the kitchen scraps of bread etc., we
could lay hands on. Unfortunately, however, our dreams of stuffing
'ourselves' with lashings of free ice cream, were dashed when we
learned that he only came home for a meal when his ice cream tub was
empty. . . He was obviously no fool.

Ice cream, in those days, was always a special but 'rare' treat. Partly
because people had less money to spare, and partly because there was
less of it about, and what there was wasn't always that good. I

remember that there was a man in the next street, Dumfries Street, who used to make ice cream in his backyard shed. He would sell it pretty cheaply, but buying it wasn't always that easy because you'd often turn up at his back gate with your penny hot in your hand to be told:

"You'll have to come back later, it's not ready yet." This would often be repeated two or three times before finally it 'was' ready – or 'sort of'. Because, as often as not, something had gone slightly wrong in his advanced ice cream shed, and it would taste more like semi-frozen custard.

Though ice cream was usually a lot better than this, it still was pretty hit and miss stuff in Barrow. It wasn't until the 'Eldorado Ice Cream' firm started sending their three wheeled pedal carts around the street, that ice cream began to taste anything like we know it today.

Doorstep milk deliveries in those days – for those who could afford fresh milk, that is – were pretty basic. There were no such things as 'bottles' of milk, at least not in Marsh Street. The milkman came around each morning with a horse-drawn cart loaded with four or five ten gallon churns. If people wanted any they simply left a jug on their doorstep, and he'd dish it out with ladles straight from the churns into the jugs.

The milkman who served the Marsh Street area was Mr Caine, he had his dairy in the backyard of his house, just around the corner in Ramsden Street. The Ramsden Street houses were bigger than those in Marsh Street, so his backyard was just about large enough to house his dairy, stable his horse and squeeze in his cart.

We could never afford fresh milk, however; condensed milk in tins was the only milk we ever used on a daily basis. The only time I can remember fresh milk being brought into the house was when someone – Henry Dixon, I think – had been given some from somewhere.

The reason I knew Mr Caine the milkman, was because he was the uncle of one of my mates in Marsh Street, Walter Caine; whose family lived three doors up the street from us. Walt and I had been pals for as long as I can remember, and used to get about together, when he wasn't involved in family activities, that is. I remember they used to go off camping quite a bit, and also had an allotment over Greengate Hill somewhere, where the whole family spent a lot of their time. I remember him coming home one day describing how they'd had to cope with a plague of cabbage white butterfly caterpillars. Apparently the only way to save the cabbages from complete annihilation had been for all the family to spend hours picking off the juicy grubs and squashing them with their fingers. Something which rather took the gloss off any idyllic ideas I might have had about gardening.

One of the other lads who I knew only slightly, lived around the corner somewhere in Florence Street. I would often see him setting off away down to the far end of Marsh Street carrying a pint jug. I found this rather intriguing, so asked him one day what mysterious mission he was on. Was it a secret?

"No," he replied, somewhat disappointingly. "I'm doing a message for my grandma. She wants some cream."

Although a bit disappointing, this mission was still fairly intriguing, since 'real' cream was something I'd never come across before. Cream, to us, had always meant the evaporated milk we had on our pineapple chunks on Sundays.

"Can I come with you?" I asked.

"Alright," was his reply. So off we went.

This mysterious creamery turned out to be in the backyard of a house in some street just off the bottom end of Marsh Street. The lad handed his jug to a lady there and a few minutes later we were on our way back up Marsh Street, carefully carrying the now full jug.

"What does it look like?" I asked.

He held the jug over so I could have a look in.

"Mmm. . ! It looks nice," I remarked. "What's it taste like?"

"Really good!" he declared. "I sometimes dip my finger in."

"Really!" I said. "Can I have a try?"

"Alright," he agreed – he was obviously a fellow adventurer.

So I dipped my finger in and tasted my first ever real cream.

"Phew! Yeah! It's great," I declared, immediately deciding this was something which demanded further examination. "Can I have another dip?"

"Alright!" he agreed; as if pleased to have found a fellow connoisseur. "I'll have one too."

And so it went on all the way up Marsh Street, until by the time we reached his house in Florence Street, the cream in the jug was looking severely depleted. I never did find out how he explained this to his gran, or how much of a clip round the ear he got, but from 'my' point of view it was worth it.

For us kids in those days the streets and backstreets were our everyday playgrounds. This was due partly to the fact that they were right outside our doors and accessible, and partly because the lack of traffic in those days made them safe, wide open spaces where we could charge about, playing our games in safety.

The most popular game was football, which simply meant a rowdy kick-about with some old tennis ball and a couple of our pullovers on the ground to mark the goalposts. Football was always played in the front street simply because of its wide open space, whereas cricket, which was played with the same tennis ball and any old lump of wood that would serve as a bat, was confined to the narrower backstreets. This was because there were fewer windows at risk there from the wild slashes of the eager boundary wallopers; which put any pane of glass within fifty yards in dire peril.

Another street game we used to play was one that I feel was probably unique to Barrow; possibly only to Marsh Street, and we called it 'Bridges'. This could only be played during the dark evenings, because it was based on the shadows cast by the old street gas lamps. These lamps had a square, tapering box shape top, to hold the gas mantle, and when these were lit, the corner frames of the glass sides cast a long shadow diagonally across the street. And since the lamp posts were placed along both sides of the street in a staggered manner, these shadows cast a zig-zag pattern across the road all the way up the street.

These were our 'Bridges', and the road became a river which could only be crossed by a bridge. The game itself was a form of 'tig', or 'tag' in which one of us would be declared 'It'. This meant that they had to stand and count to ten, while the rest of us scattered up and down the street and across the bridges to escape being 'tigged'. After the count of ten, the one who was 'It' would come chasing after us trying to 'tig' (touch) one of the others. When they succeeded, the one who'd been tigged then became 'It', and so on. The only other rule was that anyone who stepped off a bridge into the river, was automatically disqualified, and made to take over the role of 'It' and do the chasing.

At some time in this year one of my particular pals was a lad I can only remember as Derek. He was a few years older than I was, and lived in the next street. How he had latched himself on to me I've no idea, but he was a bit of a madcap, and we got about a lot together. One occasion that sticks in my mind was when he and I were playing on the big swing in the park on our own. This could carry about six kids at a time, but if you got it swooping backwards and forwards fast enough when it was empty, you could set it banging against the iron stops each way like a great hammer. On this occasion Derek had it crashing against the stops like fury, but as it swung back towards him for the umpteenth time, he didn't catch the end properly and it caught him under the chin, catapulting him into the air to land in a crumpled heap about six feet away. I felt sure he must be dead (and I still don't know why he wasn't), but when he staggered to his feet he was howling his head off, and had a great cut under his chin with blood flowing everywhere.

I don't know how we got all the way back to Marsh Street, but when we did he was carted off to hospital to be sorted out. Derek, unfortunately, never seemed to be too lucky physically, because not too long after this park swing incident he died of diphtheria. Could it be that his madcap attitude was simply a way of cramming as much life as possible into the short span he'd been allotted?

Looking back on those times now it's quite surprising to realise how many dangerous diseases there must have been around; diseases which we hardly hear of today. Diphtheria was quite common, and often fatal. Tuberculosis was another scourge which adults talked about in whispers, and which, according to what little we kids could understand, few sufferers ever recovered from. There were also many ailments which some of the 'kids' suffered from, like measles, mumps, chicken-pox, tonsillitis, adenoids etc, which we hear very little about today.

I never seemed to get any of these ailments, fortunately. Though at the time I remember being a bit envious of those kids who could boast about having their tonsils or adenoids out, while I'd been denied these exciting experiences. My mother, at one stage apparently, asked the local doctor about this:

"Why does 'he' never get any of these ailments?" she asked.

"Because he's never indoors long enough to catch them," declared the doctor.

Which probably hit the nail on the head.

Going to the cinema in those days – or 'The Pictures', as we called them – usually meant for us kids the special Saturday morning children's shows. At 2p a time to get in we thought these were great. Real rowdy affairs with lots of pushing and shoving to fight your way in, then a mad scramble for the best seats once you got past the door attendant.

Once the films got under way, accompanied by the endless racket of kids shouting at the screen, or constantly running backwards and forwards to the loo, we would excitedly follow the adventure serials of such intrepid heroes as 'Jungle Jim' fighting off dangerous animals and cannibals. 'Tailspin Tommy' – battling the enemy in an ancient, First World War fighter plane, 'Flash Gordon' – always conquering the universe in his fiery space ship. Or 'Buck Jones' – galloping the range on his trusty horse, wearing a white stetson and great woolly 'chaps' on his legs. I always thought these chaps made him look far tougher than any of the scruffy unshaven outlaws he came up against.

Every week each of these dauntless heroes would end up in a situation of dire peril, only for the picture to be suddenly cut off with

25

b

blaring music and an anxious voice calling out: "Will he escape. . ? Has he finally met his doom. . ? Watch next week." Great groans of fear and frustration would burst out from the kids. But the ploy always worked, because these impending deadly perils our heroes were in would be a talking point for the rest of the week, and we could hardly wait for the next Saturday to find out what happened.

One of the important differences about Marsh Street in those days, was that it had small corner shops – like many other streets in the town. There was a Butcher's Shop on the corner with Ramsden Street, and an Off Licence on the opposite one. While the Emmerson's Fish & Chip Shop stood on the third corner – this is 'still' a Fish & Chip Shop I believe. There was another Off Licence on the corner with Florence Street. This one was Ma Docherty's and had an ever open door which faced right down the street. We could always see the ample figure of Ma Docherty draped over the counter on duty, waiting for customers. There was another Fish & Chip Shop next door to her, but this seemed to come and go under different owners.

For us kids, however, the most important shop was Annie Booth's sweet shop, which stood on the corner with Florence Street. She lived behind the shop, like most of the shopkeepers did, and seemed to be always open. I can still hear the tinkling of her doorbell as we'd burst in to see what we could get for our ha'penny or penny. Annie Booth would always appear instantly from her back room, like a genie from a bottle. Which was only appropriate, as her shop always looked, to us, like an Aladdin's cave of boiled sweets. These were all in glass jars, stacked on shelves from floor to ceiling.

She also had a brother who ran some sort of business with a horse and cart. What this was I'm not sure, but he used to stable his horse, and the cart, in one of the enclosed arches in the back street under the Greengate Bridge.

Marsh Street itself consisted of three quite different sections. The southern one started where the double-decker buses turned into it from Ramsden Street, and ran down to where it met Salthouse Road at the bottom. The houses in this section, though still terraced, were of slightly better quality than the rest of the street. The middle section, where we lived, stretched from Ramsden Street to where the Greengate Street Bridge crossed over it. The northern section, beyond the bridge, had houses which were of similar quality to ours, but slightly different in design.

The whole street had originally been built by Clay's Wagon Works (long disappeared) as homes for their workers.

When we lived in Marsh Street the skyline beyond the bridge to the north was almost blotted out by the enormous bulk of the cooling tower rising up from the electricity works yard. This usually had a great plume of steam rising from the top as it condensed the high pressure steam, driving the generators, back into water. While most of the water was recovered some of the steam always escaped, and if the wind was in the wrong direction Marsh Street was subjected to a steady, rainy drizzle. In fact, whenever you stepped outside the house to find it raining, it was instinctive to look towards the cooling tower to see if that was the culprit.

Two other Marsh Street landmarks in those days were Casey's Brewery, which stood on a site next to the electricity works and had a tall chimney with 'Casey's Ales' written down it in large letters. And then there was a huge factory chimney which for some strange reason stood right in the middle of Salthouse Road, with railings round it, near the bottom end of Marsh Street. Because of its tremendous height, this was always known simply as 'The Big Chimney'. Along this section Salthouse Road was lined by a high wall, behind which stood enormous railway sheds and a huge area of sidings. This is probably where the old Claye's Wagon Works stood; possibly it was them who built 'The Big Chimney'.

I was still going out with my dad on his long rambles, beach combing for driftwood etc., and one of the fairly frequent outings I remember helps to illustrate just how hard it must have been for my parents, and others like them, to provide all the simple basic necessities for their families. These were our scavenging trips for coke on the rough, unmade road outside the Salthouse Gasworks. At least once a week, particularly in the cold weather, we'd stand along the side of this road, together with a dozen or more other men, waiting for the heavily overloaded coke lorries to come rumbling out on their deliveries. When they did, and hit the bumpy old road, the lorries would bounce about so much that most of the piled up coke on top would come cascading down onto the road. This is what we 'scavengers' were waiting for, and it was eagerly scooped up into our sacks. It didn't usually take long before we'd got as much as we could carry, and off we'd stagger home with enough fuel to keep the kitchen fire burning for a few days at least. I got the impression at the time that the men in the gasworks were deliberately overloading the lorries, and that the drivers played their part by hitting every bump in the road they could find.

Somewhere about this time, an event occurred that contained the first hint of what was eventually to become the 'second' of the two great pursuits of my life; namely, singing. One day at the boy's school, the headmistress came into our class to tell us about some town celebrations that were being planned. I can't remember what these were all about, but it seemed that the venue for one of the events was the Public Hall; which at that time was a fairly modern building just behind Barrow's huge, imposing sandstone town hall with its great clock tower. One of the items planned for the hall venue, it seemed, was a concert with a choir made up of school children from all over Barrow, and our headmistress was recruiting singers for this. She asked if any of us would like to be involved, and I, thinking this sounded interesting, put my hand up along with a couple of the others. An on-the-spot audition was apparently required, so I stood up and sang one of the school songs, and to my delight was accepted. What happened to the other volunteers I can't remember, but do recall that none of them were too happy singing solo in front of their classmates.

The concert itself, when it happened, was something of a letdown for me, as I discovered that I didn't get anything like as much satisfaction from singing as part of a 'group' as I did from my solo effort at the audition. An early indication, I believe, that being a 'soloist' (an individual), was always going to be my preference in life and not only in singing.

Across the road from the school was a big pub called The Waterloo which was connected to a well established school ritual. If a couple of the lads had a bit of a falling out, they'd threaten each other with the dire challenge of: "Right! I'll see you round the back of The Waterloo!"

Word would then be eagerly spread though the school about this mighty impending battle. As soon as school was let out, there'd be a great rush round to the notorious battleground in the alley behind the pub. Where, more often than not, great excitement and anticipation would turn to disappointment when either one, or both of the fearless antagonists, would not turn up. On one occasion when this happened one of the frustrated spectators decided to put on a fight himself by challenging anyone there to fight him. I, being also suitably worked up and frustrated, said, 'I' would. And for the next two or three minutes we both leapt about swinging punches at each other, none of which came within three feet of landing on the intended target. Finally, we decided to call it an honourable draw, and rather surprisingly most of the yelling crowd seemed well satisfied with the 'almost' battle of the century they 'thought' they'd seen.

SOME MAJOR EVENTS OF THE YEAR:

(1) Anthony Eden resigns over Chamberlain's appeasement of Mussolini.

(2) Holidays with pay were first introduced.

(3) First ballpoint pen made by Hungarian, George Biro.

(4) Nylon invented in the USA.

(5) WVS (Women's Voluntary Service) established.

1939 (10 years old in July)

At sometime in this year my older sister Jean and myself, with a couple of hundred other kids from Barrow, spent a great, adventurous week at a large, tented camp on the shores of Coniston Lake. This had been organised by the Co-operative Society – to give us all a bit of a treat in those rather austere times I imagine. We all had to sleep in large, army-style bell-tents; being allotted two blankets and a groundsheet each, and given 'expert' advice on how to fold these blankets into an 'excellent' comfortable bed. An optimistic claim if ever there was one, and painfully exposed when we discovered the anatomical truth, that a couple of blankets and a thin groundsheet weren't much of a cushion between the bony human body and the lumpy ground.

Another piece of expert wisdom dispensed, was that as there were to be ten of us in each tent, the only way we'd all fit in was to sleep with the narrower bits of our bodies (our feet) against the tent pole in the centre, and the wider bits (head & shoulders) out against the canvas side wall. Strangely enough we found this to be correct, even though it resulted in our heads freezing in the night, while our feet were quite warm, if somewhat cramped up.

Despite these initial shortcomings this 'Co-op Camp' week turned out to be a tremendous adventure for us kids. There were treasure hunts in the surrounding woods, swimming in the lake, tree-climbing, rambles etc. And all this with very few adults to cramp our style. We'd get up in the morning, clean our teeth and have a wash in the lake, then queue up at the one cold water tap on site to swallow the obligatory mug of Andrews Liver Salts (dispensed by a matronly figure you daren't argue with), before having breakfast. Then the rest of the day was adventure time.

In all, it was a wonderful experience, which I'm sure most of the kids there would always look back on with great pleasure, especially as it was almost certainly the first holiday experience of this kind they'd ever had.

Around late August of this year there was a strange, scary atmosphere growing everywhere, and it became obvious, even to us kids, that some sort of major disaster was looming. I remember being in the town one day and hearing all the newspaper vendors shouting out: "News of the Crisis! News of the Crisis." At the time I wasn't sure what 'Crisis' meant. But I certainly found out a couple of days later.

29

War was finally declared on the 3rd of September, and when I first heard the news I was with a group of my mates playing in what we called 'The Old Gardens'. This was a rough area of old abandoned allotments on rising ground behind the town, right next to the Grammar School playing fields. I remember quite clearly the shock of this news, and of staring out over the town with a strange foreboding of aircraft circling over dropping bombs. An uncanny preview of what actually happened eighteen months later.

SOME MAJOR EVENTS OF THE YEAR:
(1) The Spanish Civil War ended.
(2) Germany invaded Czechoslovakia.
(3) Germany invaded Poland – causing BRITAIN TO DECLARE WAR ON GERMANY.
(4) DDT discovered.
(5) The first practical helicopter flies – Sikorsky in the USA.
(6) Conscription introduced in Britain.
(7) Identity cards issued.
(8) The 'Battle of the River Plate' in which three British cruisers sank the German pocket battleship, *Graf Spee* – Britain's first major sea victory of the war.

3

The War

1940 (11 years old in July)

We were now living in the period known as the 'Phoney War', when for month after month all the expected air bombing attacks never came, so people became more and more relaxed.

With the war effort in full swing, scrap metal had now become a vital commodity, and we were always scavenging for it anywhere we could to earn a few bob. Sammy Morgan had a big scrapyard and railway sidings in the upper part of Marsh Street on the other side of the Greengate Bridge, which crossed over Marsh Street. He was always happy to take anything we could get hold of, though pretty shrewd in what he paid.

As tiny kids his scrapyard had always been a favourite playground of ours, as there was a hole in his fence round in the backstreet that we could squeeze through. I can remember playing on old scrap cars in there which must have been from the early 1900 period and today would be worth a fortune to the vintage car collector.

Our family now moved home for the first time. This was just around the corner to 1 Florence Street, which stood on the corner of Sutherland Street. This had at one time been a shop, and the old empty shop still formed the frontage of our house. It also had a cellar which we all thought was a bit spooky. I'm not sure why we moved, but it probably had something to do with our growing family numbers.

Right across the road in Sutherland Street, stood 'Cheap Johnnie's' cake shop, which was always great for a special treat whenever Mam had any money to spare.

This usually only happened on days like 'Divi Day', when the Co-op

31

paid out a dividend on the money customers had spent over the previous six months or so. Every customer had a special Co-op number, and Mam used to keep all the receipts impaled on a wire spike set in a wooden block, which always stood on the old sideboard in the kitchen. When 'divi' day approached she'd be eagerly adding up all these receipts to see how much we'd spent over that period, and trying to 'guess' how much 'divi' we were likely to get. This was 'always' a guess, until the Co-op announced how much they'd be paying out to the pound on this particular occasion.

Whatever this was, Cheap Johnnie's must have done well with its creamy creations on those days. The one special cake that I remember as my favourite was called a Chocolate Box. This was a square piece of chocolate cake, with thin squares of chocolate for sides and whipped cream on the top.

We didn't seem to live in Florence Street for very long, however, because we soon made our second move, away over the Greengate Bridge to 42 Fife Street. This was to a much better house in what seemed to us a slightly posher area. It actually had the undreamt of luxury of a bathroom with an indoor toilet. Until then we'd never had a bathroom, one cold tap over a stone sink in the back kitchen had been our sole washing facility; and the loo to us had always meant a cold, whitewashed outhouse at the bottom of the backyard.

Unfortunately, all this luxury proved to have a drawback; it came with an unwanted guest. This extra inhabitant had the inconvenient habit of locking the bathroom door from the inside. This lock was a sliding bolt, which couldn't be operated from the outside. And with the door being a slightly loose fit, you could hear the bolt rattle if you tried to open it when it was locked. There was never any answer when you asked who was in there. This was an experience which we'd all had, apparently, but never mentioned, because it was always put down to one of the younger kids larking about. One evening, however, Dad went up to the loo and came down looking pretty puzzled.

"Who's that in the bathroom?" he asked in bewilderment. "The door's locked from inside, but everybody's down here."

And so the eerie truth was revealed – we had a ghost. We all then crept warily up the stairs, to find the bathroom door not only unlocked, but standing wide open. We did hear later, from one of the neighbours I believe, that a few years earlier a former Town Mayor had lived there with his wife and that she had committed suicide in the bathroom. How true this was we never found out. However, the ghost was real enough, as Colin and I found out. The room we slept in was immediately facing the head of the stairs, and quite often during the night we'd hear footsteps coming up the stairs when no one was there.

In July of this year I moved up from the Greengate Junior School to the Alfred Barrow Boy's School in Duke Street, near the centre of the town. This was a big step nearer to being grown up, and one which I really enjoyed taking, as it provided a totally different environment in a much bigger school, laid out on three floors, instead of the previous single one.

Everything seemed bigger and better there, as if a door was being opened into a whole new wider world. Not only were the classes and subjects different, but I was now meeting lads from different parts of the town.

Strangely enough, the one new pal I remember most from this change to the Alfred Barrow School, turned out to be a lad who lived in Sutherland Street; only a couple of streets away from Marsh Street. His name was Duggie Bell. For some strange reason I always seemed to attract those who were 'characters', and true to form Duggie was a bit of a one-off. Somewhat gangly in appearance, with a shock of wavy hair, he always seemed to be living 'slightly' in a world of his own. Naturally, he and I got along very well together. Duggie's efforts at reconciling our planet with his own were a regular, interesting diversion in those early days at Alfred Barrow School. One particular event I remember was during class when we'd all been given a lecture on first aid. Question time afterwards seemed to go reasonably well, until the master came to Duggie:

"How would you recognise if somebody's leg was broken?" asked the master, hopefully.

"Well," replied Duggie, frowning deeply. "If a piece of the bone was sticking out through the skin, I'd waggle it about to see if it hurt. If it did, that meant it was broken."

How could you argue with that?

Somehow though, the master was not too impressed.

Duggie's gift for disaster sometimes extended outside school. On one occasion a group of us boys had been throwing a ball about in Dumfries Street quite safely for half an hour, until Duggie appeared on the scene and joined in. His first attempt sent the ball crashing through someone's window; and the next second Duggie was dashing off up the road like a wild hare to the safety of his own street, while the rest of us were doing likewise in the opposite direction.

These two incidents were pretty typical of what it was like being pals with Duggie. Oddly enough we stayed pals for quite some time at the Alfred Barrow school, and I later discovered that he'd actually been born on the same day as myself. Which probably means 'something', though I hate to think what.

At about this time Mam had started running something which was called a 'Money Club'. The principle of this seems to have been that you gathered 20 members, who each paid a shilling a week into it. As there were 20 shillings to the pound in those days, this meant that every week there was £1 in the kitty. This £1 would then be given to each one of the members in turn, according to the number (from 1–20) which they'd previously drawn from a hat. The person who had all the work of running it (in this case Mam), collecting the money etc., would be recompensed by receiving the pound on the 21st week, even though they'd paid nothing into it.

This money club seems to have run for quite some time, even though as far as I could see it was nothing but a constant pain in the backside. Especially to me, as I had the job of cycling all over Barrow every week trying to collect the shillings from her widely spread group of members. Every week there always seemed to be at least one door which I knocked on in vain, or where I'd receive the answer; "Can't afford it this week, I'll pay double next week." Whether they ever did I can't remember, but Mam can't possibly have made any money out of it. Especially as she was giving me sixpence a week for cycling miles doing all the debt collecting. On top of this there was always some hard-up member asking her to manipulate the draw numbers so they could get what they referred as an 'Early draw', because they needed the money 'now'. Unfortunately, Mam sometimes seemed to give in to this plea, because although on one side she had a shrewd eye for money making ideas; on the other side she was too soft a touch to be a successful business woman.

The bike I was using at this time was one bought for me sometime earlier by Mam, largely I think because I was always running around doing messages, shopping etc. It came from a shop in Dalton Road, and I chose it because it had 'dropped handlebars', which made it look to me like a real racing bike. She obviously paid for it on the never, never, because nobody was ever able to pay cash for such things in those days.

That bike turned out to be a tremendous boon to me; opening up a much wider world of exploration than I'd ever had before. Rambles and expeditions that had often meant a whole day of trudging, I could now do in a couple of hours. Places that had just been names over the horizon were now within my reach. Such places inland as Dalton, Urswick (with its Tarn), Ulverston (the birthplace of Stan Laurel), Greenodd; or places dotted along the Morecambe Bay coast road, like Bardsea and

Aldingham (with its ancient church perched right on the edge of the sea), had become regular runs. Trips through Sowerby Woods, to Roanhead, and Askam on the Duddon Estuary had now become easy. Even such relatively long hauls to the Lake District as Coniston Lake, and Bowness-on-Windermere, were looming as future possibilities.

Backbarrow is a place I always remember reaching early on because of its huge, amazing Dolly Blue Works. These works were set in a rocky ravine beside a raging torrent of a river that thundered under the stone bridge over which the road ran. Backbarrow is a very picturesque village built of natural local stone. The stunning thing about it in those days, however, was the colour. It was blue; bright blue from one end to the other. The dolly blue dye from the works had simply stained everything; the factory walls, the pavement, the houses, the roads. It looked like a beautiful artist's painting that had gone wrong. As if he'd run out of every colour but this wonderful blue.

There were many other expeditions, usually with one or other of my Marsh Street pals, to gather flowers or blackberries. The hilly woods above the estuary beyond Greenodd, were always a great place for daffodils, and bluebells. Though the bluebells didn't travel too well draped over the handlebars of a bike, and always looked a bit sorry for themselves by the time we'd got them home.

An abandoned quarry by the railway line, away out near the old iron ore mines, was a great place for blackberries. At one time we even gathered small wild strawberries along the railway embankments in Sowerby Woods.

Also in this year I have a clear memory of going out Christmas Carol singing on my own at the front doors around the Fife Street area, and going home with a pocketful of coppers – a real 'professional' from the start.

SOME MAJOR EVENTS OF THE YEAR:
(1) The evacuation of Dunkirk.
(2) Chamberlain resigned and Churchill took over the government.
(3) Home guard formed (first known as the LDV – Local Defence Volunteers, but soon changed as it became nicknamed the 'Look, Duck & Vanish').
(4) 'Fire Watching' became compulsory.
(5) Food rationing was introduced.
(6) The liner *Queen Elizabeth* (83,637 tons) was launched.
(7) Walt Disney's *Fantasia*, and Charlie Chaplin's *The Great Dictator* screened.
(8) Penicillin used successfully for the first time.

35

The so-called 'Phoney War' came to an abrupt end in Barrow on the night of April 14th. We were all awakened in the darkness of the blackout by the wailing of air raid sirens, and realised instantly that this was not just another practice, but the real thing. The long feared blitz by German bombers was finally about to descend on us.

We all clambered out of bed, scrambling to get dressed and trying to remember what we'd been told in practice. So grabbing all the warm clothes we could carry, plus candles, matches etc., we clattered down the stairs and out through the backyard.

Our back street was a dead end, and our shelter was a small one up against the fence. The shelters were built of brick, having thick walls and a reinforced concrete roof. The wooden door was protected outside by a brick blast barrier. Inside ours there were about six stacked angle-iron bunks, which we could all just about fit onto.

Once settled in, we just sat there waiting and listening anxiously. We didn't have long to wait before the distant booming of anti-aircraft guns warned us what was heading our way. Soon the bursting of anti-aircraft shells high in the sky became punctuated by the much heavier thudding explosions of falling bombs blasting the docks, railway and streets; transforming our once peaceful little town into a front-line battlefield.

As well as the ack-ack guns and bombs, we could occasionally hear the metallic pinging of shrapnel from the bursting anti-aircraft shells bouncing off the concrete shelter roof. In some strange way this seemed to bring the battle closer and make it more personal, like a direct attack on us.

How long the raid lasted I'm not sure, but it seemed to go on for ages. Eventually, though, the thunder of guns and thudding vibration of bombs gradually faded away to an eerie silence, punctuated only by the distant, clanging bells of fire engines and ambulances. We slept for the rest of that night in the shelter; emerging warily in the morning to discover how much destruction had been caused. Our immediate area of streets, it seemed, had fortunately not received any direct bomb hits; but blast damage could be seen all around. Broken glass from shattered windows, and splintered slates blown from the roofs littered the roads and pavements everywhere.

The rest of that day was spent in a great fever of activity by everybody; clearing up the deadly broken glass from both outside and inside the houses. Sweeping up the fallen slates into heaps, and blocking up the broken windows with anything that could be found.

With so much devastation to the town, school that day was

obviously out of the question, so after helping where we could, we kids were free to wander off to try and discover where all the exploding bombs we'd heard crashing down had actually landed. We soon found our attempts to do this severely restricted, as these areas were all blocked off by police, fire engines and ambulances. What we 'could' see though was scary enough, great piles of smouldering rubble, where there'd once been houses, or even whole streets; swarming demolition crews digging for survivors, and firemen still dampening down flames.

In one of the districts nearest to Fife Street, Risedale, there'd been an estate of fairly new houses the day before, but now all that was left was a great area of flattened rubble. What astonished me about this particular bomb site, though, was that all the wooden staircases of the houses had remained intact and standing, sticking up out of the rubble like a forest of distorted trees.

This violent onslaught was repeated on the nights of the 15th and 16th of April, spreading the areas of devastation to many more districts of the town. Some places seemed to get hit really hard, while others quite close by suffered little, or no damage at all.

It all seemed so unbelievably random, and pointless. Everybody had always believed that when the air attacks came, the docks, shipyard, steelworks etc., would be the obvious targets. But, although these had suffered 'some' damage, most of the bombs seemed to have landed very wide of the mark, some even miles away. I remember that our local park, a couple of miles from the docks, was absolutely splattered with incendiary bombs. These seemed to have been dropped by the hundred, and their small, burnt-out craters dotted the grass and flower beds everywhere. This proved to be a great hunting ground for souvenirs to us kids, because each of these bombs had a metal flight tail which didn't burn and was always left behind in every crater.

On the second or third of these wild nights of bombing and ack-ack fire, I remember that there came one gigantic explosion which shook the ground beneath the shelter like an earthquake. Everything inside rattled and shuddered. Things fell off the bunks and we felt certain that a bomb had landed right outside the door.

When we ventured outside in the morning we fully expected to see a pile of rubble where our house had been, but to our astonishment and relief it was sill standing. Inside, however, we discovered that most of the bedroom window frames had been blown completely out of the walls and were lying across the beds.

We discovered later, that what we'd heard was a land mine going off fairly close by. Unlike bombs, these mines were dropped by parachute and caused much more surface devastation than the bombs.

This was because they floated down and hit the ground gently without burrowing deeply into it like a bomb does. The result was a much shallower, though far wider, crater and area of devastation, because all of the blast went sideways and not into the ground.

Then, to our surprise and relief, there was a short lull in the onslaught, with almost three weeks of quiet nights.

We still went out to sleep in the shelter each night, though; just to be on the safe side, and also avoid the mad scramble of that first night.

In the days between, we kids would go out and about the streets eagerly searching for pieces of shrapnel from the bursting anti-aircraft shells. These jagged pieces of steel seemed to rain down everywhere during the air raids and were highly prized by us as souvenirs. We would often hear them pinging off the concrete roof of the shelter, and were often warned by the ARP wardens not to go out during a raid because this shrapnel could be almost as dangerous as the enemy's bombs. Our brief respite from the Luftwaffe's bombs, however, soon came to an end, when their devastating attacks were resumed in earnest on May 3rd, and lasted right through until May 10th.

During all of these raids we spent our nights tucked up in the air raid shelters, and our days sorting out any damage that had been done. Fortunately for us, however, these never amounted to anything more than a few more broken windows and fallen plaster.

Other parts of the town weren't so lucky. Vernon Street area was severely damaged, as were parts of Hindpool. Abbey Road, the main avenue entering the town, received several direct bomb hits which destroyed a whole row of houses, the main swimming baths and the Baptist Church (where the Minister and a helper doing fire-watch duty on the roof were both killed). The *Evening Mail* Newspaper offices, were severely damaged; as were the Ritz Cinema, the Plaza, the Public Library and two hotels, in one of which, The Trevelyan, several people were killed. The fine old Central Railway Station was destroyed, and the historic railway engine 'Coppernob' which stood on a large plinth in the courtyard had its large ornamental glass case shattered.

Union Street received the worst bomb blasts of all, with twenty people killed; six of whom died when their family shelter received a direct hit.

The real targets, of course, were the docks and shipyard, and although some of the workshops received shattering bomb hits, and a huge 150 ton dockside crane was demolished, none of the ships under construction there at the time suffered any serious damage. These included two huge aircraft carriers, HMS *Indomitable*, and HMS *Illustrious*; and two cruisers, *Jamaica* and *Spartan*. Submarines were also under construction at the time and none were damaged in the air raids either. (Barrow's shipyard was 'particularly' renowned for its submarines – over a hundred being turned out there during the war.)

At last the air raids came to an end, and the people of Barrow gradually began to pick up their normal lives again – at least as far as they could in their now badly damaged town. All the destruction and gaping bomb sites, however, quickly became accepted as part of Barrow's new wartime image, and people simply 'got on with things'.

At sometime in the spring or summer of this year, I and my older sisters, Jean and Joan spent some two or three wonderful short holidays in the Lake District on the shores of Lake Windermere. We used to stay in a cottage right on the edge of the lake, near the ferry, with a family called Rowe, who we called Auntie Hannah and Uncle Bill. Aunt Hannah was in fact the sister of my mother's first husband, Tetler Morrell. They had three children; a boy a bit older than me, a girl a bit younger, and a small girl quite a lot younger.

The cottage they lived in was the Ferry Cottage, because Uncle Bill was the ferryman, who skippered the car and passenger ferry on its trips backwards and forwards across the lake.

For me the days spent there were sheer magic; like the adventures of Huckleberry Finn. We used to go swimming in the lake every morning, or fishing for eels and perch with our bare hands. I always remember simply running across the road from the cottage, through a few trees and onto a short landing stage where we dived straight into the lake. The cottage being out on a sort of peninsula, the lake also lapped the shore immediately behind the cottage and you could hear this when you lay in bed at night. Sometimes we'd go off climbing the trees and steep crags behind Bowness.

Near the ferry cottage there was an old hermit living in the woods in an old makeshift hut of canvas, branches etc. Apparently he'd been there for years and was accepted as a 'local character'. We'd sometimes see him in Bowness town centre, where the shopkeepers used to keep him supplied with leftovers of bread, veg etc.

At sometime this year I joined a sort of scouting group called 'The Woodcrafters'. They were very similar to the Boy Scouts, but their uniform was more like Robin Hood's Lincoln green – which was probably what attracted me to them in the first place. They, also like the Scouts, would go off rambling and camping out; though apart from the fact that they held their meetings in a hall just above the Promenade on Walney Island and one camping expedition down the Coast Road of Morecambe Bay, I can't remember too much about them.

Sometime around July/August of 1941 we'd moved home once

more, ending up back in Marsh Street, in a house exactly opposite to 144, where most of us had been born. This was number 107, an end house a bit bigger than 42 Fife Street, but without an indoor loo or a bathroom. Once again I suspect that the size of our family was the reason for this move.

4

Another Adventure Beckons

By this time most of the eligible children in Barrow had been evacuated. Why I hadn't gone, I've no idea. All I remember is that one of my mates from up the street, George Barber, came home on holiday from the farm where he'd been billeted and told me all about it. I thought it sounded great and went rushing to ask Mam why I'd been left out of this exciting adventure. I don't remember receiving any explanation, but when she asked in surprise:

"Why. . ? Did you want go?"

"Phew! I'll say!" I exclaimed.

"Right!" she said.

And that was it. She apparently contacted the authorities who organised the evacuations, and eventually – around the middle of the year when I was about twelve – it was arranged for me to go. Not only that, they'd even managed to fit me in at the same farm where George Barber was staying. I could hardly believe it, here I was off on a totally unexpected adventure, with a whole new world looming before me.

I was eventually sent off by train to alight at the village station of Tebay in the rolling hills and fells of the Eastern Lake District. When I stepped off the train with my old case I was still some three miles from the village of Orton which was my final destination. I'm not too sure how I got to Orton on that first occasion, but assume that I must have walked; as this was always the way I did it afterwards.

The Watson's farm I was heading for was in a small, three farm hamlet called 'The Park'; which nestled at the foot of moorland hills, about a mile and a half on the other side of the main village.

When I finally got there I found that the farm itself was an old, attractive, slightly rambling looking place, built, like all the farms in the area, of the local limestone. Old Bob Watson and his wife Elizabeth ran it with the help of their teenage son Joe and daughter Eva. Eva was about a year older than George and myself, and apparently went to the same village school in Orton as George did – and which I now would attend too. Joe, on the other hand, went to Appleby Grammar School, which was about ten miles away, and was picked up by car every day by someone in the village whose son also went there.

Mr Watson (Bob) was a First World War veteran who, though very active, obviously had a slight difficulty in walking and had to wear special boots. This, I was told later, was because he suffered from what was known as 'trench foot'; caused by spending months in the freezing cold mud of the trenches on the French battlefields.

Mrs Watson (Elizabeth) was a slightly severe looking but pleasant woman who settled me in, making me feel very welcome, to what was to be my home for quite some time to come.

Finding my way around the farm and rambling buildings during those first few days, with George's help, was an exciting introduction to a whole new world for me. The Watson's farm, like most other farms in the area, was run as a 'mixed' farm, which meant, I discovered, that they did a bit of everything, from growing crops, to rearing chickens, running a milking herd of cows and fattening a pig. They also occasionally took in a flock of sheep from another farmer to fatten up on their pastures. But the main farm income, apparently, was from the milking herd.

The working powerhouse was a heavy horse called Gerry, who was a bit of an independent character, and if he didn't feel like working he'd let you know. The sheepdog was a black and white bitch called Gem. She lived out in the stable with Gerry, and they must have had serious chats at night, because she was almost as bolshie as he was – sometimes going missing for a couple of days at a time.

They had one pig which I was warned not to make a pet of – I learned why, somewhat upsettingly, later. They probably had a couple of hundred hens or so; some in a chicken-house in the main stone-built farm buildings, and more in a big shed away out on one of the pastures.

The cow-shed ('byre' in the Westmorland dialect – cows were 'Kine') was also in the main farm buildings underneath the stone barn.

The farmhouse itself was part of the main building. It had three upstairs bedrooms, a large kitchen/living room, with bacon joints hanging from hooks in the ceiling, a low, stone-slabbed cold-room (larder) a small sitting room and a rather 'posh' parlour. The parlour housed the best furniture, including a harmonium. It was also where the front door was located – which was never used as far as I can remember, because it simply led out into the front meadow.

The main 'everyday' entrance was through a tiny washroom at the back, which led straight into the kitchen. Across the path from this entrance was a low stone wall with a gate which led into a kitchen garden, where all the vegetables for the kitchen were grown. There was also a prolific damson tree and a row of gooseberry bushes in there. Up the middle of the garden was a path which led to the farm's one and only toilet. A dry one, with a trap door round the back for clearing it out. This was a specialist job apparently, as a man turned up every so often to do it.

One other family member who deserves a mention was the cat; if only for the fact that he didn't seem too sure if he was a cat or a chicken. He often used to sleep in the henhouse at night, and spent a lot of time in the day parading around the yard rubbing his head against them – much to their bewilderment.

The meals were basic country fare, but plentiful, with porridge (or podish as it was often called) served both for breakfast and supper. We had to walk to school each morning down a long, winding, muddy lane flanked by drystone walls built of rough limestone blocks. These rugged drystone walls formed the field boundaries everywhere, and as well as gates would sometimes have stones jutting out like steps where you could climb over.

The old stone-built school took up most of one side of the small square in the centre of Orton; which we learned was an ancient village with a long history. The school itself was little more than one large room divided into two classrooms by a partition. One half for the small children, and the other for us eleven plus age group. Right in the middle was a large old cast iron stove, which provided all the heating. Since a few of the pupils, like Eva, George and myself, lived too far away to go home for a midday meal, there was also a small kitchen just near the entrance. Here we would eat our packed lunches, and get hot water to make the cocoa. It was 'always' cocoa as far as I remember; which suited me because I liked it

After school in the evenings, and at the weekends, George and I would get involved in all the fascinating skills and hard work that went into the running of a working farm. We were both willing to work, and for the most part enjoyed learning about this new way of life.

At first there were the simple jobs like feeding the chickens and collecting the eggs, giving the pig his bucket of slops, and making sure big Gerry had enough hay in his stable. Soon we were helping to bring the cows in for milking, with the aid of Gem; though she was hardly needed, because when milking time approached the cows were usually all waiting at the gate of the field. This milking routine had to be done twice a day; once first thing in the morning and again in the late afternoon.

There were no milking machines around in those days, at least not on the small farms like ours, so it all had to be done by hand. I was soon joining in with this, and found it was a lot trickier than it looked, there was a knack to it and this took a while to get the hang of.

While I was learning, my biggest critics were the cows, especially the one I happened to be practising on at the time. She would swing her head round and fix me with a disdainful stare which demanded quite clearly: "What the devil do you think you're playing at?"; often giving me a smack round the ear with her tail into the bargain. Some of the more irascible of these ladies would occasionally lash out and kick the stool from under you, just to make you brighten your ideas up.

However, I did get the hang of it eventually, under the guidance of Eva and Joe; learning that the secret all lay in a special 'grip' and 'squeeze' technique. Once I'd mastered this I became quite good at it.

One thing that did puzzle me at first was why these milking stools only had three legs. On using them, however, I soon discovered that with three legs these stools were always stable to sit on, no matter how bumpy the ground was. Whereas a 'four' legged stool would wobble like the devil unless the ground was absolutely flat.

Mucking out the byre and carting it all round to the farm muck heap was another never ending task, as was cleaning out the pigsty.

The narrow road that linked the hamlet and our farm to the main road was about a quarter of a mile long, and ended on a small central green between all three farmhouses. Behind the farms the hills rose right up onto the heather covered fells which, to me, appeared to go on forever. Everywhere among the ferns and heather there were small groves of trees, some surrounding ponds of cool clear water, others hiding small ravines with streams flowing down. Whenever I was up there it always seemed like an enchanted land which stretched all the way to the North Pole.

One of the other two farms in the hamlet was run by the Hulley family, while the third was run by their daughter and her husband, who also had two lads from Barrow billeted with them. These were Bill Hindmarsh and Tom Burgess.

Neither George nor I had known Bill or Tom in Barrow, but now living in the same tiny hamlet and attending the same village school, we soon became pals. The four of us would often get about together, rambling all over the place. Occasionally we'd walk down to the village when there was anything going on there. Or maybe just to paddle in the two small streams that flowed through either side of the village; looking for the fresh water crayfish, which were 'supposed' to live there. I don't remember ever catching any though.

One of our favourite calling places in the village was the blacksmith shop to chat to big Ben the blacksmith while he worked. I'd always thought of village blacksmiths as simply shoeing horses, which he did occasionally, but most of the time he seemed to be repairing farm machinery, or welding metal gates and farm implements. I remember that he had a large, round, concave metal plate lying outside his workshop door on which he'd lay cart wheels to fit new metal rims. He was to me the typical idea of a blacksmith; big, brawny and very strong. He was also friendly, and took delight in showing off his muscle power to us kids when we asked him how much he could lift.

Apart from the village, we'd spend a lot of our free time scrambling through the heather and bracken up on the fells, or 'tops' as the locals called them, exploring all the wooded gullies, little ravines and ponds. One special place I remember going to up there, when I was with Joe Watson, was a little grove of trees that hid a large rock from under which a stream of cool clear water flowed constantly. This was absolutely delicious to drink. Joe told me that this was known as the 'Black Dub', and that it was apparently the place where Bonnie Prince Charlie had rested his Scottish army in 1742 AD when they were on their way south to invade England.

On our way home from some of these evening excursions, when the nights were drawing in, we'd all be singing at the top of our voices. One of our favourites was the marching song, 'Stout Hearted Men', sung by Nelson Eddy in the musical film, *New Moon*. We'd belt this out over and over again all the way down from the fells in the darkness, frightening the life out of any wild life within half a mile.

Not content with this, we'd often stand under the trees near the road at the bottom for another half an hour or so serenading the moon with all the old music hall ballads we could remember. Such songs as, 'If You Were the Only Girl in the World' and 'Sweet Sixteen', were our favourites. These old songs had such wonderful, singable melodies, that they were a real joy to sing, and we'd pour them out over and over again to the night sky. We'd usually sing them through together like a choir at first, then again as solos, with each of us trying to show the others just how they 'ought' to be sung, or how 'we' could sing them louder than they could, before finally trudging home to bed to rest our weary throats.

Expeditions away up onto the fells were one my favourite outings

45

at any time, but especially when George and I would scramble up there with Joe Watson and Gem, the dog, rabbit hunting. The only drawback being that we never seemed to come back with anything for the pot. This wasn't because Gem wasn't too keen; in fact just the opposite, she was so eager, that when a rabbit was spotted, she'd streak off after it like a four legged rocket, reaching it in seconds, but always running too fast to grab it, so she'd just hurtle past leaving it time to disappear underground. Joe always used to do his nut with her at this, but Gem never seemed to quite get the hang of it. The only occasion I remember her actually grabbing one, was when the rabbit seemed so startled at seeing this black and white streak flashing past, that it just froze bewilderedly, giving Gem the chance to turn back and grab it on the second attempt.

Although the Hulleys owned the two other farms in the 'park' hamlet, I don't remember that we ever got to know them. The daughter and her husband, who ran the one where Bill and Tom were billeted, we'd see occasionally out in the fields, but her parents, the Hulleys senior, I don't remember ever seeing at all. I do, however, remember Joe Watson telling me that as well as the daughter, they had a grown up son who was regarded in those days as 'simple minded'. They also had a very dangerous bull who'd attack anyone who came near. The so-called simple son, however, could apparently lead him about like a pet lamb. . . So much for animals being dumb creatures.

The Hulleys, in fact, seemed to be quite a big family in the area, because there was also a 'Hulley's' shop down on the village square, which I remember as a sort of general store, with an old hand operated petrol pump outside.

Back on the farm the milking and other jobs continued as usual. But when the weather was mild we'd often herd the cows off down the farm road first thing after the morning milking, and out along the main road, which was fairly quiet in those days with very few cars about. They'd then be herded along the main road for about a mile, with the aid of Gem, to a couple of fields which were part of the Watson's farm. One of these fields was a pasture for the cows, while the other was arable land on which they grew potatoes (tatties to the locals) or other vegetables. In late afternoon we'd have to walk out there again, and drive them all back for the evening milking and feeding in the byre.

The milk from these twice daily milkings would be put through a milk cooler in a small milk house near the farm back door. This machine looked a bit like a stainless steel version of the old corrugated, wash-day scrubbing boards. The milk was poured into the top of this machine so that it flowed down the 'outside' of the corrugations, while a constant stream of cold water flowed through the 'inside' cooling the milk. The cooled milk then flowed through a filter, to clear out any impurities, and straight into ten gallon milk churns.

Since milk was a rationed food-stuff in those days, these churns would then be carted outside the farm gate and loaded onto a milk platform at the side of the road, from where it would be collected first thing every morning by Ministry of Food lorries.

5

The Chapel

One of the other regular routines of life on the farm was the Sunday attendances at the chapel. Although there was a large C of E church in the village, the Watson's were, like many other people in the area, strictly Methodists and attended the small Methodist Chapel. Or should I say 'we children' did. For while old Bob did go 'occasionally', I don't remember Mrs Watson ever going at all, which was a bit odd since she was always the main driving force behind 'us' going.

Every Sunday morning Eva, George and I would walk down to the village to attend Sunday School in a side room of the chapel. This would last for about half an hour or more, before the adults began arriving for the main morning service. We would then go through the door into the main chapel and sit through the main service.

To me this always seemed to last forever. Most of the people who took the service were lay preachers, farmers etc., from the local area, and most of their sermons and readings just went over our heads. The best part of this that I remember were the hymns, which I always enjoyed singing.

After the morning service, we would set off back to the farm for Sunday lunch, and help with any essential chores around the farm like milking etc. These had to be done every single day of the year, of course. There are no such things as 'days off' on a working farm.

After the essential jobs had been cleared up, we would sometimes go for a walk, or if the weather was bad, we'd get around the harmonium in the lounge with Eva playing, and sing through many of the well known hymns; each having a go at singing solo the ones we liked best.

Mrs Watson had her own rather strict idea of what Sunday was all about, and we weren't allowed to sing anything but hymns, or read anything except the Bible.

George and I would often sit around the table making things out of wood or cardboard. I remember building a battle tank of cardboard once, with matchsticks glued on tape for the tracks, and a pencil for the gun – not exactly something to frighten Hitler but it kept my creative streak busy on a wet Sunday afternoon.

After tea we'd all have to get dressed up again and set off back to the village to attend the evening service at the chapel. This meant that, including Sunday School, we kids attended three services every Sunday, while the adults only attended two.

Occasionally for these 'evening' services the Methodist Minister for the area would put in an appearance, and his outpourings were usually a bit more interesting to us kids.

All in all, though, I came to enjoy the atmosphere and activities of the Methodist Chapel, and didn't mind going. They occasionally organised special concerts in which we kids were expected to take part, and I remember the first one which was held in the small village community hall; this was about fifty yards up the road from the chapel. We kids were all expected to do a bit of singing, and in this I got what was my first shot at singing solo; albeit with a slight hiccup.

One of the items in the concert was a song with five verses, each verse to be sung solo by one of us kids, and in which we sang about what we wanted to be when we grew up – farmer's boy, milking maid, soldier boy. . . etc. Each verse was interspersed with a chorus which we all sang together.

All went well until it came to my turn. I belted out manfully: "When I grow up I, er. . ? I er. . ? I er. . ? Oh! Hell, I've forgotten the words!" was what echoed around the hall to the bewilderment of a wide-mouthed audience.

I felt that this was an absolute disaster; especially in a hall full of staunch Methodists. But when the hall erupted in a great burst of laughter, followed by a bigger round of applause than anyone had got so far that evening, I suddenly felt disaster melting away into possible success. So, prompted by the lady at the piano hissing at me to the effect that it was: "A 'sailor boy' I wanted to be;" I decided to honour them with a further attempt. This time I got it all right, and the general comments afterwards were that I'd given them all a good laugh, and that once I did get going I sang it better than any of the others – due, no doubt, to my being bolstered by such an unexpected first time triumph.

49

Later that year, at a Christmas concert in the chapel itself, I got my second experience of singing solo. I sang a hymn called 'All, All, is Well', which was set to the old Welsh tune, 'All Through the Night', and received an adventure book as a reward.

My inner instinct to be a solo singer was obviously being given early encouragement during this time in Orton. Where this desire to sing came from I'm not sure. I do remember that Mam used to sing quite a lot when she was working around the house, and that she had a very good, clear voice, especially when singing all the Gracie Fields' songs, which were very popular in those days. I can't honestly say, however, that I was aware at that time of this ever arousing any desire in me to become a singer myself. But who knows; since there's no record of any other singers down our family line, perhaps it did.

The Great, Dreamy Little Village School

To say that Orton village school was 'different' to the Alfred Barrow School would be an understatement if ever there was one. Orton was a sleepy little village where things moved to the tick of a serene country clock, far removed from the clangour and bustle of a busy industrial town like Barrow. And the village school was no exception.

The first thing I discovered when settling down to lessons there, was that the curriculum was so far behind the one I'd left at the Alfred Barrow that it was like stepping back in time. I found myself having to do lessons again that I'd already done in Barrow about two years earlier. The other lads from Barrow had already come to accept this, and in fact looked upon it as a sort of bonus, since they could breeze through an hour's work in about twenty minutes, then spend the rest of the time loafing about. I soon came to accept this myself, since I had no option anyway, but still had nagging reservations about it. Wasn't school about learning something 'new', not boringly rehashing old stuff?

There were two male teachers in charge of us older kids, and a lady teacher in charge of the juveniles – whose classroom was over on the other side of the central partition. Our two masters were Mr Beale, who was a local man, and the school headmaster. He lived in the school house just across the square and had a daughter, Janet, who was around my age, and since the school was mixed sex she was in our class at the time.

Our other teacher was Mr Hobro who was from Barrow, and had come to Orton to help with the extra workload created by the big influx of evacuees. He'd brought his family with him from Barrow, and they lived in rooms above the Bowman's grocery shop in the village.

These two teachers were well aware of the curriculum problem where we Barrow pupils were concerned, but not apparently in a position to change it. Their solution to keeping the bored Barrow pupils occupied, was to allow any pupil who'd finished his schoolwork early, to select a book from a shelf at the back of the room and read. This seemed to keep 'some' of us from making a nuisance of ourselves for 'some' of the time, but not all of us. So eventually we were also allowed to go outside to burn up any surplus time and energy on the nearby playing field.

I remember that the lad I was sharing a desk with was a big, burly sort of lad; who in retrospect, reminds me physically of a kind of juvenile Burl Ives. His name was Ronnie Lanyan, and he always seemed to have a giggly, idiotic sense of humour bubbling just below the surface, so obviously he and I hit it off a treat. We seemed to spend most of our 'spare' time in class drawing potty cartoons of unlikely people in top hats hurtling down precipitous slopes on bikes, heading for obvious disaster at the bottom; or falling off cliffs headfirst with an inside-out umbrella.

These masterpieces would be passed backwards and forwards across the desk, with each of us trying to come up with a more ridiculous disaster scene than the other. Naturally, all of this was accompanied by a lot of muffled giggling, which didn't always pass unnoticed and usually resulted in us being 'advised' to go outside and share our jokes with the sheep.

There were some lessons, however, that I did find worthwhile. Perhaps the best of these for me being the English lessons. When we did poetry or composition I felt really at home with them, as if they struck a particular chord inside somewhere. In one specific poetry lesson I remember, we were all told to try and make up a poem of our own. Most of the other pupils seemed to find this a real struggle, but I had no trouble with it at all. In fact, by the end of the allotted time I'd written two; one was a great battle saga about Crusaders being locked in a deadly struggle with the Saracens. While the other, in complete contrast, was about a poplar tree.

Where the Crusader theme came from, I've no idea; but the laurel tree was undoubtedly inspired by my memory of the row of poplar trees that used to line the edge of the Barrow Park along Greengate Street, and which we'd have a go at climbing occasionally. When the teacher, Mr Hobro, came to check all our efforts afterwards, he had various criticisms and comments to make about each of them. When he came to mine, however, he asked:

"Where did you get 'these' from?"

"I wrote them," I replied.

"Are you sure you didn't just copy them from somewhere?" he asked doubtfully.

" 'Course I didn't," I replied indignantly. "You told us to write a poem, so I did."

"Well," he declared, "if that's true, then you want to keep it up, because you've certainly got something there."

This was the first encouraging comment I ever remember receiving about my writing ability, and possibly helped awaken my own awareness of it.

Mr Hobro was a teacher I only vaguely remembered from the Alfred Barrow School, so I knew little about him. He was a big hefty sort of chap, and not one to get the wrong side of. I was told that at one time he'd been a wrestler, and he certainly looked the part. He used to take care of any sports activities that cropped up, especially the indoor ones which were held in the hall next to the school.

Those I particularly remember are the ones where he decided to teach us boys the noble art of boxing. He'd set up a punchball on a heavy metal stand, which was like a coiled spring about three feet high, set in a heavy base plate which he screwed to the floor. He then proceeded to punch the living daylights out of the punchball, with a ferocity that shook the floor and sent the ball 'wanging' backwards and forwards for three feet with each thump. This was apparently a demonstration of what he expected us to do. Some hope. That ball was so hard that when we punched it, it hardly moved and took the skin off our knuckles into the bargain.

However, this apart, I think we did learn quite a bit from him about the more 'noble' aspects of the noble art, like self defence, footwork, etc. All of which we wouldn't have got back at the Alfred Barrow School. So it wasn't a waste of time.

In complete contrast, one of the other activities which we were obliged to take part in, and which 'certainly' wasn't part of the curriculum back at the Alfred Barrow School, was Country Dancing. This, I believe, was run by the lady who normally taught the juveniles. When we lads first heard that we were being dragged into this we were horrified.

"What! Prancing around like a lot of Jessies. . ! No bloomin' fear," was probably the mildest of our reactions.

However, since we were obliged to at least give it a go, we joined in reluctantly like awkward, club-footed buffalos. To my astonishment, however, once we'd started the embarrassment quickly turned into laughter, and we began to throw ourselves into it with real gusto.

Funnily enough, I don't remember that we had country dancing again. I wonder why? Perhaps we were too hard an act to follow.

Some of the most enjoyable times I remember in the school hall were the evening film shows. These were put on by Mr Beale, the other of our two teachers. Mr Beale was one of those capable people who seem able to turn their hand to anything. He apparently had his own film projector with a large screen; and having acquired a stock of old silent movies from somewhere, decided to lay on a bit of wacky entertainment for all us kids. I shouldn't think any of the kids had ever seen a silent film before. I certainly hadn't, and for me they were an absolute revelation; the most hilarious things I'd ever seen.

The antics of Charlie Chaplin and the Keystone Cops opened up a whole new crackpot world to me – though one which seemed suspiciously like the dotty one where Ronnie Lanyon and I got all our potty drawings from.

There were all the other great comic films as well, with Buster Keaton, Fatty Arbuckle, etc., but though they were good, it was Charlie Chaplin and the Keystone Cops who really carved their names on my funny bone.

One of the other diversions we'd occasionally have whilst in class was hearing the muffled banging of a shot gun not far away. Naturally this intrigued us, so in one of our many breaks Ronnie Lanyon and I eventually traced it to the garage of the George Hotel just around the corner.

"It's alright," remarked the manager emerging with a shot gun. "I was just shooting at a rat."

"Did you get him?" we asked.

"No," he replied. "But I will do one of these days."

Somehow we felt pretty glad he was a rotten shot, because all our sympathies were with the rat.

Even though Orton was buried away out in the countryside, we were still very much aware that there was a war going on, and were constantly being reminded of it. On one occasion these reminders for us kids took the form of a school competition to design a poster in aid of the war effort.

At that time there were severe shortages of all the vital commodities the country needed, not only to fight the war, but also to simply survive while doing it. Such basic things as food, clothes, fuel oil, metal for munitions etc – much of which had to be shipped in convoys across the U-Boat infested waters of the Atlantic – were of paramount importance.

Because of this almost 'siege' situation, everyone in the country was constantly being exhorted to play their part by cutting out waste and recycling everything we possibly could. Much of this message was blasted out to us from posters which were pasted up ev'rywhere. 'WASTE NOT, WANT NOT!' – 'MAKE DO AND MEND!' – 'DIG FOR VICTORY!', etc.

The aim of our poster competition was, I believe, to try and add our bit to this vast poster campaign.

After explaining what was wanted, and drawing a few design ideas of his own as examples, Mr Beale set each of us to designing our own. Many of the kids simply did their own versions of the ones he'd drawn, but some of us, including myself, went for a design of our own. I remember that saving scrap metal was the one shortage that appealed to me – perhaps my memories of Sammy Morgan's scrapyard in Marsh Street had something to do with this choice. However, I decided to draw a line down the centre of my page, in order to create two drawings of a 'before' and 'after' situation. In the left hand drawing I drew some kids pulling a small hand made buggy loaded with scrap metal, being towed towards the scrap dump. While on the right hand side of the page I drew a trailer loaded with bombs being towed towards a waiting RAF bomber. At the end of the session all our masterpieces were pinned up in a display around the classroom wall and left to be judged by some local 'notables' next day, when they'd be open to public viewing.

As in all such events there are going to be a few winners and many losers.

Unfortunately I was not one of the winners, at least not as far as the 'notables' were concerned. However, when Mr Beale pulled me to one side later and gave me a shilling, explaining that one of the visitors had asked him to give this to me, because he thought my drawing was the best, I was left feeling more than a little chuffed, because none of the 'winners' had got anything.

Another little reminder of the war situation affecting the village was that the local men had to take on emergency roles they wouldn't normally have handled. One of these was fire fighting, and though they didn't have a full blown fire engine, they did have a small trailer mounted with a motorised water pump. This they would occasionally trundle out into the square near the school to have a bit of practice with.

A few of us kids would usually watch this dramatic event, but on one occasion I think the intrepid farm worker/fire fighters must have spent a bit too much time preparing in the bar of the George Hotel, because they seemed to mistake all us kids for some raging inferno that needed dampening down; so that's what they did. The powerful blast of water from their hosepipe was directed straight at us.

We scattered wildly in every direction trying to escape the deluge, but it was no use since the enormous jet of water seemed to cover every escape route and we got soaked. I dived behind the only cover I could see, which was a telegraph pole set close to a wall. Not a good idea it turned out, since the water jet simply hit the wall near the pole and was diverted onto me hiding behind it, soaking me more than if I'd stood in front.

When I finally escaped, I squelched off to find the other kids and compare battle wounds. I don't know how many thick ears the Orton fire brigade members got from the kids' mothers. But one thing's for sure, we always kept a safer distance when watching their practice sessions afterwards.

Other reminders of the war conditions existing in the country occurred from time to time in Orton. I remember one day seeing a squadron of armoured vehicles thundering down the hill into the village. There were a couple of Bren gun carriers, and several heavy tanks in the squadron, and I particularly remember the clattering and screeching of the churning tracks as the massive tanks struggled to negotiate the narrow corner between the Post Office and Bowman's Grocery Shop.

I think that the tanks went straight on through the village, but the two Bren gun carriers stopped in the square for a while, so we had a chance to chat to the soldiers, and scramble all over these exciting war machines. One thing that sticks in my mind, is that one of the carriers had several jagged holes in its armour plating on one side.

"How did they get there?" I asked the driver.

"They're bullet holes," he replied.

This absolutely astonished me, as up until then I wouldn't have thought that any bullet could go through steel so thick.

On another occasion a fighter aircraft had apparently crashed somewhere away over on top of the fells, and an RAF recovery team had been sent up there with a sixty foot trailer to bring back what was left of it. On the way down the long, winding Scar Hill above Orton, however, the ill-fated aircraft had another crash landing when the driver lost control of the trailer, and it ended up straddled across one of the roadside drystone walls. Fortunately, the recovery trailer was itself 'recovered' eventually, and sent on its way.

The square in Orton witnessed another rather odd event, which, on looking back, seems strangely out of keeping with wartime Britain. This was the arrival of a group of gipsies. They were obviously show people, and had probably come down from Appleby, where their traditional gipsy horse trading fair is held every year. I particularly remember one hefty-looking man who was dressed in a sort of strongman outfit, with leather belts and ornamental brass studs. He was trundling around an enormous, polished cannon wheel which all us kids found fascinating. We followed him around hopefully, wondering what he was going to do with it, as it was obviously part of his act. However, we never found out, because whatever he was supposed to do with it, he didn't do it while we were there.

The only other member of the troupe that sticks in my mind was a glamorous dark haired girl in full gipsy costume. She also seemed to do nothing but parade herself about. So the whole episode just hangs in my mind like a half-remembered dream.

The nagging thought in my mind, however, still remains unanswered: How, in the middle of the war, when everybody else was dedicating themselves to defeating the enemy, was this group of people able to carry on with their traditional, wandering lives totally divorced from. 'our' reality.

6

The Farm in Winter

The usual footwear, for everyone, on the farm was clogs. At first these took a bit of getting used to, because having thick, wooden soles they don't bend like boots do, but with the soles being curved they rock foreward every time you take a step.

Surprisingly I soon found that this made them really comfortable to walk in, and much less tiring than boots because your feet stay flat and don't have to bend as they do in boots. The thick wooden soles also kept your feet much warmer and dryer than boots, so were ideal for the cold, muddy conditions we sometimes had on the farm, especially as the winter approached.

Our clogs were made and repaired by a cobbler at Tebay, and when I trudged there from the farm to get my first pair, I was surprised to find that his workshop seemed to be an old disused signal box alongside the railway line. You even had to climb up steps outside to get into it.

In the Autumn of 1941, with winter looming ahead, preparations were gradually being made to cope with this. One of the tasks involved, was the gathering of bracken from the fells above the hamlet as winter bedding for the animals. This was needed because of the harshness of winter in this northern area of the country, when the cows had to be kept in the byre twenty-four hours a day. Obviously this called for a lot of winter bedding, and the ideal bedding for this was 'bracken'. Fortunately, up on the fells there was an abundant supply. Bracken is really what's left when the vast masses of lush green summer ferns die off to a crispy brown colour in autumn, and are there for the cropping.

Bringing it down from away up there was a job for big Gerry, and since ordinary farm carts were not suitable for such rugged terrain, it had to be carried down on farm sleds. These were just like ordinary wooden sleds but far bigger and heavier built. They were about a foot high, six feet wide and seven feet long. They were dragged along on chains fastened to big Gerry's harness. Having long smooth runners they could slide easily over the very rough ground with no trouble at all.

Going up onto the fells into the fresh, clean air was always an enjoyable experience for me. That feeling of being away up above the rest of the world in a beautiful rolling wilderness of heather and ferns, little vales of trees, cool ponds and rocky ravines never failed to make me feel refreshed, and somehow expanded.

Because of the rugged conditions up on the fells, the bracken had to be hand cut by scythe. Scythes are awkward, unwieldy implements to use in the best of conditions, and on the uneven ground of the fells they could be lethal. So the scything was left to Mr Watson or his son Joe. George and I did have a go at slashing about with these deadly curved blades occasionally, but as this put every living thing within ten feet in dire peril, including ourselves, it was decided that George and I should stick to gathering it up and loading it onto the sled.

We'd pack the bracken onto the sled to a height of about five feet or so and lash it down with ropes. Big Gerry would then drag it across the rugged fells and down a steep track to the park hamlet road, and up to the farm, where we'd offload it into a storeroom. This would be repeated until the storeroom was sufficiently stocked to see us through the winter.

As it happened we were to need every scrap of this bedding, because that winter turned out to be particularly cold and frosty. The snow was so deep at times that we couldn't get to school. Everywhere at the farm was frozen solid; even the trough where we'd normally take the cows one at a time to water them was solid ice. This meant that we had to load empty milk churns onto the sled and get big Gerry to tow them around to the Hulley's farmyard next door where they had a trough set in the drystone wall which was fed from an underground spring which flowed down from the fells, and which surprisingly was never known to freeze. We'd fill the churns using buckets, then drag them back to our yard, emptying the water into our own trough, to water the cattle; making the trip backwards and forwards to Hulley's yard until all the animals had been watered. This was one of the most bitterly cold jobs I'd ever done; but it was certainly an experience.

Mucking out was another strenuous chore in winter, but not quite so numbingly cold, because you were kept warm by the hard work, and also by having to go in and out of the byre all the time. The byre had no heating, but the cows in their stalls generated so much heat, that it was always the warmest place on the farm.

Feeding the cows was much simpler because you didn't have to go outside at all. The byre was directly underneath the floor of the barn where all the hay was stored, and in one wall of the byre there was a doorway, opening into an alcove about three feet square. This was open at the top directly under the stacked hay in the barn. All we had to do was go up on top of the stacked hay in the barn and chop down through it, with what was called a hay-spade, cutting a square hole down through the hay to reach the alcove opening. The chopped hay could then be dropped down into the byre below, ready to feed the cows. This hay-spade was just like a normal pointed spade, but the two edges of the blade were sharpened like razors.

Even the empty milk churns got frozen that winter, and I distinctly remember them being placed right against the bars of the fire in the kitchen, as they tried to melt the inch thick lining of ice inside before they could pour the milk in them.

SOME MAJOR EVENTS OF THE YEAR:
(1) The Japanese attack Pearl Harbour.
(2) Conscription for women introduced in Britain.
(3) Rudolf Hess Landed in Britain on a naïve personal attempt at negotiating a peace mission. (He spent the rest of the war as a prisoner.)
(4) Terylene invented.
(5) The Gloucester Meteor Jet flew – experimentally
(6) Irving Berlin's song, 'White Christmas', came out.

1942 (12 years old in July)
The bitter cold weather lasted right over the Christmas period and well into 1942. We did still manage to get down to the village for the special Christmas services at the chapel, and there was also a Christmas party at the hall down the road, mainly for us kids. But by and large life was centred on struggling to keep the farm going during this pretty harsh time of the year.

At some time in this early part of the year, Eve and Joe's grandparents, Mrs Watson's parents, came to live at the farm. The grandmother was a little grey haired old lady who wore her hair tied up in a bun, while the grandfather, who was also quite small, had a full grizzled beard. In fact, they looked the absolute image of what kids of that time would expect grandparents to look like. I remember that the grandmother was rather quiet, and would potter around in the house helping Mrs Watson, while the grandfather was always busying himself around the farm in one way or another.

Back home in Barrow at this time they were coming under the final attacks by the Luftwaffe. The last explosive bombs fell there on January 10th causing little damage and no casualties. Overall the blitz on Barrow cost the lives of 93 people, injured 435, destroyed 600 houses and damaged 10,700 in some way. In addition many public buildings were hit; the railway station was demolished, and the shipyard and other works received some damage – though the industrial damage was small considering that these had been the Luftwaffe's real target. So bearing in mind that Barrow was a small town of just 70,000 people, it took quite a battering during 1941/2.

I made my first return trip to Barrow around this time to see the family and catch up with any of my mates in Marsh Street who might still be there. Unfortunately most of them were still away on evacuation, so there weren't many around. I did have a chance to get around on my bike, however, and visited a few of our old haunts.

I found that most of the debris from the blitz I remembered had been cleared away, leaving great gaping bomb sites where there'd once been streets, the main swimming baths, churches etc. But the countryside around was just as beautiful and inviting as ever.

There were still anti-aircraft batteries and barrage balloons stationed around the outskirts of the town, and some of the streets in the gasworks area had smoke screen burners lined along the pavements. But apart from this, life in war-torn Barrow seemed to be rolling along as busily as ever.

At the end of this visit I decided to take my bike back to Orton with me, as this would open up more possibilities for getting around up there. And as there was no charge for the bike on the train all I had to do was shove it into the guard's van and that was it. Train journeys in those days were a rare treat, and I always remember that particular line up to Tebay. The names of all the stations on that line still stand out in my memory. Ulverston, Grange-over-Sands, Arnside, Milnthorpe, Oxenholme – the junction with the main LMS line, where we'd always have to get off and wait for the mainline train to Tebay.

On this occasion, however, once we arrived in Tebay, having now got my bike, I didn't have to walk all the way to Orton, but pedalled it in a fraction of the time.

With the weather getting better, school and chapel attendances were resumed in a more regular way, and as the spring grew warmer, life on the farm gradually began to pick up its normal routines.

60

It was about this time that I learned, all too vividly, 'why' I'd been warned earlier not to make a pet of the pig we'd been feeding and looking after day after day for months. The pig, it seemed, was being kept solely to provide bacon and pork for the farm family, and the time had come to restock the meat larder. We were told that the butchering would be done by a local man who went around the farms providing this service.

This was not a very pleasant prospect for George and myself, and we looked forward to it with a mixture of fear and trepidation; plus the strange sort of macabre anticipation of a new experience.

When the day arrived, a smallish man turned up, and started preparing everything with a calm, businesslike nonchalance whilst constantly sucking away on an old unlit pipe. This seemed to make the deed he was about to commit all the more dastardly.

Firstly, a heavy low wooden bench was dragged out into the yard. This was apparently called a butchering stool. The pig was then dragged out of the sty on a rope, struggling and squealing, by a couple of the other men present, and manhandled with great difficulty up onto the stool. I'd never seen any creature so terrified before. He seemed to know that something terrible was going to happen to him, and squealed all the time in terror at a pitch which must have been heard a quarter of a mile away.

Once tied down, a bucket was put under the pig's head, and the butcher unceremoniously pulled a large broad-bladed knife, called a 'gully', from his belt, which was as sharp as a razor, and plunged it straight into the pig's throat.

The screams of agony that the pig gave out at that moment chilled me to the bone. The blood that gushed from the great gash was caught in the bucket, while one of the men stirred it with a stick.

Fortunately, the pig's struggles quickly grew weaker and weaker until finally they stopped, and its ordeal was over. It was the most awful experience I'd ever had, and for days afterwards I just couldn't get it out of my mind.

It was, of course, a lesson in reality. For although farming is obviously a rewarding and fulfilling way of life, lived out in beautiful, often idyllic countryside in touch with nature; its fundamental purpose is to produce food to feed human beings, and that includes 'meat' as well as cabbages and potatoes.

As spring progressed we found ourselves involved in all the many chores needed to prepare the ground for the summer crops. On a largely milk producing farm one of the most important crops was grass, both in the pastures for grazing, and the meadows for producing hay for the following winter feed.

One of the most basic of these chores, I discovered, was muck spreading, which I soon became involved in because in those days all the 'spreading' had to be done by hand using a fork.

All the masses of accumulated dung on the dung heap would have to be loaded onto the cart with forks and shovels and trundled out to the fields by big Gerry. Once there it would be 'splodged' out in evenly spaced heaps about ten yards apart, with Gerry constantly plodding backwards and forwards to the dung heap to reload until the whole field was dotted with heaps.

Once this was finished, the real work of muck spreading with a fork could begin; and I soon found out that scattering dung evenly over a ten acre field in this way was pretty tiring work. However, I was young and fit and at least I was learning a new skill, because like every other job on the farm 'muck spreading' had a knack to it which took practice to get right. Every time you hurled a forkful, you had to give the fork a flick with your wrist which helped to scatter it more widely and evenly. Once you'd got the hang of it, though, it got easier and easier and you developed a rhythm which you could keep up for hours.

There used to be a joke about the, 'Chinese Mystery of Who Flung Dung'? All I can say is, 'look no further', it was me in 1942.

Another of the regular jobs on the farm was keeping the drystone walls in good repair. Although these walls were pretty rugged and had been standing for well over a hundred years or so, they had no cement to bind the rough-shaped limestone blocks together so they did occasionally collapse in places – in Westmorland terminology this was referred to as the wall 'rushing'. When this happened it was simply a matter of sorting out the pile of fallen stones, and fitting them all back together.

The traditional design of these walls was fairly simple, so rebuilding them was pretty straightforward. The bottom layer was formed of large flat slabs wide enough to form a solid base. Medium-sized stones were then used to build the wall on top of this, sometimes of double thickness with an infill of small stones or limestone rubble. About halfway up another layer of large, flat stones would be laid to bind the wall in the middle, and the wall built up on top of this as before. When the required height had been reached, one more layer of large flat stones would be used to bind the top together. The wall would then usually be topped off with a layer of flat thinner slabs standing on end like books on a shelf.

Rebuilding these collapsed drystone walls always seemed an enjoyable challenge to me; a bit like doing a hefty, muscle-building jigsaw puzzle. All the pieces were there, but it was up to you to fit them together more or less where they belonged. I must have done this with 'reasonable' accuracy, because none of the walls I rebuilt ever fell down again – at least not while I was there.

When out working in the fields like this there was always a real sense of being part of the countryside, and all sorts of small incidents occurred that seemed to add to this feeling. One of these happened, I remember, when I was doing this drystone walling. This was the sight of an elderly man in the next field on the Hulley's farm, walking up and down scattering seeds. He was doing this with the aid of an antiquated 'fiddle drill', which was hanging round his neck on a strap. The drill consisted of a round metal plate hanging at about waist level from a couple of cords. Looped through these two cords was a stick, like the bow of a fiddle, which he was sawing backwards and forwards as if he was playing a tune. With each stroke the metal plate would rotate rapidly first one way then the other, while the man trickled seeds onto it from a bag he had over his shoulder. The result was that the seeds were scattered perfectly in a wide arc ahead of him as he walked. Outdated now certainly, but it filled the bill in those days.

A constant background accompaniment to virtually all these outdoor farm scenes were the birds. I particularly remember the skylarks who seemed always to be hanging high above the meadows, warbling their hearts out. Two other birds that stand out in my memory were the curlews with their long pointed beaks, and the lapwings – which the locals called pewits because of their distinctive call. These two sky dwellers seemed to swoop over the fields around the farm and fells everywhere like a permanent, moving part of the landscape.

Working out in the fields was something we did a lot of during that spring and summer. Even at times being given time off school, like all the other Orton kids, to help with the harvest. I found this open air activity really enjoyable, and a great way of working up an appetite – something I'd always had anyway – so some of the best moments for me were when the sandwiches and tea cans were brought out to the fields during haymaking, or digging potatoes ('tattie scratin' to the locals).

Where the potatoes were concerned, we didn't actually have to dig for them by hand. This was done by the plough, pulled by big Gerry, carving its way along the furrows ('splitting the stitches') to bring the spuds to the surface. Ours would then be the backbreaking job of gathering them all up until the sandwiches and tea cans arrived. These were usually brought out by Eva, or Mrs Watson, signalling a very welcome knocking off time, when we would all sit on the grass beside the stone walls tucking in to thick cheese sandwiches made with farm baked bread, washed down with lots of hot tea.

At some time around the middle of the year George Barber left the farm and returned home to Barrow for good. I can't remember now why he left, but it was probably because he'd simply had enough of country life and wanted to get back to the old life in Barrow. However, this meant that I was now on my own as the sole evacuee at the farm.

Shortly after George went home, the Watson's grandparents also left to return to where they'd come from, though I don't remember ever being told where this was. I do remember, though, that just as they were about to leave the grandfather took me to one side and gave me a shilling as a parting gift, and being quite a religious old chap, also gave me this advice:

"Always remember that the Bible is the best book. Jesus is the best friend. And heaven is the best home."

At about this time Joe Watson and I began the work of digging a narrow trench about two feet deep, across the fields towards the main country road which was about a quarter of a mile away. This was so that a better water supply pipe could be laid to connect with the water main. There 'was' water laid on to the farm, but this obviously needed improving. The farm had at one time drawn all its water from a well, and this was still there, hidden in the grove of trees outside the back entrance, but it was no longer used.

I don't know how this new pipeline turned out, as I didn't stay long enough at the farm to see it completed. This was because for some reason I was transferred from the farm, to live in a cottage in the village with an elderly widow called Mrs Whitwell. I'm not too sure why this came about; adults never did seem to consult the kids much in those days.

However, I was off to start a new phase in my life at Orton, but this time as a villager.

7

A New Life in the Village

Now that I was living down in the village, my daily life was almost totally changed. All the bustle and routine of the farm life which I'd been living, and largely enjoying for almost a year, was now completely behind me. Suddenly I found myself with much more time on my hands; which as it turned out was just as well.

My life at the school remained the same, of course, and as Mrs Whitwell's little whitewashed cottage was in a street leading down into the square, I now only had to walk a hundred yards to get there instead of the one mile trek down the lane every morning from the farm.

Mrs Witwell was a nice old lady, very kind and caring, who'd been a widow for many years. But though she'd lost her husband years before, I soon found that to some extent she still shared her life with him, as she mentioned him quite often, usually quoting him as an example whose behaviour the younger generation, like me, would do well to emulate. Despite this I liked her and we got along very well. She also had a grown up daughter who was away working somewhere; on a farm I think, possibly this was the reason she took me in.

Like most changes in life, the closing of the past usually opens up new opportunities for the future. This was definitely so in this case, because moving down to the village had given me a chance to be more in touch with one of my best mates from Marsh Street; Walter Caine. He'd been evacuated along with another Barrow lad, Ray Cook, to a house in the village owned by the Jackson family. And because I'd been away out on the farm, I hadn't seen too much of him.

The Jacksons were retired farmers and their house was over on the other side of the village, almost next door to Big Ben's blacksmith's shop. They, like Mrs Whitwell, 'also' had a grown up daughter, she was called Hetty.

Although they were retired, the Jacksons still owned a couple of large fields and a wood on the outskirts of the village, where they had a barn and stable plus a few cows, a horse and some chickens. This naturally soon became a regular stamping ground for us.

The entrance to the Jackson's fields led off the road near the village, through the little wood and across a stream; which was one of the two streams that flowed through the village. This part of the stream, which burbled its way through the wood, turned out to be quite a good breeding ground for trout, and we'd often wade along it in bare feet practicing our 'tickling' techniques. This way of catching fish; or at least 'trying to', was something we'd heard about but didn't really believe. However, this was a perfect place to try it out.

What we'd been told was that if you waded up slowly on a trout, when it was hiding under one of the rocky ledges along the bank, it would be quite happy to stay there. All you had to do then, was slowly put both your hands into the water and feel under the ledge until your fingers touched the trout. If you did this gently enough the trout would not be alarmed and would let you stroke its stomach with your fingers, seeming to become almost mesmerised by it. As you continued to do this you had to gradually work you hands along its body until one of them reached the tail and the other reached its gills. You then slowly closed your hands around it, and at the crucial moment scooped it swiftly out of the water onto the bank.

This all sounded a bit like a send-up to us, but at least it was worth a try. To our astonishment, after a few abortive attempts, it actually worked. We didn't catch many like this, and only threw them back anyway as we didn't know what else to do with them. But we had proved that, strange as it seemed, it could be done.

Walt and Ray had to go up to the barn sometimes and help clean out the cow byre etc., and the first time I went up there with them, Mr Jackson had also asked them to sort out a couple of the cows that needed milking. This seemed a bit strange to me at the time, since neither of them had a clue how to do it; so I showed them, and in fact ended up doing it for them. It later dawned on me that being a wily old country farmer Mr Jackson knew full well that I'd just spent a year on the Watson's farm, so knew that I'd be able to do it, and thus he'd get the cows safely milked.

The horse that the Jacksons kept out there was left to roam freely on the field, so whenever we could catch him we'd have a go at riding him bareback like we'd seen the Red Indians do in those old Saturday morning films. This was the first time I'd ever attempted to ride a horse and I soon discovered that it was a lot harder than those Redskins on the screen made it look. For a start, once I did manage to get on his back, he seemed a lot bigger and broader than I'd expected, and simply hanging on without a saddle or reins was difficult enough even when he was standing still, and as soon as he started to trot it was almost impossible. So this was something that we quickly gave up on.

These fields of the Jacksons, I discovered, actually bordered on woods in the grounds of Orton Manor, which is a fine Jacobean manor house dating from 1662. At that time it was occupied by some wealthy family whose name I never knew.

However, since the boundary between the two properties consisted of nothing more than a simple fence, it wasn't long before we were quietly nipping over there into the woods occasionally to explore what seemed to me a silent, mysterious world.

We never went near the house itself, in case we were spotted trespassing, but what we did discover was that there were rabbits hopping about everywhere in there.

Since we were all pretty well tuned-in to country activities by this time; both the normal and the slightly dodgy, we decided – in the ancient spirit of Robin Hood – to opt for the latter and do a bit of poaching on the 'Lord of The Manor's' land.

Getting hold of a few simple snares in Orton was easy, so sneaking over the fence one evening we set out a dozen or so in what seemed to be likely places. At the crack of dawn next day we turned up to collect our illegal quarry. To our delight and astonishment we'd snared three of the little fury creatures. Unfortunately our delight soon evaporated as we looked at the three captives uncertainly.

"What do we do now?" asked someone.

"Kill them, I suppose," replied someone else.

"How?" asked the third.

"You hit them on the back of the neck, I think," came a suggestion.

"Who's going to do it?" someone asked.

Silence all around as the intrepid hunters shuffled about, suddenly not feeling quite so intrepid any more.

"Why do we want to, anyway?" someone shrugged, as the frightened eyes of the small, helpless bundles of fur stared accusingly at us.

"Yeah! What for?" muttered someone else, guiltily. "Just let them go."

And that was it. We took the snare wires off their necks, and the great Orton Hall Rabbit Hunt ended with satisfaction all round – especially for the rapidly departing rabbits.

On one other occasion, however, things worked out somewhat differently for the Jackson farm rabbits. The three of us were up there as usual, but this time we had the Jackson's sheep dog with us; as we sometimes did. We'd been running him around as usual, throwing sticks for him to retrieve, when all of a sudden he spotted a rabbit and shot off after it like a bullet. Fortunately for the rabbit it reached the safety of a pile of rough logs stacked against the side of the barn, and the dog just leapt about barking at the logs. We all went after him to drag him away, when to our surprise three baby rabbits came scampering out form under the logs in a panic, and he went for them in a great flurry of flying legs and snapping jaws. To our dismay and astonishment, in the few seconds it took us to reach him the three little rabbits had vanished, he'd simply swallowed them all.

At first I couldn't believe what I'd seen and kept looking around hoping to find them hiding somewhere, but from the satisfied look on the dog's face, and the way he was licking his lips, I had to accept the truth. What appalled me most about this unpleasant incident, was not just the cold cruelty of the dog's behaviour, but the utter pointlessness of it, as he was a well fed dog, so 'hunger' could not be used to excuse it.

As I still had my bike with me at Mrs Whitwell's, I was able to get about quite a bit on my own expeditions as well as with Walt and Ray. On one of these solo jaunts I pedalled over the fells to the little country town of Kirkby Stephen, about 14 miles away, to visit my younger brother, Colin. He'd been evacuated there at some time after I'd been evacuated to Orton. On arrival, I discovered to my surprise, that the place he was staying at was a rather posh farm, set on a hill overlooking the old country town, with a family I can only describe as gentleman farmers. They seemed to have several farm workers around the place, and I could see a big black limousine outside in their garage. The farm itself was called 'Hartley Castle', for the simple reason that it was built on the site of what actually 'had been' a castle. In fact, a small section of the castle ruins still remained on a mound close to the rather splendid farmhouse, and they used this crumbling mediaeval remnant as a sort of cold storage cellar.

Colin was staying there with another evacuee from Barrow, whose name I can't remember. As I rolled up unexpectedly on my bike I was made very welcome by the family, and invited to stay over the weekend. I thought this was great, as it was all so different to the Watson's farm that I couldn't wait to get involved in it all.

Unfortunately it didn't turn out that way, for the simple reason that my brother Colin and the other lad were only about nine years old, and had never been expected to get involved in the daily running of the farm which was left solely to the paid farm hands. Although I was nearly thirteen I was a visitor, so the same applied to me.

However, this left us free to roam anywhere we wanted, so that's exactly what we did. The farm was perched on top of a hill with a panoramic view of Kirkby Stephen down in the vale below, and there were little valleys and woods everywhere. We explored all the farm buildings, through the woods and up onto a railway line that ran nearby over a very high viaduct. We all ran across this to the other side, stopping here and there to put our ears to the rails hoping we'd hear a train coming. But no luck, so we had to content ourselves with throwing twigs, and stones from the track down into the woods below. At the other side we climbed down into the valley beneath and practised a bit of tree climbing. All in all we had a great time, which made my cycle ride over the fell well worth it.

Back in the big farmhouse we ate our meals with the family, and though the food was good and a bit different to what I'd been used to at the Watson's and Mrs Whitwell's, it wasn't really any better. One little ritual they had which I particularly remember, was that after supper, before we went to bed they'd hand out a caramel toffee to each of us. Only the one, but in those days of sweet rationing I thought it was a great way to be sent off to bed.

The following morning, being Sunday, the whole family including us went off to church down in Kirkby Stephen. As this involved a trip in the big, black limousine I was absolutely over the moon. I'd never been 'near' such a magnificent car before, let alone had a ride in one.

The drive down to the church was almost like riding on a plush magic carpet, and to my surprise, when we all climbed out in front of the old church in the centre of the town, I discovered that we three lads were not expected to attend the service, but were free to wander off around the town.

This unexpected free time suited me perfectly, because I had only just learned from Colin that one of our younger sisters, Jill, who was only about seven years old, had also been evacuated to Kirkby Stephen. She was staying with a family who lived in the main street of the town, so now we had a great chance to go off and see her.

It didn't take us long to find the address, and I was very pleasantly surprised to find that it was also a cake shop and café, with a window bursting with the kind of delicious cream delicacies I hadn't seen since 'Cheap Johnnie's' shop in Barrow.

Our sudden arrival naturally came as a great surprise to Jill, especially 'me' being there as it must have been over a year since she'd last seen me. Once again we were made very welcome by the family, who sat us down in the little café and fed us tea and cakes. I can't remember too much about the family now, apart from the fact that they had a young daughter of their own around Jill's age who was slightly mentally handicapped in some way.

It seems odd now to think that I'd never been told about Jill being evacuated to Kirkby Stephen, but then I don't think family communications were quite as vital in those days. People knew, or assumed they knew, where each other were and that was that. Another even more surprising example of this was the fact my other sister Joyce, who'd have been about 11 years old then, must also have been living in Kirkby Stephen at the time of my visit as an evacuee with an elderly lady. This was something I only found out many years later.

Back in Orton I picked up on my ramblings with Walter Caine and Ray Cook. And one of these took us away out over the fells in a different direction to any we'd ever been before. Somehow we'd got to hear that there was an army firing range out there somewhere, where they practised firing rockets across a remote valley. We trudged out across the rugged fells for what must have been at least three miles, keeping our eyes and ears open expectantly for any distant signs of flaring rockets or violent explosions. But the fells ahead just lay as calm and peaceful as ever. Finally though, we climbed over a fern covered hill, and there lying before us was a wide shallow valley, and we knew immediately that this was the firing range. Great gashes in the opposite hillside, and long deep gouges in the earth where the rockets had landed, were glaring evidence of the explosions and flashes which had happened there recently, but which we unfortunately were too late to see.

However, we weren't too disappointed, because the atmosphere of the place was exciting enough to make our long trek worthwhile. To us it was just like wandering onto a battlefield soon after the battling armies had left.

We found bits of the rockets here and there, usually parts of the tail fins, and from these we got the impression that the rockets must have been relatively small; no more than three or four feet long. They could have been anti-tank missiles, or anti-aircraft rockets. I don't think we bothered to collect any souvenirs because the bits of metal lying about were too jagged and torn.

All in all, despite the fact that we hadn't actually seen the rockets hurtling across that valley, or heard the explosions, being where they'd 'happened' was the next best thing, so we trekked all the way back across the fells to Orton feeling well satisfied.

In the village there were just three shops. One was the Halley's on the square, which had the petrol pump outside. Another was the Post Office & Sweet Shop right on the corner where the road from Shap entered the village – this is where we'd spend our ration of sweet coupons, if and when we had any pocket money that is. And the third shop was Bowman's Grocery on the opposite corner to the Post Office.

The Bowman's being the only grocery shop, not only served all the houses in the village, but also operated a delivery service to many of the outlying farms and cottages in the area using a small car, which was driven by the daughter of the Bowman family, Edna.

One day I was asked, via Mrs Whitwell I think, if I'd like to give Edna a hand with these deliveries. Naturally I jumped at the chance, because cars in those days were only owned by people who were 'well off', so any offer of a ride in one was a rare experience. Back home in Marsh Street, where owning a decent 'bike', let alone a car, marked you out as a bit special, even old Doctor Thompson had to pop about doing his rounds on a little old motorbike – while wearing a bowler hat, I remember. In fact, if a car so much as stopped outside one of the houses, all the neighbours would be craning their necks at the windows wondering:

"Who do 'they' know who owns a car?"

On my first trip as a trainee delivery boy I soon found out why Edna needed an assistant. Not only did the boxes of groceries turn out to be heavier than I'd expected, but most of the intended customers seemed to live in awkward, inaccessible places at the end of muddy lanes, or up narrow bumpy paths. At one house the easiest way in turned out to be a scramble over the drystone wall outside, dragging the box into the garden after me. However, the car ride made it all worthwhile especially the lumpy, splodging along the winding lanes. I don't remember how many times I took part in this grocery expedition, but it was quite a few.

My adventures with Walt and Ray carried on as usual, and even took a turn for the 'unusual', when Mr Jackson decided to go visiting his farmer friends and relatives around the area. His 'preferred' form of transport was a pony and trap; the 'pony' being the big horse we'd tried 'unsuccessfully' to ride in the field, and the trap one he kept tucked away in the barn. The most important thing for us about these planned chariot rides, however, was that he asked us three to go with him.

I'd never ridden in a pony and trap before, the nearest I'd got to this had been riding on the farm carts at the Watson's during haymaking, so this chance to trot through the countryside like the gentry was an offer too good to miss.

71

On the morning of our country jaunt we all helped to harness up the horse and trap, then climbed aboard with Mr Jackson at the reins. We trotted off out of the village taking the Shap road, but soon turned off onto a narrow, hilly road which headed up towards the fells. Progress from then on ground down to a somewhat slower pace, because every time we came to a hill, we three would have to jump off and trudge to the top in order to take the strain off the horse. Since one hill now followed another we seemed to spend as much time walking as riding. However, even though the trip was turning into more of a ramble than a ride, it was still exhilarating to be wandering through all this new countryside.

Our destination was a farm somewhere in the foothills, and I can't remember if it was run by one of the Jackson's relatives, of just a family friend. However, we eventually arrived to find the farmhouse and buildings perched on the side of a narrow valley above a ravine with a stream running through the bottom.

Once we'd met all the family and had a cup of tea, Walt, Ray and myself were left free to wander about the farm valley, including a scramble down into the steep ravine and along the stream flowing in the bottom. We never saw any sign of trout in the swiftly swirling water, though, so eventually climbed back up to the farm buildings.

Looking up from the bottom, these buildings had appeared even more precariously perched than they had from the top. Especially one big, low barn of a place, which seemed almost to be hanging over the edge.

By the time we reached the farmhouse we were all starving hungry and delighted to find that dinner was already waiting for us. This was a meal I always remember, as not only were the plates piled high enough to feed a navvy, but all the vegetables had just been dug up from their kitchen garden outside the window and tasted like none I'd ever tasted before. I'm not sure why, but whenever I think of that meal I particularly remember the broad beans. Perhaps it was the first time I'd ever had them? Whatever the reason, they've been a great favourite with me ever since.

After the meal, for some reason, they were talking about the farm buildings, particularly the low barn that we'd noticed almost hanging over the edge of the ravine. It seemed that they had a problem with the roof of this building as some of the stone slab roof tiles had slipped, and because this was on the side overhanging the ravine it was going to be a rather tricky job putting them back in place, especially as nobody in the family was young enough, or light enough to climb about up on its precarious slopes. I suspect now, that in their emphasis on this there was probably a bit of a hint in there somewhere – having three young lads unexpectedly available as it were.

Anyway, we all trooped outside to have a look at the situation. On closer inspection I didn't think that sliding the roof slabs back into place looked all that much of a problem. I'd never been particularly afraid of heights, and as nobody else seemed eager to risk a sticky end on the rocks at the bottom of the ravine, I said I would do it.

A ladder was quickly found and propped up against the barn – obviously speed was of the essence before this young lad with suicidal tendencies had time to change his mind. I then shinned up the ladder as if it was the corporation wall back in Marsh Street, scrambled along the apex of the roof to where the slabs had slipped, dragged them back into place, and was stumbling back down the ladder almost before I had time to think about it. It wasn't until I looked down into the ravine afterwards that the dodgy possibilities of what I'd done really dawned on me. However, I felt rather pleased with myself; and glad that I'd at least done 'something' to earn the lovely meal we'd had – especially the broad beans.

On another of Mr Jackson's pony-trap outings we set off out along the Shap road as before, but then took a different winding road towards the fells to the last time.

Once again this led us to some outlying farm owned by a friend of Mr Jackson. Strangely enough, I can't now remember much about the farm itself or the farming family. What I do remember is that it was set among wooded hills, and that Walt, Ray and myself, were set free to roam.

We soon found a stream nearby which was tumbling down off the fells through a shady, wooded ravine, and set off to explore.

The stream seemed to be splashing down in stages, as every so often we'd come across fairly deep pools, which to our delight had trout lazing about in their shady depths. We soon had our shoes and socks off, wading in to practise our trout-tickling techniques. This turned out to be all too easy, because the trout up there were even more laid back than their dozy cousins back in Orton.

Somewhere up the ravine we came across a pool which particularly stands out in my mind. It was far larger than those we'd found so far, and much more open to the sunlight streaming down through the trees. It was also a bit deeper with a rocky bedrock bottom, and apart from trout it was alive with little glistening baby eels which darted about like small flashes of sunlight. As we waded in among them, these tiny threads of life swirled around our legs like inquisitive matchsticks.

On one side of the pool there rose a high, earthy bank dotted with

73

d

small deep holes which we decided must be the homes of kingfishers. We didn't actually 'see' any kingfishers, but felt sure that if kingfishers lived anywhere, it ought to be here, as it was an absolutely magical place.

Back in Orton we got to hear one day that somebody was starting a branch of the Boys' Brigade three miles away in Tebay, so Walt and I walked there hoping to join.

All during the walk we built up such glowing visions of ourselves strolling around in their natty uniforms, marching in parades etc, that when we finally arrived at the little village hall in Tebay we could hardly contain our enthusiasm. Unfortunately the reality proved to be something of a let-down. Hardly any other lads turned up, and what was worse, it seemed that there'd be no hope of getting uniforms, natty or otherwise, because of wartime clothing restrictions. So, another promising adventure had the door slammed firmly in its face.

We spent the long walk back to Orton trying to convince ourselves that we wouldn't really have liked it.

"Who'd want to do parades and things anyway!"

"Phew! Not me."

"Dressed up like daft penguins!"

"Yeah. . "

At the village school one day a little drama was played out that dragged Walt and myself into it, even though we didn't know what it was all about. We'd been out in the playing field with some of the other school kids, which included a few of the girls. Walt and I had been climbing the trees etc., as usual, and what the rest of them were doing we'd no idea. When we turned up for school next day, however, there was a strange atmosphere about the place. This increased when Mr Beale solemnly called a group of us boys out into the small kitchen, which turned out to consist of all those lads who'd been out in the playing field the previous afternoon.

Walt and I were bewildered by all this, but eager to know what it was all about. It didn't take long to find out. Mr Beale announced with all the solemnity of a Spanish Inquisitor:

"I have received complaints from the mothers of some of the girls who were out in the playing fields with you yesterday, that some of you boys tried to 'interfere' with them."

Walt and I stared at each other in astonishment. What dastardly goings on had we missed while we were wasting our time climbing trees?

"I have no idea which of you were involved," added Mr Beale. "So I'll just have to ask those who were to own up now, otherwise I'll have no option but to punish all of you."

The deathly silence that followed could have been heard as far as Scotland.

"Right!" continued Mr Beale, picking up a thick stick from a pile which looked as if they'd been freshly cut from a hedge. He then pointed to the first of the guilty villains, who had to bend over a table and receive six hefty whacks across his backside.

One by one we all had our backsides whacked, and though it stung a bit it wasn't as bad as I'd thought it would be. My thoughts at the time I think were, well if this is what you get for being innocent, I'm glad I wasn't guilty. However, at that time not being too sure what interfering with girls was like, who knows? Maybe it would have been worth it. I think that what peeved Walt and I most about it though, was not that we were innocent, but simply that we'd had the punishment without having 'had' the pleasure.

Orton's village doctor lived in a large house between the two streams at the northern end of the village. I'd never had cause to see him myself, but I went there once with Walt when he'd slashed his hand with a knife while cutting a stick. We didn't see the doctor, but his wife dressed the cut for him. I found this chance to see her pretty exciting, because I'd been told that the villagers referred to her as 'Minnie Ha Ha', and that she had at one time had a lot to do with the North American Indian tribes where the real 'Minnie Ha Ha' had come from. In fact, some of the villagers used to think she actually 'was' the real one. When I met her I found this somewhat difficult to believe, since she was not only white skinned, but a lot plumper than my cowboy film image of what a beautiful Indian maiden should look like.

Once or twice a week the country bus would come rattling through the village. I think it came from the direction of Appleby, and possibly departed towards Kendal. To me, at the time, it just seemed to appear from somewhere and disappear to somewhere else. And the reason I mention it is because in later years this old single decker bus became a leading character, 'Stan Ding', in one of my first children's novels, *I'll See You in Somewhere*.

Another brief memory I have is of a ramble I went on, possibly with Walt. We'd walked off down one of the narrow country roads that wind over the fells roughly in the direction of Shap, and at one point the road passed through a narrow tunnel under the main Western Railway line. We'd just emerged into a large field at the other side when we heard the distant rumble of a train approaching at high speed, so stopped to look back. To our delight and excitement we were met by the exhilarating sight of the magnificent Silver Link Express hurtling towards us like a huge, silver rocket. It flashed past us with a great roar of sound, and disappeared northward at tremendous speed. Leaving a wonderful, permanent image in my memory.

By this time in 1942 the woods around the area were well into their colourful autumn clothing and the moment was rapidly approaching of my final departure from Orton and return to Barrow. I'm not sure quite how or why this decision was made, nor do I have any memory of the train journey back. All I know is that before the end of 1942 I was back in Barrow, facing the final six months of my schooling at the Alfred Barrow School.

SOME MAJOR EVENTS OF THE YEAR:

(1) Rommel captured Tobruk, but was defeated by Montgomery at Alamein

(2) America gains hard-fought air-sea victories over the Japanese in the battles of the Coral Sea and Midway.

(3) Walt Disney's *Bambi* was screened.

(4) The Island of Malta was awarded the George Cross for its gallantry.

(5) The wartime 'National Loaf' was introduced.

(6) The REME was established – my own future regiment.

(7) The 'Mildenhall Treasure' was discovered in Suffolk (Roman silverware).

8

Back to Barrow

1943 (14 years old in July)

After the country lifestyle I'd been enjoying in Orton, settling down to life in Barrow again took quite a while. We were still living at 107 Marsh Street, but obviously things had moved on in the eighteen months I'd been away.

Fortunately the air raids were long over, though the wreckage of the bomb sites and propped up buildings everywhere were a constant reminder of the destruction these had wrought on our small town.

Some of the evacuees had, like myself, returned home, though others were still noticeably absent.

The greatest challenge that I now faced, was returning to the Alfred Barrow School after spending so long 'standing still' at the sleepy little village school in Orton. At least standing still as far as my 'formal' education was concerned, though I'd learned a great deal in other ways, and had a great many experiences I'd never have had if I'd stayed in Barrow.

Unfortunately, I discovered that as far as my formal education was concerned, after my eighteen months away I was so far behind the other pupils who'd remained in Barrow, that there was no hope of catching up in the six months I had left.

Missing so much of my schooling during this crucial, final stage of my education, has always been a source of regret to me. This was especially so where the study of English was concerned, because I now found the masters talking in bewildering detail about 'grammar', when I'd never even 'heard' of the word. With me beginning to develop the leaning I'd always had towards writing, as well as towards singing,

77

this gap in my education was something I had to struggle later to fill in for myself.

So much had moved on while I'd been away that much of that final six months at school is a bit of a muddled haze. Odd little things do stand out though, one of which is the fact that I now had school meals – something I don't remember having there before, and in which I got my first introduction to ginger pudding and custard, something which remained a great favourite of mine from then on.

One of the other highlights of that time for me was a somewhat 'cringe making' attempt by the elderly, rather staid headmaster of the time, to deliver what was intended to be a lecture on the facts of life. I'd never before seen such embarrassment in anyone of his exalted position. He muttered and mumbled his way through odd disjointed bits about the differences between boys and girls, almost whispering words like 'teets', ovaries etc, as if they were tantamount to swearing in church.

Fortunately it didn't last long and we could all breathe a sigh of relief as he left. I don't know who was the more embarrassed, the poor old headmaster, or the whole classroom of boys; any one of whom could have delivered a much more enlightened lecture on the subject than he did.

We were also doing more sports now than I remember previously at the Alfred Barrow. The main one was football, of course, and since the school was right near the centre of town, while the football field was over a mile away in the town park, this involved a long walk just to get there. Because of this, football was always scheduled as the last activity of the day; so we could all just clear off straight home afterwards. This suited me fine as the park soccer fields bordered the far end of Greengate Street, which was only a few minutes walk from Marsh Street.

Although I was never really a soccer fan, I always enjoyed these particular games. Partly because they were little more than rampaging kick-abouts, and also because the park football fields were a great play area for us Marsh Street kids anyway. As was the whole of the great rolling expanse of Barrow park itself.

At that time this side of the park was bordered by iron railings and a long line of tall, elegant poplar trees – the ones I'd written about in my school poem in Orton. Even after closing time, when the park would be cleared and locked up, we'd often shin over the fence, playing hide and seek with our main enemy, the Park Keeper, while we explored its deadly unknown jungles and swamps full of crocodiles, fought off cannibals that haunted the woods around the large boating lake, or dodged the pirates whose secret hideout, we knew for a fact, was on the island in the middle of the small one; right where the swans nested. We usually avoided the playground and swings as that would draw too much attention from our main enemy, but we'd sometimes fight battles around the bandstand, or chase after enemies up the long flight of stone steps that led up to the towering war memorial.

Unfortunately, these rousing conflicts would all too often be brought to an abrupt halt when the cry of.

"Parkie. . !" rang out from one of the fearsome warriors.

It was then a case of 'every man for himself' as we all scattered like the devil, trying to reach the nearest climbable fence before the Park Keeper spotted us.

About this time my sister Jean, who was three years older than myself, had already started working for a living. For girls in those days this often meant, 'going into service', as it was called, as a maid in one of the better off houses. There always seemed to be plenty of this kind of work around, because at that time even middle class people like doctors, solicitors, etc., all seemed wealthy enough to employ servants. Jean, however, had landed a job at one of the more aristocratic houses in the district which was the home of Lord and Lady Fell.

The only 'down' side to this, as far as 'I' was concerned, was that it was located away out in the country some distance to the north of Dalton, and I had to cycle the six or seven miles there on several occasions to take her washing which Mam did for her every week. This did, however, have a certain 'up' side to it, in that on arrival they always gave me a meal, and this is where I remember tasting 'minted' new potatoes for the first time.

Almost before I knew it, my last six months of schooling were coming to an end. My fourteenth birthday in July had almost arrived, and because the school broke up for the summer holidays about two weeks before my birthday, I actually left school while I was still only thirteen. In fact, since I started my first job almost immediately, I've always maintained that I probably started work when I was only thirteen.

With the war still raging on there was no shortage of jobs everywhere. However, because apprenticeships for skilled jobs were not available until you were sixteen, school leavers of my age had to take whatever jobs they could find, hopefully the ones that paid the most money.

For me this turned out to be at the Co-op Dairy where they were offering 21 shillings a week for boys to help on the daily milk delivery rounds. Since most of the other school leavers I knew, were taking jobs in shops for 15 shillings a week or so, I felt this was great. I was a real wage earner for the first time in my life. In fact, the only other money I ever remember 'earning' before, was the sixpence a week I got from Mam for collecting all her Money Club subscriptions; the shilling I'd once got for helping to build the dry stone wall in Orton, and 3p I'd once been paid by the organist of a church in Abbey Road for pumping the organ for his practice sessions. So £1.1/- felt like 'real' money.

Of course this was not 'my' money. In those days whatever money came in was 'family' money. Everything had to be handed over into the family pot, and you were then given something back as pocket money.

The job at the Co-op turned out to be pretty hard work, but I enjoyed it. I'd never been afraid of physical graft; having had plenty of that on the farm, and life at the Co-op turned out a lot more varied and interesting than I'd expected. The milk deliveries, it turned out, were only the morning activity. Once that was over you had a midday meal break, which most of us went home for. This was always called 'dinner' up North – lunch simply meant a packed sandwich snack.

When you returned you could find yourself being sent off to do all sorts of different jobs in various Co-op departments. Of which the dairy itself was just one in the large Co-op complex at the top end of Buccleuch Street. The others were the bakery, the butchery, and a huge food warehouse, all set around a large square which you entered through a gateway from Buccleuch Street. It was from all these departments that the many Co-op shops around the town received all their supplies.

Since many of these bulk deliveries were not only done by lorry, but also by horse drawn flat-bed carts, there was also a stable for half a dozen horses tucked away in the complex.

Apart from working in this main complex you could sometimes find yourself being sent out in the afternoon to work in one of the widely scattered Co-op grocery shops around the town to act as a shop boy.

At first I did my milk deliveries as part of a three-handed team; two boys and a man driver on one of the lorries or horse drawn carts, which served the outlying town districts. But after about three months I graduated to pushing one of the hand carts which served the town centre area closer to the dairy. At first I did this with an older boy, but was then, at around 14 and a half years of age given my own round. This consisted of about nine or ten streets on the far side of Duke Street main road, which was about half a mile from the dairy, and quite a long, hard push with a cart loaded with anything up to ten crates of milk.

I soon discovered that how 'hard' a push this was didn't depend solely on the quality of your own muscles, but also on the quality of the cart you happened to get landed with. This accounted for the mad rush I'd noticed first thing in the mornings to get the best carts. I very quickly learned to avoid the dodgier ones with stiff axle joints; because simply getting one of these out of the gate was like rowing a Spanish galleon single handed, never mind pushing it all the way to your round.

It's strange how little coincidences happen in your life which you're often not aware of at the time. It wasn't until many years later, that I learned that one of the streets on the round I'd been allotted, Duncan Street, was the street where my father had lived when he was a young man, and that one of the doorsteps I was leaving milk on during the second war, was the doorstep he'd stepped over as a young man to go off and fight in the army during the first war.

Milk, like every other food commodity, was carefully rationed at that time, which meant that every house had its own allocation according to who lived there. Houses with kids or nursing mothers would be allowed two or three pints a day, while someone living alone would probably be allowed only half a pint. Since we only used pint bottles this meant they'd get one pint every two days. Fortunately, this was all set out on my delivery sheet; and as the customer had to pay by tickets they'd bought at their local Co-op shops I didn't have to handle any money, just collect tickets.

Since this was the first time I'd had to deal directly with the public it was a great education for me, though I probably wasn't aware of it at the time. My round seemed to contain a whole cross section of customers, ranging from those I never met, and were represented solely in my mind by a couple of empty milk bottles with tickets on a doorstep. To those lonely old souls who were constantly trying to invite me in for a cup of tea and a chat.

I particularly remember one little old blind lady who lived on her own in a rather dingy little house. I nearly always had to knock on her door as her bottle was never out on the step. I soon grew to suspect that this was deliberate, and that I was probably the only visitor she received on most days. When she opened the door she was nearly always carrying something she wanted me to check; a letter she wanted me to read, etc. The item most often offered for my confirmation, though, were pairs of stockings.

"Are these two the same colour?" she would ask.

Sometimes they were, but sometimes they weren't, though I always managed to sort them into proper matching pairs for her, and this was a real object lesson to me, because it had never occurred to me before just how disabling blindness could be in the small, everyday things which I took for granted. Living on her own, she was, of course, only entitled to half a pint a day. However, as always, there was a little bit of flexibility in the system, and I made sure she didn't go short.

I had my few dodgy customers, like every other delivery man. Those who were trying to get more than they were entitled to, or who simply tried to avoid paying with the old trick:

"I haven't had time to get to the shop for my tickets; but I'll give you two lots tomorrow."

Some were genuine, of course, but you soon learned to distinguish between the two.

There were lots of jokes in those days about door to door delivery men being propositioned by bored and frustrated housewives with husbands out at work, or away in the army. But this never seemed to happen to me, unfortunately. At the time I put this bad luck down to my age. After all a 14 or 15 year old lad would hardly have been looked upon as a dashing romantic conquest by a mature woman. . . would he?

On looking back at the situation now, though, from the dizzy heights of maturity, I realise that not only 'could' I have been looked at in that way, but I can distinctly pinpoint several times when I actually 'was'. At the time I'd simply been too immature and naïve to recognise the signals that were being beamed my way.

There was, however, one exception. One occasion when I actually 'did' recognise these signals loud and clear. They frightened the life out of me, and I couldn't get out of the house quick enough. This concerned a woman who lived in a flat up a flight of dark stairs in an old building just off Hindpool Road. For some reason she would never leave her empty bottles downstairs on the step, but always upstairs on the dark landing outside the door of her flat, which was the one and only flat in the building.

Whenever I delivered the milk she always seemed to hear the clattering of the milk bottles and opened the door. The flat inside was just as dark as the landing, and she always appeared simply as a figure in the dark wearing a white, knee length dressing gown. She always seemed friendly, but a bit sleepy and always had to go back in to find her milk tickets. On the occasion in question, however, she seemed to be having difficulty finding her tickets, so asked me to step inside while she searched.

Once inside I realised for the first time that there were a couple of children in there too, as I could just make out their sleeping figures on a bed in the corner. As she finally found the tickets and came to give them to me, she let go of her tightly held dressing gown allowing it to flap wide open to reveal the first 'mature' naked female body I'd ever seen.

Then making no attempt to cover herself up she asked, in scarily inviting, seductive tones.

"Why don't you stay for a while and have a cup of tea?"

While I always 'welcomed' the odd cup of tea with my little old lady customers, I felt pretty sure that the cup of tea 'she' was offering was somewhat different from the ones 'they' gave me. So I nervously retreated towards the door, muttering inanities about being late; other customers waiting. . . Then fled down the stairs with my honour intact but the memory of her temping, voluptuous curves haunting me for the rest of the day.

Funnily enough, after that her milk bottles were always left downstairs on the doorstep, complete with tickets. And I couldn't help feeling somehow, that I'd blown my first real opportunity at genuine sex education.

In those days the central police station used to be in Cornwallis Street which was on my round. The lady there who used to be my customer, lived in a flat above it, and seemed to be a sort of caretaker, come housekeeper, for the station. She was a big Amazon of a woman, and looked as if she could have handled all the ne'r-do-wells in the district on her own. However, the main reason she stands out, is that she turned out to be the mother of one of my ex-fellow school pupils. Until I started delivering their milk, though, I never knew he lived in a police station, and meeting her explained a lot; especially why he was several times larger than the rest of us.

That winter I had my first taste of the trials and tribulations of being a milk doorstep deliverer when the weather was at its worst. Rain was bad enough, but when the frost, ice and snow covered the roads, simply getting the heavily loaded milk cart to my round became a real struggle. The first part of the journey was up Buccleuch Street, which had a pronounced upward slope; something which you'd normally have hardly noticed, but trying to push a heavy milk cart up it through six inches of snow was like climbing Mount Everest. I remember one day when the road was so bad, that I decided to manhandle the cart up onto the pavement, which had been cleared for pedestrians, and was making good progress, when an officious policeman came plodding along with a highly critical expression twisting his face.

"Get that thing back onto the road," he growled. "You're not allowed on the pavement with that."

I stopped and stared at the six inches of snow in exhausted disbelief.

"How can I push it on there?" I gasped.

"That's not the point!" he declared. "It's against the law."

"But I've got to deliver the milk," I insisted.

"Well you can't do it like that," he replied.

"Alright!" I panted, "how would 'you' do it?"

"That's nothing to do with it," he huffed awkwardly, obviously beginning to realise how stupid his attitude was. "Anyway!" he muttered, moving off, "I've given you a warning, and that's that."

"Right," I replied, continuing on up the pavement as before. At least his interruption had given me a bit of a breather.

There was quite a bit of this lousy weather to put up with that winter, which wasn't helped by the fact that at one time I also had a boil in the middle of my back, and on another occasion I was hobbling with a sceptic heel. In those days, though, people weren't expected to take time off work for such minor ailments, and I, being no exception, just had to carry on like everyone else.

One bright spot in all of this, however, came in the form of the Christmas tips I got from my customers. I could hardly believe the amount I picked up. All going into the family pot, of course, which helped our Christmas no end.

SOME MAJOR EVENTS OF THE YEAR:
(1) German and Italian forces finally surrender in North Africa, followed by Allied landings in Sicily and Southern Italy.
(2) The largest known meteorite crater (the Chubb Crater) discovered in Canada.
(3) Mussolini imprisoned, but rescued by a German raiding party.
(4) The Russians defeat the German Army at Stalingrad.
(5) Rolls Royce produce the first jet engine (the Welland).

1944 (15 years old in July)
Shortly after Christmas my afternoon work at the Co-op took a turn for the better when I was given a regular job helping old Bob Mitten, a van driver, on his daily rounds delivering grocery supplies from the warehouse to the many Co-op shops around the town. This was far preferable to being sent off all over the place doing every odd job from mopping shop floors, sloshing about the wet dairy floor in clogs, or to stacking ten-stone bags of flour up on the third floor of the bakery as they were winched up through a trap door from delivery carts below in the yard – why ten stones for flour when potato sacks were only eight I never found out. All I know is this was a tough old job.

Bob Mitten must have been well into his seventies, and but for the war, he would probably have been retired long before. He was a bit of a character who knew all the ropes, but was a nice old chap and we got along well from the start.

Everything was delivered to the shops from the warehouse in bulk in those days, and had to be weighed and bagged in the back rooms of the stores by the shop girls. Butter came in lined boxes, large, heavy cheeses were packed two at a time in rough wooden crates, dried fruit like currants etc., also in boxes, but for some reason sugar, and dried peas were always in huge sixteen stone sacks. How anyone dreamed that one up I can't imagine, because they were impossible to lift. Even wheeling them onto the van on sack barrows from the warehouse bank was hard enough; how we were supposed to get them off was apparently 'our' problem. Or rather 'my' problem since there was no way that old Bob could carry them.

However, fifteen year old lads were a lot more robust in those days than they seem to be now, and I found that once I'd got one of these hefty sacks properly balanced on my back – even though it felt like Atlas holding up the world – I could usually manage to stagger into the shop storeroom with it. Once inside, however, there was no way I could lower it down gently, so it was simply a case of letting it flop, and jumping out of the way quickly. Fortunately, the sacks seemed to survive this pretty harsh treatment OK so it seemed to work.

Of course, the inevitable was bound to happen eventually, and in one shop when I dumped the massive sack flat on its face, it split wide open. Burying the great expanse of concrete floor six inches deep under sixteen stone of dried peas.

I can't remember the exact words that shattered the air in the great howl of complaint that followed – mostly by the girls who would have to clear it all up – but I don't think they included such expressions as: "Dearie me. . !'; 'Fancy that. . !' or 'Well, I never. . !'

Still, looked at positively, disaster it may have been, but it could also be looked upon as a 'unique' experience. Something to tell their grand kids about. After all, there can't be many girls who can claim to have paddled their feet in sixteen stones of dried peas.

Another unique, but much more dramatic, disaster occurred round about this time during my morning milk round. This involved the huge anti-aircraft barrage balloons which were still floating high above the town. For even though the blitz on Barrow was long over, these monsters remained, with their long steel tethering cables acting as a deterrent to any low-flying enemy aircraft that may try again.

On this particular morning, I was delivering milk in a street near the Town Hall when a fierce electric storm suddenly burst out over the town. Torrents of rain belted down, flooding the streets, while thunder and lightning flashes were splitting the sky. Normally, this would have led to a desperate dash by the barrage balloon teams to winch the hydrogen filled balloons down to safety. But on this occasion the storm had struck so suddenly, that it was a losing battle. One balloon after another was struck by lightning, and exploded in a great blast of burning hydrogen. Soon the sky everywhere was filled with huge plumes of boiling fire, as the heavy tethering cables snaked down to earth, dragging the tattered remnants of the burning balloons down after them.

It was all over in about five minutes, but while it lasted was the most breathtaking fireworks display I've ever seen.

Although by this time the progress of the war was very definitely taking a turn for the better, it was still far from over. All around the Barrow area units of the regular army were still keeping up their training sessions. These were always a great attraction to me and my mates, particularly where gunnery practice was concerned, and we soon got to know all the best spots for watching them let rip with their blistering fire power.

One of these was down on the coast road near Rampside, where a gunnery unit would regularly set up their Bofors guns on a concrete platform overlooking the sea. The astonishing thing about this platform, was that it stood right near the edge of the road, so we could stand on the bank and watch them blast off their rounds from only a few feet away. So close, it was almost like being part of the action. Their target was a large steel plate hanging from a frame five or six hundred yards away out on the wet sands. Whenever they scored a hit there'd be a bright flash of steel on steel, followed a couple of seconds later by a faint, distant clang.

As they fired the large solid rounds the Bofors guns would spit out the empty brass cases in a great, clattering stream onto the concrete platform. And with our usual nose for souvenir hunting we always watched hopefully for any that rolled off onto the beach. But no luck, with brass being such a vital wartime commodity the eagle-eyed gunners made sure they collected up every last one.

About a hundred yards further down the coast road there was a camouflaged anti-aircraft rocket battery hidden in a field, which we'd occasionally see letting rip with a spectacular practice burst of rocket fire. These usually took us by surprise while we were watching the Bofors guns, and quite literally took your breath away, because they didn't fire single rockets, but ten or twelve together in one great salvo of searing flame. All the rockets would streak up into the sky together, and explode in a great ring of smoke and flame about three thousand feet up. Unfortunately, this rocket practice didn't take place very often, though we were always looking for it hopefully while watching the Bofors guns.

Another piece of free gunnery entertainment we'd stumble on sometimes used to take place in an old deserted sand quarry near Roose; which we were well familiar with because we always knew it as the Sandhills and it was a favourite adventure ground of ours when we were kids. Having been a working quarry, it still had several of the old, dilapidated corrugated iron sheds from its quarry days rusting away there, as well as a long-disused railway line that was sinking into the ground.

The top walls of the quarry were like great cliffs of sand sixty feet high, and leaping off the top to slither to the bottom on the soft sand was like doing the Cresta Run without a sled.

The gunners on these occasions were the Home Guard, and their fire-power was naturally much lighter, consisting usually of small submachine 'Sten Guns'. These were designed for close quarter combat and fired from the waist. Because they were cheap to make, and simple to use, these had the reputation of being somewhat inaccurate, and with a tendency to jam.

This was probably true, but when we watched Barrow's own Dad's Army blasting away with them in the Roose Sandhills they seemed pretty deadly weapons to us. And anyone who believed the old joke about, "the safest place to be when the Home Guard were practising was in front of the target," would have laughed on the other side of their faces if they'd seen the way the short, sharp bursts of crackling fire from these part-timers splintered the plywood human-figure targets to bits.

As well as all these exciting diversions to life at the Co-op, there were also a couple of disasters around this time which helped to remind me of the tragic side to the war, and the price that some people were still paying.

The first one was when we got word that a Boulton Paul Defiant aircraft had crashed 'somewhere' near Yarlside, so decided to go and look for it. The Boulton Paul Defiant was basically a single-seat fighter, which had been converted into a two-seater, by simply adding a backward facing gun turret behind the pilot. The reason for this was to try and counteract attacks from the rear, something which always posed the greatest danger to any single-seater pilot.

Apparently, the Defiant had proved a success at first, as the German pilots mistook it for a Hurricane and attacked it from the rear.

However, this success was short-lived, partly because the Luftwaffe soon latched on to the ploy, and partly because the extra weight of the gunner made the Defiant relatively slow and less manoeuvrable, so easier to shoot down from other directions.

Having tramped away over to Yarlside, the presence of military vehicles up on the hillside gave the game away as to the crash site. As we knew the area well, we realised that it must be somewhere up near the old railway branch-line cutting, which in the old days was used to transport iron ore down from the mine to link up with the main line near Roose Station.

It didn't take us long to climb up the hill through the gorse bushes on a roundabout route that brought us out just above the crash site, which was guarded by several soldiers of the Home Guard.

Our first reaction was one of disappointment, because the main wreckage of the aircraft had already been removed. However, as we looked around at all the scattered bits of wreckage still left among the gorse bushes, the 'tragedy' of the crash suddenly hit me, because hanging from the spikes of gorse everywhere were small shreds of flesh and tissue, while blood splashes stained the underlying grass. We'd come with the excited hope of seeing a crashed aircraft, but what we'd actually found was a tragic death scene.

This sudden realisation came as a shock to me, which brought home the sad reality of such disasters for those involved. I suppose it was a moment of growing up, because afterwards I never looked upon such events in the same way as before.

The Defiant in this case, it turned out, hadn't been shot down but simply crashed on a training exercise. Somehow this seemed to make the tragedy even worse.

The other aircraft disaster I remember from this time, concerned an American twin engined bomber (a Boston I think) which hit barrage balloon cables over Barrow and crashed somewhere out over Roosecote Sands I believe? But we never found out where.

Although the war was now grinding strongly in our favour, shortages of virtually everything remained part of everyday life. We were still living in a 'make do and mend' world, with Mam constantly recycling clothes on her old Singer sewing machine, and Dad cobbling all our worn out shoes to keep us plodding along. He'd made himself a tiny workshop in the cramped space under the stairs, where he kept his tools and cobbler's last.

As I was always keen to learn something new he taught me how to do it, and eventually I was able to cobble shoes almost as well as he could. I remember that on one occasion I repaired a pair of expensive high heeled shoes for a lady up the street. I can't imagine how she got on with them afterwards, but I'm not mentioning her name in case she's still inclined to sue.

Another perennial problem for most people in those days, which doesn't exist today, thank heavens, was the battle against unwanted guests, like mice, fleas and bed bugs. Mice were always a problem; setting traps etc., though the possession of a cat seemed the only real solution. Fleas I don't remember much about, but bed bugs I certainly do.

There were no interior sprung mattresses in those days. 'Sleeping' simply meant iron bedsteads head and foot, with an angle iron frame criss-crossed with steel wires as a base. This was topped off with a solid flock mattress, which was virtually impossible to clean, and apparently expected to last a lifetime. All this provided an ideal world for bed bugs to thrive in, but their most common hiding place seemed to be in the metal joints where the frame slotted into the legs. While nestling in there they were virtually impregnable.

The only solution was to regularly dismantle the bed and paint the inside of all the joints with creosote; which we always got from the gasworks in an old two pint can which we kept for this purpose. Although this did the trick for a month or so, it left the bedroom reeking of creosote for several days. . . The positive side to this, is that it probably helped to keep us free from colds as well as bed bugs.

All through 1944 my morning milk round, and afternoon deliveries in old Bob Mitten's van, had settled into a steady routine which looked set to continue right through into 1945. Unfortunately, however, something occurred in late November that brought this first phase of my working life to an abrupt end.

On that day I'd done my morning milk round as usual, but through bad weather conditions I was a bit later than normal going home for my midday meal. Since I was still entitled to a full hour's break this is what I took. When I got back, however, the manager; who was an elderly, dour, unsmiling sort of chap – who again, but for the war, would have been long retired – accosted me angrily in the yard.

"What do you think you're playing at coming back late?" he demanded.

"I'm not late," I protested. "I've only had an hour."

"Don't argue with me," he shouted.

I tried to protest, but he didn't want to listen.

"I'm not having you just coming back when you like," he ranted. "So you can just get off home."

Since I was probably one of the most conscientious and hard

working of all the lads working there, I was seething with the injustice of his astonishing outburst. But as there seemed nothing I could do about it I turned to go. Not content with this, however, he called out after me:

"I know how to deal with people like you," he shouted.

That was the final straw for me, I spun around furiously and threatened him with my fist.

"And 'I' know how to deal with people like you," I yelled. "If you say one more word I'll come back there and belt you one."

He simply stood there speechless, his eyes wide open in astonishment; but by his expression obviously convinced that saying any more would definitely 'not' be in his interest, so kept his mouth shut. And I just turned and went home.

I didn't say anything to Mam about this, and just turned up for work next morning as usual. When I arrived, however, I was told by the foreman that I was not to start, but to report to the manager's office.

When I turned up at the desk, he came out of his office looking just as sour and miserable as usual. This did not incline me to polite conversation, and definitely not to any sort of apology, so I simply demanded:

"Am I working today, or not?"

"You're not," he growled.

"Right!" I said. "Then you can 'stick' your rotten job." And that was it.

When I finally told Mam she was none too pleased, especially at the thought of losing an important part of the family income, and was rather inclined to try and get my job back. But I was having none of it, and set about looking for another job. Fortunately with the wartime conditions of full employment, I knew that there would be plenty of new opportunities.

SOME MAJOR EVENTS OF THE YEAR:

(1) D Day; The allies landed in Normandy; Liberation of Paris and Brussels; Battle of Arnhem; Battle of Monte Cassino; RAF drop 22,000lb Grand Slam bombs on German U-boat pens.

(2) Start of the German VI and V2 rocket bombardment of Britain.

(3) Failed bunker bomb plot against Hitler.

(4) National Health Service proposed in Britain.

(5) Secondary school education for all children established.

(6) Britain's largest battleship HMS *Vanguard* launched – 42,000 tons. (I later worked on its 5.25" high angle guns in Vickers Armstrongs' Shipyard).

9

The Inevitable Shipyard

1945 (16 years old in July)
With Barrow being primarily a shipbuilding town, Vickers Armstrongs' yard was an obvious first place to look for my new job, so I eventually turned up at their job's office looking for some sort of apprenticeship.

"You're not old enough yet," declared the recruitment clerk. "You have to be sixteen to start one of them. However," he added, "if you really want to work here there are plenty of other jobs you could have a go at in the meantime."

"That's great!" I said. And thus began my entry into the shipbuilding world.

It seemed that among other places, they were looking for a lad in the sheet metal shop, and as that sounded OK to me I reported there on my first day. I turned up early, as I didn't want to be responsible for holding up Vickers Armstrongs' shipbuilding production by being late – especially after my recent 'late comers' exit from the Co-op.

However, after I'd been left standing outside the foreman's office for over an hour, it dawned on me that building ships was obviously a somewhat more leisurely process than delivering milk on people's doorsteps dead on time each morning. Eventually though, a short, plump man in a dark suit and bowler hat came clumping down the stairs from the office.

"I'm Mr Dowie, the head foreman," he announced, pointing to his bowler hat. I found out later that this was traditional in the shipyard, 'ordinary' foremen only wore flat caps. He then took me off and handed me over to one of the sheet metal workers, who was busily

91

shaping a large sheet of metal by holding it against a thick lead block on a steel bench while beating it with a rubber hammer. By this time the noise in the large sheet metal shop had become almost deafening, with mechanical hammers battering heavier metal into shape or punching holes in strips, and all this to the background thump of a massive steam guillotine, which was chopping huge steel plates into smaller pieces.

The difference of this clanging working environment to that at the Co-op couldn't have been greater, but at the same time I found it all fascinating, even if slightly daunting.

The chap I'd been set to work with introduced himself as Steve and must have been in his thirties. I got on well with him right from the start, and what struck me about him most was that he looked a lot smarter than the other sheet metal workers in the workshop, because for some reason he wore a light brown boiler suit, while all the others wore the traditional blue bib and brace type. I found later that because of this he was regarded by his workmates as a bit of a natty dresser. As for myself, not possessing anything resembling proper overalls, I'd turned up in any old clothes I could find; which by contrast must have made him look even more natty.

The sheet of metal he'd been working on when I first met him was to be part of a long, convoluted box-section ventilation system for one of the 5.25 inch high-angle gun turrets, which were being built in Vickers for the battleship *Vanguard* – which was apparently under construction in some other shipyard.

So here I was straight from a milk round, right into the centre of the offensive war effort, and I thought it was great.

Making and fitting these gun turret ventilation systems turned out to be Steve's speciality, and he was brilliant at it. All the sheet metal pieces were cut out according to templates and drawings. Which, because of their awkward shapes, was complicated enough, but because no two gun turrets were 'exactly' the same size, the real skill lay in being able to modify each system to fit each individual turret. Threading all these weird shaped box sections into place among all the other pipes, speaker tubes, cables and the ammunition-hoist mechanisms for bringing up the large shells from the magazines deep below in the ship was a work of art.

My role in all this was simply to lend him a hand where and when I could, which more often than not, involved crawling in and out of all the cramped spaces in the turrets to reach awkward bolt holes.

The turrets themselves were being built in a vast building which was known as the gun shop; so this is where we spent most of our time once a particular 'vent' system had been made, carting it backwards and forwards to the sheet metal shop to do any modifications required.

Although the 5.25 inch gun turrets were large enough, they were absolutely dwarfed by some of the gun turrets the gun shop could turn out. These could be anything up to monsters the size of a bungalow, housing three or four enormous 16 inch guns. And because of all the lift mechanisms these main armament guns had underneath to hoist the huge 16 inch shells up from the magazines below decks, they had to be built over gun-pits thirty or more feet deep. The gun shop had several of these enormous pits in the floor. It was also crammed with metal working machinery everywhere, including massive lathes and huge metal-finishing turntables you could have put a bus on. Above every alleyway, overhead gantry cranes clattered along on rails, transporting castings around the huge building.

As well as helping to fit the ventilator systems into the turrets, I also helped Steve back in the workshop when he was cutting out the sheet metal sections. Generally this was OK but it did have its dodgy moments. One of my jobs sometimes involved catching the off-cuts at the back of the large steam-powered guillotine when he was cutting large steel sheets into the sizes he needed, and in my first week there I was trying to catch a rather larger off-cut than usual, when it tipped up trapping my fingers against the back of the guillotine. I instinctively snatched my hands away, but not quickly enough, with the result that the sharp edge of the plate took the skin off the backs of all my fingers; which led to my first visit to one of the shipyard's medical centres that I'd noticed dotted about everywhere.

I then spent the rest of the day hanging about painfully in the workshop, nursing my bandaged fingers and feeling sorry for myself. There was no mention of sending me home even though with sore, bandaged fingers I was obviously unable to do any work. Nor was there any suggestion of me taking the next day off in order to let my hands recover. Such small accidents, it seemed, were no excuse for taking time off. To get paid you had to turn up, even if it was just to hang about. So that's what did!

Fortunately, I managed to avoid any more accidents while in the sheet metal shop, so probably this early painful experience was a good lesson learned

Since the ventilation systems were built up from sheets of bare mild steel, once they were finished and ready for fitting into the gun turret, they had to be given a protective coating. To do this we had to cart them off to the galvanising shed and have them bodily dipped into a deep trough of molten galvanising metal.

This galvanising shed was a very tall, smoke filled cavern-like place swirling with smoke and fumes. Glaring notices outside the door warned you of the potential dangers inside, and when you went in the first thing that hit you was the searing heat, and the acrid smell of burning metal. Down the centre of the building there were two long troughs in the floor, each about three feet wide, and twenty feet long. They were both about eight feet deep, and the first one was filled with some sort of pickling acid liquid. While the other was filled with bubbling, silvery molten metal. You kept well away from these troughs, especially the molten metal one, because if you tripped and fell in there you'd never be seen again. Usually you'd find the men inside in the process of lowering metal fabrications, or long metal pipes of all sizes and shapes, into one or other of the troughs with an overhead crane. The acid in the first one was simply to dissolve away all the rust and dirt from the metal so that the molten galvanising metal would have a clean surface to bond to. Apart from the fumes this process was not particularly hazardous, but if they were dipping things into the molten metal you had to watch out, especially if it was pipes, because when pipes were being lowered into this they would often turn into lethal cannons firing great jets of molten metal in every direction.

We were always only too glad to leave our ventilation fabrication in there with them and get out; coming back later to collect it.

Another new experience for me at the shipyard was the business of clocking on and off. At the Co-op all we'd had to do was show our faces in the yard and that was it. With only twenty odd lads working there this worked OK. At Vickers Armstrongs, however, with over 15,000 employees, the situation was somewhat different. With no computers, or clocking in card system in those days to keep track of everybody, it must have been a book-keeper's nightmare.

This was compounded by the fact that the shipyard covered such a vast area, with eight or nine different gates where the workers could enter of leave.

How Vickers handled this was by using a simple brass disc system. Each employee was allotted a brass disc with their own number stamped on it, and a particular gate to enter or leave by. When you turned up at your particular gate you were handed your brass disc, which the clerk took off a hook on a large board full of discs.

On leaving at knocking off time you simply threw your brass disc into a box at the nearest gate on your way out; which, because of the roving nature of many people's jobs didn't necessarily have to be the gate you came in by. How they ever managed to get all the discs back to their correct gateways by the next morning I've no idea.

It was obviously a system that lent itself to abuse by the usual dodgy skivers there were around, who managed to find places where they could nip out over the wall for a couple of hours, and get back in time to knock off. The same applied to those who wanted to go walkabout inside the yard; to see mates in other departments, or get jobs done for something they were doing at home. The danger in this was the possibility of getting stopped by a shipyard security guard asking where you were going. One of the chaps in the sheet metal shop apparently had his own solution to this. When off for a wander he'd carry a clip-board and always walk purposefully, as if in a hurry to get somewhere. Apparently this always worked and he was never stopped by security.

Of course, there was always the possibility that they might run into some charge hand or foreman who recognised them, and knew they should have been back in the workshop. However, there was one crafty devil I heard of who'd even worked out a solution to this. He always had some ready made excuse in his head, and if spotted would make a bee-line for whoever it was and declare:

"I've been looking for you." Then trot out his cock and bull story, often to glares of suspicion. But apparently the stories were always just credible enough for him to get away with it.

One place you couldn't skive off to in Vickers was the toilet, because every toilet block had an attendant sitting behind a window at the entrance, and you had to hand him your brass disc as you went in. He would then enter your number, and time of entry, into a large ledger. You duly collected your disc on the way out, and the time would also be recorded for posterity in his weighty book. You were allowed only seven minutes for this call of nature, and if you took any longer you'd be docked fifteen minutes from your pay at the end of the week. I can't imagine how the Time & 'Motion' experts (pun definitely intended) had come up with the figure of seven minutes. But it's quite a thought to think that somewhere deep down in the vaults of Vickers Armstrongs, there probably still exists a record of every toilet visit complete with name and number – of every one of the thousands of employees who worked there throughout the war.

On one of our frequent visits to the gun shop I ran into one of my mates from Marsh Street, Willie Irwin. I knew that he worked in the shipyard but didn't know exactly where. To my surprise he was driving a bogie. These were small, flat bed, electric vehicles used for carting metal parts, supplies, etc., all over the shipyard. The flat bed on the bogie was about two feet high, six feet long and four feet wide. The driver stood on a platform at the back behind a three foot high control column.

Willie told me that all the bogies worked from a central garage, and apparently any workshop needing to send or collect something just rang there for one. He'd just delivered something to the gun shop when I spotted him.

I was fascinated by his bogie, and curious to know how he came to land the job, since none of the lads in Marsh Street had any experience whatsoever of driving.

"They told me I didn't need any," replied Willie. "They just showed me how to do it."

"Really!" I exclaimed, pretty enviously. "How long did that take?"

"Just a couple of days," replied Willie. "It's easy when you get used to it."

"Can I have a go?" I asked.

"Alright," agreed Willie, jumping off the driving platform.

"All you have to do," he explained as I jumped on, "is to press your foot on this pedal down here and steer it with the steering wheel."

"Right!" I declared eagerly following his instructions. The next second the bogie and me were spinning wildly round in a circle the opposite way to what I'd intended. I quickly spun the wheel back again, only to find the bogie then spinning round the other way, again in the opposite way to what it should. "What's the matter with the bloomin' thing!" I gasped as I jumped off.

"You were turning the wheel the wrong way," declared Willie.

"No I wasn't," I insisted. "I turned it right and it went left."

"Well, that's the way it works," insisted Willie.

"But you didn't tell me that," I complained.

"I just thought you'd know," shrugged Willie.

It turned out that this weird machine with a mind of its own, had 'rear wheel' steering, which slews the back of the machine round and not the front, so having the opposite effect to normal steering. Which may be OK when you're used to it, but a devil of a job to get your head around when you're not.

Willie, it seemed, had mastered this pretty well, and could whip it in and out of the alleyways like a demon.

Meal breaks at the shipyard, I found, were similar to what I'd been used to at the Co-op, in that you got an hour at midday. The main difference being that the whole shipyard stopped at the same time for this, 12 o'clock, and re-started at 1 o'clock. The signal for stopping and starting was a great blast on the shipyard sirens. These were placed at various points around the shipyard, and when they all went off together they could be heard for miles. In fact, people all over Barrow used to set their clocks by them.

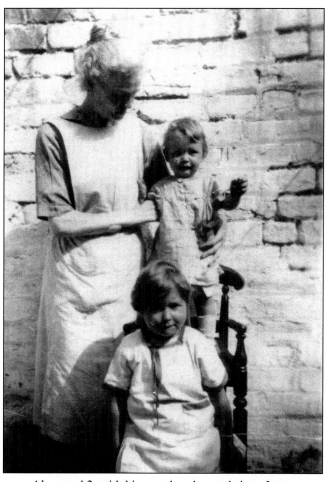

Alan aged 2, with his grandmother and sister Jean.
In the backyard of 144 Marsh Street.

Alan revisiting 144 Marsh Street in 1981.

Marsh Street, as it passes under the
Greengate Hill Bridge. *(c. 1981)*

The Infant School gate. *(c. 1981)*

Alfred Barrow School in 1994. Boys' School in right half, girls' in left half – glass stairway and new building on the extreme right didn't exist in the author's schooldays.

The sandhills and beach at Rampside, where we used
to have our picnics and gather winkles. *(c. 1981)*

The causeway out to Roa Island, along which
the steam train used to run. *(c. 1981)*

1 Florence Street – our second home. *(c. 1981)*

The cake shop that used to be 'Cheap Johnnie's' in 1938.
Still a bakery today. *(c. 1981)*

Another childhood home – 42 Fife Street, Barrow. *(c. 1981)*

The corner house at 107 Marsh Street. *(c. 1981)*

Backbarrow with the hotel that was
once the old Dolly Blue works.

Ancient Chapel Island in Morecambe Bay;
taken from the prehistoric circle on
Birkrigg Common along the coast road.

A view of the Lake District mountains across the
Duddon Estuary; taken from Roanhead.

The ruins of the 800 year old Cistercian Abbey
in the Valley of the Deadly Nightshade, Barrow-in-Furness.

Since the sheet metal shop, stood on the side of the Buccleuch Dock, right next to the High Level Bridge into town, it was only about a mile from Marsh Street; so I was able to dash home for my dinner, gulp it down and dash back again before the 1 o-clock sirens blasted out. These sirens, which also signalled the start and end of every shift, were the dreaded sounds you were hoping 'not' to hear if you were rushing to work a bit late.

This dinner break was the only 'official' break you got. Tea breaks were definitely not allowed, so if you felt hungry, crafty surreptitious snacks on the side were the only option. This was an option that somehow got taken up quite a lot. And wherever there was a burner, or coke forge capable of heating water, there'd be a constant stream of dodgy-looking characters coming and going while trying to hide their brew cans.

Although now working in the shipyard, and quite enjoying all the new experiences, I never had any illusions about this, or any other job, being my future way of life. I still nurtured my deep down desire to be a professional singer, and was determined that one day I would be. However, at not quite sixteen years old I still had no idea how this would come about.

But then a little incident occurred back at home in Marsh Street that gave me the first pointer in the right direction. In the front room at 107, which in a way had become a sort of music room, we had an old piano which Mam had acquired from somewhere. We also had a large wind-up gramophone cabinet about three feet tall. This was not only quite an attractive piece of furniture, but as an acoustic, non-electrical machine for playing 78" records with steel needles, it actually produced a very good sound for those days.

As well as a lid on the top, it had double doors on the front opening into a largish compartment underneath full of old records. These were mostly of the old music hall singers and comedians of the pre-war era. To Dad this front room had become a sort of retreat, where he'd spend a lot of his evenings relaxing away from the family crowd and listening to our old KLM radio relay set.

These radio relay sets weren't full blown radios, but simply receivers which received their programmes directly by cable from KLM's main receiving station. Because of this they didn't need plugging into the electricity mains, which was a godsend to most people at that time, because very few houses actually had electricity laid on.

KLM was the company that operated this relay system, and the name stood for Kendal, Morecambe & Lancaster – which was the area that they covered.

e

I remember going into the front room one evening and hearing this wonderful tenor voice ringing out from the radio. I was absolutely carried away by it and just stood listening in amazement.

"That," my father said, "is Enrico Caruso. He's got a voice like a bell."

And I knew from that moment, that 'this' was the kind of singing I wanted to do.

10

The Birth of a Machinist

After three months working in the sheet metal shop, I arrived one morning for work to be told that I had to report to Mr Dowie's office, so duly climbed the stairs wondering what it was all about. After all, the last time this happened I got the sack.

"How would you like to move to another job?" he asked, much to my relief.

"What job's that?" I asked.

"Well, they're looking for lads over in the East Shop," he replied, "to work on the capstan lathes."

"What're they?" I asked a bit doubtfully; since the only lathes I knew about were the monsters I'd seen in the gun shop.

"They're small machines they make all the small bits and pieces on," he explained, "like nuts and bolts, screws etc."

"I think I'd like that," I replied, immediately perking up at the thought of this interesting new challenge.

"Right!" he said. "You have to report there on Monday morning."

And that was it.

The east shop was another of the many huge workshops that made up Vickers Armstrongs. It was located right over on the far side of the shipyard, next to the Jubilee Bridge which spanned the Walney Channel over to Walney Island. One slight downside to this was that it was much further away from Marsh Street than the sheet metal shop, which not only meant a longer walk to get there, but also that it wouldn't be possible to get home for my dinner.

The capstan lathes, it turned out, were a row of six small machines, buried among a vast array of other machines of every kind imaginable.

99

There was one chap in charge of these six machines, who was a sort of supervisor/setter/machinist, because he not only set up the jobs on the machines for all us lads, but also worked on a bigger machine himself.

Learning to use these capstan lathes was a whole new experience for me. It was a chance to gain a genuine practical skill for the first time, so I found it a really enjoyable challenge and took to it straight away. Before long I was able to do most of the jobs that were handed to me without too much trouble, and at a work rate that seemed satisfactory to all concerned.

This 'work rate' turned out to be particularly important, especially to me, because operating the capstan lathes was on what they called 'piecework', something I'd never heard of before. Apparently, you were given a time to do each particular job, and if you completed it within that time you got extra money. I'd always been willing to 'work' for my pay, so this piecework idea really spurred me on. I was soon turning out screws, bolts, nuts and all sorts of other odd shaped bits of metal like nobody's business.

Unfortunately, though, it turned out that this didn't sit too well with everybody. To my surprise, one day, while beavering away at my capstan lathe I had a visit from a chap who announced himself as the Union Shop Steward. Since I'd never had any dealings with unions before, I didn't have a clue what they were all about, so he set about filling in these regrettable blanks in my knowledge. It seemed that my over-energetic industry at the capstan was something that needed to be discouraged. I was setting a bad example, and in the interests of all the thousands of other workers in the shipyard, whose jobs I was apparently putting at risk, I ought to slow down.

Since the few shillings extra a week I was earning by my hard work almost certainly left me a long way behind what 'he' was finding in his wage packet, I wasn't too impressed by his arguments, and decided that my own, and my family's needs were more important than his pretty odd attitude to work levels – after all, wasn't the country still fighting a war?

I had my feelings on this reinforced the following day, when the head foreman came down to see me. He'd obviously heard about the union man's visit.

"You're doing a good job here," he assured me. "And don't let him or anyone else put you off. Just keep up the good work."

Which is exactly what I did.

The chap supervising our six machines was a decent sort of bloke who I got on well with. He was always helpful and easy to talk to, but one day, when having a chat with him, I had one of those little life's

100

learning experiences, which for some reason tend to stick in your memory. This concerned his age. He was, I'd gathered, a bit self-conscious about his looks.

"My problem," he confided on this occasion, "is that I look older than I really am."

"Oh, I don't know," I replied, seeking to reassure him. "You don't to me."

"Really!" he smiled, looking rather pleased. "How old would you think I am then?"

"Well," I murmured, deciding to err well on the flattering side, "I'd say you're no more than thirty-eight."

As his smile faded I knew I'd said the wrong thing.

"That's the trouble," he replied. "I'm really twenty-four."

The floor never opened at that point as I hoped it would, but it was the first time I can remember making an embarrassing 'faux pas' – even though at that time I'd never even heard of this expression.

All six of us lads on the capstans got on well together, though we were obviously a mix of personalities, with somewhat different attitudes to the job. A couple of them were a bit Jack-the-Laddish and tended to pal up together. Even so, they all seemed to get on well enough with their work. So it came as a bit of a surprise one afternoon, when I returned from a bit of a wander during the dinner break, to find a couple of plain clothes shipyard security men waiting by our machines. The stony expressions on their faces, though, left me in no doubt that 'someone' was in trouble. However, I was told just to wait at my machine until the others arrived.

Finally, we'd all turned up – except for the two Jack-the-Lads.

"Where the heck have they got to?" we all muttered among ourselves.

"Don't worry about them," said our supervisor, as the sirens blasted out the end of dinner break. "Just get on with your work."

After we'd done so, the stony-faced law men came to each of us in turn asking questions. When they got to me I could hardly believe my ears. They seemed to be on bout some dynamite that was missing. . . did I know anything about it?

"Dynamite!" I exclaimed in disbelief; as the only time I'd ever heard of this before was at the Saturday morning film shows, when Jungle Jim used it to blow up his deadly enemies. "I didn't know they used that sort of stuff in the shipyard."

"Well, they do," replied the lawmen. "But it's alright," he added reassuringly, "we didn't think you'd be involved. It's just that two of your workmates have been caught breaking into the explosives store down on one of the slipways, and stealing several sticks of dynamite. We had to check you other lads just to make sure there was no more of it in the wrong hands."

Apparently, the two Jack-the-Lads had told the police that they thought the sticks of dynamite they were nicking were just some sort of fireworks. What the final outcome of this was I never heard. All I remember is that they never turned up on the capstans again.

My new longer walk to the east shop took me through the town and over the High Level Bridge, which spanned the link between the Buccleuch and Devonshire docks. Then up Michaelson Road to what we called the Old Barrow Buildings. These were huge, sandstone tenements where my paternal grandparents had lived after moving down from Glasgow in the 1890s to work in the shipyard, and where my father had been born.

At the corner of the Old Barrow Buildings I had to turn right into Bridge Street which led up to the east shop. Although both Michaelson Road and Bridge Street were broad main roads leading from Barrow over to Walney Island, they were so hemmed in on both sides by the huge buildings of Vickers Armstrongs, that they almost felt like part of the shipyard. This was particularly true of Bridge Street, half of which was taken up by railway lines, along which steam trains from Vickers and the Hindpool Steel works always seemed to be chugging, separated from the road traffic only by a light, single bar wooden railing.

Walking this route first thing in the morning was a bit like crossing the Niagara Falls on foot. You were caught up in the huge surge of the aptly named 'shipyard rush', as hundreds of furiously pedalled bicycles were swarming across the High Level Bridge, heading for the various shipyard gates. One of the hazards for all these hurrying cyclists, apart from their sheer numbers, was the fact that these roads still had the old tramlines from the nineteen-thirties embedded in them, so snagging their wheels was an ever present danger and spills were quite common. In fact, one old joke used to claim that if you got your front wheel caught in them, you'd have to pedal all the way to the tram terminus to get it out.

Another feature of Bridge Road was the submarine engine sheds. These were across the other side of the road and railway line, almost opposite the gates to the east shop. This is where they built and tested the massive diesel engines for all the submarines built in Barrow. The thing that caught your attention about these submarine sheds though, was the constant noise and vibration of the pounding engines that were being tested in there.

102

These apparently had to go through several stages of running tests before being passed as ready for submarine duty, and these included a final non-stop run of seventy-two hours. What always astonished me most about this, though, was the fact that there were several streets of old terraced houses right outside the walls of the testing sheds. How the people living there managed to sleep during these seventy-two hours (three whole days and nights) of non-stop noise and vibration I couldn't imagine.

It was about this time that I discovered from my sister Jean, much to my surprise, that she herself had at one time worked briefly in the east shop. Not only that, but she'd actually worked on the same capstans I was now working on. Quite a coincidence, considering the vastness of the shipyard, and the fact that they employed over 15,000 people.

One 'normal seeming' morning I was walking to work at the east shop as usual, and having crossed the High Level Bridge was surprised to see a large crowd of workers flocking around the shipyard gates. On getting closer I could see that for some strange reason the huge iron gates were shut, and that the men were all eagerly reading a large notice fastened to the bars. There seemed to be great excitement all around, and when I finally got near enough to read it I could hardly believe my eyes. It announced quite simply that the 'War in Europe Was Finally Over', and therefore we could all take the day off to celebrate as there would be no work at the shipyard that day.

The overwhelming relief at this momentous news spread throughout the whole town like the sunshine finally bursting through after five years of cloudy skies.

Suddenly, big celebrations and street parties broke out everywhere. Bonfires were burning on every open bomb site, as well as in the park. Crowds of people wandered about from one site to another, and it seemed as if everyone capable of playing any sort of instrument was out there having a go. One rather elderly gent I particularly remember seemed to turn up all over the place doing a soft-shoe-shuffle dance, which was obviously his party piece, and which he was pretty good at.

Strangely enough, there were apparently no official 'Town Celebrations'. Quite why, I've no idea.

Once all these celebrations had died down, life at the east shop carried on as before.

As my sixteenth birthday was now looming near, however, the time had come to chase up my original plans to take up an apprenticeship. I'd decided to go for being a shipwright, quite why this and not any of the other trades available in the shipyard, I'm not really sure. Possibly

103

it was because 'shipbuilding' being the main purpose of Vickers it was the most obvious. In any case, since whatever trade I chose was intended to be no more than an interim job until I could eventually find out how to become a 'singer', it didn't really matter.

After making all the applications in the right places I was duly accepted, and told to turn up at the head foreman's office on the slipways, first thing in the morning. Strangely enough, I can't now remember this particular head foreman's name. However, after giving me a bit of an introductory chat he took me down onto the slipways and handed me over to a shipwright called Jack Marsh (Mazzie to his workmates). I was to be his apprentice and part of his 'steel erecting gang'. This consisted of just three of us, Mazzie himself, Archie Remington (his very experienced labourer) and myself the apprentice.

Once again, I found myself suddenly plunged into a totally different working world to any I'd experienced before.

The base for our gang, and several other gangs, was a solid wooden hut on the slipways, almost underneath a large ocean liner that was under construction. This hut was an ad hoc affair, that had apparently been knocked together by the workers themselves out of old scaffolding planks and any other surplus materials they could find or scrounge.

This whole area where the actual shipbuilding took place was known as the top yard. The major part of this being taken up by a line of about six large slipways – plus a smaller special one for the submarines. These were ranged along the downward sloping shore of the Walney Channel; into which all the ships being built were eventually launched.

Along this stretch of the shore where the launches took place, the channel was little more than a quarter of a mile wide, and at low tide you could virtually wade across it. However, the tidal range was so great that at high tide the water was deep enough to launch huge aircraft carriers and ocean liners into it.

Walney Island, which formed the opposite shore of the channel, was about nine miles long, and varied in width from around a quarter of a mile to three quarters of a mile. Its far side faced the wide open Irish Sea, which meant that it formed a long, protective barrier against this sometimes wild, stormy sea; behind which the whole of Barrow, including the shipyard sheltered.

Walney is the only real island now remaining off the coast of Barrow, apart from the tiny island of Piel, with its ancient castle – which nine hundred years ago was owned by the monks of Furness Abbey who used it as a landing stage and safe storage for their provisions brought in by sea.

104

However, before the coming of the ship-building industry to Barrow in the early eighteen hundreds, all of the land on which the shipyard now stands was itself an island. This was called 'Barrow Island', and like Walney Island, was cut off from the mainland by its own sea channel. With the arrival of shipbuilding, this sea channel was eventually sealed off at both ends with lock gates, and turned into a string of docks for shipping. The three main ones being: Ramsden Dock, Buccleuch Dock and Devonshire Dock.

The slipways on which I was now starting work, were a great noisy complex of activity in which ships of all sizes were in various stages of construction. Each ship was cocooned under masses of wooden scaffolding supported in tall, fixed steel posts, the rungs of which also acted as ladders for the construction gangs. Several very tall tower cranes reached up to the sky at intervals along every slipway. Each having a long rotating gib on the top, along which clattered a hook trolley on rails capable of delivering heavy loads to every part of the growing ships on either side.

This whole bustling world of slipways echoed endlessly to the clanging of hammers on steel, the machine-gun clatter of riveting guns from every direction, and all this bathed in the dazzling blue flashes and acrid, swirling smoke of welders at work.

The ship that our steel erecting gang was working on at that time, was the one under which the gang hut lay half buried among piles of scaffolding planks and baulks of heavy timber supports for the huge hull towering over it. This ship was the *Himalaya*, a huge ocean liner being built for the 'P & O Steam Navigation Company', and at that stage less than half built.

On the slipway next to this a large aircraft carrier was slowly taking shape, and further along was another ocean liner; which I think was the *Orcades*. This, I believe, was destined for the Orient Line. Several other vessels of different types were also in various stages of creation, plus a submarine for the Royal Navy.

Under the guidance of Mazzie and Archie, I was soon clambering around the partially laid steel decks, and up and down the steel scaffolding ladders enjoying myself like an eager monkey. Heights had never bothered me, so in a way I was in my element.

The job of steel erecting consisted mainly of sorting out the prefabricated steel bulkhead sections and long curved outer rib frames on the ground, before hooking them onto the cranes and hoisting them on board where we'd temporarily bolt them into their correct places, using pinch bars, bottle screws, small metal drifts for lining up the holes, and pneumatic bolt guns. Once a particular section had been

105

finished and checked for proper alignment etc., the riveters and welders would then move in to fasten them in place permanently; removing our temporary bolts as they went.

Although it was hard work, especially when the cold wind was blowing in off the Walney Channel, as it frequently was, or when it was raining, or both; being young and fit I enjoyed all the physical activity and climbing about.

There was no such thing as safety clothing, helmets or suchlike, in those days. Everyone simply wore whatever clothes they could provide for themselves. There was also very little in the way of 'Health and Safety' as far as I can remember. These matters seemed to be left pretty much to the employee's own common sense and judgement. Which, looking back, weren't always much in evidence. In fact, such dodgy practices as riding on the steel deck plates, bulkheads and such while the crane hoisted them up sixty feet or so from the ground onto the deck was quite a common practice simply because it saved the time and effort of climbing all the way up there by the ladders.

The thick steel plating that formed the outer hull of the ships was, for some reason, not fitted by shipwrights but by special plating gangs. These large heavy plates could weigh several tons and took a lot of manoeuvring into position, so required quite a bit of skill and experience to get right. The reason I took a special interest in these plating gangs, was because I'd learned that my Uncle William had once been a member of one of them. Unfortunately, on one fateful occasion in 1912 when he was only 19 years of age, he'd been helping to swing one of these huge plates into position with the crane, when the sling holding it slipped and the plate dropped cutting both his legs off – one above the knee and the other just below. Having had a dreadful accident like this in the family was certainly an object lesson to me, and I was always doubly careful when lifting heavy, awkward frames and bulkheads to make sure that the crane cables were connected the way they should be, and to keep well out of the way into the bargain.

My Uncle William survived this dreadful experience, though he could never do much in the way of real physical work again. Surprisingly, during this enforced retirement he turned to writing, and wrote the song lyrics to several songs made famous by some of the well known singers of the period – the nineteen-thirties – including Jessie Mathews. He also, during the depression, founded the 'National Unemployed Workers' Movement', and printed a special newspaper called, *The Bulletin*, at a halfpenny a copy. Quite an accomplishment for a working class chap with no legs.

Mazzie and Archie were 'really' individual characters who I hit it off with right from the start. Mazzie was regarded as something of a hard man who nobody took liberties with. He lived away out in Ulverston, eight miles from Barrow – where Stan Laurel of 'Laurel & Hardy', fame was born. He was also a keen gardener, and I always remember him bringing in a large bunch of flowers one morning for my mother. This caused quite a sensation among his workmates, because to see the hard man Mazzie walking in to work carrying flowers was unheard of, and something it took him a long time to live down. Archie was also a strong character in his own way. He had several scars down part of his face and neck, which he eventually told me dated back to a time he'd spent in the logging districts of Vancouver, Canada. Apparently he and a couple of pals used to go out into the forests in their spare time shooting. In those days in Canada several of the wild creatures we regard as highly protected nowadays, were simply seen as dangerous pests and had a bounty on them, which meant that shooting them was not only doing a public service, but was also a profitable sport. Apparently the large eagles that haunted the logging forests of the area were one of these dangerous undesirables, and were what Archie and his pals used to go after.

On these hunting trips they had there own system, which was simply that once in the forest they'd split up and each go off in different directions. This was so they could cover a wider area and have more chance of finding their quarry. However, because being separated could also be dangerous, they operated a rule that if they ever fired at something, they'd immediately fire two more shots as a signal to the others that they were OK.

On this particular hunting trip, after they'd all gone off their separate ways as usual, Archie arrived at a small clearing and spotted an eagle circling directly overhead. He quickly aimed and fired, but the eagle just flew off over the trees, so he thought he must have missed it and carried on through the forest. A little further on, however, he came out into another small clearing and suddenly became aware of a great fluttering of wings overhead. He looked up quickly to find the eagle, which must have been following him, swooping down on him in a great flurry of claws and beak. It came down on him so fast that he had no time to aim his rifle at it. All he could do was lash out at it using his rifle as a club to beat it off.

The next thing he remembers was his mates waking him up, and finding himself lying on the ground in the clearing covered in blood. Stretched out nearby was the dead body of the eagle. It seemed his shot in the first clearing had actually hit the eagle, and though badly wounded it had followed him overhead. The attack in the second clearing had simply been its dying gasp to wreak revenge on its attacker.

The reason his pals had got there so quickly was that after his shot at the eagle, he'd simply forgotten to fire the two signal shots to show he was all right, and they'd both come looking for him.

Sounds a bit like a hunter's tall story, doesn't it. Fortunately, Archie had the evidence to prove it. Apparently the story had created such a stir at the time that the local newspaper had taken it up and printed out the whole event. They'd even printed a picture of the clearing where it had happened, showing Archie standing in front of the dead eagle; which was held up behind him by two men, with its seven foot wings outspread. Archie had carefully kept a copy of this newspaper.

Now that I was working on the top yard slipways, my morning walk to work was not so far as it was to the east shop. However, it did follow pretty much the same route over the High Level Bridge between the Buccleuch and Devonshire Docks, and up Michaelson Road. This meant that every morning as I crossed the bridge, I could always see what ships had come in for repair, or were being newly fitted out after launching.

On one of these mornings during this first year of my apprenticeship, I was crossing the High Level Bridge as usual and saw that a huge ocean liner had come in overnight. This was *The Empress of Russia*. She was painted in wartime grey, having obviously been used as a troopship or something; and I learned later that she'd been brought in for repair and refit, after having been sunk somewhere and refloated.

This refit seemed to go on for quite a while, so she became a regular sight on my morning walks to the top yard. One morning, however, when I reached the High Level Bridge I was met by an astonishing sight. The huge *Empress of Russia* was lying keeled over in the water at an alarming angle. Smoke seemed to be pouring out of her portholes and hatches everywhere, and she was surrounded by fire-boats which were pumping water into her from every angle. The great liner was so low in the water that she was obviously resting on the bottom of the dock.

When I finally reached the top yard it was to find, not surprisingly, that this incredible disaster was the talking point everywhere. "How the devil could such a thing have happened?"

Gradually, over the course of the day, the explanation – such as it was – trickled through to us. It seemed that the ship had on board two men from her original crew, who were acting as some sort of company representatives/come night watchmen. Apparently, at some time in the night they'd discovered a fire on board which was too big for them to tackle on their own, so they raised the alarm. By the time the fire boats had arrived, the fire had taken such a hold that all these could do was to keep pumping water into the ship until she eventually settled on the dock bottom.

When the fire was finally put out, it was decided that the damage was far too great to make any further repair worth attempting. What the actual cause of the fire was, and who was responsible, I never found out. However, this 'second' sinking in her unfortunate career had sadly sealed her fate, and she was eventually towed around to 'Ward's' ship-breaking dock to be cut up for scrap.

SOME MAJOR EVENTS OF THE YEAR:
(1) Hitler committed suicide and Germany surrendered.
(2) George Orwell wrote *Animal Farm*.
(3) The BBC Light Programme started.
(4) The first atomic bomb was exploded in the New Mexico desert on the 16th of July.
(5) Family Allowance introduced.
(6) Rule of the wartime government ends, and the conservatives, under Winston Churchill, lose the election (much to the surprise of the rest of the world). The Labour Party sweep to power under Clement Atlee.
(7) The Nuremberg War Crimes Tribunal held.
(8) Mussolini executed by the Italian Partisans.

11

Singers and Singing
(My Quest Begins)

1946 (17 years old in July)
My first enquiring steps along the road to my chosen future profession
left me feeling a bit like the lost hiker in the old story who asked one
of the locals if he could point out the way to the place he was looking
for.

"Ah. . ! Well," muttered the local shaking his head doubtfully. "That
be a difficult place to find, that be. An' if I were thee, I wouldn't start
from here."

This somewhat unhelpful advice the traveller received, couldn't
have been more appropriate to my own situation. Barrow, as far as I
could find, was not exactly a centre for music and the performing arts.

However, it did have a very good public library, which was to prove
my saving grace as far as this was concerned. The Barrow Library was
a fine, purpose built stone building that occupied one side of Ramsden
Square (in fact, a wide circle with a statue in the middle) at the town
end of the broad, tree-lined Abbey Road. It was apparently one of the
many such public libraries built in England by the Scottish born
American philanthropist Andrew Carnegie – I always remember
reading this as a kid on a bronze plate near the entrance door.

The library had always been one of my favourite haunts, not only
for the books, but also because it had a large museum on the upper
floor full of stuffed animals, huge fish and the like, plus models of
some of the most famous ships built in Barrow.

The extra attraction at this particular time, however, was that it had
a small, but fairly well stocked, music section. This contained quite a

good selection of full scores, books on composers, famous musicians and more; but most importantly of all, it had a surprisingly good selection of books on the life stories of famous singers of the past. So I was soon avidly following the careers of singers like John McCormack, Nellie Melba, Feodor Chaliapin, Luisa Tetrazzini, and my great hero, Enrico Caruso.

Having discovered this music section, these library excursions now had a real learning purpose. It felt as if simply being in contact with these books was helping me to move towards my chosen future, and I was soon spending more and more of my spare time searching their shelves.

In the shipyard the time was now approaching when the *Himalaya* would be ready for launching. Although she was internally just a maze of bare steel compartments. All the fitting out of the cabins, laying of teak decks, plumbing, electrics, etc., would be added once she was in the water and berthed in one of the docks.

Our gang, along with others, soon found ourselves involved in laying out the huge slipway sections underneath her on either side. Up to this point the huge ship had been standing on a long row of thick wooden blocks under her keel about eighteen inches apart all the way down her full length; the sides of her hull being supported by a forest of square wooden posts a foot or more thick, and anything up to thirty feet long. The job now was to lay the huge wooden slipway sections underneath her to form the great slides on which she would be launched.

These great slides were in two parts; a top and a bottom. The bottom slide, being laid firmly on the ground, stayed where it was during the launch, while the top part went down with the ship and floated free once the ship was in the water.

The lubrication between these two slide sections was provided by tallow – the stuff that old fashioned candles were made of – and soft soap which looked just like dark brown vaseline. The melted tallow would be poured onto the two slides' surfaces and allowed to set, before being smothered in soft soap. The top slide sections would then be jammed and wedged firmly into place against the hull on top of the bottom one.

Once this was ready, it was simply a matter of lowering the vast twenty-odd thousand ton bulk of the ship, so that it rested only on the slides. This was done by splitting out the wooden keel bocks on which she rested so that she slowly sank down onto the slide. This itself had to be done in a controlled sequence so that it was lowered evenly, and thus avoid damaging the hull by putting too much strain on any one part. This sequence simply amounted to numbering the wooden keel blocks from one to three all the way down the ship's length. The signal would then be given to split out all the number one blocks. This we did with large chisels and sledge hammers (which we called mauls), and pneumatic chisel guns for the awkward blocks where there was no room to swing the hammers.

During this process the forest of long posts supporting the sides of the hull would also be gradually removed, with the results of all this being carefully monitored to see that all went well. If it did then it would be repeated with the number two blocks, and finally the number three blocks, until all the posts and blocks had been removed and the ship was resting entirely on the two slipways ready for launch.

The reason it didn't then immediately slide down into the Walney Channel was because several of the bottom slipway sections had large triggers on top which fitted into slots in the upper slipway sections holding it back, but ready to be released by pneumatic pumps at the moment of launch.

Before the launch, great piles of heavy 'drag chains' (old anchor chains) were laid out on the ground either side of the ship. These weighed several hundred tons and were all wired together in great bundles which were fastened to the ship by thick cables to act as brakes during the launch. These were to bring the ship quickly to a standstill once it was fully in the water. This was particularly important in Barrow, because of the narrowness of the Walney Channel. Without these drag chains the launched ship would have ended up on the beach over the other side.

Launch days in Vickers Armstrongs' Shipyard were always treated as huge, special occasions, when some celebrity would arrive to officially name the ship. The renowned shipyard brass band would be there blowing their hearts out, and outsiders from the town were allowed in to witness the spectacle alongside the workers.

Since starting to work on the slipways I'd seen a couple of these exciting events before – one of them being a large aircraft carrier. Unfortunately, however, I never got to actually see the launch of the *Himalaya*. This was because when 'she' went down the slipways I was actually on board her. I'd been detailed off, much to my delight, with another apprentice and several shipwrights to be part of the shipboard gang who'd be needed both during the launch, and while she was being towed by tugs around to her berth in the Buccleuch dock.

The role of the shipwrights on board would be to handle the cables that hooked her up to the waiting tugs once she was in the water. The other apprentice and myself would be each stationed inside one of the two empty anchor chain lockers high up in the bows where the drag chain cables were coupled through the anchor chain ports. These cables were each fastened to the ship's deck inside the chain lockers by a large shackle which had a special quick-release lever. Our job was to belt these levers with heavy mauls (sledgehammers) to release the drag-chain cables once the ship had come to a standstill in the water.

We all took up our positions before the launch and waited. Through the anchor chain port in my chain-locker I could faintly hear bits of what was going on outside, particularly the shipyard band. Eventually it all went quiet and I guessed that the naming ceremony must be going on. Then suddenly the band struck up again with: 'For Those In Peril On the Sea', and I knew that the *Himalaya* was on her way.

At first there was no sensation of movement, and being enclosed inside the chain locker I couldn't see a thing. Then gradually I could feel a slight draft beginning to flow though the ship. The draft quickly grew stronger until it became a wind. I began to hear distant thudding noises echoing from all over the ship, as if doors were banging and loose scaffolding crashing to the deck. I was astonished at how smooth it all felt, because apart from the increasing wind pressure, there was no sensation of movement.

Then the downward tilt of the deck began to level off, and I realised that the *Himalaya's* stern must be lifting up as she entered the water. Seconds later there came a slight wallowing sensation as the bows also left the slipway, and the *Himalaya* was afloat – in her true element at last.

Suddenly the ship lurched as if she'd been gripped by a great hand, and the drag-chain cable tightened with a great 'twang', slowly bringing the *Himalaya* to a halt in the water. A signal shout went up from the deck above, and I belted the release lever with the maul as hard as I could. The shackle flew open instantly and the end of the cable disappeared out through the anchor chain port like a great steel snake.

My part in the proceedings over, I then scrambled up onto the bow deck above to watch the action, or help where I could.

The tugs were soon coupled up, without any help from me or the other apprentice, and we were then towed down the Walney Channel, through the lock gates into Ramsden Dock and through to her final berth in the Buccleuch Dock.

12

Fellow Travellers

One Saturday morning I went to the library to return some books as usual, and was standing by the music shelves trying to decide on my next selection, when another lad who I knew slightly from the shipyard turned up. His name was Jim Woods, and we were soon chatting away. To my astonishment I discovered that he too was keen on opera and singers. And as we chatted it soon became clear that where these were concerned we were very much on the same wavelength. He even told me he'd always wanted to be a singer himself.

"What a weird coincidence," I remarked. "Especially you turning up here at the same time as me."

As we chatted on, however, he confessed that it was actually no coincidence at all. In fact, he'd come to the library looking for me; having been primed by my mate Willie Irwin about my singing ambitions, and where he was likely to find me.

In the event, this turned out to be a fortunate move for all three of us. Jim and I because of our natural passion for singing and opera; and even for Willie himself, because even though he didn't have the same innate desire to be a singer that we had, he decided he'd like to come along with us. So from that time onwards all three of us became inseparable companions and spent a lot of our spare time together.

At the time, none of us had much money to buy records, so we now used to spend a lot of our Saturday mornings off in either Pass's big music shop in Duke Street, or Kelly's slightly smaller music shop in Dalton Road, searching through their stock of 78rpm, 10-inch shellac records. These, though state of the art at the time, gave about three minutes playing time at the most. They were also very brittle, so easily

114

cracked and broken. Pass's shop was usually our favourite, because apart from being very much larger with an advertising slogan which read '*From a Pin to a Piano, Get it at PASS'S*', it also had three of four soundproof cubicles where you could try out any record you were thinking of buying. We certainly made full use of this generous facility, and over the months actually 'tried out' a large percentage of what they had on their well stocked shelves.

Looking back this all seems a bit of a cheek, but at the time we didn't think it was dishonest, because we actually were 'thinking' about buying them – our problem unfortunately being that we didn't have the money to do so. Fortunately, the shop staff seemed to have a pretty tolerant attitude about this, and never refused to hand over any record we asked for.

Somewhere within this long period of free recitals in their cubicles, however, we did manage to scrape up enough cash occasionally to actually 'buy' an especially desirable record. My first one, I remember, was by the tenor Richard Crookes singing 'The Holy City' on one side, and 'The Star of Bethlehem' on the other. Wonderful old songs with really singable, soaring melodies and words; which remained great favourites of mine ever after, and which in years to come I was to sing many times.

I eventually also managed to get hold of a record by the wonderful Italian tenor, Beniamino Gigli, one of my favourite lyric tenors of all time, singing 'Che Gelida Manina' (Your Tiny hand is Frozen), from Puccini's *La Bohème* on one side and 'Salve d'amore' (All Hail Thou Dwelling) from Gounod's *Faust* on the other. They remain my favourite renderings of these arias to this day. Another Italian tenor Tito Schipa, with his beautifully effortless, free flowing light lyric voice also became one of our heroes. The aria 'Nessun Dorma' was one of our great favourites, though at that time the supreme version heard on the radio was by an Italian tenor called Alessandro Vallente.

We all had a particular leaning towards tenors simply because they seemed to have all the most beautiful arias to sing; so that's what we all wanted to be. At that time, however, none of us knew for certain what our voices would turn out to be. I always felt confident that 'I' was definitely a tenor, and not just any old tenor but a 'tenor-robusto', like my great hero Enrico Caruso, though I had doubts about Jim, who had a deepish sort of speaking voice which seemed destined for the baritone ranks. As for Willie, his voice was a bit indeterminate, though much lighter than mine, so possibly a light lyric tenor like John McCormack could be his fate.

Although tenors were, for us, the ultimate as far as the male singing voice was concerned, we did gradually begin to appreciate some of the baritones and basses we were hearing on the opera records in Pass's music cubicles. Among these were the Italian baritones Ricardo Stracciari, Tito Gobbi, Paolo Silveri and the American Baritone, Lawrence Tibbett, the Russian bass Feodor Chaliapin, the Italian bass Ezio Pinza. and the English basso-profundo Norman Allin; who was a real discovery for us, and possibly the only 'true' basso-profundo I've ever heard. His was a voice that flowed so easily, and was so deep that it sounded almost as if it was rumbling from under the ground.

We were also gradually adding quite a few female singers to our favourites' list. Some from the past like the Italian soprano Galli Curci, and others from the not so distant past like the English soprano Eva Turner; renowned world wide for her performances of *Turandot*. And later on the Australian soprano, Joan Hammond, whose 'One Fine Day' from Madame Butterfly was often played on the radio, and which from then on became the definitive version for us.

As well as sharing my passion for becoming a singer, my two fellow enthusiasts shared a rather sadder situation with each other; they'd both lost their mothers very early in life and lived with their fathers. As far as Willie was concerned; with him being a Marsh Street lad, I'd always known that his mother had died in a tragic fire when he was very small. Apparently she'd been bathing him and his two brothers in their tin bath in front of the open fire, when her clothes had caught fire and she was burned so badly that she died. Fortunately, he had two older sisters, Nellie the oldest, and Bessie, who took over the role of their mother, and virtually brought up Willie and his two brothers.

Jim's situation was equally sad; though, like Willie, he never wanted to talk about it, and it was some time before he let us in on it. It seemed that his mother had suffered badly with mental health problems, and had eventually been put into a mental hospital from which she never came out. He also had a sister, younger than himself, who'd been sent off to live with relatives in some other part of the country.

Jim lived with his father in the first floor flat of a bomb damaged block in Hindpool Road, the ground floor of which was just an empty, rubble-strewn ruin. The row of houses that had once stood behind it had been blown down, leaving an open bomb site; exactly across the road from the Alfred Barrow School.

Jim had somehow got hold of a small wind-up gramophone, and when we weren't playing our records on the one in our Marsh Street front room, we'd often squat on the piles of rubble in the windowless room underneath Jim's flat, holding our record opera recitals, with no one to complain but the rats.

For some reason, about this time we all toyed with the idea of joining the Army Cadets. But after attending a couple of their meetings at the Drill Hall in Holker Street, we quickly came to the conclusion that this was a complete waste of time. None of the people running things seemed too sure what we were all supposed to be doing. The meetings were pretty lackadaisical with little organisation. Perhaps with the war now over, they felt no real sense of purpose in all the drilling etc., and were simply going through the motions. Since there was also nothing in the way of equipment, rifles and suchlike, and 'definitely' no hope of getting uniforms; in the end we kicked the whole idea into touch.

However, since we all still fancied the idea of being involved in 'one' of the cadet corps, we decided to have a shot at the Sea Cadets; and this turned out to be a different proposition altogether.

They had their headquarters in part of a large old house on shipyard land, right in the middle of Barrow Island. Whether or not this house had any direct connection to the Michaelson family, who had once owned most of Barrow Island – long before the shipyard was built – and when it actually 'was' an island – I never knew. But, since Michaelson Road, which had been named after them, ran nearby, I always thought this a distinct possibility.

On the night that we turned up to join them, the Sea Cadets seemed to be in the middle of taking over two or three rooms on the ground floor, and were busily cleaning them out ready for their meetings. We three were only too willing to get involved; especially as the petty officer in charge was an energetic type with plenty of enthusiasm, so we pitched in to help out

Unfortunately we soon discovered that they too had problems over uniforms, though since a few of the lads already had them, the prospects in this area definitely looked more promising.

After a few hard-working meetings, the petty officer told me on the side one day that he was well pleased with the amount of work we three were putting in. So when I passed this on to Willie and Jim, I urged that we should keep this up, in the hope that it might 'just' help us to jump the uniform queue a bit.

Sure enough, the moment of truth came a couple of weeks later. The petty officer told us that the Barrow Sea Cadets had been invited to take part in a special town parade thirty-six miles away up in Kendal. This was to take place in a few weeks time, and he wanted us three to be part of it.

117

"How can we?" I replied in dismay. "We've got no uniforms."

"Don't you worry about that," he said. "If any of the lads deserve to have them, it's you three. So I'll make sure you get them in time."

"Great!" we all blurted eagerly, as none of us had ever been to Kendal before, and the thought of parading there in 'real' naval uniforms was a totally unexpected bonus.

The work of cleaning up the rooms was finally finished, and in the process we'd learned that these rooms were, in fact, only their main headquarters. The place where they did all their drilling and band practice, was in a large army-style hut about half a mile away, right on the edge of the Ramsden Dock. This was reached from the headquarters along a rough, narrow road which led down to where a huge, unusual-looking bridge spanned the hundred foot entrance gap between the Ramsden Dock and the Buccleuch Dock. This carried both a railway and a road across from one dock to the other and was apparently called a bascule bridge. The most surprising thing about it was that when ships had to pass through, the whole massive structure of girders, road and railway would be raised up from one end, to point vertically at the sky.

The hut itself was set near the dock edge among all the railway lines and storage buildings, and this is where we really learned to become Sea Cadets.

What appealed to me most at that time was the fact that they had a marching band, and after several requests I ended up being given a bugle, which I thought was great. After my first attempts to blow it, however, I began to feel that this might not be such a good idea after all. For, to my astonishment, all I could get out of the wide end was the same hiss of hot air that I blew into the narrow end. I'd always been under the impression that all you had to do was blow into it to produce a whacking great blast of sound that could blow down the walls of Jericho, just as Joshua did. . . the technique of blowing a raspberry into the mouthpiece was something I had yet to learn.

Eventually, though, I did master this OK and could soon blow a raspberry into it with the best of them. I even took it home to practise on, and for a brief period Marsh Street was not such a peaceful street to live in as it used to be. However, after a few complaints from our obviously non-musical neighbours I decided to confine my virtuoso efforts to the wide open spaces of Ramsden Dock.

Where the drilling was concerned we had another pleasant surprise, because the Sea Cadets actually had several real rifles to practise our arms drill with. Admittedly they weren't the 303 Lee-Enfields supplied to the British Army, but old American Winchesters. In a way, these seemed even more exciting to us, because they were the rifles we'd seen the cowboys fighting off the Indians with in the Saturday morning films. I even took one home to show off to my other mates. Peaceful Marsh Street was definitely taking on a somewhat more military aspect during this period. Whether these Winchesters were capable of firing or not I don't know, because they were only used to drill with.

We did, however, eventually have a brief go at target practice, in a large warehouse of a place, near our hut on Ramsden Dock. This had been set out as a proper firing range, and this time we did have genuine Lee-Enfield rifles to fire. The only difference being that the barrels of these had been modified to take smaller 22 bullets instead of the usual 303 rounds. I found these a bit of a disappointment, because instead of the earsplitting bang and hefty kick in the shoulder I expected when I pulled the trigger, all I got seemed little more than a 'POP', and a shoulder kick I hardly felt.

All our drilling, marching and band practice were really whipping us into shape. And soon we could belt out our marching tunes with real gusto, while at the same time keeping in step and good marching order. The date for our great debut had always seemed a long way off, but suddenly it was on top of us. Our bugles were polished and our smart naval uniforms pressed with the required number of creases in our trousers – I think these were five, which I believe represented the five oceans of the world.

The journey to Kendal by coach was itself a treat, as journeys by coach in those days were rare events. In fact, I doubt if any of us had ever been on a 'coach' before; busses, yes but coaches, no.

What was even more of a treat, was that when we arrived we found ourselves billeted in a proper army camp with huts, mess hall, parade ground, etc. This was near a village just out of town, which fortunately, since we were there for the best part of a week, had a regular bus service into Kendal town centre.

As we'd arrived early in the week, and the parade wasn't until the Saturday afternoon, this suited me no end, giving me plenty of time to get into Kendal and explore.

To my delight I found that the town was a busy, bustling sort of place with plenty of life and activity. There was also a fast flowing river (the Kent) swirling its way through the middle, with people in rowing boats battling their way up and down through the currents. Heavy natural stone bridges spanned the flowing water, and inviting footpaths, meandered along its banks.

We also discovered that the town had a special NAAFI type canteen for service personnel tucked away in one of its side streets, and because we were dressed in naval uniform, we were allowed to use it.

The day I learned about this NAAFI turned out to be a momentous day for me. I'd been wandering through the busy town centre on my own, when I spotted a beautiful girl standing on a corner waiting to cross the road. To say I was smitten would be a puerile understatement. My mind simply went: WOW. . ! She seemed the most beautiful girl I'd ever seen.

"What I wouldn't give to have a girlfriend like her!" I gasped inwardly.

As I got closer, she turned and looked at me for a second and a flicker of a smile flashed in her eyes. Then she was gone across the road and into the crowd.

I'd never had an experience like that before, and just carried on with my walk in a sort of daze. I consoled myself with the thought that although she was probably no older than I was, she looked too grown up, smartly dressed and sophisticated to be interested in a seventeen year old lad like me.

However, this dreamy state was soon interrupted when I ran into a group of other sea-cadets wandering the town.

"We're off to the NAAFI canteen," they said. "We've just been told about it, and we're off there to meet some girls we've been chatting to. Why don't you come with us?"

"Why not!" I shrugged, thinking this might help to take my mind off my recent experience.

The NAAFI canteen turned out to be down a narrow side street not too far away, and as we entered, I could see it was obviously a popular place, because there was quite a crowd in there, mostly in uniform. My mates soon spotted the group of girls they'd arranged to meet, and pushed their way through the crowd to join them.

As I followed, I stared in disbelief, because there, standing with them, was the beautiful girl I'd just seen standing on the street corner. Unfortunately, the instant burst of elation I felt at that moment, was almost as instantly wiped out by the awful thought that she must certainly be the girlfriend of one of my mates. To my amazement, however, it turned out that although each of the girls had been paired off with one of my mates, 'she' was the only one of them who hadn't.

It seemed like a dream come true. Especially when she gave me that same smile, and told me, somewhat shyly, that she remembered seeing me in the street and the way I'd looked at her. Unbelievably, it turned out that 'she'd' been having the same thoughts about me that 'I'd' been having about her. Who says that fairy tales never happen!

120

After spending a little while in the canteen getting to know each other, it was suggested that we went for a walk, and the girls, all being local, proposed a stroll along the river footpath. This sounded great to me, though 'anywhere' with my lovely new companion would have suited me fine.

She told me that her name was Cathy Dodds, and that like me she was seventeen years old. We all strolled off down to the river and along the path as a group, but I, somewhat self-consciously, took Cathy's hand and from that moment on we were in our own dream world. I do vaguely remember that the others also gradually split up into pairs, but apart from that, they ceased to exist for us. We stopped for a while under some trees and settled down on the grass, where I eventually plucked up enough courage to put my arm around her and steal my first slightly awkward kiss. It was all so wonderfully idyllic that I wanted it to go on for ever. It was also totally innocent, as teenage romances tended to be in those days.

Over the next few days we all went out several times as a group. On one of these we rambled away up a hill to the old castle ruins. On another we simply wandered further along the riverside footpath out into the countryside. These days were all a bit like a dream to me. I'd never experienced such feelings for a girl before, and even though the others were always there, Cathy and I seemed somehow alone in our own separate world; happy when we were together, and missing each other painfully when we were apart.

However, while these afternoons were passing blissfully by, our mornings back at camp had been spent clumping about practising our marching; accompanied by earsplitting bugle blowing, and ferocious big drum bashing ready for the parade on Saturday. Funnily enough, I don't remember us having any snare drums, though I suppose we must have had.

Almost before we knew it, the great day arrived. So far, the weather that week had been dry and sunny, but as Saturday morning broke, we awoke to find the skies looking somewhat blustery and foreboding.

However, we set off eagerly for the town, keeping our fingers crossed that the threatening rain would just hold off long enough for us to do our stuff.

What a vain hope. We'd no sooner begun to assemble with the rest of the parade in the lower part of the main street than down it came. At first it didn't seem too bad, just a steady trickle, which in those northern regions would hardly be noticed. As we set off marching, however, the downpour began to keep time with us, getting heavier with every beat of our big drum. Soon the rain was pouring down my

121

f

face like a waterfall, and before long our well practised bugle raspberries were beginning to sound decidedly spluttery.

At least we kept our marching going fairly well to the boom, boom of the big drum. Suddenly though this hefty boom, boom turned into a soggy, boom, splodge, boom, splodge! as one of the sodden drum skins burst with the rain. We still managed to keep splashing doggedly on though, but when this turned into a demoralising splodge, splodge, as the other skin gave up the ghost, we had a real struggle. Fortunately this is where all our practising proved its worth, and at least 'our' part of the parade reached its soggy end without collapsing altogether.

The relief was palpable. And for me there was an extra glow of satisfaction. Here I was a musician. I'd been involved in my first public musical performance. And though blowing my lungs out through a bugle could hardly be compared to singing; it was, I felt, a small step in the right direction.

That evening was my last outing with Cathy. And after a rather wistful couple of hours wandering about hand in hand, Cathy and I exchanged our addresses, reluctantly said our sad farewells, promising fervently to write, then went our separate ways. She to her home and family, and me back to a now lonely camp.

The coach journey back to Barrow on that Sunday was a somewhat gloomy affair, because after what had been the most enjoyable, and unusual week that most of us could ever remember, the prospect of dragging ourselves up for work the next morning did not hold much appeal.

Back in Vickers life soon got into full swing again. With the *Himalaya* now berthed around in Buccleuch dock being fitted out, our gang had been transferred to another half-built liner on one of the other slipways. This was probably the *Orcades*, but I couldn't swear to it.

One of the other things that changed about this time, was that the management had at long last agreed that all the shipyard workers, many of whom had to work outside in all weathers, should be allowed to have a cup of tea at mid-morning in the same way that the office staff in the comfort of their offices had always been allowed. This concession, however, referred to us having 'a cup of tea', not a 'tea-break'. Which meant that although we could 'drink' tea, we couldn't stop work to do so. The system they devised was to provide small 'hot water huts' on the slipways, each operated by a man who'd open up at the designated time each morning. We on our part had to appoint one man from each gang to take all our brew cans and get them filled up.

How we could carry on shinning up ladders, scaffoldings and bulkheads while drinking tea, nobody ever explained. However, the management, obviously satisfied that in 'laying down' the rules they'd done their job, never bothered to come round to check, we simply did our bit by ignoring them, and everyone was happy.

Our gang transferred our steel erecting efforts to the new liner, in pretty much the same way as we'd done on the *Himalaya*. No two ships are ever exactly the same, however, and present different challenges, so life was never dull. One incident I remember happened when we were fastening one of the heavy steel ribs onto the thick hull plates. We were all outside high up on the scaffolding, and I was tightening one of the bolts with a heavy pneumatic bolt gun. Suddenly, the world around me disappeared and I found myself hanging by one hand from the top of the hull plate, still clutching the heavy bolt gun with its trailing air pipe in the other. For a split second I didn't have a clue what had happened. It wasn't until I saw Mazzie and Archie spreadeagled on the next row of scaffolding seven feet below, hanging on for dear life among a jumble of fallen planks, that I realised that our row of scaffolding had simply collapsed.

We'd all been incredibly lucky to escape unhurt, particularly as the ground, some forty feet below, was stacked with jagged metal parts waiting to be fitted, so there'd have been no hope of a soft landing.

Strangely, even though I was dangling by one hand, I wasn't aware of the weight of the heavy bolt gun dangling from the other. And as Mazzie and Archie picked themselves up, I managed to lower it down onto their scaffolding by its air pipe. Once it was safely on the lower scaffolding, I let go of it and hauled myself up over the top of the hull plate and onto the deck of the ship.

As I said, life as a steel erector was never dull, and although such incidents weren't exactly everyday events, they happened often enough.

During these first few months following our parade in Kendal, Cathy and I diligently wrote loving letters to each other promising all sorts of wonderful things for when we next met. As the weeks went by, however, I'd gradually felt a growing uneasiness about this unexpected diversion which my life had taken. Until I'd met Cathy, my plans for the future had all seemed clear cut and unambiguous; I was determined to become a singer. And although I wasn't at that time clear as to how this would come about, what I did know was that it would eventually involve my leaving Barrow and going off to London. I still felt as strongly about Cathy as ever, but I'd begun to have doubts on several counts about the wisdom of getting involved in such an intense relationship at the age of seventeen when our lives had not really settled down. There was also the fact that we lived thirty-six miles apart; and although this doesn't sound far in these car-owning days, it presented much more of a problem at that time, and meant in practice that we never saw each other.

In the end I reluctantly sent her a letter, explaining my feelings about our being too young for such a strong commitment, and that we should possibly wait until we were a few years older.

When Cathy's reply arrived, almost by return of post, she was obviously upset and completely bewildered by my letter. What had happened to bring about this sudden change in my feelings towards her? She felt sure that in some way 'she' must be to blame for this. She said she 'knew' she'd been a bit shy and restrained during our outings together, 'was this it?' If so, she promised to make up for this in the future?

I wrote back assuring her that she was definitely 'not' to blame, and that I wouldn't have wanted her to behave in any other way than the way she had. In fact, that was all part of what made me feel the way about her that I did.

I doubt if my explanations made any sense to Cathy, and who could blame her. The problem for me was simply a matter of timing. Cathy had simply come into my life too early, and despite my feelings for her, I just couldn't reconcile our unexpected relationship with my other plans, which I'd had for as long as I could remember.

SOME MAJOR EVENTS OF THE YEAR:

(1) The United Nations supersedes the old League of Nations.
(2) The Third Programme started on BBC Radio.
(3) Radar echoes received from the Moon for the first time.
(4) Nationalisation of: The Bank of England; The Coal Industry; and Civil Aviation.
(5) The electric blanket invented in America.

13

A New Challenge in the Shipyard

1947 (18 years old in July)
Since starting my apprenticeship in Mazzie and Archie's gang I'd gradually learned that the trade of shipwright covered a whole range of shipbuilding skills; of which steel-erecting, laying out the slipways, launching, etc., were only a part. Most of the other shipwrighting skills only came into play once the ship was safely launched and berthed in the dock where she'd be fitted out and finished off.

As I'd now been working with Mazzie and Archie as a steel erector for about a year and a half, it was decided by the top yard office, that the time had come to move me on and widen my experience in some of these other skills.

Always keen to learn something new I welcomed this move, and found myself saying cheerio to Mazzie and Archie after work one day, and reporting next morning to the foreman in what was known as the boat shed.

I discovered that the boat shed was a long, low workshop tucked away behind the large main sawmill. And although it was still in the top yard – not all that far from the slipways – it was a totally different working environment to the clatter and clang I'd been working in for the past eighteen months or more.

The foreman took me down to the far end of the narrow shed, to where a grizzled looking man of about sixty was hacking away on a huge lump of timber perched across two trestles. The timber was about sixteen feet long by eighteen inches square section thick. The grizzled chap seemed to be carving away the square edges as if turning it into a long round boom.

125

"This is Skipper Reid," declared the foreman. "You'll be working with him." And that was it.

'Skipper' Reid's speciality – I never did find out his 'real' first name – turned out to be lifeboat repair; spar making – like the ship's derrick boom I'd seen him working on – and virtually everything else concerning the woodwork found on ships.

I sensed straight away, that here I was once again landed with one of nature's 'characters'.

The area in which he was working looked a bit like a Wild West saloon complete with sawdust, with Skipper adding to this effect by chewing tobacco; which meant that he'd spit quite frequently. 'His' version of the old Wild West spittoon, however, was the workshop floor; fortunately covered in sawdust.

This apart, though, he was undoubtedly a highly killed shipwright, and once I'd got used to his eccentricities, and 'he'd' found that I was willing to work and learn, we got along well together.

My first job was to help him finish making the boom he'd been working on, where he taught me was how to handle the draw knife I'd seen him using, plus the adze – a special kind of axe – both of which were tools specific to shipwrighting, and which I'd never come across before.

Shortly after starting work in the boat shed, I received some bad news about Mazzie and Archie's gang which made me realise how incredibly lucky I'd been in being transferred when I was. It seems that after taking on a new apprentice in my place, the gang had all been working high up on the top deck of the ship I'd just left, and were lowering a large steel bulkhead into place with a crane when the screw clamps holding it (dodgy lifting devices which wouldn't be allowed these days) lost their grip and came loose. The large bulkhead crashed down onto the deck end and started to topple over towards them. All three of them made a dash for safety in different directions, and Mazzie and Archie just made it. The new apprentice, however, was apparently in a different position and his only way of escape was to dive over the side of the ship; and because they were some sixty feet above the ground he'd almost certainly have been killed. Fortunately for him he didn't quite make it and the top of the falling bulkhead just caught him before he could jump, trapping him by the legs and badly injuring his back.

I did hear later that he'd had to spend several months in hospital, though what happened to him after that I don't know. Once again I realised that I'd been fortunate in escaping serious injury; 'this' time, however, simply because I wasn't there.

The job with Skipper turned out to be amazingly varied and interesting. We'd find ourselves doing jobs both in the workshop and out around the slipways. And since it was also part of Skipper's job to go out and about on call around the docks repairing damaged lifeboats and such when a ship came in having been hit by a storm, there was certainly no lack of variety or challenge.

One of the surprising things we often came across, where damaged ship's lifeboats were concerned, was to be told by the crew that the damage had only occurred when they were pounding their way up the Irish Sea, after crossing half the world's oceans perfectly safely.

Other jobs we'd get involved in also kept us on the move. One of these cropped up whenever there'd been a launch. This was because when a ship goes down the slipway into the water, all the 'upper' part of the slipway and supporting timbers go down with it, but float away once the ship is in the water. Most of these are quickly rounded up and towed back to shore by a flotilla of small boats, that had been out there on the water waiting. However, quite often not all of these large baulks of valuable timber are recovered from the swirling water, as some simply get swept away with the tide.

This is where Skipper and I came in, for quite often when timber had gone missing in this way, there was a good chance that it would be eventually washed up on one of in the many beaches surrounding the Barrow area: Walney Island, Rampside, Morecambe Bay, etc. Our job would be to go out exploring all of these beaches (on foot) in the hope of finding them. When we were successful, as we often were, we'd have to find the nearest phone booth (no mobiles in those days) and report its whereabouts, so they could send out a lorry to pick it up.

One of our other jobs I remember was to make and fit several six or seven foot temporary navigation-light masts on an aircraft carrier. This aircraft carrier had been built and launched in Barrow, but as the war had ended before it came into commission it had simply been berthed out of the way in Ramsden Dock until the authorities decided what to do with it. I believe she'd been launched under the name of *Pioneer*, but that this was eventually changed; though I can't remember to what.

However, it had finally been decided to send her off somewhere else, possibly Birkenhead, to be finished off and belatedly commissioned into the Royal Navy. The only problem was that she had to be 'towed' to her new destination, and never having been finished, had no navigation lights. Since these were mandatory before she could be allowed out into the open sea, Skipper and I duly obliged.

One odd thing I remember while we were erecting these masts, was watching some shipwrights working on a ship nearby. They were trying to fit a thick, seven foot length of solid oak rubbing strip to the side of the ship when the crane sling slipped and the baulk of oak plunged into the dock. To everybody's astonishment, including ours, the oak was so heavy that it sank like a stone and never came up. Whether they ever managed to dredge it up again off the bottom of the dock we never found out, but if they didn't it was a pretty costly slip-up.

During all these times of change at the shipyard, Willie, Jim and I were still holding our evening gramophone recitals in Jim's rubble strewn basement whenever we could. Or making our Saturday afternoon raids on the record cubicles in Pass's big music shop from where our small stock of 78" records was gradually being added to, as and when we had any spare cash.

However, for me the point had long since been passed when simply listening to 'other' singers was enough. I was growing more and more impatient to actually 'be' one. So feeling that any old teacher would be better than none at all, I suggested to Willie and Jim, that even though it seemed unlikely; there might just be a teacher in Barrow somewhere, who could at least 'start' us off on the right road.

They both agreed, so we set about scouring the notice boards in the music shops and looking anywhere someone might advertise, and to our surprise eventually came across one that looked promising. This was a small ad in the *Evening Mail* that had been put in by a lady piano teacher who claimed to also teach singing. So we duly contacted her, and arranged for all of us to go together, for a sort of introductory lesson.

I can't remember her actual address, but it was in a slightly posher district than Marsh Street. After showing us through into her music room, she immediately regaled us; with a certain professional flamboyance, on the details of her own musical career.

We were all pretty impressed by this; if not slightly overawed. It seemed that she'd once actually been a professional singer, and had spent some time with the D'oyly Carte Opera Company.

'Things are really beginning to look up,' I thought. 'Here we are in the presence of a real live opera singer. And even though 'Gilbert & Sullivan (which was all that D'oyly Carte Company did) was not exactly Grand Opera, it still seemed a big step in the direction of the operatic stage.

Finally we got to the point about our learning to sing.

"Right!" she said. "First of all we need to find out what kind of voices you've got."

She then started rattling off scales on the piano and getting us all to sing along with them in different keys.

128

"Let your voices go," she kept calling, "just open your mouths wider and give me more volume; more volume." The net result of us trying to follow this 'professional' advice was that our voices gradually got throatier and smaller until we were all virtually croaking like frogs.

"I can't tell what your voices are yet," she announced finally, stopping for a rest before our voices packed up altogether, "because they haven't got much range at the moment; but you're probably all baritones."

This was not a very encouraging pronouncement for three aspiring tenors to hear, especially with throats too sore to argue.

"Anyway," she continued, "why do you 'want' to learn to sing?"

"Because we want to be opera singers," was my croaky reply.

Her mouth fell open in disbelief.

"What!" she exclaimed. "You don't mean 'Grand Opera'?"

"Yes," I replied.

The prima donna just burst out laughing.

"Why!" she blurted, "even 'I' would never have attempted to sing Grand Opera."

The unspoken, but obvious, implication being, that the idea of us three 'no-hopers' imagining that 'we' could, was just too ridiculous to contemplate.

This, together with her 'sore-throat-inducing' teaching method, was even less encouraging than being told we were baritones, so we never darkened her doorstep again.

It did, however, serve as an early warning about the difficulty of finding a 'genuine' singing teacher; amply confirming my long held belief that London would be the only place to go to achieve my goal. Something which had now became Willie and Jim's goal too.

About this time Mam had somehow acquired an old, but quite good, piano. This had found a home in our front room at 107; where our favourite wind-up gramophone was kept, and where Dad spent most of his evenings listening to his KLM radio.

My young sisters Joyce and Jill had briefly taken a few piano lessons, but for some reason I hadn't. Which, since 'I' was the only one in the family at that time with any aspirations towards a musical career, seems a bit odd now, even to me.

I suppose that this was probably because I wanted to become a 'singer', not a 'pianist'; and at that time I couldn't see the value of spending my evenings after a hard day's work in the shipyard, hammering out scales on a piano.

However, I eventually decided to take Mam's advice and have a go myself. The girls' piano teacher had been a Mr Broome, so I went to seek him out.

I discovered that he lived in a big house with a front garden up in Mount Pleasant, and still remember the bell ringing distantly from somewhere deep inside when I pressed the button on the front door. This was followed by footsteps approaching down a long hall, and Mr Broome appeared on the step. He turned out to be a smart, dapper little man dressed in slightly old fashioned style with metal-rimmed specs and a wing collar shirt.

After showing me into the front room, and giving me my first brief introduction to the art of playing the piano, he explained that he was the resident organist and choir master at St George's big church near the junction of the Strand and Salthouse Road, and agreed to take me on as a pupil for an hour's lesson once a week, and that was it; my first genuine step into the unsuspecting musical world had been taken.

I had to get various books of scales and practice pieces from Pass's music shop, which I practised whenever I could, and over the following few months Mr Broome taught me the basics of musical theory, which were to be so vital to me from then on.

During these sessions Mr Broome had gradually learned about my singing ambitions; but to my relief – after our recent singing lesson fiasco – didn't offer to teach me to sing, or ask me to join his church choir. However, it turned out that he also ran another singing group independently of the church which he eventually suggested that I, along with Willie and Jim, might like to join. This was a male voice group, which performed under the name of the 'Bach Choir'.

After discussing this among ourselves, we eventually decided that it might be a useful experience, so turned up at one of their rehearsals. These were held at a school hall in Thwaite Street – just around the corner from the Co-op Dairy, where I'd had my first job on the milk round.

There seemed to be about twenty men there, and after introducing us Mr Broome explained what repertoire they were working on. He then decided that it might be best for us three to start off in the bass section. Once again three aspiring tenors found themselves relegated to growling along down in the basement. Though Jim, with his now obviously deeper voice, was managing the notes a lot better than Willie and myself.

The choir were working on a mixed repertoire at the time, though the only item that sticks in my mind was the *Pilgrim's Chorus* from Wagner's opera *Tannhauser*.

Since none of us three had a clue about sight-singing from sheet music, it was simply a question of us picking up the notes from the other basses in our section. This was not made any easier by the fact that bass sections never get to sing the melody line, but are condemned always to grunt along down in the lower harmonies, singing notes that seem to have very little to do with the beautiful melodies we could hear being poured out by the lucky tenors.

It was, however, as we'd hoped, a useful experience. Though growling our way along in our boots was hardly fulfilling our singing ambitions. So after struggling along for a few weeks we eventually gave it up as a bad job and never went again.

Mr Broome was a bit put out about this, but still continued to take me for my piano lessons, for another month or two, when I finally decided I could no longer keep this up either. It was, as I'd thought in the beginning, that practicing the piano (which I'd only ever thought of as a sideline interest) was becoming too much of a chore every evening after a hard day's work at the shipyard, so I gave this up as well.

Nevertheless, I was grateful for all the groundwork of musical knowledge I'd got from Mr Broome, and felt sure it was going to stand me in good stead in the singing world I was aiming for.

14

Down Among the Submarines

Around the middle of the year, Skipper and I were transferred from the boat shed to the submarine sheds down on the side of Devonshire Dock. I'm not sure why, but it was probably because our services were being more called for in that area of the shipyard.

For me it was a fascinating change, because working on submarines was something entirely new. Our first job was making and fitting the teak handrail ledges round the tops of the conning towers on the 'new' subs, which were 'A' class subs like the *Andrew*, and replacing them on the old long serving 'T' class subs, whose names all began with a 'T'.

The first one of these 'T' class subs we worked on was, I believe, called the *Trident*. This particular sub had come back home after a long involvement in the Pacific campaign against the Japanese, and was looking pretty rusty, worn out and sorry for itself.

At the time the war had ended in Europe, I remembered seeing one of the German U-boats coming into Barrow to surrender. What had happened to this I don't know, but there was no sign of it in the sub dock when we arrived there.

There was, however, a mysterious, somewhat smaller German sub moored alongside our wharf, with an armed Royal Navy guard on the gangway. This was something of an enigma around the dock area, and all sorts of rumours were floating about as to what it was. Talk of it having special 'jet' engines or some such were common. We who were actually working alongside it, however, were gradually able to pick up bits of the truth. It turned out that this submarine was part of a secret experiment by the Germans, in which they were attempting to create a new type of submarine with an

132

engine that ran on hydrogen peroxide as a fuel, instead of the usual diesel.

Moored alongside the sub itself, which was inaccessible, was the sub's supply ship, which was simply a cargo ship that had been modified to operate as a hydrogen peroxide fuel tanker. And, for some reason, this did not have a guard on its gangway; so skipper and I, carrying our tool bags as a blind, managed to get on board and look around.

The first thing that struck me, I remember, was the unusual chemical smell that pervaded everywhere. The only other odd thing was that each of the cargo holds was completely filled with a single huge tank from which the heavy smell seemed to be coming.

These experiments had come to a halt when Germany capitulated, so they were never brought to any sort of conclusion. Since there were apparently three of these submarines under construction at the time, the three allies; Russia, USA and Britain, commandeered one each to carry out their own experiments. These obviously never came to anything, since no such hydrogen peroxide powered submarines have ever been built.

As well as making and fitting the woodwork to the conning towers, Skipper and I got involved in a variety of other jobs in the sub dock. One of these was helping to get the subs on and off the large floating dock, which was moored out in Devonshire Dock. This floating dock was used for raising ships up out of the water, so that repairs, painting, etc., could be carried out on their undersides. It was capable of lifting quite sizeable cargo vessels in this way, but our concern was with the submarines.

The way it worked was quite simple. It had side walls and huge tanks built in underneath which could be filled with water to sink it down to rest on the bottom of the dock. The ship would be floated in between the side walls and made fast, then the water would be pumped out and the tanks filled with air. These tanks of air produced enough 'lift' to raise both the dock and the ship up until the ship was completely out of the water where it could be worked on.

Of course, the floor of the floating dock would have been laid out with supporting blocks beforehand to suit the flat bottom of the ship. This was OK for cargo ships with their wide, flat-bottomed hulls, but for submarines with their long, narrow hulls it was a bit more tricky. The subs had a long central keel underneath about three feet wide which had to be accurately lined up with the dock's pre-placed line of supporting blocks, so that as the water was pumped out, it would come to rest on them exactly.

This was achieved by having men up on the floating dock walls either side lowering long measuring poles down on ropes. One end of the pole would be held against the dock side wall, while men on the sub would hold the other end against a central line mark on the sub's deck. Other teams of men up on the dock walls with ropes fastened to the sub would be manoeuvring the sub into its central position, guided by the calls from the men on the deck.

This was a simple, but effective, way of ensuring that the sub's 'unseen' keel came to rest accurately on the line of 'unseen' supporting blocks deep under the water below. There was, however, one slight problem with this, in that very few subs were absolutely upright in the water, most had a slight list to one side or the other, which meant that the central line on the deck might be a few inches out of plumb with the centre line of the keel sixteen or more feet under the water below.

This is where Skipper and I came in. It was our job to check this by hanging a six foot long plumb-line down a vertical seam on the front of the conning tower. If this showed the sub to have a vertical lean of two or three inches one way or the other over the six foot drop of the plumb line, then over the sixteen foot drop between the deck and the keel this would amount to about eight or nine inches. So this difference had to be allowed for when using the measuring poles on the deck. If we'd got it right then as the sub settled onto the supporting blocks on the dock floor, she would gently tilt over so that the measuring poles rested exactly on the deck central line.

Late one afternoon Skipper and I were working on the conning tower of a sub, when we noticed that her mooring ropes were being cast off. Nobody had said anything to us about this, so when we enquired, we were astonished to find that she was being taken out into the centre of the dock to do some submersion tests – there was apparently a deep water trench out there, which was news to us.

As soon as she reached the spot we were told to go below because, even though she wouldn't be completely submerged, everybody had to be off the decks. So down we went, to spend a fascinating hour or more amid all the noise and bustling activity of a sub in operation; flooding and discharging its diving tanks, orders being passed back and forth on the intercom, etc. I'd seen some of this before on films, but the real thing (or almost) was something special – especially as we were being 'paid' to do it.

As it turned out, this worked out even better than we'd thought, because when we finally surfaced we were told that the sub was not going back to our dock, but was sailing right round into Ramsden Dock to be berthed there. I couldn't have been more pleased, because our normal shift was already over by this time, so we'd be on extra overtime pay for the next couple of hours or so. What a lovely way to earn extra money!

A little while after this I got another chance to get amid the insides of a fully working sub, but this time I was able to take someone along with me. This happened when one of the newly finished A Class subs was being commissioned into the navy, and they'd decided to make this an 'open day' when the men who'd worked on building it were able to bring in a family member to have a look over it. My sister Joyce, who was the nearest to me in age, jumped at the chance and spent an hour or so being astonished – as I always was – at the incredibly cramped conditions that the crew had to work, sleep, eat, and fight a war in. Scanning the outside world of the dock through the periscope, and seeing the ships in exactly the same way as the submarine commanders – on both sides – had done all through the war was quite an eerie experience.

From time to time, Skipper and I would have to go out onto the dock in a small rowing boat, usually to pick up lumps of timber floating about or suchlike, and this is where I first learned the skill of sculling a small boat.

Sculling, in this case, as opposed to rowing, is a method of propelling a boat through the water with only 'one' oar, instead of the two normally used. The single oar is placed in a slot in the stem of the boat, and worked to-and-fro sideways whilst at the same time giving the oar a half-twist in opposite directions with each stroke. It's a bit like stirring a pudding, but the effect in this case is to propel the boat along. Held in the central position this will propel the boat directly forward. Pushing the oar over to the right or left whilst doing this enables you to steer the boat wherever you want to go.

It's a bit awkward to manage at first, but simple and effective with a bit of practice.

One of the things we'd often see when out on the water, concerned the little fireboat that always seemed to be chugging about somewhere or other. Its real role was, I believe, as a sort of handy, quick response fire fighting craft. In practice it seemed to get used for all sorts of jobs, and was a sort of 'Jack-of-all-Trades'. Or with it being a boat, this should probably be, 'Jill-of-all-Trades'. One of its jobs in particular never ceased to astonish me. This happened whenever they needed to move ships about in the dock from one berth to another – which was quite often – and couldn't get a proper tug; they'd simply hook up this tiny fire boat to do the job.

The idea seemed utterly ludicrous, particularly as the fireboat was powered by a single ford V8 engine – similar to the one found in the American car, and the British army Bren gun carrier – while some of these ships were of three or four thousand tons in weight. Astonishingly, though, it worked. Once hooked up to the ship, the little fireboat would strain away with its V8 engine roaring at full blast. At first nothing seemed to be happening, but gradually the huge bulk of a ship would start to move. Once under way, all the strain seemed to ease off the tiny Fireboat, and the huge ship seemed to allow itself to be towed docilely to where it had to go.

When Skipper and I were fitting all the teak woodwork in the conning towers of the subs, we met the same problem that I'd met with the metal ventilation systems in the gun turrets, and several times since with Skipper. Namely, that no two ships, or parts of them, are ever 'exactly' the same shape.

This meant that before we could get the teak timber cut to fit any particular sub, we'd have to make mock up battens as templates for each piece of teak we needed for that particular sub. We'd make these battens out of very thin sheets of soft wood, which could be cut to shape with a sharp knife and nailed together with tacks.

Once made, we'd then take these battens to the saw mill, so that they could cut out the thick teak handrail ledges in rough form, which we'd have to finish off and fit.

These trips to the sawmill were always an eye-opener for me, because hardly any of the sawyers I saw there seemed to possess a full set of fingers. Stumps, or even half hands seemed to be so much the norm that I began to wonder if this was one of the qualifications for the job. One thing was for sure, it made me glad I'd chosen to become a shipwright, and not a sawyer.

During our midday meal breaks we'd often spend our spare time making items for home out of off-cuts of teak, oak, sycamore, etc., which were always lying about in the workshop. In the sub-shed there was a sort of loft over one part of the main workshop which was accessible by a ladder, and was an ideal place for getting out of the way, and secretly making these 'foreigners', as any unauthorised bits of useful or ornamental things for home were known. Because they were unauthorised there was always the problem of getting them out of the shipyard gates under the beady eyes of the uniformed gate security men. In point of fact it was fairly easy, and a matter of timing. Since most 'foreigners' were fairly small they could be hung around your neck on string under the ample old overcoats that most of us wore. It was then a matter of making sure you were in the middle of the great rush of bodies pouring out of the gates like a river, as soon as the knocking off (no pun intended) siren blew. I managed to make several 'foreigners' up in that good old loft, three of which I still have in my living room today. Namely; a teak fruit bowl, a teak and sycamore table lamp and a money box the shape of a cinema organ made out of about six different woods.

There was one day in the submarine dock, however, that I'll 'never' forget. On that day I was sitting in the submarine shed, during our midday meal break eating my sandwiches, when the foreman came in and told me that I was to report straight away to the main offices near the High Level Bridge gate. He couldn't give me any information as to what this highly unusual order was all about, and was as baffled as I was. However, I hurriedly packed up my sandwiches and set off. I'd never been inside any of the main offices before, so when I arrived there and climbed the hallowed stairs to the manager's office, my feelings of trepidation were growing worse.

Somebody showed me into the manager's office, where a smartly dressed, middle-aged man was sitting behind a wide expanse of desk. He had a strangely disturbing look of concern on his face as he told me to sit down.

"I'm afraid I've got some very sad news to tell you," he said. "Unfortunately, your father collapsed and died at his work place in the gun shop this morning."

I simply stood there in a state of stunned disbelief.

"How can he have?" I muttered bewilderedly. "He was all right at breakfast."

"I'm afraid it's true," he replied sympathetically. "We've already sent someone to tell your mother. So you'd better get off home now to look after her."

I then vaguely remember him giving me some advice about sweet tea being a good comforter which helped people get over such a shock, so I should make sure she got plenty of this.

And that was it! The worst news I'd ever had in my life, and all I felt as I virtually ran home was a sort of numb disbelief. As if the whole thing was not really happening.

The next couple of weeks or so were a weird sort of blur. Dad was buried in the Devonshire Road Cemetery, and some of his workmates came to act as coffin bearers. From them we learned exactly what had happened on the day Dad had died. Apparently he'd been sitting having a meal break with them, when he'd got up to go to the toilet. He set off down the aisle, but had walked only about twenty yards when he suddenly stopped, spun around and collapsed to the floor. His mates all rushed to see what was the matter, but they were too late as he was already dead.

It was obviously a big shock to them, as apparently he'd appeared absolutely normal. To us, however, this news came as a great relief, because even though life without Dad was going to be a lot harder, we now knew that he hadn't suffered. He'd simply set off happily down that aisle, and walked into the next world

SOME MAJOR EVENTS OF THE YEAR:

(1) The Crown was made liable to legal proceedings for the first time.

(2) First report of flying saucers – by K. Arnold in the USA.

(3) John Cobb breaks the world land speed record at 394mph.

(4) Britain's first atomic reactor built at Harwell.

(5) *Diary of Anne Frank* published.

(6) School leaving age raised to 15.

(7) Most severe winter in Britain for 53 years.

(8) Greenwich Observatory moved to Herstmonceux in Sussex

15

Fresh Challenges – New Experiences

1948 (19 years old in July)

Although Dad's death had left a big hole in our lives, life at 107 continued more or less as before – as it had to. Our family finances, which had never been any more than adequate, were naturally now pretty strained. This made any extra income welcome to say the least, and fortunately for me this came in the form of overtime.

Overtime at the shipyard didn't crop up all that often, but as luck would have it there seemed to be quite a bit of it on offer just at this time. This was because there were a couple of recently launched ships in the docks being fitted out and finished off.

Much of the work involved in this did not fall to us, simply because of the strict lines of demarcation that existed between trades – even right throughout the war. These, in effect, dictated that virtually all the cabin-building woodwork was carried out by 'joiners', not shipwrights.

However, this still left plenty of work for us, because all the steel work, plus all the acres of teak deck laying, handrails, lifeboats, winch-booms, masts, etc., were down to us. And this almost always meant that a lot of overtime working was needed to get the ships completed on time.

It was on these overtime jobs that I'd previously learned the skills of making and fitting handrails, how to lay decks, caulk the seams with oakum fibre, seal them with molten black marine glue (which set hard like treacle toffee) and scrape ('scrunt') this off to a smooth finish with special 'scrunting tools' which we'd make ourselves from old tempered steel files.

139

Another overtime job that seemed to crop up quite often outside normal working hours, was the fendering of large ships through the narrow gates when they needed to be moved from one dock to another, or when they were arriving, and had to pass through the lock gates into Ramsden Dock from the Walney Channel after sailing up the Irish Sea. This 'fendering' was necessary because these ships were often a tight squeeze through the narrow gates, so our job would be to dangle thick wooden fenders on ropes between the entrance wall and the ship to prevent any damage to the ship's hull if it happened to scrape the wall.

As well as this overtime in Vickers, Willie, Jim and I got wind of another bit of spare-time earning elsewhere which we decided might be worth having a go at. This was at the Barrow Paper Mills down at Salthouse, near the southern end of the docks.

Apparently, whenever timber ships came into Ramsden dock with a load of pulp logs for the paper mills, the logs would be off-loaded by the dockers into railway wagons, and towed around into the large railway siding area of the paper mills.

These logs, which were all four foot long, but anything from 8" to 18" thick, would then have to be off-loaded from the railway wagons, and piled into long lines of orderly stacks up to 15 feet high ready for use.

To do this, the paper mills would take on casual labour for the two of three days it took to off-load the ship. The most interesting bit for us though, was the fact that they were apparently paying more for a single day's casual work than 'we' were being paid for a whole week at the shipyard.

This opportunity to earn extra cash; coupled with the fact that all you had to do was turn up each morning at the paper mills gate and sign on, proved too good to be missed. So whenever we got wind of a pulp ship coming in, we'd 'go sick' from Vickers, and 'recuperate' at the paper mills by off-loading railway wagons, and stacking logs.

Shortly after this job ran out Willie received his call-up papers for National Service. He was only about the same age as I was, but was not an apprentice so couldn't get this deferred like I could. So off he went to serve king and country. Jim wasn't an apprentice either, but for some reason he never did any National Service, perhaps he had flat feet or something.

Another interesting little side-line earner came from my other Marsh Street mate Walter Caine – who I'd spent so much time with when we'd been evacuated to Orton. Walt was now working at Dawson's Wood Yard in Barrow, as (of all things) a sawyer. It seemed that one of the leading sawyers at Dawson's had somehow got a contract to do some tree felling and wood clearance up in Sowerby Woods. These lay just a mile or so out of Barrow, and had always been a favourite haunt of ours when we were kids.

He'd apparently asked Walt if he, or any of his pals, would care to help out in chopping down the trees in their spare time. Which in itself was interesting enough; but better still, he was willing to pay us a shilling an hour for doing it. This may not sound much nowadays, but at that time it was almost twice what we were earning at Vickers. And because we could do it in our spare time, usually at weekends – it all represented extra money. So for the couple of months that the contract lasted we all became lumberjacks. Mind you, since none of the trees were more than thirty foot tall by one foot thick, they weren't exactly the Giant Redwoods of North America. Nevertheless they were near enough for us.

We did all this tree felling with axes, not saws, and these axes were as sharp as razors. In fact, when we'd freshly honed them, we could pare the hard skin off our hands with them as clean as a surgeon's scalpel. This meant that they could cut into the hard tree trunks like butter. It also meant that they could be pretty lethal if you got a bit careless. One near miss incident I had makes me cringe even today. It happened when Walt and I were hacking away among the dense undergrowth fairly close together. I'd let fly a bit awkwardly at the tree I was attacking, when the axe didn't quite connect properly and glanced off the tree with a great 'WANG', swinging me round with its momentum. To my horror I had a split second glimpse of Walt aiming a similar blow at his tree no more than a few feet away, and as my axe whistled through the air it missed the back of his head by no more that three inches. If he hadn't been swaying forward at that moment with the force of his own axe blow, my axe blade would almost certainly have cut half his head off.

The shock of this almost made me feel sick, and I had to go off and find our 'billy can' of water to have a drink and try to regain my composure. When I got back Walt was still hacking away at his tree, completely oblivious about what had happened. I decided not to mention it at the time, and in fact never did afterwards. So to this day Walt has no idea just how close that lovely sunny day came to being his last.

Around this time, much to our delight, we began to get a few classical music concerts in Barrow. All of these concerts were held at the Kings Hall and often featured artists whose names were familiar to us from the radio, like the pianists Dame Myra Hess and Solomon. And although pianists weren't our prime musical interest, they definitely seemed a step in the right direction, so we went along to listen to them all.

Eventually though, singers also began to appear and we got a chance to hear genuine professional singers in the flesh for the first time, singing in the natural acoustics of a concert hall, without all the distortions of radio microphone amplification. Sopranos like Elena Danieli, Isobel Bailey, and the baritone Denis Noble were some of the first ones I remember. There was also a brilliant young coloratura soprano, Gwen Catley who was hailed by the critics of the time as the English version of the internationally famous Lily Pons.

Our first introduction to the world of oratorio also came at the Kings Hall. This was a performance of Handel's *Messiah* in which Isobel Bailey sang the soprano part she was famous for. But for me the outstanding performer of that evening was Marion Zigmunt, who I believe was Polish. He had one of the most beautiful quality bass voices I've ever heard.

Many of the musical films of the time, whilst not being 'musicals' in the sense we know today, often had well known classical singers in the cast. The duo Jeanette MacDonald and Nelson Eddy; sopranos like Deanna Durbin, Susanna Foster and Kathryn Grayson, and later on Mario Lanza were all very popular film stars. Even famous opera singers like the tenors Richard Tauber, and Beniamino Gigli seemed to get in on the film business occasionally.

However, the one who caught 'my' attention most at that time, was a tenor who appeared in the film *The Thrill of a Romance* which starred Doris Day and Van Johnson. This was because he was the first Germanic, 'Heldentenor', that I'd ever come across. His name was Lauritz Melchior, and although he was famous for singing the great Wagnerian 'Heldentenor' roles, he was actually Danish. Not only was he a great singer with a magnificent, ringing voice, he was also a great, bubbly character standing some six feet, five inches tall and weighing in at around twenty stones. He seemed to dominate every scene he appeared in simply by being there.

For me, there was something about this Heldentenor style of singing that seemed to strike a personal chord, and which undoubtedly got stored away for the future.

At some time in this year, Mam had managed to take out a mortgage on a large boarding house at number 6 Ainslie Street with the help of various bodies; including the British Legion – who'd helped because of Dad's First World War record. So we now left Marsh Street once again for a 'not too congenial' life in a busy boarding house.

As usual Mam, with her drive and energy, set about getting the

142

boarding house up and running. Soon a steady flow of boarders from every walk of life were passing through; travelling salesmen, manual workers in Barrow on short term contracts, etc., plus the odd more or less permanent resident.

Since I was working in Vickers during the day, and out with Willie, Jim or Walt at most other times I didn't get involved too much with this ebb and flow of strangers through what was, after all, still our family home. Mam wouldn't have welcomed any 'interference' from me anyway – or from anyone else for that matter. She had her own way of running things, which I didn't always agree with, especially the way the family sometimes got shuffled about to make room for boarders.

Nevertheless, since I had my own path to follow, I was quite content to hand over my wages each week, and leave the boarding house business to her.

Where the structural maintenance of the boarding house was concerned, though, running repairs etc., things were different and I was only too willing to get pitched in. I rebuilt part of the crumbling backyard wall, moulded a new concrete beam along the top, cleared out all the roof gutters and blocked yard drains. These blockages were caused by the falling leaves from a huge sycamore tree growing in the tiny back garden, whose topmost branches towered away above the roof of the three storey house.

Since it was not much use simply clearing out the roof gutters and drains, while leaving the massive cause of the problem standing to wreak its havoc every autumn, I decided it had to come down. To a recently qualified lumberjack, this was obvious; the only problem being that the massive tree was towering up from a tiny, narrow yard between two houses close together, ours and the one next door. This is where the qualified (well almost) shipwright took over. I shinned up into its topmost branches with my shipwright's hand saw and my mother's clothes line, hacked it to pieces from the top and lowered each piece down with the clothes line.

This meant a heck of a lot of climbing up and down, but eventually all that was left was a great flat stump a foot high; which as far as I know is probably still there to this day.

The little yard was stacked high with logs and branches everywhere like a timber yard, but even this gradually disappeared up our boiler chimney, as the great, beautiful tree floated gently away into the sky as smoke.

As the year went on I was growing more and more impatient about having to wait for so long before I could make some sort of 'definite' move along the road to becoming a singer. Going to concerts and

143

listening to records of singers was all very well, but I felt the time had come when I needed to take a more positive step in that direction.

What was making the situation so frustrating, was the thought that not only did I have my apprenticeship tying me to Barrow until I was twenty-one, but also that even when this ended I'd immediately become eligible for compulsory National Service, and this would almost certainly put my London plans on hold for a further couple of years after that.

All in all, I was faced with the dismal prospect of not being free to go off to London until I was around twenty-three years old, and I simply wasn't prepared to wait that long.

After a lot of thought I eventually decided that this waiting period just had to be shortened, and since I had no control over my National Service, the only thing I could do to shorten it, would be to give up my apprenticeship 'now', and get my National Service over with straight away. This would then mean that I'd be in London over a year and a half earlier than otherwise. And that was it.

Naturally Mam was not too pleased, to say the least, when I told her, especially at the loss of my wages. But, as the boarding house now seemed to be reasonably viable, I didn't feel too guilty about it, and stuck to my guns.

The authorities in Vickers were also a bit put out, and tried to talk me into staying. All except one chap I'll always remember, who after listening to my reasons, simply said:

"Well, if that's what you want to do, lad. You go off and do it."

And that's exactly what I did.

He allowed me to keep the toolbox full of tools that I'd been given, and I walked out of Vickers for the last time.

16

The World Beyond the Shipyard

I reported to the relevant conscription board on the day after my departure from Vickers and was given a couple of forms to fill in by the sergeant behind the desk. He then asked the old 'waste of time' question which had almost become a music hall joke:

"What regiment would you like to go in, lad?"

Knowing full well that whatever I said would have no bearing whatsoever on where they'd send me, I simply plucked something out of the air.

"The Parachute Regiment," I declared – probably like a couple of million others who'd been asked the same question.

"Right!" said the sergeant. "It'll probably take about three months to come through. We'll let you know."

And the next minute there I was outside on the pavement. Out of a civvy job, and not yet in the army.

Fortunately, this presented no real problem, since jobs were available everywhere at that time, and as I would only be doing it for about three months it didn't really matter what it was. I eventually plumped for one in the strip mill at the steel works, simply because they appeared to be offering exceptionally high wages.

Common sense should have warned me that there had to be a reason for this, but it didn't. So I turned up at the mill at six o'clock in the morning on my first day, not having a clue what the job was all about. The first thing I learned was that this six o'clock 'til two o'clock shift I was starting on, was only one part of a rotating three shift system, which changed every week. I would therefore have to do the two o'clock 'til ten o'clock shift the following week, and the night shift of

g

ten o'clock in the evening 'til six in the morning the week after, thus bringing me back to where I started.

This all seemed a bit odd to me, but after all, it was only for three months – and it 'would' be a new experience, so I said OK.

The huge shed I was set to work in was a great fume filled oven of a place with a massive glowing furnace taking up half of one side and filling the shed with searing heat and the acrid smell of burning metal. A line of heavy steel rolling machines were set into the concrete side by side across the floor, and it turned out that I was to be one of the team of men who operated this roller system, albeit a somewhat minor bit.

What this roller assembly was all about was producing strip steel about an inch wide, by one sixteenth of an inch thick from a white heated block of steel about six inches thick by three feet long. These blocks of steel would be put into the furnace cold at one end, and travel slowly through it on a sort of conveyer belt system, to emerge at the other end glowing white hot and ready for rolling.

To see it all working at full pitch I found was not only fascinating, but pretty amazing as it all seemed timed to perfection. As the steel blocks emerged from the furnace two men with heavy tongs would grab it and drag it across to the first rolling machine and ram it end on in between the rollers. These would drag it through to emerge at the other side twice as long, and somewhat thinner. Two men at the other side would grab it with tongs as it came through, and ram it back through the next set of rollers which would make it even thinner and longer. This backwards and forwards movement would carry on right down the line of rollers with the steel getting thinner and longer until it only needed one man behind each roller to grab it and whip it around into the next rollers like a great long snake. When it finally emerged from the last set of rollers it was the required size of about one inch wide by a sixteenth of an inch thick, and so long that it had to run down into a long tunnel. And all this had happened in less than a minute.

Oh! I forgot the most important bit. It turned out that the last operation of all was to pull down a handle and pass it between some scraper blades as it whistled out from the last rollers. This was done to scrape off any slag that might have been left clinging to the newly rolled strip, and give it a smooth clean finish. This was my job.

Simple enough really, but due to the speed at which these final rollers whistled the strip through, a bit tricky to get right in operation. If I rammed the leaver down a fraction late, I'd miss the first couple of yards of the strip, which wouldn't get scraped. This was bad enough, but if I rammed it down too early, it was disastrous, because the

146

scrapers would then trap the front end of the strip, and the whole strip would end up as a tangled mass under my machine. As this meant the rollers having to be shut down in order to clear it out; together with the fact that all the roller men were on piecework, it didn't do much for my popularity when it happened. Fortunately this wasn't very often, once I'd got the hang of it, and I quite enjoyed the job, repetitive and boring though it was.

What did begin to get me down in the end, however, was the rotating three shift system. After the first three weeks I was beginning to lose track of what day it was, or even what time. It seemed almost as if the strip mill was out of touch with the rest of the world outside. So after about six weeks I decided I just had to get off this strange 'time roundabout' and back in touch with civilisation. Therefore, I handed in my notice and went looking for some other, less disorientating 'temporary' job.

The one that turned up was at the Salthouse Gasworks, were we'd always had to traipse since we were kids, trundling our home made wheelbarrow to collect coke, or with an old can to buy creosote. It seemed that they were looking for a man to make up a shortage in their yard gang. Once again I didn't know what I was getting into, but as before I wasn't really bothered, especially as I now had only about six weeks to go before my 'rapidly approaching' call-up day.

As in the shipyard, this gang turned out to be a three man team; two well-established young blokes just a few years older than I was, and now me. As well as the big difference in age to my old mates, Mazzie and Archie in the shipyard gang, there was another difference. I sensed right from the start, that these two new gang mates of mine had a long-standing rapport with each other which would, somehow, never entirely include me. This meant in effect that we weren't really a three-man gang, but more of a two-plus-one gang.

However, as I wasn't going to be there too long I decided I could live with this. There was nothing wrong with these two. They were good workers and certainly knew their job. It was simply a clash of personalities, and although we 'worked' together, outside of that we just had nothing else in common.

One of the first jobs we got involved in was unloading several railway wagons. These had been shunted onto a railway embankment in the gasworks' sidings, and were full of what looked to me like friable red soil. It turned out that this was iron oxide for the gas filtering beds. There were several tons of it and we had to shovel it out over the side of the wagons into great piles below the railway embankment. From where it was carted off by a four wheel mechanical shovel and loaded into one of the filter beds.

147

Apparently this iron oxide acted as a filtering medium, through which the gas from the coal was pumped to rid it of all the unwanted impurities, and make it suitable for domestic gas cookers and for commercial use.

There were several of these filter beds built side by side into an unusual structure I'd often noticed as a kid when we'd walked past the gasworks on our way to Rampside, and wondered what they were for. Each bed was about twenty feet square and six feet deep with metal panel sides. This layer of filter beds was set some ten feet above the ground in a framework of steel girders, and was topped off with a roof.

Each of the filter beds had its own large separate steel lid to seal it when it was in operation; and its own mechanism for raising it up when the iron oxide needed changing. This had to be done when the oxide had lost its filtering properties through becoming choked with impurities. When this happened the old iron oxide, which had started off as soft, friable red soil by this time would have become almost as solid as concrete, which had to be dug out with pneumatic drills.

I gathered that this digging out would apparently be one of our jobs – though fortunately not for a week or two because the latest one had been dug out before I arrived, and filled with the oxide we'd just off-loaded from the railway wagons.

However, we were kept busy enough with a whole variety of jobs around the gasworks, from loading coke lorries, which seemed to trundle in and out fairly regularly throughout the day, to helping out around the coal dock on the railway embankment where the railway wagons would tip their loads of coal into the hoppers.

These hoppers were linked to the large retort house by an overhead conveyer belt system, which delivered the coal to the chutes, through which the men working there could feed it directly into the retorts. These retorts were simply large tube-shaped ovens with a heavy steel door on the front. Once filled, the door would be closed to seal it from the outside air, and the coal inside 'roasted' by the furnace underneath. Because it was in a sealed retort with no oxygen, the coal couldn't actually 'burn', it just melted, giving off its gas, oil and tar. The gas would be siphoned away through tubes to the filtering beds, while the liquids, like tar, would be drained off into tanks.

When all these had been fully extracted the only thing left behind in the retort was the red hot coke. I believe that when this process was first developed, the coke was regarded as a waste product, like slag. Eventually, however, its special value as a fuel was realised, especially in the iron smelting industry, and it became as valuable as the coal itself.

As well as our yard gang and the retort workers, there always seemed to be one or two other men working around the gasworks doing special jobs. One character I remember seemed to spend most of his time weighing up the coke into one hundredweight sacks for the steady stream of smaller customers who came in. These could be anything from small independent delivery men with horses and carts, to individuals pushing home-made handcarts looking for fuel for the kitchen fire. The reason that this particular chap stood out, was simply his size. He was around six feet four inches tall, weighed in at around twenty-six stones, and was as strong as a cart horse. When he was filling and weighing up the hundredweight sacks, he could flip the two 56 pound weights on and off the scale as if they were empty paper bags. The shovel he used was so large that nobody else could handle it, and it only took four or five shovels full to tip the one hundred weight scale.

Eventually the day arrived when another of the filter beds had to be shut down to have the oxide replaced. The heavy steel sealing lid was hoisted up by the lifting mechanism and we gathered our picks, shovels and pneumatic drills, climbed the ladder onto the solid rock-like old oxide and got stuck in digging it out. The first thing that hit me as I stepped onto the spent oxide were the heavy fumes of coal gas and ammonia welling up from under our feet. But while the gas made breathing a bit difficult, and the ammonia set your eyes watering, there was still plenty of fresh air flowing in from the sides so it wasn't too bad. As we dug away with our picks and pneumatic drills, however, getting lower and lower into the filter bed, the air coming in from the sides grew less and less, until by the time our heads were below the level of the six foot high side walls there was virtually no air at all and we were starting to suffer the effects of carbon monoxide poisoning. This meant that we had to stop frequently and stagger up our temporary wooden ladder, to hang over the side of the filter bed and clear our heads to get some oxygen back into our systems. The worst problem was, I discovered, that this carbon monoxide very rapidly affected your muscles, sapping your strength so much that if you delayed too long before climbing up for fresh air, you wouldn't have the strength to climb up the ladder.

That day seemed the longest, and worst day's work I'd ever gone through, and when I set off home my eyes were so swollen from the ammonia fumes that I could hardly see, and my legs were like jelly. I vowed there and then I'd never be put through that nightmare again.

Fortunately, the problem didn't arise, because a few weeks later – after Christmas 1948 – I finally received my call-up papers and said good bye to the gasworks for good.

SOME MAJOR EVENTS OF THE YEAR:

(1) Gandhi assassinated.

(2) Apartheid begins in South Africa.

(3) The transistor invented in the USA.

(4) The 200" Mount Palomar telescope completed in California.

(5) Nationalisation of the Health Service in Britain.

(6) The XIV Olympic Games held in London.

(7) The Russian blockade of Berlin – resulting in the Allied Air Lift.

17

A Soldier's Life Beckons

My railway travel warrant arrived in late January, and I caught the train at what was left of Barrow's bomb mutilated station, to rattle south all the way to Dorset. At the time this was the longest train journey I'd ever done, and the furthest distance away from my birthplace I'd ever been.

My destination was a REME army camp near the small town of Blandford, where I was apparently to be trained as a Royal Electrical and Mechanical Engineer. . . So much for my 'Parachute Regiment' aspirations!

The long journey itself I don't remember too much about, apart for one pretty dramatic event that occurred at Temple Meads Station Bristol, where I had to change trains for the short last leg to Blandford. I was standing waiting on the platform, along with a lot of other passengers, when a train came steaming and clattering in. This in itself would have been perfectly normal, but since ours was a blocked end platform with buffers, the speed at which it was travelling seemed a bit excessive to say the least. As the massive locomotive thundered past us, everybody moved back quickly in alarm and the next second there came an almighty crash which shook the whole station. The whole train shuddered to a shattering halt, and we all rushed along the platform to see exactly what had happened. When I got there it was to be met with the astonishing sight of the huge railway locomotive buried about ten feet into the main concourse platform belching out great clouds of steam. The buffers, which it had torn up on the way, were draped across the front of the engine looking somewhat chewed up and sorry for themselves.

I never did discover the whole story, but before our connecting train arrived, on a different platform I'm happy to say, I did hear that the driver apparently believed that he was on a through line. I couldn't help feeling at the time, that if he'd been going much faster he'd probably have made it.

I finally arrived at Blandford's small station and stumbled out onto the platform with my suitcase, to find myself surrounded by about twenty or thirty other lads about my own age, who were all heading for Blandford camp, having come, as far as I could tell by their accents, from all over the country.

Outside the station a couple of NCOs were waiting with lorries to cart us off on the final couple of miles of our journey.

On arrival at the camp we passed through the pole barrier and pulled up at a large hut just inside the gates. The NCOs told us in quite a matey fashion to jump down and troop into the large hut to get something to eat.

To my surprise we all staggered in with our suitcases, to be confronted with a room full of important looking uniforms wandering about; an officer, corporals, a couple of staff-sergeants, and one astutely observing character, whose authoritative manner as he silently weighed us all up, singled him out immediately as the sergeant major.

What caught my eye most, however, were a couple of tables which were absolutely groaning under loads of sandwiches, cakes, pies, etc., and as we were waved towards them, we all got stuck into the food which was more than welcome after so many starving hours on trains.

The whole atmosphere was strangely free and friendly, almost like 'all mates together', and the general feeling among us new arrivals was: 'Well, if this is army life, maybe it's not going to be too bad after all.' However, when I gathered from the general conversation that we were not yet 'officially' in the army, and wouldn't be until after the 'signing on' ceremony – which was to follow our unexpected feast – my suspicions were aroused somewhat.

Sure enough, once we'd all been sufficiently lulled by our full stomachs into cheerfully signing our lives over to serving King and Country, the matey atmosphere vanished like magic.

"Right! you lot," yelled the sergeant major. "You're in the army now, so outside at the double. Left! Right! Left! Right! Come on, get those feet up. . !"

These raucous cries were immediately taken up by the corporals, and we found ourselves stumbling rapidly outside, swallowing our last bits of sandwich while wondering what had happened to the 'old pals' act, and trying to work out which of our feet were which.

We then spent the next five minutes being lined up, called an absolute 'shower', and shuffled about into 'column-of-threes' – or more or less. We were then marched at breakneck speed to a hut right in the middle of the camp, and told to line up outside the door. Then, as the corporal in charge barked out the orders, we had to enter one at a time. It looked like a strangely one-ended production line, with the new recruits disappearing into the hut, but none coming out.

When it came to my turn to nip smartly though the door as ordered, the truth was revealed. There were three chairs inside, in which the new recruits were being rapidly sheared like sheep of every last scrap of their hair, and sent packing out of another door on the far side.

This didn't bother me too much, as my shipyard town hair style was short back and sides, anyway, with not too much on top. But these were the days of the Boston Hairstyle, and many of my new trainee companions were not too pleased, to say the least, at having their thick, carefully nurtured locks scattered all over the floor.

Alter being suitably sheared, which in my case didn't take too long, I staggered out of the exit door to find a seething group of bald-headed strangers complaining bitterly about this barber shop assault. However, as more and more of our squad came tumbling bald-headedly out of the door, they all suddenly began to see the funny side of it, and were soon rolling with laughter as every newly shorn victim stumbled rapidly out of the door.

It was like waving a magic wand. Half an hour earlier we were just a very different looking group of assorted strangers. But now, at a stroke, these differences had been wiped out, and we'd been transformed into a unified group of what at least 'looked like', future soldiers.

When all our group had been suitably modified to fit the army's regulations, we were marched off to the hut which was to be our home for the next six weeks. All of our group were to be billeted in this same hut, and were under the immediate command of a lance corporal, who had his own tiny room just inside the hut door.

Before we were allowed in, he informed us that we were now 'Six Platoon', and gave us a bit of a grilling on what tough times lay before us, especially for anyone who might be under the illusion they could skive off, and take the mickey out of him, or the platoon sergeant. The platoon sergeant, who we hadn't met yet, was apparently billeted in different quarters.

Blandford Camp, we quickly learned, was a basic training camp where we'd somehow be knocked into the military shape required by the British Army. The sergeant, when we met him, turned out to be a highly experienced veteran in his late thirties who'd served throughout the war. Smart and disciplined, but mellowed with experience, he knew how to get the best out of his men, and I took to him straight away.

The first couple of days were spent getting settled into our hut, collecting bedding etc, being kitted out with all our equipment, and fitted (sort of) with our uniforms at the quartermaster's stores. This last bit was something of a farce which saddled me with a problem that bedevilled me all through my army service. It concerned the fact that we were allotted 'two' uniforms. One was supposed to be an everyday 'working' uniform, while the other was slightly smarter, and intended for more dressy occasions like parades, guard duties, off duty, etc. Unfortunately, this wasn't made clear to us at the time – all we knew was 'two uniforms'. So when the quartermaster thrust two at me with an official:

"These are your size."

I just took them and moved on like the others. It wasn't until we were trying them on back in the hut, that it dawned on me that both of my uniforms were a bit baggy and shapeless, while all the other lads had one that was noticeably smarter than the other. On mentioning this to the lance corporal he told me to take one back to the quartermaster to get it changed; which I did.

"Right!" said the Quartermaster when I explained. "Well, I haven't got another your size just now. So just hang onto this and I'll sort you out another later."

Despite repeated visits to the stores, he never did. So I was doomed from then on to cut a somewhat 'less' dashing military figure when on parade and off duty, than any of my comrades. This led to my being constantly pounced on by officers and sergeant majors, throughout the rest of my army service with irate demands like: "What the devil do you mean coming on parade in your working uniform?"

And since my explanations were always met with suspicious stares, and muttered injunctions like: "Well, just try to smarten it up a bit," I learned to live with it.

As far as uniforms were concerned, for the first two weeks at Blandford we were in any case confined to camp; being unfit to be seen in the outside world until we'd learned how to wear our uniforms like proper soldiers.

We were soon pitched into endless square bashing, route marches, rifle drill, and target practice on the camp's 25 yard firing range; where I got to experience the tremendous kick and bang of firing genuine 303 bullets for the very first time. Our first task on the firing range was to 'zero' the rifles we'd each been issued with to suit our own particular eyesight. This 'zeroing' was done by fastening our rifles to a special stand which held it absolutely rigid, while we aimed it at the bull on the target and fired a few rounds. After each bout of firing the target would be examined for accuracy, and if necessary the rifle's sights adjusted accordingly. This routine would be repeated several times until you were hitting the bull consistently.

One little incident I remember when we were on the firing range concerned our sergeant and a corporal, who was training his own platoon on the range next to ours. This corporal was a bit of a bombastic bully, and although he had nothing to do with our platoon, several times in the past he'd given some of our lads a bit of a bawling out and dressing down. On this occasion he began taking the mickey out of our efforts, and started firing his rifle at the targets, shouting:

"That's the way to do it!"

Our battle-hardened sergeant took a pretty dim view of this and ordered him to shut his mouth, adding:

"Now I'll show 'you' how to do it!" And with that, he grabbed his own rifle and banged off all nine round at a target so rapidly that it almost sounded like a machine-gun. The astonishing thing about it though, was that he'd fired all of them from the hip, and with the Lee Enfield having a bolt loading mechanism, he had to work the bolt between every shot. Despite this most of the shots were on target, or not too far off. Needless to say, we didn't get much bother from that corporal again.

Most of this 'physical energy' soldiering I really enjoyed. The one thing that I found a real pain, however, was the constant 'bulling up' of our equipment; boots, webbing, etc., with blanco and polish. I think that the main reason I hated, this 'bulling up' was because the idea behind it, apparently, was to keep us constantly occupied, while at the same time drumming into us the army discipline of obeying orders without question, whether we liked them or not. None of this did I personally need, since I required no artificial stimulus to keep me occupied, or to make me disciplined. However, I accepted that a few of my more wayward fellow recruits probably did, so I had to reluctantly put up with it.

Another reason I disliked this bulling up was purely financial. We had to pay for all the blanco, polish, etc., ourselves. And since all I received out of my weekly army pay of 25 shillings was five shillings – the other 20 shillings being collected by Mam directly from the Post Office in Barrow every week – I was having to get by on a pretty 'strained' budget to say the least.

Once our two weeks 'confined to barracks' had passed, we were finally allowed out into Blandford – subject to passing a dress inspection in the guardroom on the way. Blandford, it turned out, while quite a pleasant little place, didn't hold much to excite a young soldier's interest – including mine, so I saw little of it after my first visit.

Since our camp had nothing in the way of a NAAFI, there was nothing much there either. Fortunately however, we'd discovered that there was an RAOC (Royal Army Ordnance Corps) camp not far away, which not only had a very good NAAFI but also a small cinema where they showed a different film every week. This was sited on the opposite side of the wide, shallow valley, on the edge of which our camp lay. Connecting the two camps, was a sort of ring road that ran right around the top of the valley. And being a public road, in the days before the war it had apparently been used as a motorcycle racing track.

For us now, though, this became our running track on which we did a lot of our physical fitness training. Certain targets were set which we were expected to meet, such as being able to run a mile in six minutes and walk a mile in ten minutes. Most of us managed these OK, but there were always the odd one or two who couldn't.

These lads were usually the ones from sedentary civilian jobs, or slightly pampered family backgrounds. The same applied with our tests in the gym, where we had to be able to do twenty press-ups on the floor, and ten pull-ups on the overhead beam. I was astonished to find how many of the lads had a real struggle with these. One rather weak lad in particular, I remember, could hardly manage one press-up, and as far as pull-ups were concerned he couldn't even begin. We'd lift him up to grab the bar and he'd just hang there like wet washing on a line. However, with our cajoling and egging him on, he did begin to improve considerably over the next couple of weeks.

The sergeant major had his own rather noisy way of helping to sharpen up our physical fitness. He'd laid down rules that when on camp, none of us were allowed to walk in what he called a 'slovenly manner'. Once we stepped out of our huts, we had to walk at a smart, brisk pace. And if we ever needed to cross the sacred gravel of the parade ground, as we frequently did, we had to run at the double.

We soon became accustomed to hearing his great voice bawling out: "That man. . ! Where the devil do you think you are. . ? Get those arms swinging. . ! Pick up your feet. . !"

Pretty hard on the ears, but it certainly worked.

Pay parade was another of the rituals of army life we soon became familiar with.

156

It usually took place immediately before our tea time meal, and although picking up our money was always a welcome event, it was also a bit of a long-winded affair. This was because the whole camp of around two hundred would have to line up on the parade ground in front of the paying officer, who sat at a table with all the money and a pay clerk assistant. One of the sergeants would call out each man's name from a list and that man would then have to march smartly up to the table, salute the officer and repeat his name and number. The clerk would then read out how much pay he was due, the officer would count this out on the table, the man would then step smartly forward, pick up the money, step back, salute the officer again, then march smartly off to the mess hall for tea. This was a bit of a time consuming drag for everybody, but especially so for me, because they 'always' called out the names in alphabetical order, and with the name 'Workman' I was inevitably the last man to get paid every week. This, considering the small amount I was picking up, made the whole thing seem hardly worth all the bother – particularly as by the time I reached the mess hall, half of the others had already finished their meal and were on the way back to their huts.

Although all of the lads at Blandford Camp were conscripts and not there by choice, most of us accepted it as inevitable in those days just after the war. There were, though, the odd one or two who resented it so much that they flatly refused to go along with it, and ran into headlong conflict with the military authorities. We had one at Blandford. He spent all his time in the camp lock-up, and we'd occasionally see him being exercised in the company of a couple of military police. Apparently he'd been in that lock-up for several months before we arrived, and since the authorities had no intention of giving in, it looked as if he was likely to spend the whole of his National Service in the nick.

There was another chap who we'd been told about, who tried an alternative approach to getting out of doing his stint in the army. He tried to make himself appear mentally unfit for service by blancoing the whole of his uniform as well as his belt, webbing and other equipment. Unfortunately for him this hadn't worked either. All his enthusiastic bulling up proved in vain. And after a couple of months or so he got fed up, and decided it would be easier to just get on with his National Service. If he felt the way 'I' did about bulling up, I don't blame him.

So far at Blandford we'd simply been trained in the basic skills of soldiering, in pretty much the same way as other regiments. Our regiment being the 'Royal Electrical and Mechanical Engineers',

157

however, our main role would be somewhat different from those of the infantry, tank corps, artillery, etc. As in these other regiments, we'd 'still' be fighting soldiers, but our main purpose would be the maintenance, service and repair of all the army's fighting vehicles, from despatch riders' motorbikes to massive Centurion tanks; and everything in between. Our job would apparently also include the battlefield recovery for repair of damaged vehicles, especially tanks.

As the final week of our basic training drew near we were all gradually beginning to find out what this would mean for us individually. Obviously it would involve considerable training, and as a preliminary we all had to sit a basic exam, and go through aptitude tests to determine which of the various jobs we'd be most suitable for.

As in everything else we did in our platoon, these tests showed up a wide variety of aptitudes among us – which obviously depended a lot on our working backgrounds before we were conscripted. Those from office jobs didn't do too well in the practical tests, but did well in the exams. Quite a few, like myself, did OK in both, while several didn't do too well in either. We were told that these back markers were destined for what was called, 'general duties', which apparently meant everything from sweeping up to digging latrines. Fortunately I'd avoided this fate and was told I was to be trained as a mechanic; as were quite a few of the others.

However, remembering the army's 'square pegs in round holes' reputation, and my own application for the Parachute Regiment, it was a question of 'wait and see'.

How all this was to come about, and when and where we were to be trained, we weren't told. All we knew on departure from Blandford, was that we were off to a place called Chilwell near Nottingham.

18
Moving on

At some time in the afternoon of departure day, we left Blandford by train for Chilwell more or less as a platoon, assuming that Chilwell was where we'd all be taught our various trades. However, since official information was a bit sparse, as always, we didn't really know what lay ahead.

Halfway on the journey we found ourselves clambering off the train with all our kit at some small station in the middle of nowhere, to be met by a staff sergeant with a large lorry. Apparently, for some reason, we had to do an overnight stop at a small transit camp. This turned out to be a pretty deserted wartime outpost lost in the countryside. Its only occupant being the staff sergeant, who ran it all as a sort of one-man show.

Having dropped us off at the only nissen hut that looked fit to sleep in, he pointed out the cookhouse, where we could go and help ourselves to a meal he'd apparently cooked himself, then left us to it.

After we'd eaten the staff sergeant's offerings; which were not only welcome but very appetising by army standards, he turned up again and led us to the stores, telling us to take as many blankets as we liked for our bunks. He informed us that we could help ourselves in the cookhouse that evening, and that he'd have breakfast ready for us early next morning before taking us back to the station to continue our journey.

As it was still pretty wintry we soon got the hut stove going full blast, and with our piles of blankets spent a reasonably warm night, though as it turned out, not a particularly restful one. The reason being that the hut was sited right alongside a wire fence, on the other side of which ran a main railway line to London. So with fast trains thundering past a few yards away from our bunks every twenty minutes or so through the night – rattling the corrugated iron hut like a tin can – it was a bit like trying to sleep in an earthquake zone.

Getting up early next morning was for once a blessed relief rather than a chore. And as the breakfast was not bad at all, we set off once again for Chilwell in reasonably good spirits.

Chilwell, when we finally arrived, turned out to be a fairly hilly camp attached to a large Army Ordnance Workshop complex near Nottingham, the workshops being manned by a civilian workforce.

Once we were settled into our huts, we were each put to work in the workshops with one of the civilian mechanics. The mechanic I was paired with was working in a bay with several others where they were overhauling small, warehouse-type fork-lift trucks.

This turned out to be fairly simple stuff and I quickly found myself changing hydraulic pipes and refitting all sorts of bits and pieces here and there, which I soon not only found repetitive and boring, but also a bit of a letdown.

'This can't be what training to be an army vehicle mechanic was all about, can it?' I thought. 'What about all the lorries, armoured cars and tanks?'

Most of the lads who'd come with me from Blandford were also destined to be mechanics and felt just as cheesed off as I did. Despite constantly asking everyone in authority who'd listen, however, nobody seemed any the wiser than we were, so we just had to carry on and hope.

One particular memory I have of the Chilwell workshops is of a rather odd, dour looking chap who worked in a semi-open air shed near to where I worked. He was a sort of assistant labourer to a mechanic, whose job consisted of endlessly fitting new tyres to wheels of every shape and size. Day after day I'd see this sad-looking chap standing around in all weathers, often wet through and frozen to the marrow, handing tools to the tyre changing mechanic. As I knew only too well from experience what it was like working outside in all weathers, I tended to feel a bit sorry for him. That is, until I was told one day, that about a year earlier this poor, bedraggled looking chap had actually won £75,000 pounds on the football pools (about three million pounds in today's money) and that he'd never spent a penny of it, or taken a day off work.

Chilwell was also the only camp where I ever came across ATS girls, and at this camp there was a contingent of about thirty. They seemed to be older than us; long-serving regulars, who kept very much to themselves. This was OK by us, since none of them were exactly the stuff of which young soldiers dreams are made.

It was also at Chilwell that I first came across the army's notorious pay-docking system known as 'Barrack Room Damages'. This was a compulsory system of stopping money out of the pay of every man in each hut, to pay for any alleged damage that had occurred in their hut; broken windows and the like, no matter how it had been caused. This unfair method of forcing the innocent to pay equally with the guilty was always a great bone of contention. And in this particular case was even worse, because the damage we were being forced to pay for had occurred before we even arrived at the camp.

Naturally we all protested loudly about this, but apparently such a detail was of no concern to the military authorities. As far as they were concerned, if a hut had been damaged, those who happened to be living in it at the time the damage was noticed, were the ones who had to pay for it to be put right. So our pay was docked accordingly.

The most galling thing for us about this, however, was not the amount of money we lost, which wasn't all that much, but the fact that the alleged damage we'd paid for had still not been 'put right' by the time we left the camp.

Fortunately, to our relief, this wasn't too long in coming, and after about six weeks or so in Chilwell, we were told one day that we were being moved to another camp. It seemed that we were on our way to a place called Arborfield, and since this was down in Surrey it meant we were going south again.

Arborfield was a name we'd heard mentioned occasionally, so knew it was a main REME workshop centre. 'Was this to be our training camp, at last?' As usual nobody could tell us, so once again it was a case of wait and see.

When we finally arrived we found to our delight that Arborfield Camp was set amid large, busy factory-like workshops, which were staffed almost entirely by army personnel. Just the sort of place we'd imagined we'd be taught to be vehicle mechanics.

Once settled in we were all set to work in a bay in the main workshop under the supervision of a staff sergeant. Our job was to service and repair dispatch riders' motorcycles, which were mainly 250cc BSA and Matchless bikes. And although these were the smallest vehicles used by the army – starting at the bottom as we saw it – they were at least 'army' vehicles. Another encouraging sign was that there were plenty of other army vehicles of every type being worked on in other bays. In fact, right next to our bay they were servicing huge Centurion tanks, which weighing in at 60 tons or more, couldn't have offered a greater contrast to our tiny BSA dispatch riders' machines.

I soon found myself fitting new gear boxes, clutches, brakes, etc., on the bikes, which were pretty basic machines by today's standards, and therefore easy to maintain – obviously a big advantage, considering the amount of bashing about they'd have to stand up to in rugged battlefield conditions.

With such a wide array of different vehicles in the workshop, it was always fascinating to wander off and examine them whenever we had a few spare moments. The Centurion tanks in the next bay, however, being so close, drew most of my attention, especially whenever they needed to move the huge monsters a couple of feet one way or another. They wouldn't switch on the massive engines to do this, but simply release its brakes and nudge it this way or that with a heavy tractor, using a thick baulk of timber as a sort of ram. This seemed to work OK most times, but on one occasion when I was watching, the 60 ton Centurion seemed a bit reluctant to move, so the tractor driver revved up his engine for all he was worth, with the result that the baulk of timber slipped and crunched straight through the tractor's radiator, flooding the whole bay with a couple of inches of antifreeze. I wouldn't have liked being the one who got a thick ear over that one. At least we never had such problems with our BSA and Matchless motorbikes.

Although life at Arborfield was a lot more interesting than at Chilwell, and a big step forward from fiddling about with small forklift trucks, it became obvious after a few weeks of endlessly repairing motorbikes, that this also was definitely not where we were going to get the all-round mechanical training we'd expected.

As at Chilwell, all enquiries to those in authority brought no answers. Fortunately though, also as at Chilwell, we were eventually told that once again we were to be moved. This time to a large camp away up north at a place in Shropshire called Ellesmere. And to our astonishment were also informed that at long last this was to be what we'd been hoping for; Ellesmere, it seemed, was a large training camp dedicated entirely to the teaching of vehicle mechanics.

We arrived in Ellesmere to find that the camp, which lay about half a mile outside Ellesmere village, was set in beautiful rolling woodland amid grassy glades and huge mature trees. It was almost like being billeted in the grounds of a great country estate, and even had a large tree-lined lake some two or three hundred yards wide.

The extensive camp itself was sited on a hillside, and from the number of huts I could see, it obviously housed a pretty large garrison.

As it turned out, there were about five hundred trainee mechanics there, including our new intake. One thing that surprised me initially, though, was that all the buildings were of a fairly uniform size, with nothing resembling the large workshops we'd worked in at Chilwell and Arborfield.

We soon learned, however, that Ellesmere Camp was more like a college than a workshop, and that many of the huts were fitted out like classrooms/come small workshops which housed all the equipment necessary for teaching and demonstrating everything we needed to learn.

Once settled in, we were given the very welcome news that we'd be stationed in this lovely camp for six months. And assured that although six months may not seem very long in which to learn such a highly skilled trade as vehicle mechanics, the course we were about to start was so comprehensive, with eight hours a day of full time tuition by civilian teachers, that it would be the equivalent of several years apprenticeship in civvy street.

This to me was a real bonus. The opportunity of being taught such a fascinating subject as motor mechanics, something which I'd previously no experience of, seemed unbelievable; especially as I was being paid for the privilege.

An extra plus for me 'personally' in coming to Ellesmere, was that now being back up in the North West of England for the first time since joining the army, I was within striking distance of Barrow, so the odd trip home in my time off was a distinct possibility.

One other surprise (well sort of) we had while settling in, was that several of the other lads from Blandford, who'd failed their tests and had been destined for 'General Duties', turned up to be trained as mechanics. 'Par for the course' in the army really, so the only surprise was that 'we' were surprised at all.

However, we were all glad for their sakes, because who'd want to get lumbered with an official military qualification in digging and cleaning loos.

We were soon all pitched into an intensive training routine which consisted of illustrated lectures in class, where we we'd write up all the theory into our books, followed by practical work and demonstrations on the engines, gear boxes, transmission and brake systems, etc.

All this serious training would occasionally be punctuated by the usual army chores, like guard duties on the camp's main entrance gate; which being buried away in the woods, was a somewhat spooky place to do night guard patrolling on your own.

There'd also be odd stints of cookhouse fatigues, peeling spuds, scrubbing floors and the like. Things which seemed second nature to me, having been brought up in a large family where everyone was expected to do their share, but which came hard to most of my mates who'd never peeled a spud or washed a floor in their lives.

However, these duties didn't come around too often, and as the summer was now in full flow, when off duty we'd often go swimming in the lake. Or I'd simply wander off through the woods on my own, dreaming up the odd poem which I'd jot down in an old note book. I've no idea what happened to this notebook, so the world will never know just what deathless masterpieces it lost.

Occasionally I'd walk down into Ellesmere village, especially when there was any special event on. I remember that on one occasion I went down there to hear a special talk that was being given in the local hall. In those days before television took over everything, many famous celebrities and sportsmen would often tour the country giving talks in the local halls about their exploits. The talk on this occasion was being given by three explorers who'd been members of Shackleton's expedition to the South Pole in the early nineteen-twenties. As they'd obviously travelled quite a bit further in their explorations than I had on my 'round the world adventures' as a four year old in the unexplored wilderness around Barrow, this talk by my fellow explorers was something I definitely didn't want to miss.

The hall was packed to the doors with everyone, like myself, being absolutely enthralled as the three rugged-looking explorers on the platform recounted their firsthand accounts of their incredibly desperate struggles through the wastelands of the Antarctic.

Looking back on this talk now it seems, even to me, like something out of the Victorian Era not 1949. And it's quite a thought that my childhood explorations around Barrow took place only a few years after these men were battling to reach the South Pole.

One odd little bit of kit which the army issued to all its troops, was something they called a 'housewife', which was quite an appropriate name. It was a small cloth wallet containing sewing needles and thread, spare buttons, scissors, pins, etc., so that you could do your own minor running repairs in an emergency. I doubt if many of my squad mates ever even opened it, let alone used it. Even I had only used it a couple of times to sew on the odd button.

But now, with plenty of quiet, free evenings ahead of us, I decided that this was the time to make use of it and finally tackle the one emergency repair that had been getting up my nose since my first day in the army – my supposedly 'best' tunic. Not exactly a minor repair, just a sink or swim necessity. I simply took the tunic apart and pinned

164

all the bits together until it was a much better fit. Then I trimmed off all the surplus material and stitched it all back together again by hand.

To my satisfaction, and even greater relief, once it was finally finished and pressed it looked every bit as smart as those of my mates. At last I could now appear on parade, and in public, without looking like a second-hand potato sack with polished boots.

One evening when I'd been working at my tailoring, I'd heard the sound of singing coming from the next hut to ours; someone obviously had a radio on. So I went out to investigate and found it was coming from an open window, and sat down on the grass to listen. I recognised the singer instantly, it was the Irish tenor John McCormack singing, 'The Rose of Tralee'. He sang it beautifully, and I just sat there entranced, because this was one of my favourite Irish ballads, and one of the many that I hoped to sing myself in the future. At the time, however, it simply lifted me for a while out of my army surroundings, into the career I was hoping to follow once my soldiering was done.

I took another small step in this direction sometime later, when I somehow learned that the Carl Rosa Opera Company were appearing for a week in the town of Shrewsbury, some sixteen miles from Ellesmere. 'Carl Rosa' was a famous 'touring' opera company of the time who'd been performing most of the major operas all over Britain for a great many years. As Saturday was the only day of the week that I was free to make the trip I set off on the local bus to see my first ever live opera. Which as it turned out was Gounod's *Faust*.

Because I'd never been to Shrewsbury before, I decided to get there about midday, so that I'd have all afternoon to explore the old town. To my delight I found it to be a fascinating, rambling little town, steeped in history with ancient half-timbered buildings and narrow streets everywhere. One of the things that particularly caught my imagination, was the fact that some of these ancient buildings still carried the scars of old wars, with musket ball holes visible in the walls from battles fought long ago in its streets.

By the time I came to make my way to the theatre, I was pretty weary from my wanderings and ready for a sit down in the comfort of what turned out to be a plush 'cinema' seat. This was because the theatre for the opera performance was now a cinema, having been converted – like many of the old theatres of the time – into a cinema by simply adding a screen to the front of the stage. The positive side of this being that with all of the original scenery flies, lighting booms and dressing rooms still there behind the screen, it could easily be converted back to a theatre, by removing the screen, whenever they wanted to put on live theatrical performances again.

165

Once settled in I sat experiencing, for the first time, the magical world of an opera performance unfolding. The orchestral musicians filing into their seats, the noisy shuffling of music stands, as they sorted out their music, followed by the cacophony of clashing sounds as they all began tuning up their various instruments. Finally, as if at a signal, it all went quiet, and the conductor strode purposefully in through the door under the stage. He mounted the rostrum, bowed quickly to the audience, tapped his baton on the stand to bring the whole assembly under his control, then with a wave of his hand the opening chords of the opera floated across the auditorium, and we were off into another world.

I particularly remember the opening scene as the curtain rose to reveal Faust as a disillusioned old man cursing his wasted life of futile study, and wishing be could be young again. Suddenly Mephistopheles (the Devil) appears and offers to restore Faust's youth, on condition that he agrees in return to sign over his soul to him. At first Faust is afraid and reluctant, but when Mephistopheles conjures up a vision of the beautiful maiden Marguerite to tempt him, Faust agrees and so seals his own eventual fate.

The reason that this scene had such an appeal for me was that the role of Faust is sung by a tenor. So all the way through I could envisage myself singing the part. Especially when it came to Faust's big love aria, 'Salut Demeure Chaste et Pure'. Which I knew well from Beniamino Gigli's rendering on one of the first records I ever bought from Pass's music shop.

The only slight disappointment came when Marguerite made her first entrance. Unfortunately, 'this' young maiden weighed in at around twelve stone, and looked decidedly matronly, which detracted somewhat from the illusion Mephistopheles had conjured up. However, she sang beautifully, so I was happy to settle for that.

All in all it was a memorable evening, and an early milestone on my road to becoming an opera singer.

My journey back to camp was also pretty memorable, though for a different reason. When I stumbled out of the theatre in a slightly euphoric daze at around 10.30 it was to find that the last bus going my way had already gone some half an hour earlier. My only means of getting back to camp therefore was to walk, which I did – all sixteen miles of it down the dark, empty lanes of Shropshire. In its own way it was quite enjoyable since I was in no hurry; there being no curfew on the camp gate. So strolling along through the sleeping little hamlets on the way, gave me a closer insight into the Shropshire country way of life than I'd have got from the bus, even though all of its occupants were snoring away in their beds.

One little incident on the way stands out in my memory for a very special reason. As I was tramping through one small hamlet, I came across an old water pump on the green. I stopped to take a look at this cast iron reminder of days gone by, and as it was still working, slaked my thirst under its old spout. The special reason I have for remembering this being that this rusty old pump appeared later, as a somewhat irascible character, in my children's fantasy novel, *I'll See You in Somewhere*.

Shortly after my trip to Shrewsbury we were given the welcome news that the camp would soon be closing for the best part of a week, as we were all due for our first leave since joining the army. This meant that we'd all have to get on with making our own travel arrangements for going home.

Service men were entitled to a couple of railway travel warrants each year, so travelling wouldn't cost us anything. One of the lads in our hut, however, who I only remember as Jock, told me that he was going to save his warrants for other occasions and try hitch-hiking. As the same thought had occurred to me, and as we'd both be heading in the same direction, north, for the first seventy miles or so, we decided to set off together.

Jock was a tall, rather gangling, ginger-headed Glaswegian as hard as nails, who I'd always got on particularly well with. He had a rugged sort of face, with a slight cast in one eye which made even his most friendly smile look fearsome enough to make people step back a couple of paces. This was just as well, because although he was really a friendly sort of chap, he was a born fighter, and woe betide anyone who tried to pick on him – or any of his mates for that matter.

On one occasion I remember, there was a big Canadian chap on the camp who'd apparently given a couple of our lads a bit of a hard time, and boasted openly that he was the toughest man on the camp. When Jock got to hear about this, he stalked off to find his hut, walked in to find it full of men and called out the Canadian chap's name. When he stood up, Jock just pointed his finger at him.

"Right! Outside you. . !" he ordered.

The Canadian just stared at him in bewilderment.

"What's the matter with you?" he demanded.

"You picked on some of my mates," declared Jock, "that's what. So come outside and let's see if you're as tough as you think."

Apparently, after taking a good look at Jock's fearsome face, the Canadian backed down and declined his offer. . . I don't blame him?

Jock and I set off with our backpacks on, thumbing our way along the country road outside the camp. In those days, hitch-hiking, especially if you were in uniform, was a pretty good way of getting about, and it didn't take long before a car stopped, asked where we were heading, and offered to take us at least part of the way. Since we needed to negotiate quite a network of these secondary roads for the first twenty miles or so, this relatively short lift was repeated several times before we finally ended up standing on the verge of the major highway heading north. We soon flagged down a lorry driver who, by a stroke of luck, was on his way to Scotland. This suited both of us, because it meant I could be dropped off on the way at the junction of the A590 road to Barrow, while Jock would end up right in the middle of Glasgow.

After being dropped off, I picked up a lift almost immediately for the twenty-odd miles to the small town of Dalton. And as this was only four miles from Barrow, I decided that was near enough, and finished the journey on the local bus. I felt pretty chuffed at this first effort of hitch-hiking, because I'd not only got all the way home from Ellesmere for the price of a small bus fare, but I'd done it in virtually the same time it would have taken on the train.

The first couple of days back in my old home town were pretty euphoric. I'd never been so far away from it before, or for so long, not even when I was evacuated, so coming back to my family and friends was like a real homecoming.

During this time I visited many of the old haunts I'd often thought about while I was away, and caught up with a few friends. Unfortunately, though, as the week went by my initial excitement began to fade. I found that in the relatively short period I'd been away, things had obviously moved on somewhat. Most of my mates, especially Walter Caine, now all seemed to have regular girlfriends with whom they spent all their spare time. And with Willie still away doing his National Service, and Jim working all day, I found myself roaming about on my own most of the time.

This wouldn't normally have bothered me too much, but having spent the last eight months or so living in crowded army camps, I felt strangely isolated. I found myself growing more and more impatient to go back and get my army service over and finished with, so that I could move on with my other plans as soon as possible.

One evening, in the hope of trying to liven things up, I even went to the weekly dance at the Rink Dance Hall. But although the atmosphere was just as noisy and cheerful as ever, all the other people seemed to be in pairs, or groups. So I ended up feeling even more isolated than ever, and after an hour or so took my leave and went for a walk around the town, to work out my plans for getting back to Ellesmere.

Once back at camp, life continued as before with most of us soon beginning to feel like genuine mechanics. The amount of knowledge and practical hands-on experience we were getting in this classroom-come-workshop environment was pretty astonishing. We were all now able to do most of the routine jobs of repairing and maintaining engines, gearboxes, transmission and braking systems like real professionals; bandying about such terms as compression ratios, cylinder firing orders, etc., almost like the ten times table. Even today I can still remember the firing order of a ford V8 engine almost as well as my own name.

At around this time a team of medics descended on the camp looking for blood donors. This was something I'd never come across before, but as it seemed a good idea, especially as you got a free cup of tea and a biscuit afterwards, I decided like several of the other lads, to give it a go. This turned out to be only the first of quite a few such cups of tea with biscuits I was to enjoy in the future.

Oddly enough, one of my last memories of Ellesmere is also medical, but without the tea and biscuits. It happened just as Christmas was approaching, and everyone was preparing to go home on leave for the festive season. I'd somehow managed to catch flu – something very unusual for me. However, as the camp medical officer decided that I needed to be kept in bed, there was no chance of me going home like everyone else. The problem with this being that our camp was closing down for Christmas, with no medical staff available. I'd therefore have to be sent off to stay over Christmas in the medical centre of an artillery camp in Oswestry some ten miles away.

Although not being able to get home for Christmas was a big disappointment, in the event it turned out pretty well. Because the artillery medical centre was all cheerfully decked out for the festivities, nice and warm against the cold winter weather outside, and the Christmas fare was great. Added to this was the fact that although I was feeling pretty grotty, I wasn't exactly at death's door, so probably had almost as good a Christmas as any of the other lads at Ellesmere.

SOME MAJOR EVENTS OF THE YEAR:

(1) The film *The Third Man*, screened.
(2) Orwell's Book *Nineteen Eighty-Four*, published.
(3) Russian blockade of Berlin lifted.
(4) Communist Republic of China established under Mao Tse-tung.

Shortly after Christmas our course came to an end, and we were all due for our next move to various, so far unknown, REME workshops.

h

We'd all passed out as Vehicle Mechanics Class 3 – which was as high as we'd be able to go in our short eighteen months of National Service. To reach Class 1 you'd have to be in the army for at least three years.

Proving Our Worth

When our postings finally came through I found myself on my way, with about twenty of the other newly qualified mechanics, to a REME camp near a place called Foston in Derbyshire. This turned out to be a fairly small maintenance and supply unit based on what had once been a wartime airfield, but was now just a huge park for hundreds of surplus army vehicles. These ranged from staff cars to Bren gun carriers, tanks and every type of lorry imaginable.

Although this was probably just a convenient dump for the huge mass of army vehicles no longer required once the war was over, it did also provide a reservoir to draw on whenever vehicles were needed by army units anywhere in Britain. This, it turned out, was where we came in. Whenever a request came in for a particular type of vehicle, it would be our job to search around the airfield for one that was suitable, check it over, do any servicing or repairs required and get it cleared for collection.

Being fresh from our training course, this gave us a great opportunity to put our newly acquired skills to the test. I particularly enjoyed the challenge, especially as being a fairly small 'working' unit, there was a free and easy atmosphere about the place. There was little in the way of army 'bull'. You were left to make your own decisions and get on with things; and since there seemed to be a steady flow of vehicle requests coming in, we soon found ourselves working on, and driving around in, army vehicles of every size and type.

This driving around was great, but also the cause of much debate among us, since it often involved driving lorries etc., along the main road from the airfield entrance to our camp entrance some two hundred yards down the main road. The problem with this being that 'none' of us had driving licences, so were obviously breaking the law. We brought this up time and time again with the officer in charge, but he simply brushed it to one side. Declaring that being mechanics, not drivers, we were 'not' required to be able to drive. Quite how we were supposed to move the vehicles about without driving them he never explained.

Fortunately, however, our staff sergeant could see our point, and not being the type to 'fob off' things simply because they required a bit of effort on his part, decided to give us all some driving instruction off his own bat, but although these turned out to be pretty worthwhile, they didn't get us licences, which – with future civvy street in mind – is what we were really after.

This same officer who'd refused us a chance to get driving licences, was also the one who'd have us sweeping out the huge aircraft hangars using ordinary household brooms, whether they needed it or not, on any day that we were a bit short of other work. As these hangars were about half the size of a football field it was a bit like trying to empty Windermere Lake with a bucket.

However, he probably saw it as reinforcing in us the army discipline of obeying orders, daft or otherwise, without question. So for our part we simply got on with meticulously sweeping non-existent dirt over acres of old concrete, whilst not exactly breaking out in a sweat in the process.

Although life at Foston Airfield Camp was 'usually' more demanding and satisfying than this, we began to gather from various hints here and there, that Foston camp, like all our others, was not likely to be 'our' camp for very long, the most exciting of these rumours 'to us', being that getting shipped abroad was looming as a distinct possibility.

As usual, though, we could never get any direct information on this, so just had to carry on sorting out our fascinating dump of war weary army machines, and wait and see.

There was one other little ongoing diversion I remember at Foston, which also kept us guessing – though in a somewhat different way. This concerned the activities of a large bull in the field right next to our group of huts. He had quite a sizeable herd of cows in his harem, and obviously took his job very seriously. This left him, for most of the time, looking completely clapped out and fed up with his lot. However, he was a real trier, and every time one of his harem came nuzzling up to him with a tempting look in her eye, he'd shake himself wearily out of his lethargy and struggle to make her happy. Somehow he always seemed to manage it – though often only after two or three false starts – sending her off satisfied, but leaving him looking more clapped out than ever. His problem was that every time this latest 'conquest' got back to the herd she'd obviously regale them all with her exciting experience. It would then be only a matter of minutes before they'd decided whose turn it was next, and the poor old bull would find himself being nuzzled by another amorous temptress.

This would leave him looking even more depressed, but being too clapped out to run away, he eventually had to stagger through the same exhausting routine again.

171

Our guessing in this case was simply, "How long could the poor old chap keep this up?" We never found this out either, because he was still staggering on manfully with his task on the day we packed up and left. Though we didn't give him much hope of a long life.

Finally, one day when we were all busy out on the airfield, we were called back to the office to be given the news that we'd long been expecting. We were being moved on again, and not only that, we were to be shipped abroad to Trieste in Northern Italy.

Since this would be the first time any of us had ever left the shores of Britain, the prospect of spending the rest of our army service in a foreign country was a real bonus. And for me it also had an extra special appeal, because the idea of ending up in Italy, the land of opera, during my National Service, was something totally unexpected.

19

Off to the Land of Opera

We left Foston Airfield Camp for the station on lorries, and then on to Harwich by train. Harwich was the North Sea port on the East Coast for the ferry crossing to the Hook of Holland.

At the ferry port we ended up in a huge departure shed seething with several hundred other troops; all on their way to various destinations in what was then newly-freed occupied Europe. Food was available for everyone on trestle tables, while officers and NCOs were bustling around with clipboards trying to get everything organised for this mass-embarkation.

After we'd crossed the North Sea, on the first sea trip that most of us had ever done, we set foot on our first ever foreign soil in Holland.

The long journey across Europe was slow and meandering, but absolutely fascinating. I found myself rattling along through a totally new world, with different houses, railway stations without platforms where people had to climb up steps onto trains from track level, and weird looking locomotives clattering past on other lines, often pulling ancient passenger carriages, some of which looked more like converted cattle trucks.

On this journey I discovered where the term, 'sidelined', came from, because we were constantly being diverted off the main lines to trundle along through the countryside along minor routes. I suspect that this was probably because much of the damage and disruption caused by Allied bombing during the war had not yet been fully restored.

Along one of these country lines we pulled up in the middle of nowhere, to find that a large army style kitchen had been set up in a field alongside the track. We all climbed stiffly, and hungrily, down onto the track and through a gate in the fence to be fed, leaving the train sitting there on the track, huffing and puffing asthmatically as if trying to get its breath back.

The field kitchen was staffed by drably dressed women with tired, resigned expressions – all of which was explained when we heard them speaking in German. Without realising it, we'd somehow crossed the border into the land which had been our sworn enemy for over six years, and whose land we were now occupying. Despite this, and what their country had done to ours, especially Barrow, I found myself feeling sorry for them. They looked just like normal, ordinary, hard working, family women; exactly like those we'd left back home in Britain. They were so obviously 'not' the instigators of all the death and destruction the war had caused, but victims of it just as we were. I felt as if I'd learned something very important at that moment.

Back on the train we trundled our way across Germany and into Austria, finally arriving late in the day at a freezing, snowbound place high in the mountains called Villach. Here we all piled off the train to spend a bitterly cold night in old nissen huts, as draughty as worn out colanders. The only place with any warmth was the NAAFI, though slipping and sliding your way there across the ice-covered ground was pretty hazardous to say the least. I felt at the time that this was the coldest place I'd ever been to. Compared to the winters back home it felt like the North Pole.

After trying to keep warm through a freezing night buried under piles of blankets, we finally continued our journey down to the shores of the Adriatic Sea, and along the coast to the port of Trieste.

Our final destination there was a large barracks/come workshop complex, which had apparently once been the headquarters of the Italian Military Police. It was situated in the outer suburbs of the city, only a couple of miles or so from the borders of communist Yugoslavia, ruled by Marshal Tito. This, it turned out, was the main reason for us being there.

Trieste was, in fact, a sort of border-post bulwark against the communist threat from that particular direction. We soon learned that we were just a small part of the Allied Forces stationed there, which consisted of 6,000 British troops, 6,000 American troops, plus another 6,000 Venezia Giulia Police force of Italians, which had been trained by the British Army and was under the command of British officers.

Because of this, Trieste was classed as a 'semi-active post', and entitled us to a slight (very slight) increase in pay.

Living in barracks was a real treat for us after roughing it in army

174

huts for the past year. The barrack block was built on three upper floors, each floor containing many small, four-man rooms set either side of long corridors. There were toilets on each floor, but the main wash room ablutions were away down in the basement, which meant a noisy parade of army boots up and down several flights of stairs every morning and evening.

The mess hall was in a separate building on the opposite side of a central square parade ground, beyond which were the workshop buildings. The whole complex was surrounded by a ten foot high wall with two gates. One being the main gate with a guardhouse manned twenty-four hours a day; the other being a locked gate which led into the workshop area.

Because Trieste was a semi-active post, with the possibility (however unlikely) of incursions from across the communist border, or sabotage from disgruntled Italians (who after all, had been our enemies until fairly recently), when on guard duty we'd be issued with a clip of five rounds of ammunition. However, we were strictly required to keep these bullets in our pockets unless intruders broke into the complex and our lives were in danger; a clear and obvious precaution it seemed. Unfortunately, we were also given the not so clear and obvious order that we must 'never' shoot at a woman under 'any' circumstances.

Quite what we 'were' supposed to do if a ferocious armed female communist climbed over the wall intent on shooting us, and blowing up the workshops, was never explained. And since no amount of barrack room debate among ourselves on this made it any clearer, all we could do was hope that the situation never arose.

Like everybody else I found myself doing these guard duties from time to time, carrying the almost iconic clip of five rounds – which had actually become quite polished by nestling against the inside of so many army pockets.

Fortunately on my night-time stints I never encountered any ferocious communist assassins, female or otherwise. However, there were two nights parading around on my own that I particularly remember. On the first of these I was doing the rounds on my own in the workshop area, when I heard a lot of suspicious scuffling in the region of the workshop gate. I quickly hid myself in the shadows nearby, rifle at the ready to beat off these obvious would-be intruders at all costs (well, sort of). After a couple of minutes listening to all the grunting and gasping, to say nothing of the breathless wheezing, coughing and swearing a head appeared over the top of the gate followed by a rather limp unsteady body, which flopped down inside and promptly fell over.

175

Since I'd already resisted the temptation to load the five round clip into my rifle, having suspected that I was not likely to be faced with any communist, or Italian desperado – unless they'd learned to curse and swear in drunken English – I didn't need to unload it. I just stood enjoying this rather intriguing scene for a couple of minutes before revealing myself to the wobbly shape that had managed to get to its feet and was staggering, more or less, in the direction of the barrack block.

"It's all right!" he spluttered vaguely on seeing me, I've been having a few in town and couldn't get back before the midnight curfew."

By this time I'd recognised him as the staff sergeant cook.

"Really," I replied in surprise. "Why, what time do you think it is?"

"One o-clockish," he shrugged.

"It's half past ten," I informed him.

"What. . !" he blurted, as he staggered off towards the barrack square. "Bloody hell. . !" followed by several other expletives of disgust at losing so much of his drinking time through not having his watch with him.

The other occasion on guard that sticks in my mind was one I wouldn't have wished on my worst enemy. On this night I was stationed in the workshop yard on top of a small, flat roofed building, which provided a good vantage point for viewing the whole workshop area. Unfortunately, on the previous afternoon the medical officer had given several of us a dose of medicine for a slight stomach upset that was doing the rounds. The problem was that he hadn't mentioned the fact that his dose of jollop was likely to have laxative effects. This I discovered for myself rather suddenly, whilst marooned up on that flat roof, alone in the dark, and with over an hour to go before my relief – in more ways that one – was due. The one ray of hope in this pretty desperate situation was the fact that the flat-roofed building I was standing on happened to be a toilet. So it was suddenly, 'to hell' with intruders, communist or otherwise, and down the ladder in a flash. Fortunately I made it in the nick of time, but from that moment on, guarding the workshop complex took second place to constantly dashing up and down that ladder. If only Marshal Tito had got wind of this sudden gap in our security system that night, who knows what might have happened.

Being in the REME our job, of course, was maintaining and repairing all the vehicles being used by the British forces stationed in Trieste, and we were soon settled into the workshops doing just that. Fortunately, we were not alone in this but had quite a number of Italian civilian mechanics working along side us, who we got on well with. The language barrier was a bit of a problem at first, of course, since they spoke very little English, and none of us understood a word of Italian.

However, I gradually picked up a few words of Italian, and with the help of a lot of sign language, was soon communicating reasonably well with those I was working with. At first I thought this would be a great opportunity to pick up the language properly; which after all was the main language of opera. But to my surprise my Italian workmates warned me not to, because apparently the Italian spoken in Trieste was such a distinctive dialect, that it would not be understood too well in other parts of Italy.

Because of the wide variety of vehicles we had coming in for repair or service I found life in the workshops pretty challenging, but interesting. At the time I'd arrived on the scene, the section I was put in were working on repairing a couple of Daimler armoured scout cars, which though fairly small were pretty heavy, weighing in at several tons. Our section was in the charge of a staff sergeant who was quite a character, and someone I found easy to get on with. Whenever there was any road testing to be done through the hills around Trieste he'd invariably take me along with him, and these trips were hairy experiences, to say the least. With the Daimler being such a solid, enclosed, virtually indestructible machine – like a tank on wheels – he tended to drive it like a bat out of hell, with no fear of any other vehicle on the road. The problem was that the hilly roads around Trieste, were pretty winding and narrow, and although there wasn't much in the way of car traffic on them, they were popular routes for the large fuel tankers heading for the large oil refinery down near the docks.

Time after time we had narrow squeaks with screeching brakes, and swerving near misses as some massive tanker suddenly appeared out of nowhere. The one to cap them all, I remember though, happened when he took a bend at about fifty miles an hour to be met with a huge tanker chugging towards us no more than fifty yards away. As he completely filled the narrow road there was no hope of swerving around him, or braking in time. And as the rocky hillside dropped away steeply on one side of us, and rose up steeply on the other, the options for survival were pretty limited. Fortunately, the staff sergeant decided on going up the bank rather than hurtling off into space down the other. In a split second we'd hit the bank and found ourselves looking at the sky as we careered upwards through shrubs and bracken, bouncing off one large rock after another, and being thrown around inside like peas in a pan. Somehow, he'd managed to turn the steering

177

wheel in the process, and we found ourselves heading back down onto the road, having done a complete swerve around the tanker.

What the startled tanker driver thought of all this he never stopped to find out, but as we limped on down the road it was obvious that the poor old Daimler scout car was not feeling too well. We trundled rather lopsidedly all the way back to the workshops, with the four wheel drive keeping us on the move, and the staff sergeant working out what tale he could come up with to account for us bringing the scout car back in a somewhat worse state than when we took it out. He must have come up with something good, though, because after a few somewhat incredulous frowns here and there, all we had to do was get on with renewing the shattered front stub-axle.

At sometime in the early part of the year the calm, everyday life of Trieste was suddenly disrupted by great gales of wind that came lashing up along the Dalmatian Coast of Yugoslavia, battering the town and turning the peaceful streets into hazardous wind tunnels. Apparently, this was a natural phenomena that happened every year about this time, and the locals simply called it, the 'Bora', and shrugged it off. To me it seemed to go on unabated for about two 'long' weeks, making my wanderings about down the town, or anywhere else, a real pain. In fact, I was just about becoming convinced that I'd never feel calm air again, when it ended almost as suddenly as it had began. At first the silence and stillness that descended, felt so eerie that you could almost touch it. But this was immediately followed by a great sense of relief that life could at last get back to normal again.

In my time off duty I often wandered around the old city and port of Trieste on my own, enjoying the experience of being in a foreign land. Everything was different to anywhere I'd been before; the unfamiliar language all around, the wide main shopping street with rattling trains and cars all careering along the wrong side of the road. Winding shopping alleys, and side streets completely paved with stone slabs that looked as if they'd been laid down a century before and would last forever. Hard wearing to ancient cartwheels, but apparently lethal skating rinks to modern rubber tyres when it rained. Because of this, there always seemed to be gangs of men sitting splay legged on the road along these side streets, endlessly belting notches into the stone slabs with hammers and chisels in an effort to give them a bit more grip for modern tyres. This was a scene that to me looked almost as primitive as the stone slabs themselves.

Near the town centre there was also a large indoor market that I'd wander around occasionally. It was on two floors, the ground floor being mainly a food hall, but the more interesting one being the upper, where they seemed to sell everything under the sun, and where I sometimes bought the odd cheap bit and bob that caught my fancy.

My first effort at buying here, though, I found a bit off-putting because unlike the markets back home, the price of everything was decided by haggling. Nobody 'ever' accepted the price the stall holder quoted, even if it was marked up in large bold figures; they haggled. You apparently 'had' to haggle here; while it wasn't exactly compulsory, it was expected, and if you didn't everybody looked at you as being somewhat odd. At first I felt a bit awkward and embarrassed by this new way of shopping, but once I'd got the hang of it I found it quite an enjoyable sort of goodnatured game between you and the stallholder, with both sides coming out of it feeling satisfied with the deal they'd struck.

These were still times of shortage after the war, and as well as all the legitimate goods on offer in the market, I soon learned that there were other, 'slightly scarcer', items available under the counter, if you knew which stalls to go to. One of these dodgy items was American nylons, and once I'd rumbled which stalls were the dodgy ones, I decided to get some nylons as a present to send home to Mam. These were usually only handed over after surreptitious glances up and down the aisles to make sure you weren't being watched, followed by a lot of rummaging under the counter, and a quick exchange of money for nylons – which you were expected to stuff rapidly out of sight in your pockets.

These dastardly devious deeds in foreign parts always added a little touch of extra spice to my market visits, making me feel a bit like a somewhat cash-strapped James Bond.

One surprising discovery for me early on in Trieste was the fact that our barracks had a 'Lady of the Shadows'. I only learned of her existence from hearing some of the more 'Jack-the-Laddish' types among my mates boasting of their experiences on sampling her wares. I suppose this shouldn't have been so surprising, Trieste being, after all, very much a garrison town, but it was. Possibly this was because in all my many comings and goings I'd never seen any sign of a femme-fatal lingering about near the barracks. It turned out, however, that this was because you had to know where to find her. She apparently had her patch up among the bushes on the hillside opposite the gates, which served as a sort of open air boudoir for her offerings – which also meant no doubt that this lack of overheads, 'literally', helped to keep her prices down.

Apart from a certain curiosity about what she looked like – never having seen a 'working girl' before – I didn't think anything more about her. Until one day I was strolling into town with a mate of mine from Birmingham, when he pointed out a woman walking towards us.

"This is the one they talk about," he remarked.

"The one what?" I asked.

"The one on the hill," he hissed as she drew closer.

I just stared in utter disbelief, all my visions of the beautiful temptress on the hillside shattered. The small, very plain little woman passing by looked old enough to be my grandmother. And although this probably meant she brought years of experience to her chosen profession, this would hardly make up for the complete lack of all the other attributes required. It did, however, go some way to accounting for her low prices and, more importantly, why she always worked her trade in the dark.

Although I'd been a bit disappointed over the advice from my Italian workmates 'not' to pick up the Italian language in Trieste as a step towards my singing ambitions, there were other, more positive little encouragements to be had in this direction from finding myself in the land of opera. Occasionally, when walking back to the barracks late in the evening, I'd cut through some of the alleyways, passing several small cafés used by the locals. Quite often the sound of music and singing would come floating out into the alleys from their open doorways, and I'd stand outside for a while listening to the beautiful strumming of mandolins and Italian voices singing Italian melodies. This always gave me a great feeling of being urged along my way.

'That is what I'll be doing one day,' I'd stand there day-dreaming. 'That is what my voice was meant for,' and I'd carry on back to barracks in my own little world.

The other great encouragement I'd found in Trieste towards my singing ambitions was the fact that it had a large major opera house; where at that time they were preparing to embark on their operatic season. I'd found my way to the opera house quite soon after arriving in Trieste, and wandering around outside its imposing front entrance, studying the posters of forthcoming performances, had become a fairly regular routine. At first I'd been a bit surprised to find just how many of the operas being advertised were ones I'd never heard of. The same applied to the singers, 'none' of whose names rang a bell at all. It was only then that it dawned on me just how wide a range of operas, operatic composers and opera 'singers' Italy had produced.

However, there was one opera I recognised on the posters which stood out like a beacon. This was Puccini's *La Boheme*, one of my great favourites from our evenings playing records on the old wind-up gramophone in Jim's dark, rubble-strewn cellar. I'd therefore earmarked this, along with a couple of the others whose names were vaguely familiar, to be my first operatic experiences in the land of opera – as and when the dates for their performances arrived.

One extra little boost I always got from these visits to the opera house, was that they gave me another chance for a look at a special plaque set in the front wall near the entrance. This plaque had on it the cast of the face of a famous singer. It was, in fact, the death mask of my great tenor hero Enrico Caruso, who'd apparently sung there many times.

Music seemed to figure quite a lot in the everyday life of Trieste, and there was one sort of 'café/come social club' in the main street which I'd drop into every so often. It was usually pretty crowded – mainly with servicemen, both British and American. But the attraction for me was simply that they always had live music being played there in the shape of a quartet. This consisted of a leader who played the violin, a pianist, a drummer, and 'I believe' a guitarist. Their repertoire consisted mainly of well known Italian melodies, which for me were a real treat. On my first visit I went up to the leader during one of their short breaks and asked him if they'd play one of my favourite Italian ballads, 'Catari'. He agreed readily, seeming only too pleased, and a bit surprised, to get such a request from a young English soldier. They played it beautifully, giving me a little nod for approval as they finished, I waved and gave a thumbs up of appreciation. What pleased me particularly about this little incident, was that whenever I dropped in there after that, if the leader spotted me he'd give a little smile and a nod, and the next thing they'd play would be 'Catari'.

Another odd little musical event I remember, came about through my getting wind of a small concert that was being held at an address somewhere in Trieste. Having found out from my Italian workmates whereabouts this was, I made my way there to find myself facing a large block of stone built apartments. Which all seemed rather strange, especially as the number I'd got seemed to indicate that the concert must be taking place in some apartment up on the second floor. However, having come this far I decided to investigate the mystery, and made my way up the stone stairway to find an open door with quite few people inside chatting happily. I caught the eye of one of them who came to the door, where I asked as best as I could, if this was where the concert was. This was met with a puzzled nod which seemed to say.

"Well, yes. . . but. . ?"

However, this quickly turned into a smile and she welcomed me in to what was obviously someone's home and where I found about

181

fifteen people sitting on chairs around a small platform about a foot high with a piano on one side. Everybody was very friendly and although I understood very little Italian, I gathered that this was the right place, and that the concert was being given by two young members of the Trieste Opera Company.

When the two young singers, a soprano and a tenor, made their entrance with the pianist, who was also from the opera company, they turned out to be little older than I was, and just starting out on their careers. This concert, I gathered from the introductions, was all part and parcel of their learning experience. I found this an astonishing piece of luck, because hearing these two other budding singers doing what I myself hoped to be doing one day, was also a learning experience for me.

Both singers sang really well, and although they had good voices they were not exceptional enough to make me feel at all overawed about my own potential. And after enjoying a lovely evening among friendly strangers, my feelings when I left there that evening were twofold: on the one hand my confidence had been given a boost: "Well, if 'they' can become singers in a major opera house, then I 'certainly' can." The other was a slightly guilty feeling that I'd somehow gate-crashed a private concert – I still don't know to this day whether I did or not.

As well as rambling around Trieste in my spare time, our normal army activities continued at full pace. We did a full eight hour shift in the workshop each day, as well as our regular stints on guard duty. The more typical military activities, like target practice out on the rifle range and physical training runs around the hilly roads to keep us fit, also kept us pretty busy.

Of these, the most welcome to me was always the rifle practice. This was partly because I always enjoyed these fairly rare opportunities to put my rifle to its proper use by blasting off 303 three rounds at distant targets, but also because the rifle range was away out on the hilly scrubland within a few hundred yards of the Yugoslavian border. Although no explanation was ever given to us for this siting of the range within earshot (or should it be 'gunshot') of the border, it was obviously deliberate, and probably designed to keep our communist neighbours reminded that we were there.

For me, being away up on the rocky scrubland was always a welcome change from the workshop and the bustling city, particularly as it reminded me of the Westmorland Fells above the farm in Orton where I'd been evacuated. However, although it was similar in some ways, it was also pretty different. The most noticeable of these

182

differences being the grasshoppers; they were the most enormous ones I'd ever seen, being at least three times the size of any I'd come across in England. They were also so lethargic you could catch them and hold them in your hand quite easily. Other tiny, unusual scraps of wildlife seemed to be darting about in the scrubby grass, plus tiny lizards scrambling about the rocks everywhere. So all in all, our rifle practice trips were pretty special days out.

At sometime in early May I got word from Jim and Willie telling me that Willie had finished his National Service and was now back home. Because of this, and the fact that neither of them wanted to hang about in Barrow for too long, they said they were thinking of setting off for London straight away, as a sort of advance guard.

I wrote back saying I thought this was a great idea, as they'd then be able to discover at first hand just what the job situation, accommodation, etc., was like in London; things which so far we didn't really have a clue about.

As the warm summer weather was now beginning to make itself felt in Trieste, our heavy, khaki clothes were put away and we were issued with lightweight summer uniforms. These were not only more comfortable, but a lot better fit, so for the first time since joining the army I actually felt smartly dressed.

The warm weather also meant that in our spare time we were now able to get out onto the popular beaches, and cliff-lined sandy coves along the Adriatic coast. And since the only sea swimming I'd done in the past had a been a quick dash 'into', and an even quicker dash 'out of' the cold Irish Sea – which would freeze you to the marrow, no matter how sunny the day might be – the Adriatic Sea felt like a warm, relaxing bathtub. When swimming off the beaches I always felt as if I could float and swim around in it for hours. In fact, on one occasion I found myself swimming so far out from the beach that, when I went to turn back, I had a few moments of panic trying to work out which way the shore was.

In the coves around the cliffs, however, this problem didn't arise, but the water close under the cliffs was really deep, so all our time there was spent diving off the lower ledges into its depths, which got cooler and darker the deeper down you sank.

On one of these sunny weekend days, I decided I'd like to take a trip to Venice, which was only about thirty miles away, around the coast to the north. My mate Brian from Birmingham decided he'd like to come along too so we set off by bus for this legendary city.

After an enjoyable ride around the picturesque coast on the very north eastern tip of Italy, we arrived on the quayside of the wide lagoon that separates Venice from the mainland. A short ferry trip across the water and we found ourselves standing on the main waterfront in this unique island city, only a short walk from San Marco Square with its towering Campanile, and great ornamental cathedral with the famous chiming clock. We set off wandering around this legendary place, criss-crossing its endless bridges, exploring its alleyways and little secluded squares, staring darkly for a while at the infamous Bridge of Sighs, over which convicted prisoners passed from the court in the Doge's Palace to the notorious Nuove Prison, to suffer their often grisly fate.

For the first hour or so, the endless crossing of bridges, and the complete lack of roads and traffic took a bit of getting used to, but by the time we'd reached the large Rialto Bridge on the Grand Canal the unique atmosphere of the place was beginning to descend over me like a warm, welcoming cloak, and I felt as if I could go wandering on there for hours.

Unfortunately, we were also starving hungry, but by luck there happened to be a café nearby, with tables set out on the edge of the Grand Canal; so we sat there by the Rialto Bridge to fill ourselves up with the first 'genuine' Italian Spaghetti Bolognese I'd ever tasted. The magic of Venice was now complete. I could have sat there all day simply watching the gondolas glide past. However, there was a lot we hadn't seen yet so we plunged back into the labyrinth of alleyways and bridges, roughly retracing our steps.

At some point we came across a small glass works turning out the famous Venetian Glassware, and had a quick, 'very quick', look around their gift shop. I say quick, because the prices of the samples on offer, though beautiful, set our feet rapidly heading back out into the real world again.

Eventually, we found ourselves back in San Marco Square to discover that they'd filled half the square with seats, and erected a platform for a concert that was to take place that evening – much too late for us to even contemplate. We also noticed, however, that the door of the Campanile Tower was now open for visitors who wished to climb to the top, and because we still had about an hour left before catching our ferry back across the lagoon, we decided to have a go. I can't remember if there was any charge, but if there was it can't have been very much as our, by now, slightly parlous finances would have ruled it out. So, being young and fit, we strode inside to discover that the spiral stone stairway we'd expected was, in fact, a spiral stone 'ramp'. This wound its way round and round right to the top, and proved a lot tougher on the legs than simply clumping up steps – which

184

probably accounted for the fact that we two seemed to be the only ones attempting it. However, we stumbled out at the top eventually, to find that the wonderful view out over the city and the wide lagoon with its many other beautiful islands was worth all the effort.

We lingered up in the tower for as long as we could, but finally had to make a bit of a rapid decent down the stone ramp, followed by a dash around to the quayside, just in time to catch our ferry back to the mainland, and our bus back to Trieste.

Shortly after this Venetian outing, the date for the first of my selected operas, *La Boheme* finally arrived, and after lining up among all the eager Italian opera fans I managed to get a seat up in what we'd have called 'The Gods' back home. I was pretty familiar with the music and plot of *La Boheme* from our record recitals in Jim's old cellar, but having never seen it staged I was bursting with anticipation. I'd never heard of any of the singers, however, so could only hope for the best. I was not disappointed, as both the singing and stage settings were wonderful, creating the colourful but poverty stricken world in which the leading characters struggled to find love and happiness; only to have it all taken away by tragedy in the end. As I left after this wonderful, but sad experience I felt as if my 'withers had been well and truly wrung'. Nevertheless, I was also longing for the day when I too might have the chance of singing the part of Rodolfo, even though he does lose his beautiful Mimi so sadly.

All of the singers sang their parts wonderfully, but strangely (or perhaps 'not' so strangely in the circumstances) the only singer's name I remember now is that of the tenor, his name was Gianni Poggi, and I've never ever heard of him since.

The only other operatic evening I managed to get into in Trieste was when they were doing two of Puccini's one-act operas, *Il Tabaro* and *Gianni Schicchi*, neither of which I knew much about, although the aria, 'O mio babbino caro', in *Gianni Schicchi* was a well known soprano party piece. *Il Tabaro*; a dark and gloomy drama set on a canal barge, though very well performed was not my cup of tea – possibly because there was no memorable singing in it for the tenor.

There was one other name on my operatic list, which I'd intended to see but never did, this was called *La Wally*. Why I'd chosen this one I've no idea as I'd never heard of it before. The reason I never saw it was due to a problem which we'd run into ever since arriving in Trieste – the Italian currency. Probably because of the war, the Italian lira didn't seem to us to be worth very much at that time. In fact, the one thousand lira note was worth less than an English ten shilling note. Which meant there were over a hundred lira in a single English shilling. This wouldn't have been too bad in itself, but for the fact that it was nearly all in paper money, and they didn't seem to issue many coins. Which meant that you'd end up with a pocketful of small value lira notes, which quite literally weren't worth the paper they were printed on. In fact, we'd often find ourselves throwing some of the smallest value notes away as being about as valuable as used bus tickets.

What was even worse, however, was the fact that whatever value the note, if it was damaged or stained in any way it was immediately regarded as worthless by the Italian treasury and your loss. And since 'they' wouldn't redeem its value, neither would the shopkeepers. Therefore, if you happened to get lumbered with a damaged note, it was not spendable and just tough luck on you.

This is why I never got in to see *La Wally*. The girl in the ticket office spotted that one of my notes had a tiny tear in it, which I hadn't noticed myself. Naturally I wasn't too pleased about this and made my irritation felt about being conned in this way by the Italian treasury. Who, it seemed, could just print out as much paper money as they liked, knowing full well that they'd never have to redeem a single lira of it, just leave it all out in circulation until it got damaged, as it inevitably would.

There was an Italian policeman on duty in the foyer and he came over to see what the problem was. He was very friendly and sympathised with me, but shrugged and said unfortunately that was the way things were in Italy at that time, and there was nothing they could do about it. The crowning annoyance in this for me, however, was the fact that without this damaged note I didn't have quite enough money to buy my ticket, so had to give up on *La Wally* and head back to barracks.

By this time we were well into June, with the end of my National Service rapidly approaching.

Before this actually arrived, however, our Sergeant Major somehow discovered that in all my time in the army I'd never been on a 'charge' for any sort of misdemeanour. Being a bit of a hard-bitten, sceptical type, he'd adopted a philosophy that every man 'ought' to be have been up on a charge at least once during his army service, and if he hadn't this didn't mean he was innocent, but had simply managed to get away with it. So he made a personal point of ensuring that they didn't.

In my case he used the infamous Section 40 of the Army Act to put me on a charge. This Section 40 is a rule that can be used to cover all those cases which do not fit into any 'specific' misdemeanour. It simply states that, 'Any action contrary to good conduct and military discipline' can be regarded as an offence if those in authority wish it to be. Which, of course, gives them the power to put you on a charge for absolutely 'anything' at all. It's a sort of crafty, 'cover all' device they use when they want to punish someone but can't find a 'genuine' reason for doing so.

In my case the Sergeant Major used his daily inspection round of our rooms – which he carried out every afternoon while we were away in the Workshops – to make sure that 'I' didn't escape out of the army without getting clobbered by Section 40.

I only discovered that it was 'my' turn when, on the way in after work, someone pointed out to me that my name was up on the notice board in 'Daily Orders', as one of those on a charge next day.

I was completely baffled by this, as I hadn't the slightest clue what it was all about. After climbing up the stairs and entering our room, however, the truth was revealed. All my kit, which was normally arranged neatly on a shelf above the bed, like everyone else's, was scattered over the floor. This was the Sergeant Major's well known way of showing disapproval, though I was still pretty bewildered about it because I knew that my kit had been just as neat and clean as it always was.

Next morning I duly reported, along with a couple of other alleged villains, all properly dressed in our best uniforms, to the corridor outside the captain's office. A corporal waiting there took our names and told us to wait. Fortunately, I appeared to be first on the list, so when the sergeant major's voice bellowed out from inside, the corporal ordered me to take my cap off, then ushered me inside. The captain was sitting behind his desk, with the sergeant major standing stiffly to his right like a prosecuting council; with what looked to me like a self-satisfied smirk on his face.

"ATTEN... SHUN!" he snapped. "State you name and number."

"22105205. Craftsman Workman, Sir. . !" I shouted, just as loudly as he had.

"You know why you're here, of course," stated the captain.

"No Sir!" I replied.

"Well," declared the captain, "the sergeant major claims that on his inspection rounds yesterday afternoon, he found that your kit was in a filthy condition. What have you got to say about that?"

"It 'wasn't' in a filthy condition, Sir," I insisted. "It never is."

"I see!" replied the captain with a frown. "Well, that's a bit of a problem isn't it. It's your word against the sergeant major's. Have you got anything else to say in your defence?"

187

"No Sir," I replied. "There's no point."

"Why's that?" asked the captain.

"Because you're going to accept the sergeant major's word, Sir, whatever I say."

"I believe you're right," declared the captain, after a thoughtful pause. "You'll do three days of fatigues, starting tomorrow morning. Next man, Sergeant Major."

I was marched out smartly, past the others awaiting their fate, still contemplating what my next three days were going to be like.

As I'd never done 'punishment' fatigues before I didn't know what to expect, and in the event they turned out to be a lot more of a pain in the backside than I'd imagined, which, of course, is what they were intended to be. I found myself having to drag myself out of bed in the morning an hour before everybody else, then dress in full kit with webbing, back-pack, ammunition pouches etc, to attend an inspection on the parade ground with my fellow criminals. Once we'd passed the inspection by the sergeant in charge, we'd then be given marching drill in full kit for about half an hour or so, before being dismissed with five minutes to get back up to our rooms, change into our working clothes, and get to the canteen to grab what was left of breakfast. It was then back on parade in time to march off to the workshops and do a full day's work. As soon as my shift had ended, when everybody else was starting their main meal, I had to shoot back up to my room, get washed and changed into full kit again for more marching drill on the parade ground. This over, it was then a dash back to my room to change into my working clothes again, and get over to the cookhouse to grab a quick meal, before starting an evening of cookhouse fatigues, cleaning the place up ready for the next day. If you were lucky you might get to bed before midnight; with the same routine waiting for you every day. For me, at that time, Section 40 of the Army Act certainly had a lot to answer for.

In early July we all packed our kitbags, said our last goodbyes to Trieste and boarded the train heading back to the Hook of Holland. Our final destination being the major army base in the South of England, Aldershot – from where we were due to be demobbed and released back into Civvy Street – or 'almost'. Because although we'd be civilians again, having done our eighteen months as 'full time' soldiers, our conscription terms committed us to doing a further three years, as 'part time' soldiers in the Territorial Army.

20

The Future Beckons

On arriving in Aldershot and settling into our huts; which seemed a bit of a come down after six months in a comfortable barrack block, we were left pretty much to ourselves. There were no parades or duties of any sort; in fact, nobody seemed interested in us any more. Although the military life of Aldershot was bustling all around, for us it was like hanging about in a busy departure lounge, where they were simply waiting to get us off the premises.

After about a week we were finally given our departure documents plus railway warrants, and sent on our way back to civilian life. As I boarded the train with a wonderful feeling of at last being free again, I sat on my seat reflecting on the odd coincidence that the date was the 20th of July 1950, which as well as being my first day of freedom, was also my 21st birthday; most of which I was to spend travelling on the train from Aldershot to Barrow – I couldn't have wished for a better birthday present.

I arrived in Barrow late in the day, looking forward to seeing my family again after being away so long. Instead I was met at the station by a staff sergeant in a fifteen hundredweight Bedford. He'd apparently been detailed to take me straight over to an army camp on Walney Island, so that I could hand in all my kit – apart from my uniform, which I'd need for my TA service.

He seemed to think I'd be doing it in Barrow, so I quickly told him that I definitely wasn't, and that I'd be heading for London as soon as I could.

"That's OK," he shrugged. "Just contact the nearest TA unit when you get there, and sort it out with them." He then gave me a receipt for all my surplus kit, and drove me home to Ainslie Street and a happy reunion with my family. Or, at least, those who were still living in Barrow. My two eldest sisters Joan and Jean, who were often away anyway, were by this time living down in London. Joyce, Jill and Jacqueline were still living quite happily at the boarding house. Colin, my younger brother, was also still living there, but not exactly happily, and I got the feeling that he didn't get on too well with Mam, which didn't surprise me, or with his job on the railway which did, as I'd thought that he liked it there. He'd only started work there a short while before I'd left to go in the army, and I remember the interview he'd had at the station on leaving school at fifteen, as it was typically Colin.

The manager sitting behind the desk had asked, staring doubtfully at his rather smallish frame:

"Just what job are you looking for, lad?"

"Station Master," replied Colin confidently.

"Really. . !" blinked the manager in astonishment. "Well, I'm afraid that job's already filled."

"Oh!" replied Colin disappointedly.

"However," added the manager, "I could probably give you a job as an office messenger. Perhaps you could do that in the meantime."

"Right!" said Colin. And that was it.

Perhaps his disenchantment 'now' stemmed from the fact that after two whole years as an office messenger they still hadn't made him the Station Master. The fact remained, though, that he wasn't happy. So when I told Mam that I was off to London – something she must have been aware of but wasn't too pleased about – she immediately declared, pointing at Colin.

"Well, if 'you're' going, you can take 'him' with you."

I was a bit taken aback, but under the circumstances I thought, 'Why not'. So I asked him:

"Would you like to come?"

"Phew, I'll say!" he exclaimed. And that was it.

Colin and I eventually arrived in London by train and caught the underground to Archway, where Jim and Willie were living in a bit of a grotty bed-sit. They'd agreed to let us kip down with them for a while (unbeknown to the landlady) until we could get settled into a place of our own. Their flat was just near the bottom of Highgate Hill, where we discovered a plaque on the pavement marking the spot where Dick Whittington is believed to have stopped to look back when he was quitting London, and where he heard the voice saying "Turn Again Whittington". Which he did, and eventually became Lord Mayor of

190

London. Under our present circumstances, I couldn't help feeling that this was a good omen for us.

Bedding down in that one tiny room was not exactly luxury living, especially as we had to be careful how we came and went to avoid attracting the attention of the landlady. Fortunately, she had several bed-sits in the building, and since she obviously liked a drink, didn't seem too sure most of the time who belonged there and who didn't.

"We'd no intention of staying there any longer than necessary, however, so finding a place of our own was a priority. But since this took money, which we didn't have much of, getting jobs would be our first aim.

Jim and Willie, who by this time were well settled into London life, both worked at a large hotel, 'The Regent Palace', in central London just off Piccadilly Circus, and felt sure they could get us jobs there. In London, at that time, there seemed to be jobs available everywhere, especially in the catering trade. So Jim and Willie had a word with the hotel staff manager, and Colin and I went along for an interview.

As predicted, he was keen to take on staff, so signed us on immediately. Colin being younger and smaller, was given a job down in the kitchens, while I joined Willie and Jim on the backdoor goods delivery entrance. This involved unloading all the lorries and vans that rolled up constantly throughout the day with loads of potatoes, veg, meat, fish, bread, etc., which with all the smaller deliveries of special delicacies to suit the various tastes of the several hundred guests passing through there at any one time, seemed enough to feed an army.

This was a totally new world to me and an exciting introduction to the pace and bustle of central London. The wages weren't great, being only about £4 a week, but as we got all our food as well, three good meals a day, it suited our bed-sit situation perfectly. And because we could even go in for meals on our days off if we wished – which we always did – for those first few weeks we didn't have to worry about food at all.

We were soon wandering around London with Jim and Willie, getting to know all the famous landmarks: Marble Arch, Buckingham Palace, Hyde Park, Trafalgar Square, Theatre Land – which began in Shaftesbury Avenue just around the corner from the hotel, taking in all the theatres from Charing Cross Road, Leicester Square, The Haymarket, The Strand, Drury Lane, and culminating right over at the wonderful Covent Garden Opera House, with its large, noisy vegetable market bustling along right beside it.

After working at the Regent Palace for about three months, we all felt flush enough to start looking for a better place to live. By this time life in the grotty bed-sit had become pretty intolerable, and we couldn't get out quick enough.

SOME MAJOR EVENTS OF THE YEAR:

(1) The Korean War started.

(2) McCarthy's 'Un-American' persecutions began in the USA.

(3) The Labour Government was returned in a general election.

(4) India became an Independent Republic.

(5) The aircraft carrier 'Ark Royal' launched.

(6) Rover built the world's first gas-turbine car (experimental).

Alan in stripey jumper, with his older sister Joan
and the three Rowe children, outside the ferry house
window on Lake Windermere in 1939.

The ferry and ferry house on Lake Windermere in 1981.

The Watson's farm.

Orton Village, with the road from Shap
coming down the hill on the right.

The Community Hall where Alan sang solo
in public for the very first time.

Orton – the village below the fells.

The Methodist Chapel where Alan sang solo
in public for the second time.

Mrs Whitwell's corner cottage in Orton village.
(c. 2007)

Alan during his army days – on the cliffs
above the Adriatic Sea.

Alan as Prince John in the dressing room
at Dundee, waiting for his stage call during
his first professional performance.

Opera A Challenge

William T. Wilson again in a leading role. Like Mr Macdonald, he gave the impression of being really " inside " his part, and his singing throughout was particularly notable for the clarity of his diction.

As Alice Ganwell, Miss Mabel Petrie gave a beautifuly restrained performance. At times the orchestra proved rather overpowering for the softer quality of her lower register, but the charm of her lovely contralto voice can never be denied.

Two of the company's best singers were also well cast last night.

David Imrie is always a joy to listen to, and his portrayal of the jovial Friar Tuck proved entirely successful. As Little John, we also had the real pleasure of hearing George M. Ogilvie once again.

In Alan Workman the company have discovered a tenor of great promise. His voice is still a little inconsistent in quality, but the upper register promises a brilliant future for this young singer.

James M. Graham, as Richard Coeur de Lion, gave one of those completely satisfying performances which have made him one of the most dependable and enjoyable singers in the Dundee company. As the Abbot of Doubleflask, Alistair Gordon showed a real flair for comedy.

Although the tenor section seemed a little outnumbered at times, the men's chorus coped admirably with some very difficult music.

Particularly effective were the church-styled choruses for the men and the concerted effect of the angry "Drive Him Away." The hymn, " Heavenly Father, sing we praises ", is surely one of the finest things contained in the whole score, and was memorably sung last night.

In complex writing such as that of " Maid Marian " it is not always easy to keep the balance between singer and orchestra. At times the latter proved a little too powerful, but such moments were rare, and all the orchestral players must be warmly congratulated for the very workmanlike job they made of this really difficult music.

Alan's first professional performance; in which he played Prince John in *Maid Marian*.

A fabulous standard

A FAT frolicking Falstaff led a first rate cast through three hours of rollicking fun at The Adeline Genee Theatre last week in The Merry Wives Of Windsor.

Actors alternated the leading roles to avoid strained voices and to assure a week-long run for Nicolai's fine opera based on Shakespeare's play.

Wednesday's Sir John, an arrogant would-be suitor to two married women, was Patrick Ward, amply filling a well-rounded part.

Mrs Page, Jennifer Simpson, and Mrs Ford, Veronica Gilbert, led to an elaborate plot to humble him.

This whipped up Mr Ford, Tag Caisley, into an inferno of jealousy because he was not let into the plot for quite some time.

The sub-plot involved a more serious bid by the impoverished Fenton the family's least favoured of three potential partners, to marry young Miss Page, Fionnetta Ryan.

Fenton was played by Alan Workman, fortunate enough to possess the sort of voice that shone even in distinguished com-

His rivals for Miss Page's hand were two larger-than-life characters, the sly Dr Caius and the bumbling Slender. Two good performances from Dennis Shearman and Russell Phillips.

Another great singer and stirling peformer was Frederick Harrison as Mr Page.

This was a production where all the departments got it right. There were no weak links in the performance chain and a fabulous standard of singing from all concerned.

Ripe for praise were the mobile Tudor sets which put the final

A review of *The Merry Wives of Windsor*
in which Alan played Fenton.

'Viennese Evening'— at Camberley

FAITHFULLY capturing the legendary city's atmosphere of song, laughter, and love, "Viennese Evening" provided the Camberley Civic Hall audience on Saturday with a first-rate musical programme.

Star of the show, Marion Studholme, has a beautiful soprano voice that captivates from her very first note and a charm of manner to match. Her every note and word is clear and true, her actions and expressions so fitting and well-timed as to enrich everything she does. Her rendering of the Laughing Song from Strauss's "Die Fledermaus" must be among the most delightful ever.

A real cavalier of song, Robert Bateman is a dashing, debonair figure, equally at home in opera, operetta, or musical comedy. To a fine tenor voice he adds touches that prove him no mean actor, as he very effectively displayed in his two songs from Mozart's "Don Giovanni."

Marion Studholme. "Love! What has given you this magic power?" Alan Morrell's rich baritone voice evoked inevitable memories of Richard Tauber; but Mr. Morrell is a widely experienced artist and has his own individual style that made him a valuable asset to the programme.

At the piano, John Parry was equally impressive, both in his solo items and when providing unobtrusive but sensitive accompaniment to the singers.

Featuring the works of Beethoven, Mozart, Lehar, Schubert, and the Strausses (Johann II and Oscar), this was an extremely well balanced, varied programme, admirably suited to the talents of its performers.

A well filled hall made it evident that music of this kind is much to the taste of Camberley audiences. Their spontaneous acclaim of every item left no doubt of their genuine enjoyment of this most delightful, exquisitely performed en-

A review of the Viennese Evening in which
Alan appeared with Marion Studholme.

The 1958 21st Birthday Show at Coventry Theatre,
where Alan was a member of the Mitchell Singers.

21

London's World of Singing

1951 (22 years old in July)
In those days, the best way of finding accommodation in London was to get on the tube to the area you fancied, and walk around the main streets scanning all the notice boards outside the newspaper shops.

On this occasion, for some reason, we ended up away over in Peckham on the south side of the River Thames, where we found a small flat which gave us more room – which was fortunate, because our group of four had suddenly become a group of five, when one of the other porters at the hotel (Bob 'Dusty' Miller) had decided he'd like to join us. Which was a bit odd, because he'd shown no interest in music or singing – perhaps being alone he just enjoyed our company. However, we all got along OK so that was it.

Because Peckham was quite a distance from central London, this now meant a long, cold, clattering early morning journey to work each day, on the old, rattling double-decker trams. A thing that always astonished me about these old double-decker trams, was that on one of the routes along the Thames Embankment they turned into a tunnel under one of the Thames bridges, and travelled underground through the tunnel for about a quarter of a mile, before emerging out of the ground again up a steep slope right in the middle of the road in Kingsway.

Now being more settled into London life, with a regular job and a reasonable place to live, I felt I could at last start turning my attention more towards what I'd come here for in the first place. Jim and Willie felt somewhat the same, but seemed to have their own slightly less urgent agendas than mine.

j

So, having no idea where to start, I began visiting the music shops in central London near the hotel; Chapel's in Bond Street, Riccordi's in Upper Regent Street, etc., looking for some sort of information on singing teachers, but couldn't find any. However, I did pick up odd books of scales and vocalise on the way, though how and where to practise these I'd no idea. Finally, however, I came across 'Weeks' Music Shop' in Hanover Street near Oxford Circus, where I found the solution to this last problem, at least. They had a dozen or more practice studios on the three floors above the shop, each equipped with a piano, which you could hire by the hour. So for about one shilling and sixpence you could howl your head off for sixty minutes, in competition with all the other aspiring singers, pianists, etc., to your heart's content. And as the studios stayed open until about nine o'clock each evening all I had to do was slip up Regent Street after work, and add my bit (quite a lot actually) of howling to the general cacophony.

Another bonus of going to Weeks was that you gradually got on nodding terms with some of the other disturbers of the peace, and I gathered that some of them were receiving lessons from teachers there who had their own permanently rented studios.

However, remembering our singing-teacher experience in Barrow, I was definitely not inclined to rush in this direction. What I did do occasionally, though, once my own howling was over for the evening, was to wander around the corridors listening outside the doors where I knew teaching was going on. Unfortunately, nothing I heard exactly inspired me to knock on any of the doors demanding lessons. So I just bided my time.

Although Jim and Willie still seemed to be in no hurry to follow my lead, we did get about fairly often together to concerts at the Kingsway Hall and the Wigmore Hall, given by well known Leider singers of the day, like the German soprano, Elisabeth Schwarzkopf, or famous opera singers like the Russian bass, Boris Christoff. Our favourite musical outings, however, were the large orchestral concerts in the huge Albert Hall – often with famous solo singers and choruses. We also had occasional excursions to Covent Garden Opera House, where we'd queue up hopefully for seats away up in the Gods; from where the stage looked almost a bus ride away. Nevertheless, we enjoyed the magical atmosphere of being in such a great opera house, listening to our favourite music and singers, and gradually attuning our ears to the sound of what live singing was all about; as a opposed to the distorted, amplified version we'd previously been used to on our records.

At some time in this year I came across an advert in the *Stage* newspaper which caught my eye. It was advertising what was

194

described as a 'Silent Method' of voice production, by which you could apparently exercise, and develop the muscles used in singing, without having to sing endless scales, vocalise etc. Although rather sceptical, I was intrigued enough to want to learn more. And as it wasn't very expensive I sent off for it. The 'Method', when it turned up a few days later turned out to be a sort of two pronged plastic fork which you placed under your tongue, together with instructions on the tongue-exercises you had to practise with it. It also explained how this magical device had come about. Apparently the inventor – whose name I can't remember – had been a singer himself, and had noticed while watching many famous singers perform, that when they were singing with beautifully, ringing open tones, their tongues not only remained flat, but also formed a deep groove down the middle from front to back. This seemed to have the effect of opening their throats, so he'd concluded that this flat, deeply grooved tongue was the key to producing a lovely, open-throated voice.

As there was no fear of this simple tongue exercise doing any physical harm, I therefore put it to the test, and very quickly found that with the aid of the plastic fork, I could produce this easy, relaxed tongue groove at will. And once I'd got the feel of it, could also do it without the aid of the fork at all – which was obviously the whole idea behind it.

Because I still didn't have a singing teacher, and as this new found skill had made my throat feel nicely relaxed and open when practising, I thought that the chap who'd invented the idea, might just be worth a shot as my first singing teacher.

He lived away out in Coulsdon, which is a suburb of South London. So with a feeling of having nothing to lose, I called him up on the phone. He sounded a friendly sort of chap, and the moment he spoke I detected a slight North Country accent. When I explained why I was calling, he replied that he didn't usually take on pupils for actual singing lessons; but if I thought it might be useful in getting me started, he was willing to give it a try. So we arranged a time.

On the day appointed I caught the train out to Coulsdon, and turned up at his house; a pleasant semi-detached in a nice modern street about ten minutes walk from the station. After being introduced and led into his music room, his wife brought us in a cup of tea, and we all had a pleasant chat. He then tinkled out some scales on the piano which I sang to give him some idea of what he was dealing with.

To my delight he congratulated me on having what sounded like the makings of an exceptionally good voice.

"Do you have any songs you'd like to try?" he asked.

"Well. I could try, 'O sole mio'," I suggested.

"That's just the thing," he replied, "but this time we could try using this," he added, going over to some sort of box on a small table, which I'd assumed to be some sort of gramophone. "I doubt if you've ever seen one before."

"What is it?" I asked.

"A recording machine," he replied. He then lifted the lid to reveal a machine with two spools on the top, one of which was wound full with what looked like fuse wire, the other end of the wire being coupled across to the other empty spool.

"How does it work?" I asked fascinated.

"Well, it's a 'wire' recorder," he replied. "When you switch it on, the wire winds from one spool to the other, passing over the recording head on the way. The recording head then transfers the sounds of your voice – which it's picking up from the built in microphone – onto the wire. And when you wind it back and play it, you can listen to what you've just sung."

Never having actually heard my own voice before, at least what it sounded like to other people, I was naturally intrigued by this odd machine. So I sang 'O sole mio' at the machine, and waited in great anticipation as it was wound back. When it started to play, however, I discovered the awful truth – which everyone does on hearing their own recorded voice for the first time. I simply couldn't believe that it was me. It sounded nothing like the voice I was used to hearing in my own head, and my first reaction was great disappointment.

"Is that 'really' what I sound like?" I asked in dismay.

"Well, yes!" he answered. "The recording's a bit 'tinny', but it's you all right."

I stood listening in disbelief, trying to come to terms with this 'new' voice I'd just had inflicted upon me. As I listened on, however, I began to think, 'Well, even if it doesn't sound like 'me' it's not too bad. . . I'll just have to get used to it, that's all."

We tried a bit more recording on his machine, during which I discovered that the wire had a tendency to break. This seemed no problem, however, because he simply tied a knot in it and off it went again.

I went over for a few more lessons with him during the next two or three months which I don't think he charged me anything for; not even the cup of tea. But I quickly realised that although I'd definitely benefited from the experience, he wasn't really able to teach me anything further, so I called it a day.

As this was the first year after my demob from the army, I'd had to find out where to report in London to start my compulsory three years Territorial Army service. This turned out to be a TA barracks in Shoreditch, down in the East End.

When I'd first reported there I'd been told that all I was required to do each year was attend one 'parade' a month at the Shoreditch Barracks, plus an annual camp for a week's full time training; which could be anywhere in the country. The good thing about this last bit, was that wherever you were working at the time, your employer was forced to not only let you go, but to pay you your full wage for that week as well.

All in all this hadn't been too bad a prospect, and the monthly parades I'd attended so far that year had been little more than an evening out for a bit of a recap on army procedures, plus bringing us up to date on any changes, new equipment, etc. – which since the armed forces were being wound down rather than up – was virtually non-existent.

The first of the annual camps, however, was now looming up, and somewhere around the middle of the year we all trundled off out of London in army lorries, heading for the huge military training ground on the rolling moors of Salisbury Plain, away over in Dorset.

Our main base was at a place called Tilshead Lodge where we were billeted for the first couple of nights in army huts. Most of our time after that, however, was spent living and sleeping out on the moors taking part in what were quite large army manoeuvres, involving troops from other regiments, infantry, artillery, etc. Being a REME workshop company our job was to move around the battlefield area, setting up and camouflaging our workshops wherever they were needed. This involved constantly striking camp and moving on to a different location every time a radio call came in from HQ to do so. Since our unit consisted of about fifty men, all our transport lorries, workshop equipment, a radio truck plus a heavy Scammel tow truck and trailer with a tank on it, packing up and moving this lot at a moment's notice was a frenetic scramble – and one we had to do several times during the days that the make-believe battle was raging all around us.

On one occasion we'd buried all our unit in a wood, camouflaging it in our usual way, because we'd been warned that spotter planes would be buzzing the area trying to find us. But even though the wood was fairly small, we'd had so much practice at fading into the landscape that they never did and, in fact, refused to believe that we were actually on the plain at all.

Although there was no 'real' enemy facing us out there, we'd been

197

warned that several units of the SAS had been let loose on the plain to create havoc and keep us on our toes. Whether this was true or not we never found out because they never came near us. I must admit, however, that the thought that they might be out there somewhere in the dark certainly sharpened up our vigilance during the nights.

After spending such an exiting and adventurous week away out in the wild moorlands, we headed off home to London to try and get back to normality as best we could.

At some time in this year Colin and I left the Peckham flat; which was proving a bit crowded for the five of us, and moved in briefly with our two elder sisters, Jean and Joan, at their flat in the Westbourne Park area of North Kensington. This was much handier for getting into central London than Peckham had been.

My eldest sister Joan, had also blossomed into a keen singer after leaving Barrow, and proved to have a very good soprano voice. She'd sung in various amateur shows whilst living down in Guildford for a few years, and had also sung professionally in one or two summer shows down in Weston-Super-Mare, Devon. Jean also had a good soprano voice, and both she and Joan sang for a while in a choir in London. Colin and I went to hear them once when their choir sang at a sort of armed forces entertainment theatre just off Trafalgar Square.

At the time we moved in with them, Joan was taking singing lessons with a teacher called Louise Trenton, who had her studio in Cavendish Square, just above Oxford Street in central London. And since I still hadn't found a regular teacher, I decided I'd like to give her a try. Joan arranged for me to go along and meet her, and a course of lessons was arranged at her rather 'posh' studio; which was only to be expected, since most of her pupils seemed to be somewhat older than I was, and from the better off classes, such as bankers wives, etc., for whom singing was obviously only a hobby. The only two I remember who were anything like my age were a brother and sister, who I believe came from some minor aristocratic family.

None of this particularly bothered me as they were all very friendly people when I met them. This happened once a month when Louise Trenton held a sort of master class for all of her pupils. In this, several of the more advanced pupils would sing something they'd currently been working on and the rest of us would be invited to offer comments and criticisms on their performance afterwards. It seemed a good system and I quite enjoyed these monthly sessions, especially as quite a few of the female pupils had really good voices, particularly one large, expensively dressed soprano with a powerful Wagnerian voice which could have blown the windows out. Unfortunately, where the male singers were concerned, not only did there seem to be 'fewer' of them on Madame Trenton's books, but even those she did have didn't strike me as particularly impressive. However, I carried on going back for lessons feeling sure that 'I' could prove to be at least 'one' exception.

Colin and I were still working at the Regent Palace, although I was getting a bit fed up with the routine work on the hotel back door. However, I had to earn my living somewhere, and as well as having all our meals provided the back door did have certain other compensations. For one thing, being almost in theatre land, I was constantly seeing famous faces from the theatre and film world passing by the door; and although these were not exactly what I was aiming for, this did give me a feeling of being right in the heart of where everything theatrical was happening.

Another unexpected 'experience' of London life I got through working at the back door, arose from the fact that the pavement running past it was actually in Soho, and formed part of the territory of the local 'working girls', who had regular beats around there. This gave me an intriguing glimpse into their world, because when work was a bit slack for them, they'd often stop for a chat; seeming to regard us simply as fellow workers in Soho. To my surprise I found that they were mostly pleasant, friendly girls, who looked upon their profession as simply a job like anyone else's. They'd often talk about their lives and families almost as if we were next door neighbours.

These chatty conversations, however, would always come to an abrupt end if they spotted a potential client approaching.

Eventually, though, I spotted an advert somewhere about a job vacancy at a taxi garage in nearby Notting Hill Gate, who were looking for someone with mechanical experience to take on the job of helping to service their fleet of London cabs. This was an opportunity too good to miss; because not only did it offer me the chance to put my REME skills to good use, it also offered wages about twice what I was earning at the hotel. So I went along to see them and was offered the job on the spot.

I walked away from humping sacks of potatoes, and boxes of wet fish at the hotel to become a mechanic. Well, sort of; because my job consisted mainly of keeping a check on the cabs' tyre pressures, topping up the gearbox and engine oils, radiator coolant, etc., and generally keeping a chart on how they were running. Colin still carried on work in the hotel kitchens, because he'd taken a liking to working there.

A few weeks after starting work at the garage, I decided it was time to find a place of our own. Living at Joan's flat had only been a temporary arrangement anyway, because it wasn't really big enough for the four of us.

We found a large boarding house only a few streets away which had a top floor double room available. Unfortunately, the room was right away up under the roof, had sloping ceilings, and no form of heating. But, as the weekly rent included breakfast and an evening meal, we decided that on balance it might be worth a shot, so we moved in.

The room turned out to be a lot colder than we'd expected, especially at night. So I bought a small oil stove and sneaked it in and up the stairs without the old boy who ran the place noticing. This warmed the place up a treat, especially after I'd found an old chrome wheel disc at the garage which just fitted over the top, helping to radiate the heat sideways into the room instead of it all rising up under the roof. During the day, when we were out, we'd hide the stove in the roof space through a small door in the wall.

Unfortunately though, some of the other boarders began to comment to the landlord about the mysterious smell of paraffin that had started to waft though the upper rooms at night, and the old boy decided to investigate. He never discovered who the culprits were, but it was obvious we couldn't use our secret furnace any more, and just had to weather the Arctic attic conditions as best we could.

I carried on my singing lessons with Louise Trenton during this time; travelling down to Weeks' Music Studios in the West End to do my practising on most evenings. Unfortunately, I was gradually coming to the conclusion that she was doing nothing worthwhile for me. Also, in the monthly Master Class too, I was beginning to feel a bit awkward and out of place among the other smartly-dressed, well-off pupils. This was emphasised every time we met, because they, like the friendly people they were, would always hold out their clean well-manicured hands to shake mine; which, having been soaked in dirty engine oil and grease all day, looked as embarrassingly grimy as if they hadn't been washed for weeks. They were all much too nice to notice this, of course, and I certainly felt no sense of inferiority; just an awareness of the rather wide gap between their everyday world and mine.

One little incident that served to emphasise this somewhat, occurred when we were all arriving for a Master Class one day. One of the lady pupils came bustling in, excitedly talking about a wonderful bargain she'd just picked up on the way. . .

"I was just passing Debenhams," she explained eagerly, "when I spotted this in the window, and just 'had' to have it." She then opened a paper bag she was carrying, to reveal a tiny fluffy sort of hat. "Isn't it lovely!" she added. "And it only cost thirty-five pounds."

As this was equal to about five of my weekly wages, I can't say I shared her enthusiasm.

Eventually, after about six months, I finally decided to face up to the fact which I'd suspected early on, that Madame Trenton was not really a teacher for the male voice, especially mine. So I said my thanks for her efforts, and set off to find one who was.

SOME MAJOR EVENTS OF THE YEAR

(1) The diplomatic traitors Burgess and McLean defected to Russia.

(2) The Witchcraft Act of 1793 was finally repealed (unbelievably, due to the dictatorial 'back room' powers of the established Church in Britain, this cruel, medieval act under which hundreds of people had been tortured and put to death, had been kept in force until 1951); it was replaced by the Fraudulent Mediums act.

(3) The musical *South Pacific*, by Rogers and Hammerstein was staged.

(4) The films *Oliver*, *African Queen* and *The Lavender Hill Mob* were screened.

(5) The Festival of Britain opened by George VI.

(6) The Festival Hall opened.

(7) The first three-dimensional films were shown at the South Bank Festival.

(8) Submarine disaster; the *Affray* sank off the Isle of Wight.

(9) *De Havilland Comet*; the world's turbo-jet aircraft flew.

(10) The first ever 'peaceful' atomic energy produced at Harwell Atomic Research Centre. The Conservatives, under Churchill, win the general election by 17 votes.

22

My Search Continues

1952 (23 years old in July)
I was still keeping in touch with Jim and Willie, even though they were each living in their own bed-sits elsewhere in London. We'd still occasionally go out together to Covent Garden, or when any particularly interesting concerts cropped up at the Wigmore or Kingsway halls. At some time during this period, one of us spotted an advert somewhere about a singing teacher away up at Swiss Cottage in North London. She was apparently an ex-professional singer, with the Russian-sounding name of Olga Slovodska (or something like that). And as this sounded rather intriguing, we decided to give her a shot.

After telephoning her and fixing an appointment, all three of us (reminiscent of our Barrow epic) found our way to her front door. Which turned out to be a large Victorian house, in which Madame Olga occupied a ground floor flat. Madame Olga, herself, proved to be a rather large, Brünnhilde of a woman, full or vigour and enthusiasm, who was more than a match for her even larger grand piano. She rattled away on this while getting us to sing various scales. Stopping only to regale us with bits of advice from her own varied experience. Which as far as I could gather was rather more to do with somewhat out-dated musical 'shows' than anything classical or operatic.

Despite these all too familiar warning signs, and because we'd spent time and bus fares getting there, we decided to stick it out. Fortunately, this didn't last too long, and after about an hour we found ourselves out on the pavement again, without too much in the way of sore throats; due almost entirely to the fact that Madame Olga had done most of the singing herself.

As far as Jim and I were concerned, it was a case of one more lucky escape and a vow never to return. For some strange reason, however, Willie – obviously a sucker for punishment – decided to go back again, which to Jim and I was totally incomprehensible. Eventually, though, after a few of Olga's exuberant lessons, even he managed to escape before it was too late.

After this Swiss Cottage excursion, I decided that if I was going to make any real progress with my singing I needed to be based back in central London, where everything musical was happening. My first step in this direction was to give up my garage job in Notting Hill, and offer my services back to the Regent Palace Hotel, where Colin was still working in the kitchens.

The garage owner was sorry to see me go, and even offered to take me on as a full blown mechanic, if I was prepared to stay – a real tribute to my REME training, which I'd had ample opportunity to demonstrate at the garage. However, I stuck to my plans, and as the hotel were glad to have me back in my old job, that was it, back to square one.

To complete the move I also needed more central accommodation for Colin and myself, and as it happened, Jim and Willie were also thinking along the same lines. Somehow we came across a bed-sit house in Victoria which was ideal. It was within walking distance of Piccadilly Circus, and the lady who owned it happened to have several bed-sits available, so we all moved in. Colin and I in a double right up a narrow winding staircase at the top of the house, while Jim and Willie had separate rooms lower down. Dusty, who was still working at the hotel, also decided to rejoin us. So once again our little group was back together.

One slight disadvantage we discovered about our new address, was that our windows overlooked the junction with Vauxhall Bridge Road, which was a major road into London and therefore a busy tram route. These rattling old trams could be heard approaching the junction from several hundred yards down Vauxhall Bridge Road. And as the clattering of the steel wheels on the tracks grew louder and louder we'd sit there hoping that they'd get through the junction before the lights changed. Because when this happened they'd jam their brakes on with such a shuddering crash, that it sounded as if a head on collision had taken place. At first we'd find ourselves dashing to the windows to see, but very soon got used to it and it just became part of the normal traffic background.

My pleasant daily walk to work took me through St James's Park, over the bridge on the lake, into The Mall then up Lower Regent Street

203

to Piccadilly Circus, so the feeling of being right at the heart of what London had to offer couldn't have been greater. So many of the major events and parades took place on this route, especially along The Mall from Buckingham Palace to the Admiralty Arch, that I would often find myself wending my way through crowds lining the pavements watching some great spectacle or other. The one I remember above all others at this time happened in February after King George had died. I stopped amid the crowds that day to watch the horse-drawn gun carriage go by bearing the coffin of the man who'd been our king all through the dark days of the war.

I soon caught up with my regular practising at Weeks' studios, which was now much easier than when we were living away out in Westbourne Park. And, as it happened, things took an almost immediate turn for the better. A notice appeared one evening on the board at Weeks by a lady singing teacher who was now taking pupils at the studios. After my previous experiences of such notices, I would normally have been pretty sceptical, but somehow I felt that this one was different. Her name was Maria Linker, which sounding German was in itself promising. More importantly, however, she was also apparently a retired professional opera singer.

I put my practice session on hold that evening and immediately made a beeline for her studio. As all I could hear from outside was a tinkling piano she obviously didn't have a pupil there at that moment, so I knocked on the door. When it opened I found myself facing a pleasant looking, middle-aged woman who I immediately took a liking to.

"I've just seen your notice downstairs," I explained, "and I'd like to see about some lessons."

"Ah! Good," she replied inviting me in and waving me to a chair. "First of all," she added after I'd introduced myself, "tell me why you want to learn to sing?"

"I want to be an opera singer," I replied.

"Really!" she declared, with an approving smile. "That's quite a big ambition."

"I know," I replied, "but it's what I've always wanted to be to be."

"Well in that case," she added going over to the piano, "we'd better find out what sort of voice you've got. Did you bring anything with you?"

I pulled something out of my music case, though I'm not sure what – possibly 'O sole mio' or 'Santa Lucia'.

"Will this be alright?" I asked.

"That's fine," she replied, rattling off the introduction.

I belted my way through it in my best 'tenor robusto' style, and as I finished she stared at me in astonishment.

"My word!" she declared to my delight. "You really 'do' have a voice. It still needs a bit of work, of course, but I feel sure we can certainly make an opera singer out of 'you'."

And that was it. We fixed up a time and date for me to start lessons, and I walked elatedly down the stairs and out of Weeks' Studios feeling that at long last I'd taken a real step in the right direction.

Over the next few months I turned up for my weekly lessons at the studios, working on scales, arpeggios, and various vocalise of her own, which all gradually began to make my singing easier and more fluent. One thing I felt particularly happy about, was that she didn't believe solely in practising endless, boring scales to develop the voice, but also in using arias, or 'phrases' from arias for this purpose as well. I already knew a few arias from my own practising sessions at Weeks, and this gave me the chance to learn one or two more. One particular tenor aria which she came up with was one I'd never come across before. This was 'Ah! dispar vision' from Massenet's opera *Manon*, and it was obviously one of her favourites.

"This aria," she declared, "is not only beautiful, but very difficult to sing. If you can sing this well, then you can sing anything."

She was certainly right about it being difficult, and we always used it as a sort of 'test piece', to see how I was progressing.

By my own choice I was also working on other arias like 'Celeste Aida', 'Amor ti Vieta', and especially the 'Prize Song' from Wagner's opera *Die Meistersinger*, a heldentenor aria which I had a particular leaning towards. My greatest reward for all this work finally came about six months later, when after singing through our test piece as usual, and the last piano notes were fading away, she looked at me with great satisfaction, and said:

"Most tenors would find that extremely difficult to sing, but you now sing it as if it had been written for you."

Despite having reached this encouraging point, I knew only too well that it was just a milestone, and that I still had quite a way to go, and much to learn before I'd be anything like ready for the professional singing world.

My monthly TA meetings had been fitted in as usual this year, and the annual camp was soon on top of us. This time we were off to a camp near Thetford in Norfolk and found ourselves in a totally different type of landscape to Salisbury Plain – fairly flat and heavily forested. The camp itself was exactly 'that', and we found ourselves living in tents, with makeshift ablutions, toilets and mess tents. We

205

also found ourselves sharing the camp with a platoon of 'Z' men reservists. These were ex-REME squaddies, who were slightly older than us, and because they'd only been called up towards the very end of the war, were required to stay on the 'reserve' list after 'demob', and attend annual training camps as we did.

Most of he training routines were fairly basic REME recovery exercises. The main recovery task we were set, however, was far from routine. This consisted of dragging up a heavy battle tank from the bottom of a tree lined gorge some twenty feet deep, where it had been dumped – supposedly damaged in battle. Since none of us National Service conscripts, or the 'Z' men, had ever faced such a hefty job before this turned out to be a real challenge. We knew the 'theories', of course, and under the guidance of regular army instructors set to work hammering dozens of four foot long spikes into the ground to act as anchors for our steel cables and pulleys, then clearing away all the broken trees, shattered stumps and shrubs that were in the way before coupling up the winch on our heavy, Scammel towing truck. When we turned on the power, however, it soon became obvious that dragging some forty tons of battle-tank up from this steep sided gorge was going to be no easy task. Firstly, the towing cables kept digging into the ground on the lip or the gorge, so we had to lay baulks of timber from the broken tree trunks under them to stop this happening. Then all our anchors for the pulley cables started tearing out of the ground under the tremendous strain, so we kept having to stop and hammer in more and more. Eventually, however, all our struggles began to produce results and the great forty ton monster slowly began to move. Little by little we edged it up from its tree bound tomb, until after several hours of hard graft, its nose slowly rose above the lip of the gorge and it flopped down with a great cloud of dust onto the flat earth outside.

As well as the purely REME training at this camp there were also basic army exercises like drilling, but the one exercise that stands out for me was a particular 'map reading' test they'd devised. This was something they'd kept quiet about and sprung on us as a surprise. We were gathered together on parade one morning, split up into teams of three men, and told that a three mile map-reading trail had been laid out through the woods and surrounding countryside. Along this trail, apparently, about a dozen map references had been hidden at various points together with a code word. Each one giving the map reference to the next one. We were only given the map reference to the first one, from where we'd find the next one plus the code word. To add a bit of extra incentive, the first team to arrive at the end with all the code words would be declared the winners, and receive a special prize.

The two squaddies I'd been put with happened to be brothers, and as one of them was a lance corporal, he was in charge. It soon became apparent, however, that he hadn't a clue about map reading, and since his brother was no better it was left to me to find the first location on the map from the reference we'd been given. So off we all set in various directions with each team trying to find their own shortest route. A few were heading in the same direction as us, so when we reached the first map reference it was a question of searching surreptitiously for the next hidden map reference, without giving its location away to the other searching teams. We found it fairly quickly, and the lance corporal jotted down the next reference and code word, hoping the other teams hadn't latched on to where it was. When none of the other teams followed us we thought we'd pulled a fast one on them. Until, that is, we reached the map reference the lance corporal had written down, because we could find nothing there that fitted the hiding place described.

We were just about to give up when a farm worker who'd been watching us asked what we were looking for.

"Ah! well," he replied, pointing to a nearby dry stone wall when we told him. "I did see some of your fellahs stickin' somethin' in that wall earlier on."

Although this hiding place didn't match the clue we'd got written down, we decided to have a look. And lo and behold, there it was! But just as we were congratulating ourselves on this stroke of luck, we discovered to our dismay that the map reference and code on it were, in fact, for the third reference point, not the second. Our lance corporal had obviously misread the map reference on the first one we'd found, and by some weird coincidence, this had led us to within about thirty yards of the third one.

"Well, that's the end of 'our' map reading saga," we thought, because without the code word we should have picked up from that 'second' map reference, we couldn't prove that we'd done the whole course.

By this time other three-man teams were coming into sight, so we just tagged on behind them going through the motions of collecting the map references and codes from then on. One of these other chaps was a bit talkative about the course so far, and we managed to wheedle out from him the information we were missing from map reference two. By this time, of course, any hope of coming in among the leaders was out of the question, but at least we wouldn't have to explain how we'd missed the second map reference point.

Eventually we were approaching the last but one reference point with all the other teams stretched out for some three hundred yards ahead of us. There was a fairly extensive wood coming up on our left hand side, and we saw the leaders stop and search around near the edge of the wood – obviously looking for the hidden clues to the final destination, then set off again straight ahead up the outside of the wood. Most of the other teams had obviously settled down to simply making a note of the hidden information, and following on after them.

We, being the last by now, were in no hurry, so had a proper look at this last map reference – as we'd done at all the others.

"Hang on a minute!" I said, as I rechecked this on the map a couple of times. "I can't believe this."

"Why? What's the matter?" asked my two team mates.

"They've gone the wrong blinkin' way!" I exclaimed in disbelief.

"They can't have!" insisted my mates.

"I tell you they have!" I insisted, pointing at the map. "That's where we're making for, over the other side of this wood. They've all gone straight on, when they should have turned left along the bottom of the wood."

"You sure?" they both replied doubtfully.

" 'Course I am!" I insisted. "Come on."

We scrambled over the wall and made our way along the bottom edge of the wood for about three or four hundred yards before suddenly emerging into a small, grassy meadow, where we just stopped and stared in amazement at the staff car and lorries all waiting for our return.

As soon as we were spotted, the staff sergeant beckoned us over and checked the details of our efforts on the record sheet we'd kept.

"Everything checks out all right, Sir," he announced.

The officer gave a satisfied smile.

"Congratulations!" he declared. "Well done. You are the first ones to arrive, and seem to be well ahead of all the others."

To say we were 'embarrassed' was an understatement if ever there was one. But at the same time it was so utterly ludicrous, almost like a scene from a Laurel and Hardy film, that we had a job to keep straight faces. Unfortunately, to confess the truth was out of the question, because the situation had now taken on a momentum of its own.

Before long the other map-reading groups began to arrive from the opposite direction to where we had – obviously having traipsed a very much longer route right around the outside of the wood. The first of these turned out to be a 'Z' man group, who trooped into the grassy meadow with confident smiles on their faces, obviously feeling sure that they'd won the prize. When they spotted us three sitting there all innocently, they just stared in disbelief

"Congratulations on coming second," declared the officer. "You were only beaten by about five minutes. But well done anyway."

The prize turned out to be a pack of about 200 cigarettes, and the journey back to camp in our particular lorry became a bemused quiz show, with everybody demanding to know how the devil we'd got there first, when most of them distinctly remembered passing us on the way.

We obviously made the most of all this bewildered questioning, by insisting that it was all down to our superior map-reading skills and tactics, and so managed to get back to camp without revealing the farcical truth. After all there 'was' a tiny element of truth in this wind-up of ours, because they 'had' all made a mistake over the very last map reference reading, while we hadn't. And it was this that left the way open for us to steal a march (literally) on them all.

However, although we played the joke for all it was worth, we knew full well that we were 'not' the genuine winners and had no intention of keeping the prize. So that evening I took the 200 cigarettes around to the tent of the three 'Z' men who'd come in second.

"Here you are," I said handing them over. "These belong to you."

They all stared at me in bewilderment.

"How do you make that out?" asked one of them.

"Because you were the 'real' winners," I replied, "not us."

"Well that's very honest of you," said one of the others taking the fags happily.

"But how did you do it?" asked the third. "You were miles behind when we last saw you."

"Yeh!" agreed the second. "That's what I can't work out."

"Neither can we really," I shrugged walking off, and leaving the whole farce unexplained.

In fact, it remained a mystery for the rest of that week.

Back in London I settled down to picking up the strings again, and life returned to normal.

At about this time Colin, who was now eighteen, became due for his National Service call up, something he was quite looking forward to. He'd realised by now that there was no future in the hotel job he was doing, and as he had no 'other' reason for staying in London, in the way that I had, the idea of going off to a whole new life in the army looked really exciting.

Eventually his papers arrived and he went off cheerfully for the usual preliminary medical. When he came home afterwards, however, he was looking pretty dejected.

"What's the matter?" I asked.

"They've turned me down," he replied.

"What!" I exclaimed in disbelief. "But why. . ? What was wrong?"

"They wouldn't tell me," he shrugged. "Just said I wasn't fit enough."

Although I felt sorry for him, it dawned on me then that deep down I shouldn't really have been all that surprised. He'd always looked rather pale, and perhaps not quite as tall and robust as he should have been, but until that moment I'd never thought it was anything more than that.

"Well, we can't leave it like this," I declared. "We've got to find out what's wrong with you."

"How?" he asked.

"We'll see our own doctor," I replied, "get him to find out. They wouldn't tell 'you', but they're bound to tell him if he asks them."

"Yeh! That's right," agreed Colin, brightening up. "Maybe they would."

The following day we called in at the surgery and explained the situation to the doctor. Fortunately he agreed that Colin had a right to know, and said he'd find out. A couple of days later we got word to call in to see him.

"Well, I've got the results of your medical," he declared to Colin. "Unfortunately, they discovered that you're anaemic, 'very' anaemic. Which, I must say, doesn't surprise me."

"Can anything be done about it then?" I asked.

"Oh yes!" agreed the doctor confidently. "In fact, I've already started making arrangements to get him into Westminster Hospital. I feel sure they can sort it out."

Within a week Colin was admitted into the hospital, where they explained that it was a matter of getting his very low blood count up to where it should be. This took them about three weeks, by which time he was already looking fitter and healthier than I could ever remember.

This unexpected hospital stay turned out to be a life changing event for Colin in more ways than one, because before discharging him altogether they sent him off to spend another week or so in Chartham Park convalescent home, down near Lingfield in Surrey. Whilst there he got to know one of the local people who worked at the home, and on discharge ended up going to live with his family. Eventually he found a job down there, and never came back to London.

A perfect example of how simple, unexpected events can so often effect the whole direction of your life.

Just after Colin had left I got to hear from somewhere; possibly on the Weeks' grapevine, about an amateur operatic group who were rehearsing for their next operatic production, and were looking for new singers. What particularly interested me about this, was that although they were putting on their opera away down in Isleworth, South London, they were actually doing a lot of their rehearsing in some music studio in Soho, just below Oxford Street. The opera they were staging was, strangely enough, *Faust*, the first opera I'd ever seen performed away up in Shrewsbury while I was in the army.

I decided that this was worth a look, so turned up at one of their rehearsal evenings. As I'd gathered that an audition would naturally be required I'd brought my music case.

They seemed a very friendly group, with an excellent lady musical director, and a very fine pianist/répétiteur. They were keen to hear me sing, so I had my first ever chance to perform one of my party-pieces to an audience. I'm not sure which party piece but it was 'probably' 'The prize song' from *Die Meistersinger* – not exactly appropriate, but at least it gave me a chance to show off.

This was exceptionally well received by all those present, and was followed by an apology from the musical director.

"We'd love to have you with us," she declared, "but I'm afraid that the leading roles have already been cast."

"Oh! I see," I replied, putting on a slight air of disappointment, though the thought of being offered the leading role had never entered my head. "What a pity."

"But we 'could' offer you the 'understudy' of Faust," she added quickly. "If you'd be willing to help out in the chorus in the meantime."

"Oh, alright," I agreed, trying not to sound too condescending.

And that was it, my first offer to 'cover' a major operatic role, and I'd never set foot on a stage in my life.

From that moment onwards, as it quickly dawned on me exactly what I'd agreed to take on, my singing activities took on a more urgent and hectic pace. I not only had my normal lessons with Maria Linker to fit in, but was now faced with the pretty daunting task of learning a full operatic role, as opposed to the odd aria here and there as I'd done in the past.

My first move, obviously, was to get hold of a full vocal score of the opera and start learning the part. This in itself turned out to be a real learning curve, because although I could learn the notes myself by tinkling them out on the piano in Weeks' studios, learning the words was a different matter. This was because *Faust*; being a French opera, the original libretto was in French, so what we'd be singing would be

211

an English translation. Unfortunately, I discovered, there was more than one of these, so the question for me was 'which'?

However, I did eventually manage to find a second-hand score with the correct translation in Foyle's bookshop in Charing Cross Road – so at least I'd be singing the same words as the rest of the cast.

Throughout this time I was still working during the day at the Regent Palace Hotel, though I was now growing somewhat fed up with the routine again. And since Colin had left there, and Jim and Willie had also drifted away to other jobs, I began thinking of making a move as well. The final thing that put the tin hat on it for me, happened one day when they asked me to 'see in' a lorry load of coal for the boilers. This involved going down into the cellars and shovelling the coal away from the chute among clouds of swirling coal dust as it was tipped down; the purpose being to make sure the whole load of several tons would fit in. It was like working in the depths of a coal mine, and by the time I'd finished I looked like a miner who'd just done an eight hour shift. When I emerged from the depths of the Regent Palace's coal mine, I immediately handed in my notice and threw myself back on the jobs market.

I quickly found another job in a Lyons' Tea Shop somewhere in Westminster, not far from the Houses of Parliament. This lasted all of three days, because on the first morning I turned up the manageress greeted me with:

"Now what I'd like you to do today, is give all the windows a good clean, both inside and out."

"Since I'd always found window cleaning the most soul-destroying job imaginable, coupled with the fact that this particular tea shop was on a corner, with what looked like acres of glass stretching away down the streets on either side, this did not bode too well.

'However,' I thought, 'it's only the first day, so give it a chance. I therefore got my water bucket, chamois-leather, polishing scrim, and got on with it. There was so much glass that I was at it all day before she was satisfied with the results.

'Ah well!' I thought as I trudged home wearily, 'it was only the first day after all, it's bound to be different tomorrow.'

A vain hope if ever there was one, because I arrived next morning to be met with:

"Now what I'd like you to do today, is give all the windows a good clean and polish."

I just gritted my teeth in disbelief.

'This can't go on forever,' I assured myself, and just set off on the window cleaning marathon once again.

I soon found out how wrong I was when I turned up for work on the third day to hear:

"Now what I'd like you to do today is. . . etc. It was like listening to a gramophone record, and I vowed there and then that my days as a window cleaner were coming to an end at tea time that day. I simply collected my three days' pay and departed, vowing never to look another plate glass window in the face again.

I walked into another job almost immediately when I learned that a place called the Berkley Court Restaurant, right near Baker Street Station, were urgently looking for a kitchen porter, so I headed off there and was once again given the job on the spot.

Fortunately this turned out to be a much more interesting job altogether, because as well as doing all the usual kitchen porter chores, I was also apparently required to be an assistant to the 'veg' chef. And since this not only involved peeling and cutting up all the vegetables, but actually helping him to cook them, it was a fascinating chance to try my hand at something new. I was quite familiar with cooking ordinary veg on an everyday scale, of course, but learning how it was done on a commercial scale, and with a greater variety of veg than I'd ever come across before, was quite an eye-opener.

The veg chef himself turned out to be a really likeable chap, in his late twenties, with quite a pronounced accent. He came from Liverpool – or at least that's what he told me at first. Later on, though, he confided that he was actually Irish, but because he didn't like the bad reputation some of his fellow countrymen had got in London, he'd decided to pass himself off as a Liverpudlian. Strange as it may seem this was fairly easy to get away with, since there 'was' a certain resemblance between the two accents.

Working with him I soon learned the basic Berkley Court routines of veg preparation and cooking; which was done in large, deep trays in the upright steam chests built along the wall like fridges. Mashing up the creamed potatoes with their industrial sized masher was simplicity itself, because this could whip up about half a hundredweight of spuds in seconds.

All the fancy cooking, of course, was left to the other chefs with their tall, bobbing white hats and frenetic activity.

As it turned out, the thoroughness of my Liverpool/Irish tutor was just as well, because after I'd been there about three weeks I arrived one day to be met by the rather anxious looking manager.

"The veg chef's gone down with the flu," be declared. "Do you think you could fill in for a while?"

"Well. . . I suppose I could," I replied, somewhat taken aback by this sudden offer of promotion.

"Oh, that's great!" sighed the relieved manager thankfully. "All the 'other' chefs will keep an eye on you. . . Help you out if you need it."

"Alright then!" I agreed. And that was it. For about a week I became the veg chef at the Berkley Court Restaurant. Unfortunately, though, they didn't give me a tall white hat. And I still had to mop the floors as well.

After my Liverpool/Irish tutor got over his cold, I was unceremoniously demoted to being a lowly 'assistant' again.

The only other thing I remember about the Berkley Court Restaurant was when the manager told me one day that he had an all night job coming up, cleaning and disinfecting the whole kitchen to comply with health and hygiene regulations; apparently this had to be done at regular intervals, and was now due.

"Would you like to give me a hand?" he asked.

Since it paid double time I said OK.

On the night in question, I turned up again late in the evening after the restaurant had closed its doors to the last customers, and went down into the kitchens, which were at basement level – having pulley-operated dumb waiter lifts up to the restaurant level. I was surprised to see all the gear that was already laid out; hose pipes, high pressure spray guns, large canisters of disinfectant and insecticide. The insecticide was the one thing that didn't surprise me, because I'd learned from all the other places I'd worked in that 'cockroaches' were an absolute menace in large kitchens, and virtually impossible to eradicate completely. No matter how much strong soda I'd flood the kitchen floor drains with, 'some' colonies of these ugly little creatures would always survive.

On this occasion we were obviously going to town in a big way. Firstly we got clothed from head to foot in boiler suits, hoods, gloves, masks and goggles. Then we just blasted away with the high pressure hose pipes and spray guns. Walls, ceilings, floors, every nook and cranny under or behind everything got the full treatment. It took us nearly all night to get it all done and washed away, and by the time we'd packed all up and left for home, the whole kitchen looked, and smelled, as clean as an operating theatre – for a little while at least.

As the day for the performance of *Faust* was growing nearer I was growing a bit concerned about my progress – or lack of it – in learning the role of Faust, which I was supposed to be covering. The reason was simply lack of rehearsal. The singers actually playing the leads had been finding it such a struggle to get their parts right, that they'd taken

214

up all the rehearsal time available, leaving none at all for the understudies. The crunch came, when with only about one week to opening night, the tenor singing the part of Faust was having a particularly bad time and got really panicky.

"I'll never get it right in time!" he blurted turning to me. "I can't do it! You'll have to go on."

"What. . !"I retorted in disbelief. "Not on your life! You've been rehearsing the role for weeks, and I haven't had the chance to rehearse a single note of it."

With a few other voices joining in, he gradually realised how ridiculous he was being, calmed down and tried it again until he eventually got it right.

Despite all this, on the opening night the 'Faust' conquered his nerves and we managed to get through the opera without any major problems. With the initial pressure now off, the rest of the week's performances were more relaxed and enjoyable.

All in all, not a very auspicious introduction for me to the world of operatic performance. But it did give me my first practical experience of what was involved in learning and performing a major role – even though I'd never actually got to sing it myself.

Towards the end of the year I gave up kitchen portering at the Berkley Court Restaurant, and took a job at Watney's 'Stag' Brewery in Victoria. The reason being quite simply that they were not only offering much higher wages than the Berkley Court, but being in the centre of Victoria, the brewery was only about five minutes easy walk away from the bed-sit.

The centre of Victoria itself was built around the famous railway station, and as well as the brewery, whose main gates were just off the main road, was always a busy, bustling place with main roads leading through it up into central London; which wasn't all that far away. At the time we were living there the Victoria Palace Theatre, just near the station, was presenting the long running Flanagan & Allen 'Gang Show'. And while a huge modern Odeon Cinema dominated the main shopping area, just down the road was a tiny, single-storied 'flea pit' of a cinema called (I think) the 'Biograph' which was a real remnant of the very early days of cinema. Built to show the very first silent films, it was 'still' showing films – although watching them was a bit like sitting in an old barn with creaky tip-up seats.

The job at the brewery consisted of working with a team of men rolling barrels of beer about down in Watney's extensive cellars. These seemed to extend forever underneath that part of central Victoria, and although manhandling these hefty beer barrels was pretty hard

215

physical work, it made a welcome change from the heat and hassle of the steamy Berkley Court kitchen.

For some reason, which I can't recall, I was only there for about three months. It can't have been the work that made me pack it in, because I quite enjoyed it. Or the men I was working with, as they were a friendly, interesting bunch. Three of them I particularly remember were a big bruiser of a chap with a face like a prize fighter, who spent all his meal breaks knitting clothes for his four kids; another was a rather well rounded sixteen-stoner, who apparently only worked at the brewery for about six months each year, because for the other six months he'd be away up in the North of England playing football for 'Accrington Stanley'; the third one was a shortish, powerfully built chap in his thirties who loved to show off his strength. His party-piece used to be putting his middle finger through the metal 'spare bung' ring on the top of a full nine gallon 'firkin' and hoisting it up waist high with that one finger. Since a full firkin weighed around 120 pounds, most men would struggle to lift it an inch off the ground with both hands.

SOME OF THE MAJOR EVENTS OF THE YEAR:
(1) King George VI died; Elizabeth acceded to the throne.
(2) Wartime identity cards abolished, also the 'Utility Goods' system.
(3) Agatha Christie's play, *The Mousetrap* opened in London. The films, *High Noon* and Charlie Chaplin's *Limelight* screened
(4) Farnborough Air Show disaster, 30 killed.
(5) John Cobb killed in his speedboat on Loch Ness.
(6) De Havilland jet flies faster than sound.
(7) Jodrell Bank telescope under construction.
(8) Radiocarbon dating used for the first time.
(9) Coelacanth caught alive off Africa – thought to have been extinct for 50 million years.
(10) Farewell journey of the last London tram.

23

From Beer Barrels
to Hospital Trolleys

1953 (24 years old in July)
Once again I found myself kitchen portering, but this time at St Thomas's Hospital, a huge Victorian building which stretched right along the South Bank of the Thames, exactly opposite the Houses of Parliament.

The reason, I suspect, boiled down to the old attraction of having all meals provided on the job – which cut out the hassle of cooking in the bed-sit, and the shopping that went with it – and so leaving more time free to get on with what I'd really come to London for.

In the hospital I found myself working in the bakery department, which was a sort of annex off the main kitchen run by a single pastry chef. As at the Berkley Court, I was his only assistant, although unfortunately this time I didn't get to do any of the actual baking. My job was mainly to keep all his equipment, mixers, baking trays and other tools clean and ready for use, from one batch of baking to the next, as well as the usual floor mopping, etc.

The pastry chef himself was quite an independent character, who'd brook no interference from any of the other chefs, including the head chef himself. He was such a whiz at turning out great cakes and pastries, however, especially on the scale needed to keep several hundred patients happy, that everybody just left him to get on with it.

Although I never had anything to do with the baking, I did learn one fundamental truth from his baking philosophy:

"You only get out of the oven what you put into it," he'd often declare. "Put crappy ingredients in; you get crappy cakes out."

217

k

The proof that 'he' didn't put crappy ingredients in I tasted often enough for myself in his sponges, and pastries, which were made to his own recipes and absolutely scrumptious. And even though they seemed to be lashed up on what seemed an industrial scale, and baked on huge trays, I never knew him to have a failure.

One particular morning near Easter, however, I arrived to find the whole kitchen pervaded with a heavy, spicy smell that you could almost have grabbed by the handful. At first it seemed quite sweet and pleasant, but after a few minutes began to make your head spin. This turned out to be bun spice, and was explained when I found the pastry chef up to his elbows in dough, making hot cross buns.

From the strained faces, and comments of the other kitchen staff, I gathered that this was one day of the year they didn't look forward to, because ten minutes of breathing this heady bun spice was enough to give everybody a throbbing headache, which didn't lift until the bun baking was over.

I soon found myself in the same state as they were, and for two or three years afterwards I could hardly look a hot cross bun in the face.

One of the other jobs I'd occasionally get lumbered with whenever they were a bit short of staff, was helping to deliver the meals up to the many wards that the St Thomas's had. These were on about four upper floors, each of which had one long main corridor down the centre which seemed to stretch for miles. Along these long corridors all the ward entrances were laid in a regular pattern on either side.

The meals themselves were all housed on shelves inside large trolleys with sliding doors, which were kept heated in the kitchen by being plugged into the mains. My job, when elevated to the role of trolley-pusher, was simply to unplug them, push these via the lift to the correct floor, then along the corridor; plug them into the mains again outside the correct ward, report the success of my mission to the ward nurse, and traipse back down again for the next one. Not a task that required a university degree, or the skill of an experienced 'mopper-upper', but it made an occasional change, and did, after all, help to keep the patients fed.

All during this time I was still carrying on with my weekly evening routine at Weeks' Music Studios of one lesson with Maria Linker, and two or three other evenings practising on my own. I'd known from the start that developing my voice to the level of a full-time professional without the aid of a music school or college would be a long job. But since, as far as I was aware, there were no scholarships or grants available at that time, certainly not from my home town of Barrow, I was quite resigned to making my own way there, no matter how long it took.

218

Although at times this did seem a bit like trudging slowly down an endless road, I did occasionally get a bit of encouragement here and there – quite often from one of my fellow hopefuls at the studios. One Polish chap in particular, who I'd bumped into several times in the corridor after my lessons with Madame Linker, gave me a surprising boost one evening when he explained that this bumping into me was no coincidence.

"Whenever I hear you singing arias in your lessons," he said, "I always come to listen outside the door, because you are now one of my favourite tenors."

Praise indeed, especially as he was, apparently, a tenor himself. And although I didn't exactly let this go to my head (well not much), it 'was' confirmation of my faith in my voice; and being completely unasked for, good to hear.

All during this time in London, and before, my other creative urge, 'to write', had never been far below the surface. And although I'd never been able to devote 'much' time to it, I did from time to time manage to keep the flame burning by jotting down bits and pieces in small, floppy-paged exercise books. The word 'exercise' in this case being pretty appropriate, as that's just about all they were. At first they'd be attempts at simple poems, but it wasn't long before I'd written this out of my system and graduated to more satisfying things like short stories. I'd found these much more in line with what I 'really' wanted to write, and had already got a few plotted out in my floppy books.

In my attempts at writing I'd discovered early on – as I had with my singing – that creative writing was a 'skill' as well as a talent, and this had to be 'learned'. Simply having the desire to write was merely the beginning. The basic techniques, the dos and don'ts had to be gathered along the way. In my case from reading the work of other writers, and from the occasional 'Guidance for Writers' articles I'd come across.

However, just as with singing, where all the desire in the world to sing would come to nothing unless you had a good natural vocal instrument to start with; all the urge in the world to write would be pointless, unless you had something, interesting or creative to say. Which I felt I did, simply because characters and plots for stories were always rolling around in my head.

I was now in the third and 'final' year of my compulsory Territorial Army service, with the monthly parades away over in Shoreditch being ticked off steadily. For me these were now just a rather boring count down routine, because with the end in sight, any sense of purpose they'd had at first had wilted away. We seemed to be accomplishing nothing on these evenings now, but simply filling in the time by rehashing old training routines.

There was, however, one evening I remember which really did go down well with me. I turned up as usual to be met by the sergeant who immediately detailed myself and two others to take the fifteen hundred weight Bedford truck and report to a REME unit away over in Wimbledon on the other side of London.

Although we were all delighted at this welcome change to say the least, we were also somewhat puzzled.

"But none of us have driving licences," I pointed out.

"That's exactly the point," declared the sergeant. "You're going over there to get them. It's an army driver-training unit."

"Great!" we all agreed.

"But who's going to do the driving to get there?" I asked.

"Just share it between you," declared the sergeant.

"But we haven't got driving licences," I repeated.

"Oh! Don't worry about that," declared the sergeant, brushing off such a minor problem breezily. "You 'will' have on the way back."

We all just shrugged and set off, deciding among ourselves that we could blame him if we were stopped by the police because, after all, we were only obeying orders.

We swopped over the driving several times on the way through the traffic of central London, and fortunately arrived at the Wimbledon Army Driving Centre without being pounced on by the law. The test itself was, by today's standards, a bit of a joke. All that the staff sergeant doing the tests did, was chat to us for a few minutes, about nothing in particular, then get each of us in turn to drive the Bedford up a quiet lane near the driving centre, do a three point turn, and drive it back again.

When all three of us had completed this, he gave a little nod of satisfaction and declared:

"Right! You can all get off back now."

"Is that it?" we all asked in astonishment.

"Yes," he declared. "You've all passed."

"But what about the licences?" I asked.

"Don't worry," he replied breezily, "they'll all be sent through to Shoreditch in due course."

'Where've I heard that one before,' I thought, as we all set off back to Shoreditch in the Bedford, still minus our licences.

Of course the licences never did turn up. For me, it seemed, army driving licences were destined to remain forever in 'never-never land'.

For some reason this year, we never did our annual week's training camp. I don't remember being given any explanation for this, but it was probably all to do with the atmosphere of winding down that I'd already felt. However, whatever the reason, by halfway through the year I was finally free of the army for good.

Somewhere around the middle of May, I found myself getting a bit fed up with the routine at St Thomas's Hospital, and decided it was time for a change. I'd got wind from somewhere that they were looking for 'all-night' staff at Lyons' big 'Corner House' in the Strand and thought that might be worth a try. The idea of working through the night and having the whole of each day free to do what I wanted, had a special appeal. So I applied for the job and was taken on straight away.

Lyons, of course, were the owners of the Regent Palace Hotel where I'd already worked twice, as well as several other big hotels in London, plus all the many tea shops they were famous for – including the one which I'd endured three tortuous days cleaning windows.

Their big 'Corner Houses', however – of which they had more than one in London – were large buildings with a tea shop café on the ground floor and large restaurants on each of the two or three floors above. The one I worked at in the Strand, however, was the only one with an 'all-night' restaurant – which was right up on the top floor, and was, I believe, the 'only' all-night restaurant in central London.

I turned up on the top floor on my first night to find myself working in a large, noisy kitchen, with cooks and kitchen staff bustling about cooking and preparing meals everywhere. A long serving counter ran along one end of the kitchen, which on our side was split into several separate areas, with women in each, busily serving the customers as they filed through into the restaurant on the other side.

My job, along with a couple of other similarly aproned and white jacketed men – both quite a bit older than myself – was to be a helper out, fetcher and carrier, mopper and sweeper up; plus any of the other dozen-and-one tasks that might crop up needing urgent attention; including occasionally helping out at the counter or clearing tables.

It was certainly different to any of my other temporary kitchen exploits. There was never a dull moment, and nights there seemed to pass like lightning.

We seemed to get quite a fascinating, and varied, array of customers passing through during the night. For the first couple of hours or so, these would range simply from theatre goers on their way home, to various film celebrities and well known actors and actresses winding down after their evening performances. I soon noticed, however, that as the night wore on the type of clientele we were serving had a

221

decided tendency to dip 'somewhat' from the ordinary and famous towards the slightly less ordinary and decidedly dodgy. In fact, I got the impression at times, that by the early hours there probably wasn't a crook left out there in central London – they were all drinking coffee in our corner house.

Strangely enough, there was never trouble or rowdy behaviour from them. It was almost as if they regarded the all-night restaurant as a sort of club house where they could catch up with all their fellow ne'r-do-wells, and woe betide anyone who broke the club rules by getting stroppy – especially towards us staff. I saw this in action quite early on, when one big bruiser of a chap started giving one of the serving women a bit of a hard time at the counter. In seconds a couple of the 'club' fraternity in the queue grabbed him by the arms and saw him very rapidly off the premises, warning him not to come back.

My first reaction at finding myself working in what appeared to be an underworld melting pot was to ask:

"Where the heck are the police. . ? Why don't they just close this place down. . ?"

The answer I found was, surprisingly, that far from closing it down, the police were actually in favour of it. Because with this 'early-hours' gathering den of villains great and small, they knew exactly where to look 'first' if they wanted to find someone for a particular job.

On one of the nights during that first week I was detailed to help out the woman in the tea and coffee area, because her usual helper hadn't turned up. She seemed a pleasant friendly type and showed me all the routines of filling and operating the coffee percolators, tea urns, etc., and although quite a bit older than myself we got along very well. She told me her name was Barbara, and that she'd been working there for several years, so obviously the whole of this somewhat intriguing all-night scene was second nature to her.

Now that I was working in the Strand, my usual walk to work from Victoria in the evening, and home again in the morning, was pretty much the same as when I'd worked at the Regents Palace Hotel; across St James's Park and down The Mall. But instead of turning up the Duke of York Steps, I now carried on along The Mall, through Admiralty Arch and across Trafalgar Square into the Strand.

On June 2nd, however, instead of spending all of the day in bed as usual after my night shift, I got up early and did an 'extra' walk along this way. The reason for this was pretty special: it was the day of the Queen's Coronation, and her procession from Westminster Abbey, after the ceremony, was due to pass along much of this route.

As I made my way through St James's Park, I could hear the many-gun salute being fired away over in Hyde Park, and the distant Westminster Abbey Crowning ceremony echoing across St James's Park as it was relayed on speakers set up in the trees.

Being familiar with most of the best vantage points; when the ceremony ended and the procession got under way heading in our direction, I was able to see most of the parade from St James's Park and The Mall. I'd seen quite a few big parades pass along this route before, but on this occasion the military bands, marching guardsmen and household cavalry, all in their most stunning ceremonial uniforms, was the most magnificent, colourful and joyful spectacle I'd ever been involved in. I say 'involved in' because that's exactly what it felt like. And when the young, radiantly smiling Queen in her huge, glittering Coronation Coach passed by amid the clattering of horse's hoofs and the deafening cheering of the crowds no more that thirty yards from where I was standing, it was like watching a scene from fairyland.

As the coach passed on up the Mall, with the following stream of commonwealth carriages and marching bands, one other carriage stood out from all the others. In this open carriage sat the beaming figure of Queen Salote of Tonga; who, despite the rain which had started pouring down, had refused to have her carriage hood put up, and just sat there in the rain waving at the crowds as she passed, with such a huge, happy smile that it was almost like the sun coming out.

Although Jim, Willie & Dusty were still living in our bed-sit house in Victoria, we were now all working in different places, and our lives had diverged somewhat. Jim had a job in the wine cellar at the big, fashionable Trocadero restaurant in the West End, Willie was off working in a hotel kitchen somewhere, while Dusty who'd never shared our singing ambition's, of course, had somehow landed himself a job as an operating theatre porter at St George's Hospital on Hyde Park Corner, and was hopeful of moving up the ladder to bigger things.

Unfortunately, 'I' seemed to be the only one of our original Barrow 'would-be singers group' still actively pursuing this ambition. For Jim, who had an excellent baritone voice, and could undoubtedly have made it to the professional ranks, the time was 'never' quite right to start. He loved talking about singing, but it was always 'next week', or 'the end of the month', that he planned to get down to finding a teacher and begin serious training.

For Willie, however, the reason was somewhat different. He was always willing enough to try having lessons – and on a couple of occasions actually did – but unfortunately was not blessed with as good natural voice as Jim and I were, so these always came to nothing. Jim and I had been aware of this shortcoming right from the start, suspecting that he'd only joined in with us because we were his mates, and wanted to do what we did. But since his decision had been made entirely off his own bat, with no encouragement from us, there was little we could do about it.

Although we did still go about to concerts together occasionally, that was about as far as it went. One rather odd little thing happened around this time to emphasise this going our separate ways. Jim had picked up with a young married couple in London who he'd known from Barrow, and would occasionally go off to visit them, often coming back to tell us all about them, referring to them simply as 'Morris and Sheila'. This had been going on for about three months when one day he just happened to remark:

"By the way, it's a funny thing, but Sheila's maiden name was Workman, the same as yours."

I just stared at him in disbelief.

"Do you mean to say," I exclaimed, "that you've been going to see them all these months and you didn't think this worth mentioning before?"

Jim just shrugged. "I just never thought about it," he replied.

As it turned out she was my cousin Sheila, who I last remembered seeing when we were kids. And although I never actually got to meet her again in London, this contact with her through Jim did 'eventually' lead to a renewal of contact with my other cousins and extended family in Barrow – who for some unknown reason I knew very little about.

SOME MAJOR EVENTS OF THE YEAR:

(1) Korean War ends.
(2) Stalin dies.
(3) The Coronation of Queen Elizabeth (televised).
(4) *Guys & Dolls*, Musical staged. Films *Genevieve* and *The Cruel Sea*, screened.
(5) BBC TV Centre at Wood Lane opened.
(6) Hillary and Tenzing conquer Everest (Sir John Hunt expedition).
(7) Myxomatosis epidemic wipes out the rabbit population.
(8) Disastrous floods on North Sea coasts of Britain and Holland. Smog hits Britain.
(9) Piltdown Man exposed as a fraud by chemical tests.
(10) Structure of DNA molecule elucidated by Crick (English) and Watson (American)

24

Unforeseen Developments

1954 (25 years old in July)

Since the night time job at the Strand Corner House was fitting in surprisingly well with my singing and practice routines, I found myself staying on longer there than any other job in London so far.

My lessons with Maria Linker were also still progressing well, though I was beginning to suspect that this might not be going on for very much longer. I got the impression from little things she said from time to time that she'd reached the point, and the age, where she was just about ready to give up the routine and responsibility of teaching, to have more time to spend on her family and other things in her life.

Another reason for staying on so long at the Strand Corner house was that Barbara on the tea counter and I had got on so well that we'd eventually started going out occasionally in our time off. She even came to the Weeks' music studio's sometimes, and took a real interest in my ambitions and plans.

Barbara, it turned out, had a son, Lewis, of eleven or twelve years old. However, Lewis seemed to spend most of his time with his father, so she didn't have much in the way of a life outside work. And with Colin gone, and Jim and Willie now off doing their own thing most of the time, neither did I. So we were company for each other.

Barbara lived in a flat in Islington not too far from the Sadler's Wells theatre, and just around the corner from the old Colin's Music Hall, which was a real throwback to the old music hall days. At that time they were still putting on live shows every week, and on our nights off together we'd occasionally drop in to one of their boisterous old fashioned variety shows. Walking into the noisy, cheerful atmosphere at the Colin's was almost like striding into a noisy, cheerful wild west saloon, with the audience laughing and drinking, and constantly trooping off to recharge their glasses at the long, brightly lit bar which stretched right across the back of the auditorium.

At some time in the middle of the year Barbara's son, Lewis, went off with his father to live in Ireland with his Irish relatives. Now on her own, Barbara gave up her flat in Islington and took a bed-sit in the house in Victoria where Jim, Willie, Dusty and I were staying.

Shortly after she'd settled in with our crowd, the manageress at the Strand Corner House recommended her for a job at Orchard House, which was the London headquarters of Lyons; apparently they needed a waitress to work in their small dining room, to look after their top executives. Since this was a step up the ladder for her, particularly financially, she took the job. The only downside to this being that it was a day job, which meant that she'd be working on days, while I'd be still on nights.

However, as I'd just about had enough myself of being out of step with the rest of London life in this way, this was no real problem. I simply left the Corner House to take a daytime job 'briefly' in the kitchens of the University College Hospital in Gower Street.

Oddly enough, the only thing I can remember now about working there, is the 'coming' and 'going'. This is largely because as I'd go in through the staff entrance I had to walk down a long sloping corridor to basement level. At the bottom of this there was a large metal stand with an upright disc contraption on it about four feet in diameter. The disc had about two hundred numbered holes around the edge, and a long rotating arm in the centre like the hour hand of a clock, but with a sort of peg on the end. To clock on for work you had to rotate the arm and push the peg into the hole near your staff number, and apparently this registered your time of arrival, or departure, somewhere inside the machine.

As a piece of 'Heath Robinson' machinery it was quite fascinating. As a clocking on system, though, it didn't seem to have much going for it, since anyone could walk up and plug in any number they felt like, or any half dozen for that matter. And the poor old machine would be none the wiser. However, since some poor soul must have thought this a natty device to have in the hospital I went along with it; though after my experience of the simple old brass disc system in the Barrow Shipyard, I couldn't help feeling it was a bit over the top.

I stayed at the University College Hospital for no more than five or six weeks before packing it in. I think the reason was simply that I'd finally had enough of mopping floors in kitchens as a way of life, and needed to move on.

However, since I seemed fated to earn my living and pay for my singing lessons by working in either hotels, hospitals or breweries I, almost inevitably, ended up in another brewery. This time it was Truman's Brewery in Brick Lane, just off the Mile End Road away over in the East End of London.

This old brewery really did have its roots away back in London's history, because it was founded in 1666; the year of both the plague, which wiped out thousands of people in the East End at the time, and the Great Fire of London which followed, destroying a huge area of crowded housing and small businesses and to some extent helping to wipe out the aftermath of the plague.

Brick Lane was also at the heart of 'Jack the Ripper's' territory in later years, so if the walls of that old brewery could speak they'd have some pretty awful tales to tell.

As at the Watney's Brewery, my job boiled down to rolling beer barrels about, or I should say – my being by this time a 'professional' beer-roller as it were – 'casks', because that's what they're called in the trade. A beer 'barrel' is actually a 36 gallon cask. The casks by size are a 'Pin' (four and a half gallons), a 'Firkin' (nine gallons), a 'Kilderkin' (18 gallons), a 'Barrel' (36 gallons), a 'Hogshead' (72 gallons, and the largest cask that can be rolled about). There's also one called a 'Butt' (108 gallons = to three barrels), but this is far too large and heavy to be man-handled, and is usually used for static beer storage. There you are, now we 'all' know!

The difference for me at Trumans, however, was that I was now working out in the open as part of a three man 'yard' gang, not down in the cellars, and was rolling 'empty' casks about, not full ones. This is because I was now at the beginning of the beer producing chain and not at the end.

Our job was simply to keep the supply of clean, freshly washed casks flowing down a ramp and onto a conveyor system through a tunnel to the large brewing house over on the other side of Brick Lane. The number and size of casks we had to supply, and the order in which we had to roll them off down the ramp, varied from day to day, so we had to work from a daily order sheet.

Four or five large cask washing machines filled one side of the yard, which were like long, automated production lines. Each of these had about six upward-facing, high pressure spray nozzles placed at intervals along its length, and every cask, large or small, had to pass through the machine from beginning to end, being lifted by automatic arms from one nozzle to the next, until by the time it rolled off at the other end it had been given six thorough washings. These machines

227

only needed three men to operate them, with two loading the casks on at the beginning, and one rolling them off at the end. As this last man tumbled them off, he'd roll them away onto one of the many narrow railway lines set into the yard's concrete floor, leaving them bung-hole down to drain.

Before 'we' could collect them, however, they had to pass a 'smeller's' inspection. This 'smeller', was an experienced yard man who'd been trained to sniff at each bung hole to check for any of six or seven unwanted smells. These included such smells as, sour, mouldy, acid, etc., and were all clear indications that the cask could not be used, and needed to go back for further washing, or special treatment, before it could be used for beer. If the 'smeller' detected any of these he'd simply put an appropriate chalk mark on the cask and roll it to one side to be sorted out.

The three man yard gang I'd found myself in consisted of, 'Sam'; a chirpy, flatcap Cockney about forty years old, 'Jock', a stocky, slightly tubby Scotsman of about the same age, and now me. Both Sam and Jock were seasoned yard men, and easy to get on with.

One of the first things I'd discovered on turning up at Truman's, was that every man working there was allocated two pints of beer a day. This 'had' to be drunk on the premises, and the only way you were allowed to take it home was 'inside you'.

Since I didn't drink I just gave it away, and as Sam was only a moderate drinker, this only left Jock to dispose of it. Fortunately, Jock could have drunk for Scotland, and not only did he take care of my two-pint allocation, but performed the same service for several other non-drinking yard men as well. I began to think after a while that the management had better keep an eye on Jock, or they'd never get any beer out of the gates.

The most astonishing thing about his ability to make Truman's product disappear like magic was that it didn't seem to have any effect on him whatsoever. He never seemed in the least bit tipsy, was always nippy on his feet and full of energy. As well as drinking Truman's dry, he apparently also carried on this mission outside work, helping to do the same for other breweries; and even on his way home from work would often call into their pubs to do his bit for them.

He told me once that the only problem he had with all this, was that if he ever wanted to go out in the evening to the cinema, he had to try and work out a route to get there that didn't involve passing a pub. Since this was virtually impossible, he hardly ever made it to see the films intended, but ended up in some drinking den on the way.

According to the other yard men, the only time they'd ever seen him

228

even remotely intoxicated, was one year on his birthday when he brought in a large bottle of whisky to supplement his usual meagre twelve pint plus daily beer ration. This, apparently, did give him a 'slight' extra 'glow' that day, but that's about all.

Apart from our yard gang, the 'Smeller' and the washing machine crews there were several other yard men pottering around doing various jobs here and there. Jan was a big Polish chap whose English wasn't too good. Still, it was better than our Polish, so we could hardly criticise. Strangely enough he was a skilled Cooper (Cask-maker) and his job was to sort out any of the casks whose steel hoops had become a bit loose; something that happened quite frequently. These hoops which hold the casks together are not actually fastened to the cask, but are jammed on hard as a sort of shrink fit, and so long as there's beer in the cask to swell the oak sides, are almost impossible to move. If a cask has been left empty for too long, however, the oak dries out and shrinks, so one or more of the four hoops can become loose. When that happened it was Jan's job to tighten them up with a hammer and special chisel.

Another rather unlikely-looking two man team, Dan and Bert, also worked around the yard doing general work, and compiling special orders, etc. Dan was a tall, raw-boned sort of chap. Slightly slow, he had a rather vague look about him most of the time, as if his brain was about two steps behind everyone else's. Bert, on the other hand, was a tubby, shortish, bossy sort of chap, who obviously kept the team on track.

Despite the fact that they were constantly losing patience with each other, and in a constant state of argument they also seemed to have a certain awkward sort of rapport which appeared to work. Dan, though a bit slow, was exceptionally strong, and Bert always took a pride in getting him to demonstrate this to the other yard men. Their favourite trick involved Bert, who was a chubby fourteen stone, standing on a shovel while Dan lifted him up as easily as lifting a shovelful of coal.

Apart from his strength Dan was also noted for his odd adventures while trying to negotiate his way home after work. By this time of day, having disposed of a bit more than his fair share of Truman's allocation during his shift, he'd be even more in his own vague dimension than usual. He'd manage to catch the Underground train from East Acton all right, but this was often the last thing he remembered about it, until somebody woke him up and threw him off at his station. Unfortunately, however, there'd occasionally be nobody on the train who knew where he should be thrown off, so he'd wake up somewhere away down the line and have to catch the next train back to where he belonged. This worked out all right so long as he didn't fall asleep again and end up back at East Acton. All this was fairly everyday stuff to Dan, but his crowning achievement, which he'd sometimes talk about, was the time he fell asleep on the train and didn't wake up until the early hours of the morning to find himself in a darkened carriage parked up in the sidings at the terminal.

Like several of the other major breweries in London, Truman's still kept links with their past by using traditional horse drawn drays for 'some' of their fairly close local deliveries, and also up into the nearby City of London. These were partly for keeping up with old tradition, but were also great advertising; as the sight of these massive shires trotting through the London traffic with their beautiful, jangling harnesses and brightly painted beer barrel laden drays were real eye-catching head-turners and drew a lot of attention.

The stables for these magnificent horses were quite near to the yard where we worked, and we'd see them coming back into the nearby loading bay to offload their empty casks after their trips to the city. Sometimes it was quite obvious that the odd drayman here and there was somewhat the worse for wear when he pulled up – having obviously accepted a bit too much hospitality from the various publicans on the way, and he would just sit on his seat contemplating the problem of climbing down off it as something of a challenge which he wasn't too confident about. However, this was apparently quite a common occurrence, so someone would eventually get him down from this towering cliff, and see him and the horse safely back to the stables.

Something which wasn't such a common occurrence, but had happened from time to time apparently, was that a horse would come trotting into the yard with his drayman fast asleep on the seat, having brought the dray on its own across Tower Bridge, right through the busy traffic in the city, and all the way back to the yard with the drayman out to the world all the way.

One thing that had struck me quite early at Truman's was the number of long-serving employees they had. As apart from Jock – who'd been away in the Parachute Regiment during the war, spending much of it in a prisoner of war camp after being captured at Arnhem – most of the men I worked with seemed to have been there for most of their working lives. In fact, it was a bit like working for an old family firm where all the employees were like family retainers. This impression was confirmed one day when I had to go into the main office for some reason, and saw that the walls in the entrance hall were lined with large polished rolls of honour, listing the names of all the past employees who'd done over 'sixty' years continuous service with the company.

This I found pretty astonishing, for two reasons; firstly because sixty years is far longer than the whole of an average working life today, and secondly, because there must have been a couple of hundred names there of men who'd spent this long working solely for Truman's at a time when life expectancy was supposed to be far shorter than it is now.

One other event I remember in the brewery yard that year about this time, was seeing my first ever eclipse of the sun. We'd all known it was coming, of course, because the newspapers had been full of this impending phenomenon for days, warning everybody against trying to look at the sun directly, or even worse through binoculars. However, looking at it through dark glass was apparently all right, so most of us had got hold of broken pieces of brown beer bottle glass from the bottling plant ready for the great moment.

Shortly before the eclipse was due, unfortunately, we were splattered with a great deluge of rain, and thought that as far as we were concerned the whole event was doomed to be a soggy, disappointing wash-out. In the event, however, the sky cleared just in time, and not only that, we now found that we could actually watch the whole of the eclipse quite safely and clearly reflected in the large puddles left in the yard by the rain.

At sometime towards the end of the year I got word from my sister Jean, who was still sharing a flat in Westbourne Park with my oldest sister Joan. Jean now worked in a chemist shop near their flat, and had apparently just been offered an unfurnished flat of her own from one of her elderly customers. As the flat was a bit too big for her on her own, she asked me if Barbara and I would like to share it with her.

This couldn't have come at a better time for us; because with Barbara now working at Orchard House in central London, and me at Truman's away out in the East End, getting to work on the tube would be much easier for the both of us, especially as Westbourne Park tube station was virtually at the end of the street where this flat was.

So we all went to have a look at it, took it on the spot, and moved in within a week. During that week we managed to gather together enough furniture to enable us to move in. Barbara and Jean had single beds in the large bedroom, while I made do with a sort of put-you-up in the lounge; it was all a bit sparse at first, but at least it was a start.

This move to Westbourne Park proved to be one of those unexpected turning points in life for me; especially the connection it gave me with the chemist shop where Jean worked. It turned out that the lady who owned and ran the chemist shop had at one time been a professional singer. Not only that, but in the flat above the shop she had an elderly gentleman tenant, who'd apparently been connected in some way to the old opera companies of the early nineteen hundreds.

When all this came to light, and the chemist learned from Jean about 'my' singing ambitions I was invited along to meet her tenant. When I climbed the stairs to his flat for the first time, it was like walking into an old, crowded Victorian music room, complete with grand piano, and huge lacquer cabinets around the walls that reached almost to the ceiling.

The tall, slim elderly man who welcomed me in, introduced himself as Mr Thomas Fairbairn; a name that meant nothing to me at the time, but which I was soon to learn had been quite a well known one in the world of music and opera some forty or fifty years earlier. In the conversation that followed I gathered that he'd been a member of the 'old' English National Opera Company working as a producer, come singing and dramatic coach. He asked me to sing a few scales for him, then an Italian ballad, and from his enthusiastic reaction to all of these I knew that I'd found my next teacher.

I began studying with him almost immediately, and used to slip around the corner to his flat about twice a week for lessons. Once again I found myself being taught by a real professional, and soon began to feel that I was back on the right track, and moving on from where Maria Linker had left off.

Mr Fairbairn came across as a fairly lonely man, and I got the impression almost immediately that in taking me on as a pupil he was getting almost as much out of it as I was. He'd apparently lost his wife some years earlier, and from the way he talked about her obviously missed her very much. He told me that she'd been born in Germany and was a very fine operatic soprano.

All the time he was coaching me on singing, he'd be constantly regaling me with stories from his time at the English National Opera Company, as well as tales about many of the other famous international singers from the old days he'd worked with, or come across on the way. Names like Alexander Kipnis, the great bass cropped up, and Beniamino Gigli – one of my own favourite tenors. He remembered hearing the great Enrico Caruso in his prime, and even Caruso's great tenor predecessor Tamagno – who'd reputedly possessed one of the most powerful tenor voices ever.

Perhaps his own crowning glory, however, had been the performances of *Hiawatha's Wedding Feast* which he'd dramatised and staged at the Albert Hall for Samuel Coleridge Taylor between the wars.

These had been highly successful, sell-out performances apparently, and he told me that on one of the evenings he'd had a rather odd experience in the foyer just before the performance was due to begin. A rather flamboyant lady swept in and up to the ticket office. He recognised her immediately as the famous operatic diva Nellie Melba. She seemed to be having a bit of an argument with the girl in the ticket office, so he went over to see what was wrong.

"Can I help, Madame Melba?" he asked.

"Yes!" she declared. "This girl tells me that there are no tickets left. Which is ridiculous!"

"I'm afraid she's right," replied Mr Fairbairn.

"Nonsense!" retorted Melba. "Nobody 'ever' sells-out at the Albert Hall!"

"I assure you it 'is' sold out," emphasised Mr Fairbairn. "And has been all week, but I'd be more than happy to let you use my private box, if you wish."

"Definitely not!" retorted Melba. "If I can't pay for my seat I don't want to go in," then she swept out. And that was it; his one and only encounter with the great Nellie Melba.

SOME MAJOR EVENTS OF THE YEAR:

(1) Roger Bannister becomes the first man to run the four-minute mile.

(2) Decision made to develop Gatwick Airport as the second London Airport.

(3) Food rationing ends. Television act sets up ITA.

(4) Vertical take-off 'Flying Bedstead' makes its first flight.

(5) Eclipse of the Sun over England – apparently the next one's not due until AD2115.

(6) McCarthy's 'un-American persecutions' finally banned in the USA.

(7) Films: Walt Disney's *Living Desert* and *On The Waterfront* screened.

233

25

The Winding Road Leads On

1955 (26 years old in July)

My lessons with Mr Fairbairn were by now going well, and I felt that I was learning a lot and moving steadily towards my goal; though unfortunately at a somewhat slower pace than I'd have liked. This was partly because my studying was, as always, on a part-time basis due to my need to earn a living, and partly because of Mr Fairbairn's insistence that I shouldn't try to enter the singing profession until I was absolutely ready.

Of course he was right, but I was getting a bit frustrated with the seemingly endless routine of singing to myself and four walls in empty studios, or occasionally in the flat whenever all the other occupants of the house were safely off the premises. However, a way of slightly relieving this frustration occurred to me one day when I was reading the *Stage* newspaper. The columns in this usually carried notices about auditions for singers from various companies planning shows in London. None of these shows were really of any interest to me at all; but I felt that this needn't stop me from going along to try them out and gain a bit of audition experience, whilst airing a few of my party pieces at the same time.

I therefore started turning up at one or two of these auditions here and there, along with all the stage-struck hopefuls desperately trying to get into 'show biz', and it was a real experience for me. Naturally most of these sang song bits from the most recent shows, or at least attempted to, because quite a few of the hopefuls were pretty obviously no-hopers. There were always the odd one or two, though, who stood out as promising, or even very good. My own efforts, however, always

234

provided a sort of light relief among all these serious aspirations. And although I was usually aware of a sort of 'square-peg' atmosphere out in the auditorium of: "What the devil's 'he' doing here?" They were always polite, and the pianists were usually excellent. So I'd walk off the stage back into anonymity, having enjoyed the experience.

A couple of these exploits, however, stand out from all the others. One of them was, of all places, a nightclub cabaret venue where I've never seen people more bewildered at my offerings before or since. The pianist, however, was a West Indian, and a brilliant player. He gave me a little smile as I collected my music from the piano afterwards, and whispered:

"I really enjoyed that."

"So did I," I answered, as I thanked him and walked off.

The other show-biz audition I had a go at and will never forget, took place at the large theatre in Edgware Road (the Empire, I think?). They were as usual looking for male singers for their forthcoming show. I hadn't taken much notice of what the show was all about, simply because this was of no consequence to me anyway.

I turned up backstage, to find a larger number of young chaps than usual standing about in the wings waiting to do their stuff. Eventually an announcement came over the Tannoy.

"Will all those auditioning please go and get ready."

This was a bit unusual, but since as far as 'I' was concerned I 'was' ready, I ignored it.

A few minutes later my name was called out, and I walked out onto the stage to belt out my offering to them. As I finished, the usual polite "Thank you," echoed up from somewhere out in the darkened auditorium. When I walked back into the wings, however, I suddenly found myself surrounded by beautiful girls in stunningly Glamorous costumes.

'Where the devil did they all come from?' I thought in astonishment. 'There wasn't a sign of them when I went on to sing.' Then a couple of them spoke, and the penny dropped with a thud. These beautiful girls were, if fact, all the young chaps I'd been talking to earlier. I'd been auditioning for a 'flamin' drag show!'

That was one show I was 'especially' glad to be turned down for, and I couldn't get out into Edgware Road quick enough.

During most of this year I was still working at Truman's Brewery with Sam and Jock, and managing to fit all my singing practice and auditioning activities around this.

Babs and I finally decided to make our partnership permanent, and late in the year we got married. We'd occasionally been attending a small Methodist Church in nearby Notting Hill – due no doubt to my Methodist Church experiences when I was evacuated away up in Orton – so this is where the wedding took place on 15th of October.

We decided to spend our honeymoon in Blackpool, a place that Babs had never been to, but which I was familiar with as it was up on the same part of the Lancashire coast as Barrow. At that time Blackpool was the largest seaside holiday resort in Britain, and though it was mainly a family 'day out' sort of place for the people of Barrow, families from all over the North of England and Scotland used to flock there for their summer holidays. On a clear day, when I was a kid in Barrow exploring the beaches of Walney Island, we could often just about make out the famous Blackpool Tower, sticking up like a tiny pencil away down the coast across Morecambe Bay.

Unfortunately, our honeymoon there turned out to be a soggy nightmare. We'd booked a week in a boarding house, which someone had recommended, and caught the train from Euston Station in the rain. The train chuffed and puffed its way northwards through the darkness at what seemed a snail's pace, being delayed umpteen times for reasons we never found out, and arrived late in a rainy Blackpool well after midnight.

The rain seemed to have followed us every step of the way from London, and now soaked the darkened streets of an out of season Blackpool. Somehow we found our way to the boarding house to find it locked up and in darkness. Our banging on the knocker brought the sleepy looking, slightly irate landlady to the door in her dressing gown. Our explanations about the delay simply wafted over her head as she showed us to our room and promptly went back to bed. We'd had virtually nothing to eat all day, apart from a few sandwiches we'd managed to pick up on the way, so were expecting at least a cup of tea; but no such luck.

The room was unheated, which wasn't uncommon in those days, though being so tired we managed a fitful sort of sleep. A bang on the door woke us up early next morning, and we gathered that something was being left on the mat outside the door.

'Ah!' we thought, 'at last a cup of tea.' I opened the door to find one small cup of hot water sitting on the doormat.

"What's this for?" I called out after the retreating figure who'd left it.

"For you to shave with," came the reply. "Breakfast in half an hour."

I'd like to say that things got better after this, but unfortunately they didn't. Far from being glad at having out of season guests, we got the impression we were almost a nuisance who were interrupting their off season activities.

Add to all this the fact that it kept on raining, and very few entertainments or eating places were open in Blackpool, we threw the towel in after two days and set off for Barrow, hoping to spend the rest of our honeymoon more congenially there.

Since I now had none of my 'immediate' family living in Barrow; all of them having moved to London – including Mam, who'd eventually been forced to give up the boarding house. My idea was to seek advice on a boarding house to stay in from the in-laws of my half-brother Charlie. They lived in Ainslie Street, only a few doors away from where Mam's boarding house had been.

As it happened this turned out to be the best move we could possibly have made, because they were not only very pleased to see us, but insisted we go off to see their daughter and Charlie, who'd now got a new house on the outskirts of Barrow, feeling sure they'd be pleased to put us up for the rest of the week.

So this is what we did, and what had started off as a disastrous honeymoon, ended up being a wonderful one spent with Charlie, his wife and two lovely little girls, while at the same time giving me the chance to get to know a branch of our family which I'd previously never known much about.

On our return to London we settled back into the flat with Jean, and slightly different sleeping arrangements. However, this didn't last long as shortly afterwards Jean had an offer to join the NAAFI, and went off to Egypt to work in a canteen serving British forces who were still stationed there after the war had ended.

I resumed my lessons with Mr Fairbairn as usual, but just before Christmas something rather unusual happened to give me an unexpected boost along the way. I was in the middle of a lesson when the phone rang, and when Mr Fairbairn picked it up it turned out to be a call from Dundee, away up in Scotland. I wasn't too surprised at this, as I knew that Mr Fairbairn had a particular connection with Dundee, and spent about a month there every year producing an opera for the local operatic society. He was, in fact, due to go up there for their next production early in the new year.

From what bit of the conversation I could hear I gathered that they were having some sort of problem. After a minute or so of discussion, Mr Fairbairn just said:

"Hang on a minute." Then he turned to me and asked, "How would you like to go up to Dundee and sing a part for them?"

"Really. . !" I exclaimed in astonishment. "Phew. . ! I'll say!"

237

"Right!" said Mr Fairbairn, handing me the phone and going back to the piano. "Just sing a few notes for them."

He then rattled off a few scales that seemed to run up to some exceptionally high notes; which I sang into the phone as ordered. When I'd finished Mr Fairbairn took the phone and asked the Dundee end:

"How did you like that, then?"

Apparently they liked it a lot, especially the extreme high notes, and offered me the job on the spot. I could hardly believe it – after all there can't be many singers who've been offered a major role by singing down a phone to adjudicators 550 miles away.

The reason behind all this turned out to be that the part they were offering me had several high D flats – half a tone higher than a top C – which is usually regarded as the top note in the tenor's range. Because of this, they'd been unable to find a tenor anywhere up there willing to take on the part. And with the opening date for the production only six or seven weeks away, they'd been getting pretty desperate.

The up-side of this for me was to be suddenly offered this wonderful opportunity to make my operatic debut; the down-side, however, being that it only left me six or seven weeks to learn the part from scratch. This wasn't helped by the fact that the opera they were tackling wasn't one of the familiar operas found in the standard repertoire, but a brand new work by a London based Scottish composer named Colin MacCleod Campbell. The name of the opera was *Maid Marian* and the libretto was based, surprisingly for a Scottish composer, on the English Robin Hood legends.

Another thing I discovered, which made this Dundee production pretty special, was that it wasn't only 'my' debut, but the 'opera's' debut as well; since it had never been performed before as a fully staged production; only as a concert version once in London. This, therefore, was to be its 'World Premiere', and as such, the names of all the original cast would be printed in the score – including mine. . .

"Please. . ! No pushing in the queue for autographs."

Also unusual for an opera, was that the roles of both the hero, Robin Hood, and the villain, Prince John, were written for tenors – guess which one I was. . ? You're right! Still, starting off my operatic career as a villain was better than not starting it at all. And it did have the slight compensating factor of not being quite so 'long' a part to learn as the hero Robin Hood; which under the circumstances was just as well.

As Mr Fairbairn was to be the producer and director, he already had

238

a copy of the full orchestral and vocal score. So for me, just as Christmas was approaching, it was now an urgent matter of getting down to learning the part. This I did by going through the role bit by bit with Mr Fairbairn in his flat, and endlessly note bashing on my piano at home.

SOME MAJOR EVENTS OF THE YEAR:
(1) Films: *The Dam Busters* and Disney's *Lady and The Tramp* screened.
(2) Plans made for 12 nuclear power stations in Britain.
(3) New 'Salk' Polio vaccine developed in the USA.
(4) The infamous 'credit squeeze' introduced in Britain.
(5) 'Bill Haley & the Comets' give birth to the Rock & Roll era.

26

North of the Border

At some time in late February, Mr Fairbairn and I set off north on the all-night sleeper from London, and after a brief stop off in Edinburgh to change trains, arrived in Dundee around noon the next day. I'd never been north of the border before, so Scotland was a whole new country to me. We were met at the station by members of the Dundee Operatic Company and driven off to our accommodation. Mr Fairbairn being dropped off at a small hotel in central Dundee, while I was whisked away out to Broughty Ferry in the outskirts. The small commercial hotel I was to stay in was right on the edge of the River Tay Estuary, with the sea and lovely beach directly across the road from the front door.

My room was up on the first floor, and the most abiding memory I have of the hotel itself is that it had a towering grandfather clock on the wide landing just below my room which chimed, somewhat disturbingly every quarter hour, day and night. Still, this soon formed just a sort of musical background to everyday life there, so I eventually got used to it.

The meals were pretty good, and the hotel itself had all mod-cons, so it came as a bit of a surprise when I went out for a walk that first night to find a long row of toilets at the end of a nearby street of small terraced houses. Each loo was locked and carried the number of one of the houses. I'd thought life in Barrow was bad enough, with many houses having their loos out in the backyard, but the thought of having to get up in the middle of the night, take a key off a hook and walk down to the end of the street just to use the loo made the mind boggle. . ! Thank God I'd been billeted in the hotel on the sea front!

We were scheduled to be in Dundee for three weeks in total, with the first two weeks dedicated to rehearsals, and the last to the performances. These rehearsals were, of course, just the 'final' rehearsals as far as the local cast, chorus and orchestra were concerned, because they'd already been rehearsing the opera for several months.

So on the morning following our arrival I made my way into Dundee to meet the rest of the principals and start my first rehearsal at the theatre.

The venue turned out to be a large Gaumont Cinema (former theatre) in Dundee's main street. Like the one I'd seen *Faust* performed in years before in Shrewsbury, it still had all the old theatre dressing rooms, scenery flies, etc., in place behind the cinema screen which had simply been removed for our forthcoming performances.

Mr Fairbairn, who was already well known to everybody there, introduced me to the rest of the cast, including the other tenor who was to sing the part of Robin Hood. He turned out to be from the Covent Garden Opera Company, and had arrived up from London the day before, just as we had. His name was Kenneth Macdonald and I soon found that he possessed a fine lyric tenor voice. Like Mr Fairbairn, he'd worked with the Dundee Opera Company before, so 'unlike me' was no stranger there. However, with 'both' of us being London based tenors working 'north of the border', we hit it off immediately, so rehearsals got under way very well.

For the first couple of days I was working only with the other principals, and had my first chance to see Mr Fairbairn in full flow as a producer, director and musical coach at first hand. Despite the fact that he must have been well into his eighties, now that he was in his real element, he became a dynamo of creative energy, and seemed to know everyone's part better than 'they' did, both musically and dramatically. Furthermore he didn't simply 'advise' them on how to get the most out of their characters, but was constantly demonstrating just how they should deliver a particular line, or how to walk and present the character physically. He even did this with the female characters, and to see him acting as a demure young girl one minute, and a severe old matron the next was pretty incredible.

As a raw newcomer to all this I certainly wasn't spared, and had to put up with quite a lot of stick from my mentor. I felt sure, however, that his putting 'me' through the mill a bit more than the others, was all part of preparing me for a future which he felt sure I was heading for. So I accepted it all with as good a grace as possible, like a patient swallowing grotty medicine, because he knew it was intended to do him good in the long run.

241

l

Although the rehearsals were hard work they were enjoyable, as were the make-up sessions and costume fittings. These gave me a beard, buried me in a magnificent costume of chain mail complete with a sword, stuck a rather splendid crown on my head, and suddenly Prince John was born. When I saw this grandiose figure staring back at me from the mirror for the first time, I could hardly believe it was me.

'Well, I certainly "look" the part,' I thought in astonishment, 'The thing is it's now up to me to make sure I "sing" it as well as I look.' If I'd needed any extra spur in that direction, which fortunately I didn't, this would certainly have provided it.

While I was involved in the rehearsals on 'most' of the days in those first two weeks in Dundee, I was not required on days when they were rehearsing scenes which didn't concern Prince John, so I had a day off here and there to get out and about in the Dundee area. Since Scotland was a whole new world for me it obviously needed exploring, so that's what I did.

Most of my wanderings were in and around Dundee itself, and on one of these free days I was invited out for a meal by another member of the company who was also not needed that day. He just happened to be a policeman which couldn't have been better, because he knew every beat in Dundee like his own backyard. So, after we'd had our meal with his wife and family, he took me out on a short guided tour of this lovely old town.

As we set off, the truth of the old claim about a policeman 'never being really off duty' quickly became obvious. Because as well regaling me with information on the interesting sights of Dundee, he was also throwing in fascinating little asides here and there about the odd dodgy local citizen he'd spot along the way. To me, none of these looked any different from all the other people going about their daily business, so it was like having a secret lid lifted occasionally which separated the dodgy from the un-dodgy.

The one piece of lid-lifting which I particularly remember happened when we were wandering in some gardens near the River Tay Railway Bridge, which snakes out for two miles over to the other side of the estuary. He'd just pointed out the broken piles of the 'old' railway bridge; still sticking up out of the river alongside the present bridge, and was explaining how the old bridge had collapsed one stormy night in 1879, plunging the night train into the depths of the river and killing 79 people, when his attention was diverted again to some middle-aged chap sitting on a bench near the children's play area.

"Hang on a minute," he muttered. "I want to keep an eye on him."

242

So for the next five minutes we wandered casually around the gardens with both of us casting surreptitious glances towards our suspect – my policeman friend knowing 'why', I not being in on his dastardly deeds – could only guess.

Fortunately the chap soon latched on to the fact that he was being watched, got up from his seat, and disappeared through the trees back to the underworld.

All in all it had been a fascinating and unusual morning. I mean, who could have guessed that in coming up to Dundee to sing my first operatic role, I'd end up shadowing paedophiles in a park with the police.

The rehearsals at the theatre were now progressing well. I was growing more and more confident in the role and more importantly, was beginning to sing it well too. The music had proved to be well within my vocal range, even the unusually high top notes, so I was actually starting to enjoy it.

Outside the theatre other unexpected diversions also turned up which really brought home to me the intense Scottishness of this land across the border. On one evening in particular, when we had a short break from rehearsals, I went along with Mr Fairbairn to a sort of Burns Night celebration laid on by some members of the company. Since the 'official' Burns Night of January 25th had already passed, this must have been some special Burns celebration laid on in honour of Mr Fairbairn.

The great pride which the Scots take in Robbie Burns was a real eye opener for me that evening. They even had a piper to pipe in the Haggis, and several of them took turns at reciting many of his best known poems. But the real revelation of the evening was Mr Fairbairn's contribution, which consisted of reciting reams of Burns' poetry from memory, and talking about Burns and his life in a way that held all these avid Scottish Burns' fans absolutely entranced.

On another occasion one of the members of the opera company took Mr Fairbairn, myself and Ken McDonald on a car trip to Pitlochry away up in the Highlands, where they had a Festival Theatre which he thought we'd like to see. Pitlochry turned out to be an attractive touristy place; very popular with summer visitors, when the theatre was a big attraction. As we'd turned up in March, however, the theatre was closed, but as luck would have it, the caretaker (manager or whatever) spotted us trying to peer in through the glass entrance doors. Our driver beckoned him over, told him we were from the theatre in Dundee and he immediately invited us in to have a look around.

The theatre was a lovely little place, but on entering the auditorium

I was pretty astonished to see that the walls and ceiling were completely draped in sheets of cloth.

"It's just like being in a tent," I remarked in bewilderment.

"Because that's what it 'used' to be," explained the man who'd let us in. "The original Festival performances were to be held in a large marquee. And this was so popular, that when they finally built a proper theatre for it, they decided to keep the traditional marquee atmosphere by making the inside look like the old tent."

While this seemed an attractive idea, Ken and I being singers, were both a bit sceptical about what this would do to the acoustics of the place. So, much to the astonishment of our guide, we both spent about ten minutes belting out top notes to check this out. The results seemed OK to the others, but Ken and I both felt – as we'd suspected – that the lack of resonance would make singing there pretty hard work.

On our journey back to Dundee our driver stopped off at a couple of other well known landmarks along the way. One was the Pitlochry river dam which had a 'fish ladder' to enable the salmon to get past the dam on their way up river to the spawning grounds. The Pitlochry fish ladder was a bit special, apparently, as it consisted of a tunnel with a glass panel so that visitors could watch the salmon on their way through. Unfortunately, as with the theatre, we were there at the wrong time of year, so saw no fish.

The other stopping-off landmark was on the edge of a deep ravine with a fast flowing river surging through it. This was the Soldier's Leap, where an English soldier, desperately trying to escape from pursuing Highlanders was reputed to have leapt across the ravine from a high rock; only managing to escape because none of his pursuers were willing to attempt the leap after him. When I stood up on the high rock from where he was supposed to have jumped, I just couldn't imagine how anyone could have leapt off this high point with any hope of landing on the far bank away below, without breaking most of the bones in his body. Still, as the alternative was to be cut to pieces by the claymores of the fearsome Scots chasing him, it would probably have seemed worth having a go.

Back in Dundee the rehearsals continued as before, though getting more and more intense as the opening day of performance was drawing near. Before this arrived, however, I had the chance of one more unexpected diversion, when a travelling salesman up from Edinburgh arrived at the hotel in Broughty Ferry. He told me that he dealt in household wares, crockery etc, and came up once a month to do the rounds of all his village-shopkeeper clients throughout this part of Scotland.

"What a great way to explore the Highlands," I remarked.

"I suppose it is," he replied, seeming pleased at my interest. "I'll tell you what!" he added. "If you've got any spare time why don't you have a run out with me tomorrow?"

As it happened I 'was' free the next day, so that was it.

We set off early the next morning, with him wondering how much trade he would be able drum up among the canny Highland villagers on this trip; and me eager to see how it was all done, while enjoying a free guided tour of the beautiful scenery at the same time. We drove on and on along rambling country roads through hilly woodland for mile after mile, calling in at every village on the way large enough to boast its own shop. At these business stop-offs, my salesman guide proved to be a really gifted 'charmer' with his customers, especially the ladies, and was greeted everywhere almost like a member of the family. This was obviously a great sales technique, because after dropping off the deliveries from previous orders he'd taken, he always seemed to wheedle out plenty of new orders to make his next trip worthwhile.

We'd covered quite a large area of that part of Scotland during the morning, before finally ending up at the busy fishing port of Stonehaven away up on the North Sea Coast where we had a welcome meal break. He then did the rounds of his last few customers there, before we motored off all the way down the coast road, back to Dundee. A really great 'free' day out touring the beautiful countryside of Scotland, with the added bonus of watching a natural born salesman in full flight.

At long last opening night finally arrived, and I turned up at the theatre to find it now buzzing with a noisy atmosphere of excitement and expectation. People were milling about everywhere; checking out their costumes, queuing up at the make-up room, or just generally chattering nervously, wishing each other luck and expressing the hope that it was all going to go off well. The odd distant voice could also be heard warming up in the dressing rooms – a sound that was absolutely evocative of what I'd always imagined life in an opera house to be.

I was soon caught up in all this nervous activity, and before I'd had time for the nerves to start jangling, I was costumed, made up and sitting in my dressing room ready to sing the role of Prince John for real at last. Almost immediately, I heard the distant sound of the orchestra striking up and the whole adventure was finally under way.

As Prince John didn't appear until well into the opening scene, I just sat in the dressing room listening to the singing of the chorus and other principals coming through on the Tannoy, and waiting for my own call. After all the rehearsals, this couldn't come soon enough, and as the hollow whisper of the stage manager's voice broke through above the music:

"Prince John, on stage please!"

I was out of the door and up in the wings like a cork out of a bottle. Strangely enough, I didn't feel particularly nervous; just eager to get involved in what we'd been rehearsing for so long.

Suddenly, the musical build up to the Prince's entrance began. I could hear everyone on stage rushing about excitedly, calling to each other:

"Prince John is coming! Prince John is coming. . !"

The next moment I strode purposefully through onto the stage, to find myself standing imperiously on top of a flight of stone steps in an arched doorway. A vast sea of faces was staring up at me from the darkened depths of the huge, packed auditorium; while the milling crowd of singers on stage were bowing and giving forth with greetings, also with their eyes fixed on me. Hardly a subdued entrance for my first solo appearance on the operatic stage.

Oddly, I still don't remember feeling particularly nervous. This was undoubtedly largely due to the fact that we were so well rehearsed that things just fell into place. But also, I suspect, partly due to the 'fools rush in' principle – I simply wasn't 'experienced' enough to feel nervous.

As my musical cue arrived I simply let rip with full voice exactly as I'd done in rehearsal, only this time with such a large audience in front of me, I now felt a real sense of performance.

The whole opera then rolled on just as we'd rehearsed, with the packed house seeming to enjoy it and giving us a very enthusiastic reception all the way.

Suddenly, it seemed, the performance was over and the curtain came down to genuine applause on what everybody agreed had been a very satisfactory first night.

The next day, when the local newspapers appeared, they gave the performance an excellent write-up, with every one of the principals being given their own encouraging mention. What particularly pleased me about this, was that I'd not only been given my first ever newspaper write-up, but that they'd singled me out as a young singer whose extreme high notes made me destined for a fine future career.

From here onwards the daily performances went by with pretty much the same sort of enjoyment and excitement for us on stage, and encouragement from the Dundee audiences out front. Almost before I'd had time to 'really' take it all in, the curtain came down on the last night, and it was all over.

The following day it was an early start on our long train journey south, back to the realities of everyday London.

27

Back to the Grindstone

I now found myself back to Earth in London trying to pick things up from where I'd left off three unbelievable weeks before. And since I'd given up my job at the brewery before heading off for Dundee, it was a case of, 'Where do I go from here?'

After the last three weeks as a singing 'professional', I didn't feel inclined to go plunging straight back into yet another odd job in London. However, the bills had to be paid; and although Babs was still working at Orchard House which was a big help, I had to find some way of earning a living again; preferably in some way helpful towards becoming a 'full time' professional singer.

Fortunately, the answer came quicker than I'd expected. I happened to read an article somewhere about Butlin's Holiday Camps, in which they went into detail about the 'Redcoats'. Although I'd 'heard' of these Redcoats before, up to this point I'd known little about them. From the article, however, I gathered that they were a cross between hosts and entertainers, and more interestingly, that quite a number of well known singers and comedians had originally honed their talents as Butlin's Redcoats.

While this didn't exactly seem as if it would lead me down 'my' particular road, I thought it might be a useful way of temporarily earning a living, while gaining more experience as a professional singer into the bargain. In any case, it would be a heck of a lot better than mopping greasy floors in steamy kitchens. I therefore mentioned this idea, rather diffidently, to Mr Fairbairn at my next lesson.

"That could be just the thing," he replied much to my surprise.

"Really?" I declared relieved. "Right. . ! I'll try to find out where to apply then."

"Don't worry about that," replied Mr Fairbairn. "Leave it to me, I think I know just the right person."

It turned out that Mr Fairbairn's 'person' was a certain Major Green; a longstanding acquaintance from his theatrical days, who just 'happened' to be a personal friend of Billy Butlin himself. With such impressive, high-flown connections it was no surprise that the answer 'yes' came back almost immediately. What 'was' a surprise, however, was that even though most of Butlin's staff for the coming season had apparently already been engaged, I was still given the option of choosing 'any' Butlin's Camp I liked, and could start there at the opening of the season in a few weeks time. As if this wasn't enough, they'd obviously got wind of the fact that Babs was in the catering trade – presumably from Mr Fairbairn – and offered her a job as a dining hall supervisor if she wished to come along for the season as well.

As this would be a totally new venture for 'both' of us, Babs was just as keen on going as I was. And since Butlin's had seaside camps all over the country to choose from, we quickly settled on Clacton, simply because it was the closest one to London.

At some time in late April we arrived in Clacton by train to start our first summer season anywhere. Never having seen a Butlin's Holiday Camp before, we were pretty astonished by its sheer size. Covering a huge area stretching right along the beach, just beyond the pier, it looked to us almost like a small town in its own right, and once through its large entrance gate we found ourselves amid what seemed acres of solidly built chalets, plus a theatre, cinema, ballroom, concert hall, dining hall, swimming pool, sports centre, tennis courts and more.

Having been told previously that we'd be going to the camp right at the start of the season, I was a bit surprised to find it already buzzing with happy holidaymakers. However, I let this go as not being all that important. We were here now, and that's all that mattered.

When we reported to reception, though, I was again slightly bewildered by a slight coolness towards me I detected by one or two of the other Redcoats there. Not towards Barbara, but to me personally. When one of the female Redcoats was detailed to take us off to the stores to be fitted out with our uniforms, and shown to our chalet. I took advantage of the right moment to bring this up with her. At first she seemed a bit reluctant to make any comment, but eventually admitted there was a reason for this, and told me that during the previous week one of their male Redcoat colleagues – who'd apparently been a popular chap – had been transferred to another camp to make room for me, even though he didn't really want to go.

While I was somewhat taken aback by this, and felt pretty sorry for the chap, I didn't feel particularly guilty about it, simply because it was none of 'my' doing, and in fact I'd never had the slightest inkling this was going on. However, for me it was one more lesson learned – namely that when 'influence' plays a part, for every 'winner' there's always a 'loser'.

One other thing we discovered on that first day, was that with Babs being a 'Blue Coat Supervisor', and I a mere 'Redcoat Host Entertainer', she'd be on a higher wage than I was – which pleased her no end.

The day after our arrival we were both pitched head long into camp activity. She to take over a section of the large dining hall, with about a dozen girl waitresses under her, and I being shunted about everywhere with different, experienced Redcoats trying to get the hang of the place. This meant that from that moment on we didn't see an awful lot of each other during the daytime; apart from briefly at meal times when I'd be sitting at my allotted table acting as mealtime host to four or five campers, and she'd be busy supervising her flock of young waitresses.

For Babs to even 'think' of taking on such a position was a real tribute to the strength of her personality, because she was actually dyslexic and unable to read or write. Even having to sign her own name in public would bring her out in a cold sweat. How she managed to be a waitress never ceased to amaze me, since being able to write down the customer's orders was such an essential part of the job. However, as so often seems to happen, nature had compensated for this by giving her an astonishing memory. No matter how many orders were thrown at her she would remember them all perfectly; including the table and customer who'd made them. She could probably have described what they were all 'wearing' as well if you asked.

As for myself, the first instruction I'd been given by the Redcoat manager on arrival was that I, like all the other Redcoats, had to head for the office first thing each morning to discover which duties I'd been detailed for that day. These were pinned up on the notice board, and could be anything from helping out with the outdoor field sports and swimming pool, organising a snooker tournament in the sports hall, being an usher at the Repertory Theatre or a host in the Dance Hall, etc. It soon became obvious that whatever 'else' life at the camp was, it certainly wasn't going to be dull.

However, I was soon beginning to wonder where and when my

singing was going to fit into all this. After all, 'that' was my main reason for coming here. The nearest I'd got to exercising my vocal cords 'musically' so far, had been when I was detailed to run a sing-along for about two-hundred happy, beer-guzzling souls in the 'Jolly Roger Bar', which was not exactly what I'd had in mind. Not only that, when I turned up to enter this lion's den I discovered that I had to do it on my own, with the help of only the bar pianist; and that the session was expected to last about one and a half hours.

Since I knew no more than three of four songs which could be even 'remotely' regarded as sing-a-long material, the prospect was pretty daunting to say the least. However, there I was standing on the platform, so decided that the only thing I 'could' do was start off with a couple of the better known of my own 'tenor songs'. At least 'these' would prove my credentials as a 'genuine' singer. Where things would go from there on was anybody's guess.

To my great relief 'O sole mio', 'Because', and 'The Rose of Tralee', went down an absolute treat with my large, semi-inebriated audience. So having got them on my side, I then threw in 'Bella Notte', from the film *Lady and the Tramp*, Nat King Cole's 'Mona Lisa', and 'Lonely Ballerina', all of which were really popular songs at the time with lovely, singable melodies, so also went down well with my happy, noisy audience; particularly 'Bella Notte' and 'Mona Lisa', both of which I had to sing about three times.

Although this helped to fill in 'some' of that one and a half hour marathon looming before me, having now exhausted my repertoire of 'popular' ballads, it still left a long way to go. Fortunately, the pianist was an experienced bar player, so began rattling off all the popular sing-along tunes, some of which I was able to join in with. And as the audience got happier and louder I decided to try dragging one or two of the rowdier ones up onto the stage, thrust the mike into their hands and let them have a go. In this way the whole sing-along session miraculously passed by, until finally it was all over – the longest one and a half hours I'd ever spent in my life.

Once clear of the lion's den, I vowed that I'd never be caught out like that again, and that on our next day off, it would be a case of, down to the music shop in Clacton to stock up on some of the other more 'singable' of the popular ballads of the day.

By this time I'd also gathered along the way that as well as the likelihood of being pitched into other such 'Jolly Roger' situations; by simply being a 'Redcoat' I'd be on duty (or on call), virtually from first thing in the morning until last thing at night. In fact, if you were 'on camp', even on your day off, you were regarded as being 'available' to help out if the need arose. Fortunately, these emergency call-outs usually only happened when sudden rain washed out a lot of the outdoor activities, forcing a hurried scramble to set up indoor activities to take their place.

Finally, one morning, I was detailed to report to the main theatre for a rehearsal of something called *Pot Pourri*. This was apparently going to be a regular, once a week, light musical concert by the resident orchestra, which was to include several instrumental soloists from among the orchestral musicians, plus myself as the one and only singer. At last I was going to get a chance to do some proper singing.

I duly turned up at the appointed time clutching my music case, to find them already well on with their orchestral rehearsal. Simply walking back into a genuine musical atmosphere again was a real treat for me, so I just sat in the stalls to listen. I eventually presented a selection of my songs to the conductor.

"You realise that it's only a 'light music' concert," he remarked looking through my offerings quizzically, "so none of these heavier things would really be suitable."

"That's all right," I replied. "What about the others?"

"Well, 'O sole mio' would be fine," he said, "and 'The Rose of Tralee', I think. I'm sorry it's only two," he apologised, "but because we've got several instrumental solos to fit in as well there won't be time for more than that."

"Oh!" I replied, feigning the slight disappointment I sensed he expected. "That'll be all right I suppose." And even as I said it I was suddenly struck by the ludicrous contrast of being apologetically restricted to two here, whereas in my previous singing effort at the Jolly Roger, a 'hundred and blinkin' two' would have been barely adequate – a rapid rise from the ridiculous to the sublime if ever there was one.

However, I ran through my allotted 'two' to everyone's satisfaction, then got back to my other Red-coating duties.

On the night of our first concert I arrived fairly early, even though I knew I wouldn't be on for the first twenty minutes or so, and sat in the dressing room listening to the orchestra on the Tannoy. Suddenly I got my call through the speaker and, as I set off for the stage I heard the orchestra strike up with the Dam Busters' March, which I knew was the orchestra's big showpiece before my spot, and I stood in the wings listening to it. It was a pretty rousing piece of music, and rather a nervous one to be following, especially as the tumultuous applause at the end indicated that I was about to walk on stage to an absolutely packed house. Suddenly it all went quiet, and the next second the intro

251

to 'O sole mio' was ringing through the theatre and I strode out onto the stage with my fingers crossed hoping to do it justice.

Fortunately, I needn't have worried, because as soon as I opened my mouth to sing the notes just poured out effortlessly, and I found myself instantly enjoying the experience. Both of my offerings went down really well with the audience, and before I knew it I was taking my bows and walking back into the wings with great relief that my first serious singing performance at Butlin's had gone down so well.

One of the most pleasing spin-offs for me about both this concert, and the Jolly Roger marathon, was that I now found myself being 'recognised', not only by the campers – who'd often buttonhole me around the camp to say how much they'd enjoyed hearing the songs – but even more importantly by my fellow Redcoats, who now accepted that I was there on 'merit', whatever doubts they may have had at the time of my arrival at the camp.

As for myself, I'd already discovered that virtually all the Redcoats at the camp had some definite qualification for the job. Some were musical entertainers or singers like myself; some were simply good 'hosts' who could get on with people and organise events etc; while others were skilled in some branch of sport.

One of the latter was Sammy Sullivan, an ex-professional light-heavyweight boxer, who just happened to live in the next chalet to ours, so I got to know him pretty well. Sammy came from a well known boxing family, and his older brother, Johnny Sullivan, had actually been the middleweight champion of England.

Sammy told me that at one time he'd been involved in touring all over Britain with a boxing booth, and had quite a few tales to tell about his experiences. They'd apparently go from town to town, setting up their boxing ring in a large marquee at funfairs. They'd then fill the marquee with paying customers to watch the team of boxers putting on a few 'preliminary' demonstrations among themselves to warm things up. Then they'd get to the main purpose of there being there, which consisted of throwing out a challenge to all the local boxers or hard men who fancied their chances, to get up into the ring and have a go. The bait being that any man who could last for three rounds with one of the team would win a worthwhile purse.

Despite the fact that they always got plenty of local hopefuls eager to get their jackets off and have a go, virtually none of these ever got the money, simply because the booth manager always made sure that the particular boxer they pitted against each of these hopefuls was more than a match for him in size and strength.

I say 'virtually', because Sammy told me about one occasion they actually did have to pay out. This happened when they were on a tour of Ireland. It was Sammy's turn in the ring, and he being one of the heaviest of the boxing team, it was usually his job to deal with the bigger of the challengers. On this occasion he was just waiting in the ring for his opponent to appear when a big, brawny chap began climbing into the ring.

"As soon as I saw him," explained Sammy, "I knew there was something familiar about him. Then as he turned to face me the truth suddenly dawned; it was Paddy Slavin, the heavyweight champion of Ireland. The next minute he was coming at me like a tank, and I've never moved so fast in my bloody life. I back peddled round and round that ring like a mad hare so fast for three rounds that he couldn't lay a glove on me. . . He got his money all right, which didn't please the boss, but at least 'I' was still in one piece."

I would often bump into Sammy first thing in the morning outside our chalet when I was off to the office to check my duties for the day. It was at these meetings that I first noticed a certain vagueness about him which made me suspect that he may have taken a few more punches during his career than he ought to have. More than once after saying good morning he'd frown and ask:

"What am I doing today?"

"I don't know, Sammy," I'd reply. "You've got to go and look at the notice board."

"Notice board?" he'd repeat vaguely. "What notice board?"

"The one by the office," I'd reply. "It gives you your duties for the day."

"Ah!" he'd murmur as his thoughts began to sort themselves out. "That's right. Is that where you're goin'?"

"Yes." I'd reply. "Come on," and off we'd go together.

There were other little incidents which I'd heard about from others, which unfortunately seemed to confirm my own suspicions. Apparently he'd been put on evening hosting in the dance hall a couple of times, but they had to take him off this particular duty because he seemed to get the idea that he was there as a sort of 'bouncer', and when he thought that one of the campers was beginning to get a bit rowdy, he'd go over and threaten to 'stick one on him' – which didn't 'quite' fit in with the 'happy-go-lucky' spirit of a Butlin's Holiday Camp.

This was a great pity, because underneath all of this confusion Sammy was a really nice, friendly bloke.

As well as Sammy, one or two other well known sports personalities turned up at the camp. One I particularly remember was the table tennis star Diane Rowe, who along with her sister held the Ladies World Doubles Championship. Why she was there without her sister I never knew. I personally came into contact with her when I was detailed – in true 'square pegs in round holes style' – to organise a table-tennis tournament in one of the sports halls. I arrived there to find this very young girl waiting for me. She introduced herself as Dianne Rowe – something that I'd gathered the moment I set eyes on her because of all the photos I'd seen of her and her sister in the newspapers.

She told me that 'she' (a world champion) was there to help 'me' (who didn't know one end of a table tennis bat from the other) to run a table tennis tournament. Images of my 'Jolly Roger' nightmare instantly flashed before me, only this time I wasn't going to be able to sing my way out of it. It simply looked like being a case of the sublime leading the ridiculous.

Unfortunately, there was no way I could bluff my way out of it either, so I simply had to confess that I was somewhat 'less' than a table tennis wizard, so would be relying pretty heavily on her.

Fortunately she saw the funny side of this, and between us we managed to scrape together some sort of tournament between the fairly large number of keen players who'd gathered, both to meet her and to have a go at thrashing the daylights out of each other on the tables.

I had a similar experience a little while later in the snooker hall (why me? I was beginning to wonder), when the world billiards champion, John Pulman, paid a short visit to us in Clacton. The purpose of this was for him to combine a few billiards and snooker demonstrations with a tournament between all the avid snooker fans on the camp. By this time I was beginning to get quite competent at making the most of my incompetence. Although in this case I actually 'did' know one end of a snooker cue from the other – if only just.

To my relief, as with Diane Rowe, John Pulman turned out to be a friendly, easy to get on with professional, and we got through the tournament with no problem.

My days as a sporting tournament organiser finally came to an end one day when I was detailed off to organise a tournament out on the tennis courts. Tennis was a sport I'd never played in my life, so I knew even 'less' about this than table tennis or snooker. It seemed pretty obvious to me now that my somewhat less than auspicious career as a sporting mastermind was taking an even deeper, possibly fatal dive than ever. Fortunately, however, this tennis outing turned out to be a rather lower key affair than the previous two. There were no celebrities involved, and only a handful of racquet wielding campers turned up.

So we had a little chat between us as to who would play who; during which I declined their offer that I should take part in the ball belting procedures – out of modesty, of course; and that was it. I just left them to get on with their playing, doing their own umpiring, and deciding who won. So everyone went back to their chalets in time for tea quite happily in the end.

Our *Pot Pourri* show was by this time quite an established musical evening each week, and although quite enjoying the challenge of all the other activities, it was *Pot Pourri* that kept me in touch with the main reason I'd come to the camp in the first place.

However, there was now one other weekly show at the theatre which I'd become involved with – though not as a performer. This was a top class 'Variety Show', which once a week featured well known acts from London; TV comedians, singers, dance acts, etc. I came to be involved in this when they were having trouble finding someone to operate the spotlight from away up in the back of the gallery. This powerful beam of light, which could flood the whole stage with light, or focus down to illuminate a pair of dancers in a circle of light as they whirled around the stage, or even focus right down to a 'pin spot' on the face of a singer on a darkened stage, was a crucial lighting effect for many of the acts. Unable to find anyone else to operate this fascinating device, they decided for some reason to ask me if I'd do it. Naturally I jumped at the chance; after all, operating the spotlight from the gallery of a theatre is not something that comes around more than once in a lifetime; in fact, for millions of people it probably never comes around at all.

On the morning of the next Variety Show, I spent about an hour up in the gallery with the stage electrician, getting some tuition on how to work this fascinating piece of equipment. It looked just like a two foot long, by one foot wide searchlight and was mounted on a swivel so that it could be easily directed at any point on the stage away below. Although it worked by electricity it had no light bulbs in it, just two carbon rods placed end to end on two separate, movable mountings, but separated by a gap of about two inches. When the electricity was switched on nothing would happen so long as this gap was left between them. If the carbon rods were wound nearer together, however, a point would be reached when the electricity would strike across the gap in an arc, giving a continuous, intensely bright white light. This would be maintained so long as the carbon rods were kept close enough to keep the arc flowing across the gap between them. Wind them apart a fraction, however, or let the carbon rods burn down too far and its light would shut off.

That evening, at my first attempt at doing it for real, I had the stage electrician with me to keep me on track. After that, however, I was on my own, trying to keep all these visiting celebrities firmly on the end of my great beam of light, and following their lighting cues in the way that 'they' wanted it to be. So from then on I was spending 'two' of my evenings each week at the theatre.

The season at Butlin's felt almost as if it was going on for ever, but then quite suddenly it dawned on me that things seemed to be running down. The number of campers was growing steadily less every week, until the point was reached when the full complement of Redcoat staff were no longer needed. The outcome was pretty obvious, and with about three weeks of the season left to go, the management began laying Redcoat staff off. As it turned out I was fairly lucky in that I didn't get my marching orders until about a week before the camp's final closure.

Babs was even more lucky as they asked her to stay on right to the end because of all the clearing up that would be needed in the dining areas. At first she wasn't too keen on this, but we both agreed it would be a good idea, as it would give her an extra week's pay, which could be handy.

I finally packed my bags and set off back to London alone to wait for Babs; having enjoyed Butlin's, but glad to be getting back to the centre of things once again.

28

Picking Up the Threads Again

Now back in the flat and unemployed, my first priority while waiting for Babs was to set about finding myself a job again to pay the bills. However, London being London, there was no lack of opportunity. I somehow didn't fancy going back to any of the old type of jobs, so I cast around for something a bit different, and soon spotted an advert that seemed worth a shot. It was for a job at a large branch of the 'International Stores' in Baker Street, central London. They were apparently looking for a male assistant to look after their veg counter, and as both the pay and the hours seemed pretty good I went along to see them.

The manager, Mr King, came across as a decent sort of chap who I felt straight away I could get along with. However, when he told me that the job entailed not only 'selling' all the various types of veg, but running the counter completely, including doing all the ordering from the suppliers, presenting the displays, keeping the records, etc., I had to admit that I knew nothing about all this.

"Don't worry!" he declared, much to my surprise. "I can teach you all that."

"Well, in that case," I answered, intrigued at again learning something new, while at the same time earning my living, "I'll take it. When do you want me to start?"

"Tomorrow morning, if you can," he replied.

And that was it. I'd hardly been home five minutes and I'd landed myself with what looked like being an interesting job, which not only paid good money, but had working hours that would fit in perfectly with my singing lessons with Mr Fairbairn, and my evening practice sessions at Weeks' Music Studios – which were only about fifteen minutes walk away from the shop, on the other side of Oxford Street.

Once I'd started the job I soon learned why he'd been so keen to get a fit, able bodied man to run the veg counter; it was a job that called for quite a bit of heavy lifting and humping stuff about, especially when taking deliveries of sacks of spuds, boxes of fruit and the like. All of this Mr King had been forced to do himself before my arrival, as well as managing everything else in the large shop, simply because there were no other able bodied men on the premises. The International Stores being such an old established shop, most of the staff looked as if they'd been there for donkey's years, and the majority of these were women. The only two other men on the counters were not exactly 'able' bodied; one being elderly, and the other, though quite young, was rather small, and not in the best of health.

Shopping in those days was very much different to what it is today. Our shop in Baker Street, like every other grocery shop of the time, was laid out with several separate counters, each with its own counter assistant and till serving only certain items. This meant that shopping could be a pretty long-winded business – especially at busy times. Because to get all the items they wanted, the customers had to plod from one counter to another, queuing up and paying separately at each one.

There was one counter for bread and cakes, another for fresh meat, another for dairy products – eggs, butter, cheese, etc., one for bacon and cooked meats, another for tinned goods, one for tea, sugar and coffee – which had to be ground on the spot as there was no such thing as 'instant' coffee at that time. I particularly remember this coffee machine, because when it was roasting and grinding away in full flow it filled the whole shop – and the street outside – with such a delicious, overpowering aroma of coffee that you could almost lean on it.

Finally, at the end of the line, there was 'me' on the veg counter trying to sell my spuds, cabbages, fresh fruit, etc., to all the mainly 'posh', middle-aged, ladies of Marylebone. Most of these were quite pleasant, but there was the odd one here and there, who'd breeze in with a superior air intent on treating you like one of their below-stairs servants. The other staff had obviously learned to accept these types as being all part of the job, but that didn't wash with me, I'm afraid, and on a couple of occasions I objected to their attitude, and flatly refused to serve them. At these times Mr King, who being the manager had to indulge these old biddies, usually came to the rescue. Giving me a little wink and taking over serving them himself.

One of these genteel ladies I particularly remember, came in one day complaining bitterly about some potatoes I'd apparently sold her the day before.

"Why, what's wrong with them?" I asked in bewilderment as she tipped the potatoes out of her bag onto the counter.

"Well, just look at them!" she declared. "They're all the wrong shape."

"Really?" I asked staring at them curiously, wondering what I was missing. "They look just like normal potatoes to me."

"Of course they're not!" she insisted, obviously frustrated at my lack of expertise on such a vital subject as the shape of potatoes. "Just look at these two here, they look like a pair of great flat feet."

"Well, I'm afraid that's just the way they grow in the fields, madam," I shrugged, beginning to wonder if she thought they were made in a factory, and that the moulding machines had gone wrong.

Fortunately, at that moment Mr King appeared on the scene, so I left him with the job of finding her some potatoes that 'were' the right shape – whatever that was.

Being in the rather posh area of Marylebone our shop offered a delivery service to any customer living in the vicinity of the shop. Our delivery service was in itself a bit special, since it consisted of one delivery 'boy', George (about forty years old), whose delivery vehicle was a two wheeled, upright sack-barrow. George would stack the boxes of groceries on his sack-barrow every day, and set off bravely through the wild jungle of London traffic pushing it before him. This in itself would have been worthy of a medal, but what made it even more special, was that George was registered blind. He could hardly see anything at all more than four feet away from him; and to read the customer's name off his delivery sheet, he'd have to stop and squint at it about an inch from his nose. To see him weaving his way through the busy Marylebone traffic, pushing the sack-barrow with one hand, while waving his white stick in the other was a sight to behold. Despite all this dicing with death, however, George somehow managed to survive, and get all the boxes of groceries to their correct doorsteps every day – though how much traffic chaos he left in his wake in the process, I can't imagine.

All during this fascinating time at the International Stores I'd been continuing my lessons with Mr Fairbairn, as well as managing to get down to Weekes' Music Studios most evenings to do my practising. I'd also been invited, along with Mr Fairbairn, to spend two or three enjoyable musical evenings at the home of Major Green; the man who'd been instrumental in arranging the season at Butlin's for Babs and myself. Strangely enough, Major Green and his wife lived in a rather posh apartment block right near the Baker Street Station, only a stone's throw from the International Stores, where I was dishing out fruit and veg all day – possibly to some of their neighbours.

On these special musical occasions there'd usually just be Major Green and his wife, a few of their friends – one of whom was a very good lady pianist – Mr Fairbairn, and myself. I was obviously the singer of the group, and together with the lady pianist we got through quite a number of Italian and German songs, plus her piano pieces, over the course of each evening.

The thing I enjoyed most about these was feeling that they reminded me strongly of similar evenings I'd read about in the biographies of some of my old singing heroes like John McCormack, and Enrico Caruso. In their day singing at such social evenings was quite a regular part of their professional calendar.

There was also a certain amount of quiet discussion on the side between Major Green, Mr Fairbairn and myself about what could be done to help my singing career on its way. Major and Mrs Green, I'd discovered, were the parents of Hughie Green, whose talent show, *Opportunity Knocks*, was one of the most popular shows on television at the time.

"Why don't you have a try on the show?' suggested Major Green at one stage. "I feel sure that you'd have a pretty good chance of winning if you did. And think what a boost that would give your career."

Unfortunately, although I was very grateful for this offer of help, I wasn't too keen on the idea, as I felt it would be heading me off more in the direction of 'Show Business', than the world of opera, so I reluctantly turned the offer down.

There was another suggestion made, however, that sounded more interesting. This concerned the possibility of arranging a few auditions for me, which they thought 'might' lead me more in the direction I wanted to go. They didn't say who these auditions would be for, but after the way Major Green had arranged our season at Butlin's I decided to give it a go; if only for the experience.

The first of these auditions turned up a couple of weeks later when I was invited to attend an audition being held by the Jack Hilton Organisation somewhere in central London. Since the Jack Hilton Organisation was one of the big names at the time in the theatrical/musical world, it proved that Major Green was not only being true to his word, but true to form as well.

Having managed to get time off from the shop, I turned up at the address I'd been given to find myself in a small first floor waiting room at what seemed like a suite of offices. There were two other people already in the waiting room, a man and a strikingly pretty petite blonde. They seemed to be together, and I assumed they were aspiring auditionees like myself. There was little time for conversation, however, so apart from telling me they were piano duettists I learned nothing about them before they were called in to the audition room, leaving me on my own. Almost immediately, the sound of beautifully played, dynamic piano music came echoing from the other side of the door, flooding the waiting room with sound. And although I enjoyed it, I couldn't help feeing slightly apprehensive that they were going to be a pretty hard act to follow.

I didn't have much time to worry about this, however, before there was a break in the music, and the next moment the pretty blonde came hurriedly out into the waiting room looking slightly agitated and closing the door behind her.

"God, these pants are killing me," she exclaimed, hoisting up her skirts to waist level and adjusting her underwear before dropping her skirt with a great sigh of relief, and hurrying back into the audition room.

I just sat there staring in disbelief.

"Phew. . !" I gasped when I'd got my breath back. 'Well it was worth coming here today just for that. If my singing goes OK too, that'll be a bonus.'"

In the event I did sing quite well – once my blood pressure had dropped to normal. But I still had the uncomfortable feeling throughout, that this was not taking me down the road I wanted to go, so I wasn't really bothered about the outcome.

As to the pianists, I don't know what happened to them after this, but I was told later that the male pianist in the duo was actually Richard Bonynge, Joan Sutherland's husband, who at that time was trying to make a musical career of his own as a duo pianist. How true this was I never found out, but he did, of course, become well known as Joan Sutherland's own personal musical director, and eventually a conductor in his own right.

A second of these introductory contacts arranged by Major Green arrived a little while later, but this time it didn't contain details of an audition, just a phone number which I was to ring to 'arrange' one. To my astonishment the number was that of the office of the man who was at that time the director of the London Palladium.

Once again I found myself wondering why the heck I was constantly being given these wonderful opportunities in a direction I most definitely didn't want to go, when London must have been swarming with young show-biz hopefuls who'd give their eye-teeth for half the chances I was getting.

However, since those arranging all this had obviously put themselves out quite a lot on my behalf, I felt I had no option but to go along with it all – for the moment at least.

The problem this time though, was that having no phone at home, and no access to one at the shop; not for such private conversations, anyway, it had to be a public phone box. As the appointed time approached I managed to slip away from the veg counter to the nearest phone box; having made sure that I had plenty of the right coins to feed it with.

Dead on time I fed the slot with coins, dialled the number, and after explaining who I was to the girl who answered was told to hold the line. The next moment a friendly male voice came on the line, and I found myself talking to one of the most important and well known men in the London theatre world.

Strangely enough I immediately felt at ease with him, and was soon chatting away in a perfectly relaxed manner. He seemed genuinely interested in what I'd done so far in the profession, and what my plans were for the future. But although I tried my best to sound enthusiastic about the show business world in general, while skating carefully around what my real singing aims were, in the end I felt so guilty about repaying his very obvious kindness by deceiving him in this way, that I simply had to put my cards on the table.

"Thank you for showing so much interest," I declared uncomfortably at last, but I'm afraid that what I 'really' want to do is become an opera singer. It's what I've always wanted right from the very beginning, and I still do. I'm just sorry that you've had so much of your valuable time wasted like this, and I don't want to waste any more of it.

"Oh! I see. . ." he replied, obviously somewhat taken aback. "Well, thank you for your honesty. If that's what you really want to do, you go off and do it. I can only wish you luck."

And that was it. I'd just turned down an offer from one of the most important men in the theatrical world, and was setting off back to the Baker Street shop to carry on selling veg to the posh old ladies of Marylebone.

I couldn't help feeling how utterly ridiculous this all seemed. Deep inside, however, I knew I'd done the right thing for two reasons: firstly because I had no interest whatsoever in being involved in 'show business' – which in itself would have been reason enough – and secondly, because of this lack of interest I'd have had no talent for it anyway. Therefore any thoughts that I might just have thrown away the possible chance of a glittering career on the stage, was nonsense, and I knew it.

One effect it did have, though, was that I never received any more of these special auditions or contacts that Major Green had so kindly been arranging for me. Which in a way was a relief for me, and I hope for him, too.

Life at the International Stores carried on as before, and as Christmas was now almost on top of us I found myself wondering what the New Year would bring.

SOME MAJOR EVENTS OF THE YEAR:

(1) Films *The King and I* and *Around the World in Eighty Days*, screened.
(2) Frogman Commander 'Buster' Crabb disappeared in Portsmouth Harbour during a Russian Naval visit.
(3) Grace Kelly married Prince Rainier of Monaco.
(4) Premium Savings Bonds introduced by McMillan.
(5) The Road Traffic Act brings in vehicle testing, and parking meters.
(6) Gaming Act legalises Bingo and Lotteries for the first time.

29

The Singing Profession Looms

1957 (27 years old in July)

After a pretty busy time at the shop over the Christmas period, the early months of the year at the International Stores settled down to being pretty much as they were before. The only unusual event during this period being that we had a burglary. We all turned up one morning to discover that thieves – or I should say 'would be' thieves – had broken in through the window into the basement by climbing over the railings on the pavement outside, and dropping down into the sunken area in front of the window.

Although the window had bars, these had presented no problem to the intruders who'd simply levered them apart, broken the glass and squeezed through.

Their target was obviously the safe, which was kept in a small office down there, and was used for keeping all the day's takings overnight, ready to be paid into the bank next morning. The intruders must have been aware of this routine, and feeling well pleased with themselves at getting in so easily. When they also found the safe unlocked, they must have 'really' thought all their birthdays had come at once. Unfortunately, however, they'd reckoned without Mr King, because there wasn't a penny in it. Having in his own wily way anticipated such a possibility, he'd found his own 'safe' for keeping the day's takings in. This was an old empty biscuit tin, which he'd hide among all the several hundred other biscuit tins stacked in the very crowded basement along with all the other great piles of groceries.

Whether they ever caught the unsuccessful culprits for this I don't know, because shortly afterwards I decided it was time to move on

264

from selling potatoes – both right shape and wrong shape – to the ladies of Marylebone, most of whom I liked and got on well with, and take a more positive step towards my professional career.

All through this 'International Stores' period, as well as the auditions, etc., arranged by Major Green, I'd continued my weekly lessons with Mr Fairbairn and my regular practising at Weekes' Music Studios, so was feeling more than ready to plunge into earning my living, full time, with my singing.

I'd been keeping an eye on the adverts for singers in the *Stage* newspaper for some time, but most of these were for West End Shows, so nothing really appealed. However, I eventually came across one that I felt might be worth a shot. It had been put in by George Mitchell, who was well known for his Male Voice Singers on radio and TV. Apparently he was looking for singers to join his smaller male voice groups, which he provided every year for many of the summer seaside shows at resorts all over the country. And although not 'exactly' what I was looking for, I'd always enjoyed the 'middle of the road' songs they did, and felt that I could live with these as a sort of stepping stone on the way.

The advert was announcing an audition session for these groups at an address somewhere just out of the centre of London, so I made my arrangements at the shop so that I could get away and give it a try.

I arrived at the address to find myself in a street of large old Victorian terraced houses, each with railings around a basement area. The house that I wanted caught my eye immediately, simply because to my surprise I could see a large group of youngish men queuing all the way up the front steps and filling the doorway. It became pretty obvious to me at that moment that I was not only going to be facing a lot more competition than I'd expected, but that I'd have to queue up for ages, just for the privilege of trying.

However, I joined the queue at the bottom of the steps, and almost immediately felt like an outsider. Most of those in the queue seemed to know each other, calling out greetings and chatting about previous shows they'd been in, etc. With all this show biz chatter going on around me, I was soon feeling like an inexperienced amateur among real professionals.

I couldn't actually 'hear' any of the audition efforts from outside on the steps, but every so often a young chap would emerge from the doorway above carrying his music, and squeeze his way down past the queue having done his stuff. The odd one here and there looked a bit bouncy and pleased with himself, but most of them looked decidedly subdued, which seemed to indicate that the standard required was pretty stiff, and they hadn't done too well.

265

m

As the queue moved slowly up the steps into the hallway, I could see that a couple of yards along it the queue turned through another door and down some stairs into the basement. Once in the hallway, I began to hear the singing offerings of the auditions echoing up faintly from below. As I progressed along the hall and down the stairs, however, I began hearing them more clearly, and any concern I might have felt about all this 'professional' competition grew less with every step nearer, so that by the time I reached the door of the audition room I could hardly wait to get in there.

I was at last ushered in to find myself facing George Mitchell himself, plus a couple of other people and the pianist. One of them took my name, and George Mitchell asked me what I was going to sing.

" 'Ch'ella mi Creda', from Puccini's opera *Girl of the Golden West*," I replied. I'd chosen this because it was a short, but very 'telling' showpiece. Though after what 'they'd' been listening to so far that morning, I wasn't surprised to see a few raised eyebrows, and hoped that I hadn't gone a bit over the top.

"Really!" came the slightly surprised reply from George Mitchell. "Good! Let's hear it then."

I handed my music to the pianist, told him how I wanted it playing. Then gave it all I'd got in real tenor robusto style.

When I'd finished, George Mitchell stared at me quizzically.

"Are you 'sure' you want to sing in one of my groups?" he asked.

"Well, yes," I replied.

"In that case," he declared, "you've got a job. Where would you like to go?" he added, reeling off a list of seaside venues. Among which I spotted Blackpool.

"Blackpool would suit me fine," I replied, hardly able to believe my luck. "That's my part of the country."

"Right!" he said. "We'll send you a contract and all the details soon. I'll look forward to seeing you up there some time."

And that was it; suddenly I was a full time professional singer. And although it wasn't what I really wanted, it was at least a start.

As I squeezed past the remainder of the queue on my way out, I was 'definitely' one of the bouncy ones feeling pleased with himself.

Back at the shop I didn't mention any of this to anyone, simply because I wasn't too sure myself yet what the exact starting date of my Blackpool contract would be. I did know, however, that it couldn't be more than three or four weeks away, so I just got on with my job, counting off the days as patiently as I could.

The only other event, that for some strange reason sticks in my mind about this waiting period, was the day when one of our regular customers came in talking about a new type of grocery shop that had opened somewhere in London. According to him, it was a shop where the customers didn't have to queue at counters to be served, but simply went around helping themselves to goods off the shelves.

Having only known the traditional counter system of serving customers, we thought this sounded absolutely preposterous.

"How could you 'possibly' run a shop by letting the customers just walk in and help themselves?" was my own reaction.

"The idea's just too ridiculous," agreed most of the other staff, dismissing the story as some sort of joke.

Of course, what we were hearing about, although we didn't know it at the time, was the tentative birth of the huge, supermarket shopping system we have today.

Eventually my contract from George Mitchell arrived by post, and I learned that I was to be part of a four man George Mitchell group in *The Hylda Baker Show*, at the Palace Theatre, Blackpool, which was apparently on the seafront promenade, right near the Blackpool Tower.

I therefore had to say cheerio to Mr King and my fellow assistants rather sadly, as I'd enjoyed working with them. I was particularly sorry to be leaving Mr King like this, because he'd been a good chap to work with, and I couldn't help feeling a bit guilty about leaving him in the lurch.

However, there was nothing I could do about it, except hope that he'd find someone else to take my place fairly quickly.

30

Back to Blackpool

Babs and I set off by train to spend the next four months or so in the place we'd 'tried' to spend our honeymoon, hoping we'd find it considerably more comfortable than on that occasion.

We didn't have any accommodation fixed up in advance this time though, but had been told to ask at the theatre, as 'they'd' have a list of 'theatrical digs' we could try.

In the event this turned out well, because after the long, weary journey north we ended up in the pleasant home of a nice little old lady within walking distance of the theatre. She lived in a quiet street, had a double room to let with use of all cooking facilities, etc; she told us to call her Edna, and we were soon settled in for the season.

When I arrived at the Palace Theatre next day for our first rehearsal, and my eyes fell on its large, beautiful auditorium, I fell in love with it straight away. Its splendid ornamental balconies, red plush seats and velvet curtains looked absolutely magical.

'This really "is" a place to sing in!' I thought.

There seemed to be quite a crowd of people sitting there in the stalls already, chatting away and getting to know each other.

I soon singled out my three fellow Mitchell singers, however; a couple of baritones, one of them noticeably older than the rest of us, and another tenor like myself. Almost immediately we struck up an easy-going rapport, which seemed to bode well for the season ahead.

Also in the stalls were a couple in their thirties sitting with another man, all of whom sounded French, and were, I gathered, an acrobatic balancing act trio. The couple had a lovely little girl of about four who was happily running around trying to say hello to everybody in her own unique version of the English language.

At the front of the stalls stood another man, obviously the musical director, because he was discussing some sheet music with a youngish West Indian chap named Victor Soveral; whom I guessed was a singer of some sort.

A group of about a dozen sixteen to eighteen year old girls were draped around the stalls. These I knew must be the Joan Davis Dancing Troop; all local girls according to the posters I'd seen outside. Sitting with them was Joan Davis and her female choreographer assistant. Joan Davis, it turned out, would also be responsible for arranging all the stage routines of the show, including those 'we'd' be involved in.

Hylda Baker herself turned up eventually with her tall, female impersonator stooge; both well known figures from TV at the time. And after a brief introductory chat from her, plus a rundown of the show, and rehearsal schedule from both Joan Davis and the musical director, it was down to business.

For the rest of the company, including the girls, this simply meant polishing up already well rehearsed routines. For us four Mitchell singers, however, who'd never met before, this meant going off with a pianist to sort out the songs and harmonies already received by the musical director from George Mitchell.

All this show-biz scene was a new but enjoyable experience for me. And as the songs were all typical of the George Mitchell style, with good singable melodies, I found myself quite at home with them – not exactly thrilling stuff, but pleasant enough.

The show itself, being a typical Summer Season offering, was built mainly around the comedy scenes of the star, Hylda Baker, with her rather dim-witted female impersonator stooge. The other acts, like the balancing act trio family, the West Indian singer Victor Soveral – who turned out to be a lyric tenor with a very good voice – our George Mitchell Singers group, and the troop of dancing girls, were all there to fill in the space between, and add variety and movement to the show.

The only times when everybody would be on stage together, would be at the 'all singing and dancing', opening curtain. And the equally 'all singing and dancing', finale at the end.

Rehearsals went well, despite the fact that in one of the routines which Joan Davis had worked out for the girls, she'd co-opted us four singers as their partners. I now, therefore, found myself having to become a dancer (sort of) as well as a singer.

269

'Hardly a hardship to be waltzing around a stage with a dozen pretty girls,' I thought, 'and it is, after all, a chance to learn something new.' So I just put up with it manfully, and tried not to enjoy it 'too' much.

With only a relatively short rehearsal period, the opening night seemed to arrive all too quickly, and to everyone's delight and surprise went down really well.

Considering it was the opening night of the season, we had a reasonably full house and a very receptive audience, so things had got off to an excellent start.

From the show business point of view, Blackpool during the season was almost like London-on-Sea, having at least seven theatres, all featuring famous names from the West End and TV. 'The Palace', 'The Hippodrome', the 'Opera House', 'The Winter Garden Theatre', one on each of the three piers, plus a repertory theatre which put on a whole range of plays.

The town seemed to be packed with celebrities, and it was quite common to see them around the town during the day. One I particularly remember seeing quite often was Tommy Cooper, who must have been staying quite near our digs, because I'd often see him standing at the bus stop when I was on my way to the theatre. Others in town included Cliff Richard, Morecambe & Wise and Bob Monkhouse, at that time part of a comedy double-act.

Another well known 'non-theatrical' celebrity who I'd also see around the town occasionally – simply because Blackpool was his home town – was Brian London, who at that time was the heavyweight boxing champion of Britain. A title that his father, Jack London, had also held before him.

Our weekly schedule at the Palace was for six evening performances, which left our Sundays completely free. Quite early on I got to hear that there were several social clubs in Blackpool who put on entertainment every Sunday; and that they were usually looking for performers, especially singers and comedians.

Sensing the chance to earn a few bob on the side – it had to be 'on the side', because my George Mitchell contract forbade any 'moonlighting' of this sort – I went along to the nearest of these, 'Bloomfield Bowling Club', on the next Sunday to see about getting a booking.

As they didn't know me, they were a bit sceptical at first. So drawing on the hard won experience I'd gained from being thrown in at the deep end in Butlin's 'Jolly Roger' pub, I offered to sing a couple of songs for them, there and then, free of charge to prove my credentials.

270

They accepted my offer, so feeling almost at home in this Jolly Roger type club atmosphere, I gave it my all, probably rattling all the glasses behind the bar for good measure. The result of all this was that I got two bookings for the club, plus bookings at three other Blackpool clubs; whose concert secretaries happened the be in the club that night. These were: the CYMS Club, The Bagot Street Club, and the Winmarith Social Club. So it looked as if my 'moonlighting' was off to a good start, and that most of my Sunday evenings in Blackpool were going to be pretty busy. Not only would this be bringing a few extra bob into the family coffers, but even more importantly, it would be keeping me in tune with myself as a solo singer.

The fees paid by these clubs were only about £3 for two spots of three songs – about twenty minutes work. Which wasn't bad, considering that most of the club members I was singing to would at that time only be getting about £12 for a full week's work.

As well as the show performances, and my Sunday moonlighting, I was keeping up with my writing whenever, and wherever, I could. I even used to take my notebooks to the theatre with me, and was forever scribbling away in them during our breaks in the show. Although for me this was just normal activity, my three fellow singers found this pretty intriguing, and a bit baffling.

"How can you sit there writing away at your stories with all this noise and chatter going on?" was one of their regular comments.

"What noise and chatter?" I'd reply, equally mystified, because when I'd got my nose in my scribbling books I was off in an undisturbed world of my own.

The story I had roaming around in my head at that time, and trying to get down on paper was, *I'll See You in Somewhere*, my first attempt at a full-length children's novel.

Almost at the same time that I started my club singing, Babs decided she'd like to do a bit of seasonal work herself, and after looking around, soon found a job as an evening waitress at a large café restaurant on the sea front called Doddino's. This turned out to be an ideal arrangement, because her hours at the café coincided almost perfectly with our evening show at the theatre. This meant that we could walk down to work together, and since the end of her shift at the café was slightly later than our final curtain, I'd have time to get changed and meet her for our walk back to the digs.

Since nearly all of the theatre shows going on in Blackpool were evening shows only, this left the afternoons clear for the managements to put on special performances by other artists. At our Palace Theatre, these were virtually all well known pop artists of the time. The first of these I remember was Tommy Steele and his group, and although pop groups were not exactly my kind of music, I slipped into the theatre one afternoon to watch them from the wings just out of curiosity. To my surprise, even though, as expected, the actual singing did little for me, I was completely taken aback by the sheer energy of their performance, and the wild enthusiasm this worked up in the fans out front. What also impressed me about Tommy Steele himself, was that when required he could tell quite a good story in song. And for me 'that' is what singing is all about – telling a story. So at least I'd learned 'something' about the up and coming pop scene. And even though I could never be enthusiastic about it, I now understood why their fans were.

Another group who took over our dressing rooms for these afternoon sell-outs, were Lonnie Donegan and his skiffle group. Now these I actually found a bit more to my taste, largely I think because of their comedy send-ups like, 'My Old Man's a Dustman', and 'Does Your Chewing Gum Lose its Flavour on the Bedpost Overnight?'

A third musical group who shared our dressing room during the day for the best part of a week were, 'The John Barry Seven'. I particularly remember these because they used up all my make-up removing tissues. However, at the end of the week they did replace them, and leave a note of thanks.

At some time in the middle of the summer season, Hylda Baker went down with a severe cold and had to drop out of the show, causing panic stations all round. Fortunately, however, one of the other acts appearing in Blackpool agreed to step into the breach by 'doubling up' between his own show and ours. So we found our show being topped by Jimmy James, a well known comic from the old 'Music Hall' and 'Variety Show' days.

This 'doubling up' obviously meant rearranging the running times of both shows, because he had to dash backwards and forwards with all his 'stooges' between theatres trying to fit it all in. However, it all worked out OK, and for me it was an extra treat, because it gave me the chance to see this old comic – who I'd often heard on the radio – at first hand.

Many of the old comedians had their own band of stooges as foils for their comic routines, and Jimmy James was no exception. In fact, he actually had three or four; one of the most noticeable being a tall, gangling idiot of a character played by Eli Woods – who was obviously a real comic actor in his own right. Out of the others, the only one I remember was dressed incongruously as a somewhat undersized, bossy policeman. I used to talk to him occasionally in the wings when

272

he was waiting to go on, and he seemed to be a friendly, naturally funny sort of chap. He told me that his name was Roy Castle; unknown at the time but destined to eventually become one of the best known names on television.

Hylda Baker eventually recovered enough to take over the show again, and everything returned to normal. Babs was still happy with her evening job at Doddino's Restaurant, and my Sunday moonlighting was going so well that I found myself with more offers of club bookings than I could fit in.

The tiny four year old daughter of the French balancing act, was by now everybody's favourite, and quite a comic. She was always coming out with her version of odd bits of English she'd latched onto, especially the calls she could hear coming over the Tannoy. The one we always used to wait for in the dressing rooms, was when the last call of the evening came over and she'd go running along the corridor peering through the ventilation slats on the bottom of all the dressing room doors shouting: "Banana Peas. . ! Banana Peas. . !" which was the nearest she could get to "Finale Please!"

Whenever I heard this coming over the Tannoys in the future, my mind automatically translated it into 'Banana Peas!' Which, carrying as it does that French touch of individuality, albeit of a four year old, I think I preferred.

As the end of the season was rapidly drawing near, my thoughts were automatically turning to – 'What comes next?'

This question had been at least 'partially' answered, when the concert secretary of one of my moonlighting venues happened to ask if I wanted to carry on doing club work when I left Blackpool. He then went on to tell me that if I did, then one of the best places for getting regular bookings all the year round was the Sheffield Area of Yorkshire. He even gave me the name and phone number of the best man in Sheffield to contact. This was a Mr McGregor, who was apparently the 'Secretary', of the 'Concert Secretaries Association', for the whole of the Sheffield area.

Although this didn't really appeal to me at the time, it struck me as being a useful standby if nothing else turned up when I got back to London, so I quickly noted it in my diary.

Finally, the last night of the show arrived after what had been not only a very enjoyable season for both Babs and myself, but a real learning curve of practical, theatrical experience for me. And even though my attitude 'against' a 'showbiz' career was now even stronger than ever, I was still very grateful for all that this season among the professionals had taught me.

273

On the last night, Hylda Baker, who'd always been a friendly, down to earth top of the bill, went around the dressing rooms giving out small presents to everybody in the show. Mine turned out to be a tie of slightly startling colours. I never wore it; just hung it up in the wardrobe to frighten the moths – cruel I know, but at least it seemed to work.

31

Home Again to London

Once again settled into the flat in Westbourne Park, it soon became obvious that unless I was prepared to take on another ordinary job to keep our heads above water, I'd have little option but to follow the suggestion made by the concert secretary in Blackpool. I therefore eventually rang Mr McGregor in Sheffield – albeit somewhat reluctantly – and explained my case.

"Well, it sounds as if you've been doing alright in Blackpool, lad," he replied. "So what I'll do, is fix you up with a week's work up here to see how you go, and we'll take it from there. How does that suit?"

"That's fine," I replied. "When will that be?"

"Straight away," he answered. "Best time to start's the weekend. So if you can get up here on Friday, I'll have some bookings worked out. All right?"

"Right. . ! Right. . !" I agreed, somewhat taken aback by the speed at which Mr McGregor did business. And that was it; the wide world of club land was about to be opened up before me, all for the price of a three-minute phone call.

By this time the early signs of winter were beginning to show, and as I set off for Sheffield the weather was turning decidedly Icelandic. Snow had been forecast for the North of England, and unfortunately they were right, for as our train pulled into Sheffield Station the flakes were falling steadily, adding relentlessly to the three or four inches that already blanketed the ground everywhere.

Not exactly a warm welcome for the start of my new venture, especially as I didn't have anywhere to stay. My first move, therefore, was a beeline for the station telephone box and its directories. After dumping my suitcase outside in the snow, I made a few unsuccessful calls before finally coming across a boarding house that had a bed available – providing I was willing to share the room with a travelling salesman. Since the price was reasonable, and it was pretty central – plus the fact that I was rapidly turning blue in the draughty phone box – I accepted it gladly.

Fortunately, there was a lone taxi standing outside in the snow, so off I went for what looked like being my abode for the next few days at least.

Luckily I was just in time for the evening meal, after which I was shown to my room, where there was no sign of my unknown room mate, though his suitcase and belongings marked out which bed was 'his'.

Since I'd never been to Sheffield before, as soon as I'd settled in – which took me all of ten minutes – I set off to explore what I could of this famous old 'steel town'. I must have wandered for miles, because in some ways I felt almost at home, especially near the steel mills, which reminded me strongly of the Hindpool Steelworks area of Barrow. A big difference, however, was that Sheffield itself was a lot bigger than Barrow, and much more hilly. It also had old double-decker trams clattering about everywhere through the snow; even up and down the steep hills, which I found pretty astonishing.

When I'd worked my way back to the boarding house it was fairly late, and I found my unknown room-mate was just a snoring lump in his bed. Next morning, I awoke to find he was up and gone, though his suitcase was still there, so he was obviously not gone for good.

After breakfast I rang Mr McGregor, and he reeled off the names and addresses of four different clubs, plus times and dates, together with brief instructions on how to get to them from where I was staying, which trams to take, etc. – all of which I scribbled down in my diary as rapidly as I could. He then wished me luck, told me to ring him later in the week for other possible bookings, and rang off. I was now apparently clocked on as an artist of the Sheffield Club Circuit, which from the club addresses I'd been given obviously covered a pretty wide area.

As the first club on my list was for that night, I set off with my music case and climbed into a freezing cold tram which rattled me down into Foster Square, where I had to change onto one that would drop me off as near as possible to this 'fairly central' club. This turned out to be a big, crowded, obviously popular venue, where I discovered, fortunately, that I'd be sharing the bill with three other acts.

Almost immediately I got the impression, from listening to the other acts, that this was a sort of introductory testing ground where new acts were tried out.

I wasn't first on, so having given my music to the organist – most clubs I'd found had an organist and drummer as accompanists, usually pretty competent and versatile – I sat back to listen to the others do their stuff. There was a young married couple singing act performing the latest popular songs, a stand-up comedian, and a young chap strumming on a guitar. All of them were pretty good performers, and as none of them clashed with me, it looked like being a pretty well-balanced show.

When it came to my turn, I held forth with my newly established 'Blackpool repertoire', which now consisted of the odd operatic aria, plus one or two of the better known tenor ballads, interspersed with a couple of the more 'ballad style' popular songs of the time.

Everybody went down well, and it was an enjoyable introduction to the Northern Club World for me. What I found particularly satisfying was, that apart from going down well with the audience, I'd been approached by a few concert secretaries from other clubs trying to book me for their clubs.

However, since I was being booked through McGregor, all I could do was thank them, and refer them to him.

I arrived back at the boarding house fairly late, to once more find my room mate just an unrecognisable, shapeless lump under his bed blankets. And as before, when I got up next morning he'd gone off doing his travelling salesmanship somewhere.

This first day pretty well set the scene for the next three days. I'd wander around during the day exploring Sheffield, getting back in time for tea. Then I'd set off by tram at around 6.30, into some outlying district looking for the club of the day. All of these clubs were different in size and lay-out, but they all had good organists and drummers, and large enthusiastic audiences, which as far as I was concerned was what really mattered. Another bonus, which made them enjoyable for me – apart from the fact that I always seemed to go down well – was that they always had at least one other act on the bill; unlike the smaller Blackpool clubs, where I'd always had to carry the show on my own.

During the week I'd always given Barbara a ring each day to keep her up to date on how things were going. But on the morning of my last club, I was about to ring McGregor about further bookings as arranged, when to my surprise 'she' rang me.

"I was hoping to catch you in time," she declared eagerly. "I've just had a call from George Mitchell. He wants to know if you'd be interested in doing a pantomime for him. I told him you were away for the week, and he said will you ring him as soon as you get back.

Although this came as a real surprise, it also brought a great sense of relief, because even though I'd enjoyed the challenge of my brief tilt at the Northern Club scene, it was purely a side road, and definitely not one I'd want to follow for too long.

32

Next Stop Pantoland

Once back home in London, I had a good night's sleep in a warm, 'dry' bed, then rang George Mitchell first thing in the morning. As before, it turned out that he was providing singing groups for quite a few theatres around the country, so offered me a choice, reeling off the names of several, and to my astonishment the last one was the Lyceum Theatre in Sheffield.

"That one will do for me," I declared quickly, hardly able to believe it as the possibility of a bit of 'Blackpool type' moonlighting loomed on the horizon as a bonus.

"Good," he replied. "They're putting on *Sleeping Beauty* there this year, with Ronnie Hilton in the leading role as the Prince, so I think you'll enjoy it. I'll get your contract in the post."

So there I was, hardly having had chance to brush the Sheffield snow off my boots, and I was already booked to go back.

A week or so later my contract came through, and as before I was to be part of a group, only this time it was a slightly larger one, with both male and female singers; two tenors, two baritones and three sopranos.

As the panto was only scheduled to run for about ten weeks, and because Babs had just got herself settled into a job which she didn't want to lose, she decided she'd rather stay behind in the flat, and just pop up to Sheffield here and there whenever she got the chance.

Although this wasn't ideal, it was something that went with my being in the singing profession, so we both accepted it. In any case it actually made things a lot easier for me, because with her staying at home in the comfort of our flat, I only needed to worry about digs for myself – this time, with any luck, minus a travelling salesman.

279

In the event I managed to fix myself up with theatrical digs by ringing the Lyceum Theatre for any they had on their list. Once again I found myself lodging in a house run by a little old lady – what 'would' the theatres do without them.

Fortunately I had a comfortable room of my own, with a dry bed, and the theatre was only a twenty minute downhill walk away – down hill both ways would have been better, of course. Still, you can't have everything, so I settled for that.

Our first rehearsal at the Lyceum was a bit of an eye-opener after Blackpool, because it brought home to me just how different the world of pantomime was from the traditional seaside show. The main difference, of course, being that pantomimes are plays, not variety shows. In Blackpool we Mitchell Singers had been for the most part a separate act; coming on, doing our bit, and going off like all the other acts. In Sheffield, however, we now found ourselves involved in the plot, and that most of our singing and acting was concerned with the ongoing story. I personally thought that this was great, because it struck me immediately as being somewhat akin to the format of opera, and therefore much more enjoyable.

Another difference that quickly became obvious, was that the cast we were now working with were 'not' variety performers, but seasoned pantomime 'actors', well known in the business for the characters they played. All of these were brilliant in their roles, with possibly the most striking being the middle-aged actress who played the Wicked Witch, whose name I can only remember as 'Fan'. Playing witches and medieval old crones, apparently, were her speciality and she'd been making her living out of them for years.

The two exceptions to this, apart from the dancing girls and ourselves, were the Princess played by a pretty young blonde singer, and the Prince played by Ronnie Hilton; who at that time was at the height of his fame as a pop singer; having just made the charts with his hit version of 'Magic Moments'.

Despite being a big celebrity in the pop music world, Ronnie Hilton was not only a very friendly, down to earth sort of chap to work with in the theatre, but if you ever bumped into him out in the street he'd stop for a chat, or even suggest going for a coffee. The one thing that impressed me most about him, however, was that unlike most of the other pop singers of the time, he wasn't just a microphone crooner, but had a really good, natural singing voice, which even without a mike could carry to the back of the auditorium.

As his hit, 'Magic Moments', was currently high in the charts it was naturally included in the panto, and we Mitchell Singers had to fill in the harmony background to match the record. To get this right we had to work with his own personal musical director, who to my surprise was called Will Fyffe Junior, and turned out to be the grandson of the great old Scottish actor of the 1930s, Will Fyffe, whose old black and white films I'd seen at the cinemas in Barrow years before.

Once the rehearsals were over and the show up and running, I rang Mr McGregor to put him in the picture about my sudden return to Sheffield, and he fixed me up with my first couple of Sunday bookings straight away. From then on I found myself traipsing about every Sunday evening to various clubs in the outlying districts of Sheffield, or the nearby towns of Rotherham and Barnsley. In fact, my way of life in Sheffield was turning out to be somewhat busier and more hectic than I'd expected, especially on the Sundays, because not having my own transport, I had to find my way out to all these far flung venues on whatever public transport happened to be running.

However, with Babs not being there for most of the time, this club work did help to keep my 'solo' singing in pretty good shape; as well as occupying my otherwise empty Sundays. It was also bringing in useful extra money to help bridge the earning gaps between shows which was something we'd come to expect.

Christmas was soon on top of us, and with pantos being very much aimed at the kids, special children's Saturday afternoon performances were laid on just for them. These were great, noisy affairs with lots of foot stamping, shouting and yelling going on between the kids and the cast on stage, especially whenever the Evil Witch appeared.

Babs managed to get up from London for a few days over the Christmas and New Year period, sharing my room at the digs and seeing the panto a couple of times, as well as traipsing out on one of my club expeditions. These were outings that she was well used to by now and enjoyed, so all in all we spent a good Christmas and New year together.

SOME MAJOR EVENTS OF THE YEAR:

(1) The Death Penalty abolished.

(2) *My Fair Lady* was staged.

(3) The book, *Parkinson's Law*, published.

(4) First British hydrogen bomb exploded on Christmas Island.

(5) Jodrell Bank, and Cambridge Radio Telescopes completed.

(6) The first British Radar traps used against speeding motorists.

(7) Russia launches the first ever artificial satellite, Sputnik 1. This was followed by Sputnik 2 which carried the dog Laika. (Babs and I watched this pass over London from the roof of 24 Aldridge Road Villas, like a bright moving star. The dog Laika, of course, didn't survive.)

281

33

Goodbye To Panto

1958 (29 years old in July)

After Babs returned to London, *Sleeping Beauty* carried on as usual playing to pretty full houses. But gradually audience numbers began to tail off, and after a very good run of about 16 weeks, the Sheffield Lyceum finally closed its doors on us, and I was once more on my way back to London.

Fortunately, on this occasion I wasn't going home quite so empty handed as far as singing engagements were concerned, because George Mitchell had already offered me the chance of doing the Blackpool Summer Season again if I wished. An offer which in the absence of anything else at the time, I'd accepted.

As the Blackpool show wasn't due to start for a couple of months or so, there was once more the inevitable earnings gap. However, as we'd managed to top up our coffers quite a bit with my club earnings, and Babs still had her job, this didn't loom as too much of a problem.

It also dawned on me that since I was now a full time professional singer; even to the extent of being a member of Equity, that during these flat spots I should be entitled to sign on the dole in just the same way as any other temporarily unemployed person. So off I went to my nearest unemployment office and found that this was perfectly true. In fact, as it turned out, there was actually a slight advantage in my being a 'stage' professional, because the staff there could only offer 'skilled' people work in their 'own' trade or profession, and couldn't force them to take on anything else. And since they didn't deal with jobs in the theatre, I was simply signed on, and left to find work for myself.

As I'd never claimed any sort of benefit before in my life, had always worked for a living paying income tax, national insurance, etc., I didn't feel at all guilty about this. Especially so, after coming across the queues of men in the labour exchange drawing dole every week, when I knew from my own experience that just outside the door London was awash with jobs for those willing to look for them.

One benefit of having these few weeks of enforced break I found, was that it gave me a chance me pick up on my vocal practising again. This I felt particularly in need of, because singing constantly in performance – especially the kind of things you have to sing in panto – is no substitute for real vocal practice. And even though my stints in the clubs certainly helped keep my voice more in shape, never having anywhere to practise properly was always a real drawback.

Another benefit of being in London for a while, was that it enabled me to get back in touch with Mr Fairbairn again. He was still not too much in favour of my singing in the kind of shows I 'was' singing in. But then, neither was I, and as he could suggest no immediate alternative, he came to accept them as mere stepping stones along the way, just as I did. In any case he had to admit that they were certainly better than mopping hotel kitchen floors, or serving veg to elderly ladies in Marylebone, so didn't press the point too much.

My contract for the Blackpool Palace Theatre finally came through at sometime in May, and I discovered that this time I was to be adding my vocal efforts to *The Dave Morris Show*. Once again I was to be part of a male voice 'foursome', with two tenors and two baritones.

Babs decided that she wouldn't come with me right at the beginning, but would wait until the show had settled down and then come up to join me. This seemed a good idea to me, so I booked my digs in Blackpool with Edna again on this understanding.

After a long, tedious train journey up north on my own, I settled down into our old room, then had a brief walk along the sea front to get a few breaths of the good old North Sea air that I'd grown up with. Then it was back to Edna's for a good night's sleep before the first rehearsal next day.

I turned up in the Lyceum Theatre next morning to find, as in the year before, that most of the cast, the musical director, Joan Davis and her assistant choreographer, with their troop of local dancing girls, etc., were already scattered about in the stalls of the beautiful red plush auditorium, chatting away eagerly about this year's new show.

Singling out my three fellow George Mitchell singers, was obviously my first priority. As it turned out, 'none' of us had ever met the others before, so it was a case of getting to know each other from scratch. However, even in those first few minutes we developed an easy going rapport, so all looked good for another season.

Dave Morris, the star around whom our show was built, was one of the old school of natural born funny men. Short, stocky and short-sighted he could make an audience laugh simply by walking onto the stage and staring at them myopically through his thick, bi-focal specs. As I looked around, he was sitting there in the stalls cracking gags with his own gang of assorted idiots, and obviously enjoying himself. Like Jimmy James – who I'd met during the last Blackpool show when Hylda baker went down with flu – Dave Morris's act was based largely on sketches and running gags with his own picked gang of stooges. He was himself, however, just as funny a character off the stage as he was on, and before the show he'd often stand outside the stage door in his straw boater hat, buttonholing unwary passers-by to try out new gags on them.

The final two members of the cast sitting there were both women. One was a bubbly, glamorous blonde, whom I guessed from seeing the posters outside must be Odette Christal, a French classical soprano. Classical singers were very popular on the variety stage in those days, and every show seemed to have one. The other woman was Margo Henderson, a likeable 'personality' singer of the more popular ballads of that time.

When all the introductions had been completed, and brief details of the show's running order explained, we all split up and rehearsals got under way. Joan Davis and her dancing girls made their way up on stage to start practising their routines, while we four Mitchells went off with the musical director to find a room with a piano and begin working on the songs George Mitchell had sent him.

After two weeks of solid rehearsal our show got under way in early June. By this time Blackpool was already beginning to buzz with a holiday atmosphere, and we opened to a pretty enthusiastic first night audience. This created a great atmosphere in the theatre and got our season off to a really promising start. As if this wasn't enough we were then told that our show was to go out 'live' on BBC Television on one of the nights during the second week, and that for this we'd each be paid a fee by the BBC amounting to almost an extra week's wage.

On the day of the TV show the camera crews moved in to set up their cameras out in the auditorium, and dot their microphones around the stage area as unobtrusively as possible. By the time we arrived for the show in the evening we could hardly make out where the stage mikes were. So we were all given a quick run down of their locations, and told where to direct our voices for best effect. This was particularly important for our singing spots, because if we got it wrong our 'wonderful' vocal efforts would probably disappear into the wings, and the television viewers would think they'd all gone deaf. Once the show got under way, it all passed off just as usual with us hardly aware that the show 'was' being televised.

Now that the show was up and running, I decided it was time to start chasing up some Sunday club work. I rang the club secretaries of all the clubs I'd appeared at during the summer before, and soon had quite a few dates scribbled in my diary. So everything was now on course for another busy summer.

At some time in the first few weeks of the show the musical director approached us about doing a charity concert. It seemed he'd been asked by the Blackpool Blind Association if he could get Odette Crystal to sing at a concert for its blind members which was being held at a big hall in the town. Apparently Odette had agreed, and he thought it might be a good idea if we Mitchell Singers would be willing to go along and do our bit as well. My three fellow singers agreed straight away, but I hesitated, not feeling too happy at being so obviously categorised as simply part of a 'group'.

"Well, I'd be more than happy to come along and sing," I replied, "but 'not' simply as a Mitchell Singer. I'd want to sing a solo as well."

"Oh! Really. . ." said the musical director in surprise. "Well, alright! That'd be great. Just sort out what you'd like to sing and let me have the music."

"Right!" I agreed happily; already racking my brains as to what vocal offering would adequately fit this sudden exciting challenge. "I will."

On the afternoon of the concert we all turned up at the hall to find it packed to the doors with blind people and their helpers, all happily enjoying the refreshments and sing-along music that was already in full swing. We were all invited to join in the fun, which we did until the time arrived for our spot in the show. As arranged, we Mitchells were on first to open the concert with a selection of the songs from our show at the Palace, paving the way for the star of the concert Odette. She sang several of her songs from the show, which she put over beautifully to an absolutely captivated audience. Then, just as a special treat for 'us', she added a couple of other songs which we'd never heard her sing before.

We Mitchells then sang a few more excerpts from our Palace Theatre repertoire, and suddenly it was my big moment. For some reason I'd chosen to sing 'Che Gelida Manina' (Your Tiny Hand is Frozen) from Puccini's opera *La Boheme*. Which under the circumstances was a somewhat risky choice, because although an absolutely beautiful aria to sing, it has a sustained, full voice top 'C' in the last phrase that makes it quite a challenge. Fortunately, however, it all worked well, much to the delight of everybody in the hall it seemed – especially me.

The most important moment I remember about that concert, however, was when I walked off the platform to be suddenly met by an astonished looking Odette.

"What are you doing, singing with these. . . these. . . 'Mitchell' people?" she demanded in her heavily broken English. "Why, with your voice. . . If you were over on the continent. . . you'd be going 'right' to the top. . .

Coming from such an accomplished singer as her, I found all this pretty flattering as well as totally unexpected. It struck me immediately though, just how much her comments echoed those of both Mr Fairbairn, and my other major singing teacher, Maria Linker. I could almost have been listening to them.

The trouble was, unfortunately, that although I found myself flattered and encouraged by them all, I was still stuck with the fact that I 'wasn't' over on the continent, so could only make my way forward a step at a time, according to how the 'right kind' of opportunities presented themselves 'here'.

In the meantime, as far as solo singing was concerned, it was back to the clubs. These were going down well, with bookings for every Sunday as far as the eye could see. However, although enjoying the clubs as a change from the show, I was getting a little fed up with all the public transport jaunts I was having to put up with simply to 'reach' the various club involved. As in Sheffield, I was rapidly coming to the conclusion that if I was to continue with this club work, or any other solo work that might crop up in future, then having my own transport was going to be essential.

This time, though, I decided that it was time to do something about it, so I started looking around tentatively at what 'second hand' cars Blackpool's car dealers had on offer. It had to be 'second hand' for two obvious reasons, the first, and 'most' obvious being that the cost of a new car would have been way beyond our means. And the second, that new cars were so scarce after the war that even if we 'could' have afforded one there was about a year's waiting list.

I was still in the early stage of this second hand car exploration, when Babs decided she'd had enough of her job in London, and came up to spend the rest of the season with me at Edna's. Since we'd never owned a car before, she fortunately took to the idea as eagerly as I had, so now both of us could go off wandering around the car lots and show rooms together.

Our early wanderings were not too promising, since nearly all of the cars on offer were old pre-war bangers which looked as if they'd floated off the ark after a pretty rough voyage. Some of them even looked as if they'd probably been 'second hand' even when Noah bought them. Even the few more presentable ones we found turned out to be either too big, or still a bit too expensive.

However, we did eventually come across one that really caught our eyes. This was a pre-war (1937-8), MG (VA) Sports Saloon. For some reason this was actually in the showroom window at a price of around £100. Although even this was a bit more than we were hoping to pay, we both knew it was the one for us, especially as the price tag stated that HP terms were available. We went inside to have a closer look and that settled the matter. With lovely sleek sports saloon lines, wire spun wheels, one of which was mounted on the mudguard, leather upholstery and huge chrome headlights it had obviously been a real quality car in its day, and still looked a treat. I guessed that there would probably be some work to do on it, but with my mechanics training in the army I felt sure I could handle all that. And with the £100 repayable over a couple of years, we signed the papers, were told we could come and collect it in about a week and off we strolled back to Edna's place, the proud owners of our very first car.

There was only one small problem with all this. For despite being a mechanic in the army and used to driving all kinds of vehicles from huge lorries, to motor bikes, Jeeps, Bren gun carriers, etc., and actually 'passing' a driving test at an army driving centre in Wimbledon, I still didn't actually have a driving licence. I'd long since given up trying to chase up the army licence; as apparently all trace of the licence records for that particular period had been lost.

My first step, therefore, had to be applying for 'another' driving test straight away, and so getting a valid licence once and for all. However, since I hadn't driven for quite some time, and wasn't really used to small modern cars anyway, I decided it might be a good idea to take a few lessons just to get the feel of things again. There was a small driving instructor's office in the main street just around the corner from Edna's place, so I booked myself in for a few lessons with him.

In the meantime, I duly collected the MG and parked it up in the street outside Edna's, and began giving it the once over. Having originally been a fairly expensive model it had quite a few built-in extras, not all of which still worked properly. Some of these I was able to put right, like the indicator arms which should have shot out from

287

each side, 'but didn't'; and a complete hydraulic 'self-jacking' system, that 'wouldn't'. This particular, pretty intriguing extra, was a system by which you could jack up the whole car in one go simply by attaching a lever to a hydraulic pump under the bonnet and pumping it backwards and forwards. This pumped hydraulic fluid though a maze of copper pipes to the jacks under each corner of the car.

Unfortunately, this system had obviously given up the ghost long ago, and was now just scrap metal weighing the car down. Surgical removal was the only answer, so I bought myself a simple car jack and stripped the whole system out, pump, tubing, jacks and all,

All this amounted to a lot of dirty, awkward crawling about underneath in the street. But by the time I'd finished we had a car that not only worked well, but really looked immaculate.

My driving lessons had also been going well, and after five lessons over about three weeks, my instructor decided that I didn't need any more, and booked me in for a test. To my surprise, on the day of my test, the instructor picked me up in a totally 'different' car to the one I'd done all my practising in.

"I'm sorry about this," he apologised, "but I couldn't get the other one to start this morning."

The car was so different that my heart sank. 'Here we go again,' I thought, trying to sort out the unfamiliar controls, while feeling that this looked doomed to be yet one more abortive attempt at getting a licence.

"But I'm sure you'll be alright," he added, not very convincingly.

When we pulled up at the test centre, the examiner emerged carrying his clipboard.

"Oh! It's him," muttered my instructor as he got out, in a tone that did nothing to brighten the situation.

The examiner got in, and after the usual pre-test questions and instructions we set off around the streets of Blackpool, with him doling out his orders, and me doing my best to sort out the controls and follow them.

Finally, after what seemed a marathon run, we pulled up back at the test centre where he finished writing up his notes before asking simply.

"How do you think you did?"

"Well, 'I' think it went alright," I replied.

"So do I," he replied much to my astonishment. "Congratulations, you've passed."

When I told my instructor, he gave a huge sigh of relief, obviously just as astonished as I was.

"When I saw who the examiner was," he admitted, "I thought you

Alan as Count Borsa (with sword),
in *Rigoletto* with Sadler's Wells.

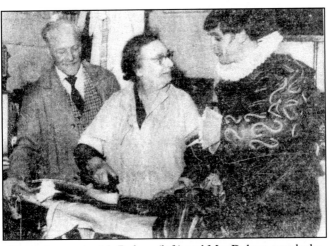

Wardrobe master Mr Delroy (left) and Mrs Delroy, wardrobe
mistress, talk with Alan, playing Borsa.

Sadler's Wells – signatures for my monthly Oxfam collection.

Newspaper cutting from Alan's home town of Barrow-in-Furness on his return there with Sadler's Wells.

Alan during his time with Sadler's Wells Operatic Company.

Alan and Babs in their Dormobile. This became
their home for about three years during
Alan's touring period with Sadler's Wells.

The Dormobile at Cheddar Gorge.

One of the spectacular scenes from the Granada production of Offenbach's " Orpheus in the Underworld " to be televised on Wednesday, with the original Sadler's Wells cast.

Newspaper cutting of the televised *Orpheus in the Underworld*.
This Sadler's Wells production, in which Alan
appeared, was filmed by Granada Television.

Alan's wife Babs on the lawn.

The Dormobile on Southsea front, Portsmouth.
Babs in the background.

One of Alan's hand-out photos during his freelancing days.

Alan rehearsing his role as Faust for
the Bel Canto Opera Society.

had no chance, because he's never passed 'any' of my pupils at their first attempt before."

However, at long last I'd finally got my own licence, plus a car to go with it, so the roads were all out there, just waiting for us.

Almost before we realised it, the summer season was running out, and after a run of about 16 weeks this second Blackpool Summer Show was rapidly approaching its end. It had been a pretty enjoyable, and eventful season in its way, so we were all sorry to see it close.

However, to round the season off on a more positive note, George Mitchell had already offered me a contract for a show in Coventry which was called simply *The Coventry Birthday Show*. This was apparently an annual event put on to mark the anniversary of the opening (or re-opening) of the Coventry Theatre, after rebuilding some years before. And since this was due to start in only about three weeks, there was to be no long 'payless gap' to fill in this time.

To make this even better, the *Birthday Show* was to be immediately followed at the same theatre by their annual Christmas panto; which this year was *Robin Hood*, which all meant that I'd be in work well over into the New Year.

With no train involved this time on our journey back to the London flat for our short, welcome break, Babs and I loaded up the car with all our luggage and set off on the open road, heading south for the great metropolis over 400 miles away.

In those days there were no such things as motorways, and even stretches of ordinary dual carriageway were few and far between, so progress along what were mainly country roads was pretty 'steady', to say the least. Ring roads, were also pretty much a thing of the future, so we found ourselves wending our way right through the centre of every hamlet, village, and town that lay on our route, all the way to London. However, after what seemed about a week, though was possibly only about fifteen hours, we trundled into the outskirts of the capital and made our way right through it, to finally switch off the engine outside our flat in Aldridge Road Villas, Westbourne Park.

n

34

A New Theatre in a Rebuilt City

After about two weeks of welcome relaxation, and catching up with things in London, for me it was then a case of loading up the MG and setting off to yet another new venue.

Although I'd never been to Coventry before, its name was only too well known because of the terrible destruction it had suffered during the blitz. Being a vitally important engineering town during the war, just as Barrow was, the colossal battering it had taken by the Luftwaffe over the course of a few dreadful days and nights had virtually laid the whole town to waste. The blitz we'd suffered on Barrow had been bad enough, but compared to that inflicted on Coventry, we'd got away very lightly.

Fortunately, by the time of this first visit of mine, I found that there were surprisingly few visible scars remaining. Most of the destruction seemed to have been cleared away and replaced by bright new buildings. The most outstanding example of this being the great modern cathedral built right alongside the ruined shell of the ancient Norman one. This battered sandstone remnant of the once magnificent Norman Cathedral, still displayed the temporary cross of charred timbers set up among the rubble by the rescue workers, right where the old altar would have stood.

Quite nearby stood the brand new Leofric Hotel, obviously named after Earl Leofric of Mercia; the husband of Lady Godiva who, according to legend, rode through the streets of Coventry on horseback naked, in order to get the taxes reduced which her husband was inflicting on the people of Coventry.

The Coventry Theatre, which was to be my place of work for the next few months, was in the centre of the town just a short walk away from the two cathedrals. It was a bright, modern building, looking somewhat like a cinema, even though it was a genuine, purpose built theatre.

From the posters outside the theatre main entrance I discovered for the first time that the star of the show was to be David Whitfield, a popular recording artist, somewhat in the Mario Lanza style, whose big hit at that time was 'Cara Mia'.

Also on the bill was Jimmy Wheeler, a well-known stand up comedian of the old school; The Kaye Sisters, a top line singing trio; The Three Monarchs, a popular harmonica act; Lauri Lupino Lane & George Truzzi, a comedy act; Grace O'Connor, an Irish singer; a large troop of dancing girls, and we Mitchell Singers.

My digs, which I'd managed to get via the theatre stage door office as usual, were only about a mile away, in a pleasant semi-detached house, which even had a drive where I could park the car.

Rehearsals got under way fairly quickly, and with the *Birthday Show* being a normal variety show, as well as doing our own spot, we Mitchells found ourselves involved in several of the big special scenes with David Whitfield, the Kaye Sisters, and the dancing girls, plus the big opening scene and finale. So, all in all, we had to put in quite a lot of work to get things right, and needed every bit of the seven days' rehearsal time allotted.

However, the dress rehearsal and first night both passed off without any real problems, and this latest *Coventry Birthday Show* was up and running; and judging from the audience reception looking set for a successful run.

The big difference for me this time though, was that unlike Blackpool and Sheffield, Coventry was not noted for its club scene, so for a change all my Sundays would be relaxing days off.

With Babs not being with me, I made the most of any leisure time I had by wandering around exploring Coventry on my own. Since I enjoyed looking at great buildings, one of the first places I made a beeline for was the new St Michael's Cathedral. This had come in for quite a lot of criticism in the press as being too modern in design, but as soon as I set eyes on it I found this criticism utterly ridiculous. To me it was simply a wonderfully beautiful, inspiring building, both from the outside, with Epstein's great bronze sculptures hanging on the walls near the main entrance depicting St Michael battling against the forces of evil; and on the spacious inside, full of light and colour which streamed in through the long, narrow window slots of brightly coloured glass stretching from floor to ceiling all the way along the

291

side walls of the nave. The stunning effect of all this as you entered, was to instantly lead your eyes away down to the far end where the huge symbolic painting by Graham Sutherland completely filled the whole of the wall behind the altar. As a modern version of what a great Christian Cathedral should be, for me it was just perfect.

In complete contrast, I also came across another type of building that was a long lost relic of the past; or at least I'd thought so until I stumbled on it just down the road from the theatre; this was a 'British Restaurant'. These were set up by the government during the war when food was strictly rationed, as a way of allowing people, under certain circumstances, to get a meal without having to use their ration books. Since rationing had ended several years ago, I'd thought these had disappeared along with the ration books. However, there it was, large as life, and since they served quite a nice cup of tea, I resisted the temptation to inform them that the war was over, and would occasionally drop in for a sample.

Our show at the theatre was still going down well with the Coventry audiences, and backstage a friendly sense of camaraderie had developed which made for an easy-going working atmosphere.

The star of our show, David Whitfield, was obviously very popular with the public at that time, especially since his recent big hit song, 'Cara Mia', had shot up the charts. He himself, while quite easy to get on with, was a bit of a rough and ready character, whose extrovert personality fitted his role as a popular 'chart' singer perfectly. According to the media publicity machine, he'd been a worker on a building site who liked to sing as he worked. Apparently, someone from the musical world was passing by one day, and was so impressed by what they heard that they persuaded him to become a professional singer. How true this was I don't know, but at least it made for good publicity, which undoubtedly helped him on his way.

The Kaye Sisters, who actually 'were' sisters, were one of the most popular female vocal threesomes of that time. All of them were attractive girls in their twenties and although very friendly and fun loving, they always stuck very much together, as if to discourage the unwanted attentions of any predatory males who might fancy their chances.

Our other leading act, Jimmy Wheeler, was a well known stand up comic from the old Music Hall and Variety Show days. I'd heard him on the radio in Barrow several times, but had never seen him in performance before. He'd obviously learned his trade the hard way, and liked to chat about how tough and poorly paid life had been on the boards in his early days compared to what they were now. In fact, I rather got the impression that it was the 'money' more than the 'fame' which he regarded as the real measure of his success, because he would often boast about how comfortably off he was now compared to those early times.

"Nowadays," he'd often say, patting his back pocket with a wink, "I never go out with less than seven hundred pounds in there."

Since seven hundred pounds at that time was the equivalent of a whole year's wages to most people, I always felt that keeping quiet about his 'back pocket' bundle, would have made more sense. But then, it could be that he felt there was no point in being well-heeled unless you let everybody know it.

At sometime in November I got the chance of an unexpected short trip to London when one of my fellow Mitchells, Gerry Toner, told me he was making a quick run down to London on his motorbike, and asked me if I'd like go with him on the pillion. The plan was to set off straight after the show on a Saturday night, reaching London in the early hours. As this would give me the chance to spend the whole of Sunday with Babs, before setting off back on the Monday afternoon I jumped at the chance.

Gerry's bike was a 250cc BSA – similar to the dispatch riders machines I'd worked on in the army. And although these were just about adequate to plod around a muddy battlefield delivering messages, they were decidedly lacking in punch when it came to lengthy trips on the open road, especially with two on board.

'Still,' I thought optimistically, 'it'll probably be alright.'

When we came out of the theatre that night all ready to go, however, and found that the temperature outside had plummeted to freezing point, my earlier misgivings about the bike's ability to get us to the Capital were not exactly improved – since we now faced the added possibility of being frozen to death in the attempt.

This wasn't helped by the fact that in those days such things as weatherproof leathers, boots and crash helmets were virtually unknown to the ordinary motor cyclist. Gerry certainly had none of this gear; his only concession to motorcycling was to wear bicycle clips on his trouser bottoms so they wouldn't get in the way as he changed gear with his foot. As for me, 'I' didn't even have bicycle clips.

So we set off into the arctic darkness heading for London bare headed, with our only protection against the elements being scarves wound tightly around our necks, and overcoats buttoned right up under our chins.

The BSA popped along steadily through the well-lit streets of

293

Coventry contentedly, and even when we left the outskirts to plunge into the empty darkness of the countryside it didn't seem to be doing too badly – so long as we were on the flat. As soon as we came to anything remotely resembling a hill, however, it struggled so much that I was tempted to get off and walk. But, as this would 'probably' have meant me having to wait at the top of the hill for Gerry and the BSA to catch up, I just sat tight trying to 'will' the struggling bike on with mind over matter. Unfortunately, this seemed to cut no ice with the BSA as 'it' obviously didn't mind, and 'we', apparently, didn't matter.

Even when we 'were' making a bit of progress, we were so frozen, that we'd have to stop every few miles and stamp up and down the grass verge just to get some sort of circulation back into our legs. As if all this wasn't enough, it turned out that the gear box on the BSA had a tendency to leak away its oil; something that Gerry hadn't thought worth mentioning before. So every so often we'd have to stop so he could top it up from a small can he'd kept hidden in one of the panniers.

Eventually, however, after what seemed one of the longest nights I could ever remember. We finally chugged out of the darkness into the welcoming flood of street lights in the outskirts of London.

Gerry dropped me off outside our flat, and disappeared away into the London gloom in the direction of his own place somewhere over Earls Court way.

After spending a lovely day and night with Babs, Gerry picked me up early on Monday afternoon for our trek back. Fortunately, the temperature was quite a bit higher by this time, and also, being in daylight, we made much better time, arriving back in Coventry in plenty of time for curtain up.

The end of the *Birthday Show* was now in sight, after a very successful run of about seven weeks, and our thoughts were turning more and more to the panto looming on the horizon to follow it. We'd learned that it was to be *Robin Hood*, and that the only 'star' names involved were to be Jewel & Warriss – one of the top comedy double acts of the day. Quite how 'they' would fit into the Robin Hood story I couldn't imagine.

The last night of the *Birthday Show* finally arrived, and as we Mitchells and the dancing girls were the only ones moving over into the coming panto, we said our goodbyes to all the other acts after what had been a very friendly, enjoyable show, and looked forward to what the panto would have to offer.

As there was only about a week between the two shows, all the panto cast arrived on the Monday, and we found ourselves immediately involved in rehearsals again. As in the Sheffield panto, apart from the two stars, Jewel & Warriss, all the other characters were to be played by experienced pantomime actors, who were not exactly household names. Working with these well practised pantomime professionals was very easy and the rehearsals all went very smoothly; rehearsing with the two star leads, however, was a bit more difficult. Ben Warriss, the 'straight man', was a keen professional with a good sense of humour and got on with the job properly, but to my surprise Jimmy Jewel, ostensibly the 'funny one', was a moody, morose individual who obviously didn't like rehearsing, and simply 'walked' through every scene with his hands in his pockets looking glum.

The producer obviously didn't take too kindly to this, and tried repeatedly to get him to rehearse properly for the sake of everyone else, but without much luck. However, since most of their scenes in the panto were based on their own well practised routines, and didn't involve the rest of us much, it was left like that.

When the panto finally got under way, however, to my astonishment the opening night went exceptionally well, with Jewel & Warriss right up to their old form as a pair of robbers. It was just like magic, once in front of an audience Jimmy Jewel suddenly blossomed into the funny, slightly gormless clown of the team we'd all expected him to be, and they went down a bomb.

Apart from our singing role, we Mitchells found ourselves involved in most of the swashbuckling Merry Men scenes, including the well known archery contest, where we had to fire arrows right across the stage at imaginary targets in the wings at the back, all to the accompaniment of rousing cheers from the crowd on stage.

Once again I found the 'running storyline format' of pantomime much more enjoyable than that of the straightforward variety show, where separate acts follow each other on to do their stuff. Only coming together 'perhaps' at curtain up, and a grand finale at the end.

Christmas was now almost on top of us, and Babs decided she'd like to come up to spend a few days with me. This gave her the chance to see the panto a couple of times, as well as take her first look at Coventry, with its cathedral, shops etc. We had such a lovely few days just wandering around exploring together, that by the time she set off back home to pick up her job again, we were almost into the New Year.

SOME MAJOR EVENTS OF THE YEAR:
(1) Alaska became the 40th state of the USA.
(2) The novel *Dr Zhivago* published. / The musical *West Side Story* staged.

(3) Britain's rocket Black Knight was fired.

(4) Herstmonceux Observatory completed.

(5) The Van Allen belts round the Earth discovered.

(6) Reports of the Abominable Snowman (Yeti) received from
    Central Asia.

(7) Munich air crash kills seven Manchester United footballers.

35

The World of Opera Looms

1959 (30 years old in July)
The panto continued on into January, still doing well and playing to pretty full houses. However, at some time early in the month I decided that after spending almost two years gaining professional stage and singing experience with the George Mitchell Singers – which I was certainly grateful for – the time had finally come to get off this show-biz 'side road', and set my feet onto the operatic 'main road', where I wanted to be. I therefore wrote off to Sadler's Wells Opera Company asking for an audition. To my delight, after a couple weeks of hopefully checking the post every day, a letter finally arrived inviting me to an audition for their chorus in the following week. Fortunately, this was scheduled for the morning, which meant I'd have plenty of time to get down there, and back in time for the evening show afterwards.

When the day arrived I drove down from Coventry to London very early in my old MG. Which, as usual, rattled and complained for most of the way, but got me into Islington's Roseberry Avenue and the Wells Theatre in plenty of time.

The audition turned out to be up on the top floor, in the large mirror-lined rehearsal come ballet-practice room. I'd been to Sadler's Wells Theatre plenty of times before, of course, but only as a paying customer, and this was the first time I'd ever had a chance to see behind the scenes, so this in itself was an exciting experience.

I don't remember seeing any other audition candidates there, though I suppose there must have been. However, I was called in to find myself facing a group of unknown adjudicators, plus a pianist at the piano.

After a brief introduction one of them asked: "And what have you brought along to sing for us?"

"The 'Prize Song' from *Die Meistersinger*," I replied.

A few eyebrows went up as they glanced at each other.

"Will that be all right?" I asked.

"Oh yes. . ! Yes," came the reply. "That'll be fine."

I gave my music to the pianist, then belted my way through what was my favourite party piece quite well. When I'd finished the pianist gave me a nod and a smile of approval. And from the looks on the faces of the others I felt I'd made a pretty good impression.

"Thank you for coming," said the one who appeared to be in charge. "Well, I think it's safe to say that we'll be offering you a position. It's in the chorus, you realise?"

"Yes," I replied, "I knew that."

"Good!" he said. "We'll drop you a line with all the details next week."

I thanked the pianist, gathered up my music and was off down the stairs to the car in a wonderful haze of achievement. At long last I was actually about to join a famous professional opera company, just as I always felt sure I would.

When the details finally arrived, I found I was being offered a year's contract, and although it was only in the chorus, it was at least a foot on the first rung of a ladder which I felt I could eventually climb.

There was, however, one problem that had to be solved before I could take up their offer. I was still under contract to George Mitchell for another month, and the Sadler's Wells contract gave me a starting date for about two weeks time. Fortunately, George Mitchell, who had singing groups all over the country, just happened to be visiting the Coventry Theatre that week. So I button-holed him at the first opportunity and put my case to him, asking to be released from my contract early. George Mitchell, being the decent chap he always was, agreed to do so, provided I could find some other singer to fill my place for the last two weeks of my contract.

As luck would have it, I happened to know that one of my former George Mitchell Singer friends, who'd been appearing in some other theatre, had just come to the end of his contract. So I contacted him and he was only too pleased to come up to Coventry and take over; especially as it meant a couple of extra weeks work for him. Once he'd arrived and settled into my place in our four man group, I was able to leave Coventry behind and head back home for London.

One other change I'd decided to make on this transition from showbiz, panto and the clubs was my name. I'd felt for some time that the name 'Workman' didn't exactly fit the image of a romantic operatic tenor. Fortunately, there was another name in our 'family' which I felt had a much more appropriate ring about it, so I plumped for that. This was the name 'Morrell', which was the name of my half-brother and sister from my mother's first marriage.

I'd informed the Sadler's Wells management about this when I sent back my signed contract, so right from the start I was known as Alan Morrell. Fortunately, this didn't seem to come as any surprise to them, as apparently quite a few of their other singers had adopted professional names for the stage.

The first thing I discovered in my first week, was that the company I was joining, was in fact the old 'Carl Rosa Company', which Sadler's Wells had only just taken over as a 'second' company. This, apparently, was to enable Sadler's Wells, to take over Carl Rosa's role as a National Touring Company, as well as running the permanent one in London. The policy was that both companies would be equal in status, and would alternate between the London theatre and touring the provinces approximately every three months.

Since the very first opera I ever saw was the Carl Rosa's performance of *Faust* at Shrewsbury when I was in the army, it seemed a rather odd coincidence that here I was, now joining what was 'ostensibly' that same company.

As this Wells/Carl Rosa branch of the company were already in the process of rehearsing for their next tour of the country, I had quite a bit of catching up to do. This meant that my first job on arriving was a visit to the theatre's music library to collect scores for the four or five operas we were about to take out on the road.

As far as I can remember, these included *Rigoletto*, *Magic Flute*, *La Boheme*, *Barber of Seville*, *Samson & Delilah* and the operetta *Orpheus in the Underworld*. Rehearsals while in town, I found, were usually held in the large top floor ballet practice room where I'd sung for my audition, so at least I was no stranger to that. My first impressions on this occasion, however, were somewhat different, because when I walked into that room this time I found it absolutely packed with singers. It was only then that it dawned on me, just how large a group of singers I'd now be singing with compared to the mere handfuls I'd been used to in the George Mitchell groups.

Made up of six fairly equal sections of sopranos, mezzos, altos, tenors, baritones and basses, we numbered about fifty in all. And while quite a lot of them were, as I'd expected, former Carl Rosa singers, several others had been members of the D'Oyly Carte, Gilbert & Sullivan Opera Company, and one or two had even been freelances, like myself.

The chorus master in charge of us all was John Barker, an unassuming, but highly competent musician. He was so well regarded in the company that even some of the orchestral conductors would sometimes confer with him about odd technicalities in the score. His sight reading at the piano was legendary, and some of the other music staff claimed that you could put a piece of music 'upside down' on the piano in front of him, and even if he'd never seen it before he'd play it through 'note perfect'.

What mattered most to me, however, was that he was also very easy to get on with, so there was a good working atmosphere in the chorus.

The best part of that first week was spent up in the ballet room with our scores, learning the chorus parts from all the operas in our coming repertoire by endlessly going over the notes until we'd got them right – 'note bashing' we called this. Once we'd reached this stage, the scores were put aside and we'd then have to practise singing everything from memory.

For the next phase of our rehearsals we were all assembled down on stage to try everything out with 'our' Sadler's Wells Orchestra – there were actually two of these, one for each company, with around sixty musicians in each. Once this was satisfactory, we were then pitched into 'production' rehearsals with the various producers responsible for the different operas.

At some stage in all this we were fitted with our costumes for the operas, followed by dress parades to make sure that the producers and wardrobe staff were satisfied with the results. Finally, there were full 'dress rehearsals' on stage for each of the operas, with scenery, lighting, orchestra, etc., to make sure everything was working as it should do, and ready for our impending invasion of the provinces.

At sometime during all this frenetic activity, I decided that I now had no further use for the old MG. And as I didn't want to leave it rusting away in the roadway outside our flat in Aldridge Road Villas, I drove it to a car auction room somewhere over in Brixton where they sold it for us; happily getting us back just about what we'd originally paid for it.

When the day finally arrived, the whole company of singers and musicians set off by train to begin what was my first operatic tour of the UK; leaving the stage hands and their great furniture vans loaded with scenery, hampers of costumes and everything else needed for the production, to follow on by road.

As far as I can remember, our venues on this first tour included: the King's Theatre, Southsea; Bournemouth Pavilion; Bristol Theatre; Grand Theatre, Wolverhampton; Bradford Alhambra; York Theatre; Newcastle Theatre Royal and the Glasgow Alhambra.

This travelling around the whole of the UK staying in different digs every week, and singing our six different operas in different theatres every week, opened up a whole new, slightly hectic, world of theatrical experience for me. We usually did six evening performances every week, plus a matinée on the Saturday – which was normally a repeat of the operetta.

The opera I particularly remember was *Rigoletto*, because I'd been given the minor role of Count Borsa in this, which although small was, I felt, a promising start. I'd also been given the even more minor role of Apollo in *Orpheus in the Underworld*, which I suppose added 'slightly' to this impression.

After our fairly long busy tour performing in a great many different theatres in towns and cities all over the UK, most of which I'd never been to before, we arrived back in London for our first season at Sadler's Wells itself, much to the delight of Babs who'd been left behind in the flat all this time, because we'd now be able to pick up on something like a normal life again; for the next few months at least.

The beautiful Wells Theatre on Roseberry Avenue, which had originally been the home of the Sadler's Wells 'Ballet Company', had such a wonderfully resonant auditorium that every time I walked out onto its stage and heard its acoustics, I felt like bursting into song. Since it was also the first London Theatre I'd ever appeared in, I felt as if I'd really arrived at where I wanted to be.

With the other company now setting out on tour to carry on where we'd left off, we were soon plunged into performing our touring repertoire for the audiences of London. During the daytime we also began gradually working our way through the repertoire for our next tour in the late autumn.

After our last long separation, Babs and I were determined to work out some way that she could travel with me on tour in future. As an interim measure, however, we decided that for the next tour she should travel up to join us occasionally, staying in the digs with me until we could come up with a better solution.

One of the regular routines that cropped up during this summer period were obligatory auditions. Apparently these were an annual event we all had to go through in order to guarantee our next year's contract. I didn't mind this at all, as it gave me another chance to prove my worth. On this occasion I sang 'Celeste Aida' from Verdi's opera, *Aida* which I felt went well, and secured my contract for the following year. I also got quite a few encouraging comments on my singing from members of the music staff afterwards, but unfortunately 'none' from the only person whose opinions really carried any weight at the Wells, the 'director'. Was this an early warning against being too optimistic about my future chances at the Wells. . ? If it was, then I let it go, because I had too much confidence in my own voice to be put off by such things.

During these early performances at the Wells I'd picked up on my occasional dressing room story-scribbling again, just as I'd done in the Mitchell shows. As before, this aroused quite a bit of curiosity among my fellow singers, but was soon accepted as a normal part of our dressing room activity. This was especially so when one of my fellow choristers, an Australian baritone called Bob Eddy, also began making use of his gift as a talented artist to turn out brilliant stylised portraits of the other singers in the company in their full costumes. So our dressing room became quite a creative workplace between scenes, with writing and painting going on intently against a background of Grand Opera filtering faintly down through the Tannoy from the stage above.

By the time the other Wells Company arrived back from their tour we'd just about got the operas for our autumn outing ready to go. Before this started, however, the theatre closed down for the annual holiday, giving us all a welcome break for about three weeks.

At some time in this autumn period our landlady, Mrs Samuel, sadly died, and 24 Aldridge Rd Villas was sold off to a new Irish landlord who immediately set about turning what had been her ground floor flat and basement into a drinking club.

Although this was no direct threat to us in our flat on the top floor, and the landlord was putting no pressure on us to leave, it soon became obvious from the noise and late night music that we weren't going to be able to stay there much longer. On the plus side, it did spur us on to find a way in which we could both go off on tour together without having to worry about keeping a permanent flat in London.

One other positive side in this was that whilst our new landlord obviously had no interest in having tenants in the building, he didn't seem too bothered about collecting rent either, because whenever I tried to pay it he'd keep putting it off with:

"Not just now. Give it to me later," until in the end we owed him about three months' rent.

Our autumn tour eventually got under way, and because of the flat situation Babs spent quite a lot more time travelling with me than we'd originally planned. However, being together actually worked out to our advantage, because when we were about half way through the tour we suddenly found what seemed the complete solution to our touring problem. A married couple who were in the orchestra unexpectedly turned up one week with a motorised caravan that they'd just bought. These compact caravans were apparently fairly new on the market, and were based simply on the ordinary fifteen hundredweight delivery vans which could be seen charging along the roads everywhere. To us they seemed an absolutely brilliant idea, and exactly what we were looking for. One of these would give us both our transport and living accommodation in one compact vehicle which was not that much larger than the average car, and just as easy to drive.

When my orchestral colleagues gave us the chance to inspect their new pride and joy, we made up our minds instantly. However, as we were still only halfway through the tour, bringing it about would have to wait until we got back to London. This was partly because we'd somehow have to raise the money to buy the van, but also to work out the best way of getting out of the flat in which we had quite a bit of our own furniture.

Under the circumstances, waiting for the tour to run its course seemed an eternity. For me it wasn't too bad, because I was involved every evening in a whole new repertoire of opera productions, plus the odd rehearsal here and there during the day. For Babs, though, the waiting must have seemed endless.

However, our final performance was eventually over, and we found ourselves heading back for London.

Once back in the flat, our first priority was the motor home. London was the place where you could get absolutely 'anything', and after searching around we discovered that there were actually several different types of these van-caravan conversions available, each being put out by different van manufacturers. The only one we'd seen so far was that owned by the orchestral couple which was a Volkswagen, but after viewing some of the alternatives, we finally came across the Vauxhall Bedford long wheelbase Dormobile. This was not only much more roomy, but had an extending roof which could be raised up when parked, giving you enough headroom to stand upright and walk about.

The main Vauxhall dealers we found were somewhere in the upper part of Edgware Road and couldn't have been more helpful, fixing up the whole deal, including hire purchase, on the spot. We had to wait for delivery though, because the actual caravan conversions were done to order by the firm of Martin Walter away down in Folkstone.

After about three weeks, however, we collected our lovely new caravan and phase one of our venture was complete.

Phase two, however, was a little more tricky, because before we could get out of the flat we had somehow to sell off our furniture, and hopefully recover at least 'some' of the money we'd paid out for it.

After running around trying to find someone interested in it, we finally came across a second hand furniture dealer somewhere in Westbourne Park who agreed to come and have a look. On the day appointed he turned up, made a list of everything, including carpets, and made us an offer for the lot. Naturally, it was a lot less than we'd hoped for, but was at least better than simply walking away and leaving it, so we accepted. He went off to get his van straight away, and turned up with another chap to help him clear the whole lot out; after which he gave us our money and that was it.

Since we'd already cleaned the whole place up, and the landlord still showed no interest in collecting his rent, we simply left the keys in the lock, climbed into our new four-wheeled home and drove off into the sunset (well, sort of).

SOME MAJOR EVENTS OF THE YEAR:
(1) Street Offences act clears prostitutes from Britain's streets, especially London's.
(2) Communists, led by Castro, seize power in Cuba.
(3) The first section of the Ml motorway opened.
(4) The hovercraft invented by Christopher Cockerell (on the Isle of Wight).
(5) The driest summer for 200 years.

36

Life On the Open Road
(but not just yet)

1960 (31 years old in July)
Since the 1959 Christmas break was now almost upon us, we decided to take a bed-sit for a week or two while we got the Dormobile fitted out properly. It already had a Calor gas cooker, storage cupboards, sink with water tank, interior lighting and curtains, fold down bed, and a radio. So all we needed to get were kitchen utensils, crockery, pots and pans and food, plus warm bedding and a Tillie high pressure paraffin heater to keep us warm on cold nights.

The bed-sit we found on this occasion was in a street just around the corner from Arsenal's Highbury football stadium and only about a ten minute drive from Sadler's Wells Theatre. The landlady was a friendly Irish woman so this made a comfortable base until our next tour was due.

About this time I decided to do something more positive with my writing efforts by trying some of it out on magazine editors. Short stories seemed to be quite popular at the time, and although these weren't the sort of writing I felt drawn to I'd actually scribbled out one or two purely as practice pieces. Before I could send any off, however, they needed to be typed out properly, so getting myself a typewriter was obviously a first priority. Fortunately there was a small stationery shop in the Highbury area where they were advertising secondhand machines. So I managed to get myself a compact little 'Empire Aristocrat' portable, which would stow away very neatly in the Dormobile, and began clattering away in my spare time, learning how to use it.

At first I found this pretty frustrating, because unlike modern word processors, where you can simply delete any mistakes and type them again, with these old typewriters this wasn't possible, and any typing mistake meant that the whole page had to be scrapped and retyped. There was, in fact, a white liquid you could buy called Tipp-ex which you could use to cover up these mistakes, but this was pretty noticeable and left the page looking a bit of a dog's dinner.

Another problem with these old typewriters was that if you were sending your work to an editor, you obviously had to keep a copy of it for yourself, and since there were no such things as photocopiers in those days, the only way you could get a copy was to make a 'carbon' copy. To do this you had to make a sandwich of two sheets of typing paper with a sheet of special 'carbon paper' in between them, and wind the whole thing into your typewriter. In this way everything you typed on the top sheet left a carbon imprint on the one underneath. Although these carbon copies were a bit messy, and mistakes on them couldn't be rectified, at least they provided you with a copy of your original work in case the top one disappeared in the post, or was never returned by the magazine editor.

By the time we were ready to set out on our next Sadler's Wells tour, my typing, though still somewhat laborious, was coming along quite nicely. I'd managed to type out a couple of what I regarded as the better of my short story efforts, and decided to send one off to see what happened. This was titled *The Trial*, (appropriately enough) and for some reason, which I can't quite recall, I sent it off to an Australian magazine named *Pocket Man*. Perhaps I thought it might be safer to start on the other side of the world and gradually work my way back this way, I don't know. However, off it went over the horizon, while we booked out of our bed-sit, and set off to tour yet more of Britain's theatres, while looking forward to our new gipsy life on the highways in the Dormobile.

One of the first things we learned, almost immediately, was that parking overnight on lay-bys or similar stopping places, was not quite as simple as we'd thought. No matter where we decided to rest our weary heads, we always seemed to attract the attention of the local police patrols. In fact, being knocked up in the middle of the night to find a couple of curious bobbies shining torches through the windows became quite a regular event, especially if we'd returned to the same place more then once, which we frequently did.

Fortunately they were never over-officious, and usually explained that it was part of their job to keep tabs on everything unusual that they came across in their area. In fact, one of them even gave us a couple of tips about the best way to park up for the night without being disturbed. The first one being, 'don't park on the actual lay-by', as this was technically part of the highway and 'restricted', but to park on the grass verge as this wasn't. Secondly, if we planned to come back for several nights, it was best to let the local police know and then we could be there all week without being disturbed.

This travelling the highways and byways was a whole new way of life for us, especially for Barbara, who'd never travelled much beyond her home town of London before she met me. And now, with the van being our home, we were able to sleep in a different location every night if we wished, which gave us more chance to see the countryside around the towns we were playing in than if we were living in digs.

Another bonus on this tour was that there were now about three other couples in the company travelling in motorised caravans of various makes. This led the company to occasionally get permission for us to park up on empty sites owned by the local council. Aberdeen was one of these, where we settled down for the week on a site right behind the theatre free of charge, with all the theatre washing and toilet facilities close at hand.

The one site that stands out, however, was the one in Sunderland where we were playing the Empire Theatre. The council gave us permission to use their car park on the seafront, which at that time was home to a large travelling funfair. This turned out to be an unexpected new experience for us because we found ourselves parked up for the week in our small Dormobile right in the midst of 'real' travelling show people with their large, beautifully appointed caravans. Fortunately they accepted us immediately as fellow travellers just like themselves.

The head man of the travellers was a 'tough as nails' but friendly individual who was obviously a born and bred 'traveller'. His own impressive caravan was one of the largest on the site, and didn't look like a caravan at all, because it was in two separate parts set out in a 'T' shape; which must have come apart for towing.

He loved talking about the traveller's way of life. Of being constantly on the move from one fairground location to the next and never quite knowing what to expect when they got there. Would it be sunshine and good crowds, or a rainy, muddy wash out. Would there be any trouble on the Saturday night with drunken local rowdies looking for bother – something which he assured us he and his men were more than capable of sorting out with their own swift brand of summary justice. Judging from the look of the other male travellers on the site, you'd need to be pretty drunk to try tangling with them.

He invited Babs and I into his caravan a couple of times for a cup of tea, and with this being a 'T' shape, with two rooms leading off sideways, once you stepped into its beautifully ornamented interior, all done out in polished woodwork, glass cabinets and mirrors, it was more like being in a miniature palace than a caravan.

As usual, once the tour had got under way, rehearsals during the day became part of the weekly routine. These were mainly to keep our evening performances up to scratch and iron out any problems that might have crept in, but also to give understudies the chance to run through the parts they were covering. Unfortunately, as far as we choristers were concerned, the only understudy opportunities that came our way seemed to be for the minor roles – of which I usually had a couple. One of these being Monostatos in Mozart's *Magic Flute*, which I actually got a chance to perform on one occasion when the singer doing it went down with a cold.

I found this 'cover' situation particularly frustrating, because although these little crumbs were better than nothing, they were far below what I knew I was capable of if given the opportunity. Sadly I wasn't alone in this, as there were four or five other singers in the chorus, male and female, with exceptionally good voices whose vocal talents seemed to be consistently ignored.

In the end I got so fed up with this management attitude that I put in a request to them, via our chorus master John Barker, that they should consider giving certain 'suitable' members of the chorus the opportunity to cover the major roles as well as the minor ones. I pointed out that this would produce a two-fold benefit, in that it would not only give 'us' the encouragement we felt we ought to be getting, but would also provide the company with 'extra' understudies in case of emergency.

After a bit of a delay, an answer finally trickled down from the heights to the effect that they thought it might be worth considering, and that they'd probably give it a try later on at the Wells Theatre when we were back in town. Despite this semi-positive response, or rather because of it, I couldn't help feeling at the time that they weren't exactly bursting with enthusiasm about the idea. However, we'd have to wait and see.

At some time in the season I received a reply from the *Pocket Man* magazine in Australia, forwarded on from Sadler's Wells Theatre in London – which was the address I'd given them – telling me that they'd accepted my short story, and enclosing a cheque for what amounted to almost a week's pay at the Wells.

Success at my first attempt. . ! I could hardly believe it. And even though I didn't regard short stories as anything more than basic writing practice – children's adventure novels being what I really wanted to write – this confirmation of my writing ability was a big boost.

When we finally arrived back in London after this spring tour, Babs and I were faced with the problem of finding accommodation for the following season at the Wells Theatre. As we were by now quite accustomed to living in the Dormobile, we decided not to bother looking for a temporary bed-sit immediately, but would try living in it for a while in town. Since there was obviously no way of sleeping in it overnight on the streets of London, this meant driving out into the countryside each night just as we'd done everywhere else. With London being vastly bigger than 'everywhere else', at first this seemed a pretty tall order. However, we eventually managed to find a few quiet country roads away out near Elstree, where nobody seemed to notice our late night comings and our early morning goings. So that was it – for 'this' period in London at least.

After a little bit of prompting about our 'understudy' request, the management did finally set up a few sessions with a couple of the répétiteurs on the music staff as promised. But these turned out to be such uninspiring affairs, with the répétiteurs obviously just going through the motions, that we suspected them immediately of being no more than a ploy to keep us quiet. Consequently, as these sessions were on a voluntary basis, we all decided that we weren't going to fall for this, and gave them the boot as a complete waste of time.

One result of this was that the company lost two exceptionally fine soprano voices when two of our 'would be' understudies group, turned down the renewal of their contracts that year and went off to Covent Garden where they were immediately offered contracts with much better future prospects.

As the summer holiday was soon looming, those of us who were staying were once again having to face up to our annual auditions. For some reason these were not being held in our own Sadler's Wells Theatre this year, but in the Haymarket Theatre in central London. However, as it gave me the chance of trying out my voice in another of London's famous theatres, I enjoyed the challenge. In the event it all went well, so my contract was safe for another year.

Once the summer holiday was over, which we'd spent cruising around the South Coast holiday resorts in the caravan, it was back to London to continue our season of evening performances at the Wells, while at the same time rehearsing our new operatic repertoire during the day for the autumn tour.

At some time during this period I somehow came across a leaflet for the charity Oxfam, which up to then I'd never heard of. However, I was so impressed with the work they were doing in tackling the dire poverty that existed in the more deprived areas of the world that I sent them a donation. This resulted in them sending me other, more detailed leaflets, emphasising just how great was the need for all the different kinds of aid they were trying to provide, and asking if I'd be able to help in this by making a small 'regular' monthly donation.

After some thought, and bearing in mind our own far from affluent financial situation, I decided we probably could, so long as it 'was' small. Furthermore, it occurred to me, that if I could persuade some of my fellow singers at the Wells to do the same, then perhaps between us we might be able to raise a slightly more worthwhile contribution to send off every month.

My first move, therefore, was to pin a note suggesting this on the notice board in the staff entrance at the theatre. I also pinned up a very persuasive Oxfam leaflet and a large sheet of paper for the signatures of all those willing to take part. I thought that at best I might, with luck, get about a dozen or so. But to my astonishment, within a fortnight I found myself faced with the pretty daunting prospect of having to collect monthly contributions from around a hundred and fifty people. Among them being some of the best known opera singers in the country, and a couple of conductors with international reputations. (Copies of these lists are in a photographic section of this book).

Having set the whole thing in motion, however, I had no option but to see it through, and began doing the rounds collecting contributions almost immediately. The problem was that because of the frenetic nature of life at the Wells, with people constantly on the move and spread across the two different companies which were hardly ever in town at the same time, it was almost impossible for me to pin everyone down for their contributions each month. Unfortunately, what had seemed a good idea, was soon proving to be a something of a nightmare.

Fortunately, though, with people passing on their contributions to me via others, etc., it gradually began to work. 'Most' of their contributions seemed to be reaching me in time each month, so I was able to send them off and pin the receipts on the notice board for all to see.

Our autumn season soon got under way, and we found ourselves once more out on the open road performing in quite a few new theatres as well as a couple of the old ones that had a particular meaning for me. One of these turned out to be the Lyceum Theatre in Sheffield; my old stamping ground for panto and the clubs. While the other was in Dundee, Scotland, where we played the same theatre that I'd made my solo operatic debut singing Prince John in *Maid Marian*.

310

Our final new venue for this year was The Shakespeare Memorial Theatre in Stratford-upon-Avon, where we spent around two weeks over the Christmas period conveniently parked up on the theatre car park. A real 'extra' bonus of being there just then was that the great American film star singer Paul Robeson was due to appear there with the resident Shakespearian Theatre Company in the role of Othello, and they were at that time in the process of rehearsal. We'd often see him strolling around the gardens outside the theatre in discussion with other members of the cast. To me, seeing this great iconic figure from such exciting adventure films as *Sanders of the River* – which I'd seen as a kid on screen in Barrow's old cinemas – actually walking past me in the flesh, was just incredible.

SOME MAJOR EVENTS OF THE YEAR:

(1) American U2 spy plane shot down over Russia.
(2) John Kennedy becomes the US President.
(3) *Lady Chatterley's Lover* (unexpurgated version) published.
     Hitchcock's *Psycho* screened.
(4) The farthing withdrawn from use. Stiletto-heeled shoes in fashion.
(5) Britain's last tram service comes to an end in Sheffield.
(6) Princess Margaret and Anthony Armstrong-Jones married.

37

Touring, Singing & Scribbling

1961 (32 years old in July)
After our usual Christmas break we ended up back in London to prepare for the spring tour, which added several different operas to our repertoire, plus the operetta *Orpheus in the Underworld*. In this I was given the small part of Apollo, which I suppose seemed a 'slight' indication that I was being singled out from the crowd to some extent – but not very much.

From time to time since joining the company I'd received quite a few favourable comments and encouragements about my voice from various members of the music staff, répétiteurs, etc., even from one of the conductors, so had hoped that sooner or later this may lead to bigger and better opportunities. Unfortunately, I'd already learned from the experiences of other promising singers, that the opinions of none of these people carried any real weight at the Wells, and that the only opinions which did were those of the director himself. Since he was an establishment appointee, with neither musical nor vocal qualifications, his judgements proved pretty obviously to be based 'less' on a singer's vocal talent than on their social background and connections – the criteria by which he himself had got his job.

One glaring example of this, I heard about from some of the music staff, concerned one of the auditions which the company occasionally held in some of the towns we were playing while out on tour. The Wells were apparently obliged to hold these auditions around the provinces, simply because we were a 'National' opera company, subsidised by the Arts Council, and not a purely London one. At these auditions the director himself usually presided, with members of the music staff to act 'ostensibly' as a sort of jury. On this occasion, however, the standard of singers hadn't been all that high, until one particular baritone began pouring out his offering in an absolutely superb voice. The music staff were all knocked out by his singing, so were astonished when, at the discussion later, the director simply declared:

"Well, I didn't think any on them were any good."

"But what about the baritone?" protested all the music staff, in disbelief.

"I don't like his teacher," replied the director.

And that was it; the explanation of why we'd so often seen singers being brought in on principal contracts whose voices were nowhere near as good as half the members of the chorus.

I remember one soprano who'd been brought in to take over a particular principal role, whose singing was so dire that it prompted one of the chorus sopranos – a big, down to earth type, with a really fine voice herself – to declare in disgust afterwards:

"I could 'fart' better than that!"

Whether she could or not, 'fortunately' I never found out.

Despite all this, however, Sadler's Wells 'did' have some very fine principal singers on their books at the time, including a few of real international standard, like the tenor Charles Craig; the sopranos Ava June, Rita Hunter, June Bronhill and Victoria Elliot; the mezzo-soprano Joyce Blackham and her baritone husband Peter Glossop; plus bassos Howell Glynne, Owen Brannigan, and for a brief period a Polish bass called Marian Nowakowski who had one of the most beautiful quality bass voices I'd ever heard.

Incidentally, I'd actually heard this Polish bass several years before when he'd come to Barrow to do a concert. In those days, however, he was singing under the name of Marian Zigmunt. I never did find out why he'd changed his name. Perhaps it was for the same reason that many of the Wells singers had done so – including me.

To my amazement, one of the early venues of our spring tour this year turned out to be the Coliseum Cinema in my home town of Barrow-in-Furness. I say amazement, firstly because Sadler's Wells had never to my knowledge ever performed in Barrow before, but also because to me the Coliseum – which was one of the most beautiful and impressive buildings in the town, being built of ornamental white stone with a dome on the top – had only ever been associated in my mind with the rough and tumble Saturday morning film shows as a kid. However, like most other cinemas in the town, it had originally been built as a theatre, so still had the original stage, flies and wings hidden away behind the screen.

313

o

When the Barrow week eventually arrived, we turned up with the Dormobile in the fading daylight to look for a spot on Walney Island beach where we could park up for the week. Eventually we came across what had once been the site of a wartime army camp right on the seashore. All the huts had long since disappeared, but fortunately the concrete bases were still there, which made ideal parking platforms for the Dormobile.

As it was very late when we arrived, I managed to park up for the night on one of these bases in the darkness and got out for a quick look around. As I stepped off the concrete base, however, expecting my foot to land on grass, I discovered somewhat too late that on this side of the platform there was a drop of nearly two feet onto a pile of broken bricks.

The intense pain that shot through my twisted ankle, and the impressive somersault that followed, left me lying flat on my back in agony on the pile of jagged bricks, without quite realising how I'd got there.

As I dragged myself up and hobbled painfully into the van, my first thought was: 'What a preposterous way to begin my first operatic visit to my home town. How the devil am I going to get through the week hobbling about the stage with an ankle which was rapidly swelling to the size of a turnip?' To make matters worse another, more immediate, problem quickly struck me: 'How the devil were we even going to get to the theatre, since Babs couldn't drive?'

This led to us bathing my swollen lump for half the night in hot and cold water, trying to get it down to something resembling a human ankle. This probably helped to some extent, but when we set off very gingerly the next morning heading for Barrow's North Lonsdale Hospital to see if they could improve the situation, my foot pedal technique was pretty unorthodox, to say the least.

However, we eventually arrived in the hospital courtyard and I hobbled hopefully into the accident and emergency department. These hopes were quickly dashed, however, when the doctor on duty looked at it with a frown and demanded:

"When did this happen?"

"About midnight last night," I replied.

"Well, there's nothing I can do with it now," he declared flatly. "You should have come in straight away."

"What? At midnight!" I retorted. "The hospital wouldn't have been open then."

The doctor just shrugged unconcernedly and walked off.

Before I could blow my top, however, the nursing sister who was

314

also there gave me a little sign to say nothing. And as soon as he'd gone she bathed it, bound it tightly with a bandage and gave me a few tips on how to cope with it.

Fortunately, following her advice, I managed to hobble through that week's performances without too much hassle, and things 'generally' took a turn for the better.

Firstly, we had a visit from an *Evening Mail* photographer eager to get a shot of this unexpected local 'celebrity' who'd arrived with the company. This photo, plus the article that appeared in the paper with it that evening, led to several messages being left at the stage door from people who'd known me or our family. One of these, Mrs Naughton, whose family had only lived a couple of doors away from our house at 144, actually worked in the large garage right next to the theatre, and called in to see me, greeting me almost like a long lost son.

Another surprise was a note left by my Uncle William – my dad's brother who'd lost his legs in the shipyard accident – inviting us to call in for a visit. The surprise in this case being not only very welcome, but intriguing, since, strange as it may seem, it dawned on me at that moment that I had only the vaguest of childhood memories of my uncle, or any of my other relatives in Barrow for that matter. Why this should be I had no idea.

Uncle William, it turned out, lived in the top end of Marsh Street on the other side of the Greengate Bridge – which spanned the street making both halves seem almost like different districts.

The first thing that struck me on meeting Uncle William was just how much he resembled my father; the same looks, the same manner of talking, even the same sense of humour. The one difference being that he looked quite a bit taller than my dad had been, though since he had two false legs they could have made him as tall as he wanted to be.

The second thing I gathered, was that Violet, the woman he was living with, was not his original wife so not really my aunt. . . Could this 'rift' in the family account for the somewhat vague early memories of my Barrow relatives? I don't know.

However, in the course of the couple of hours we spent with them, this gap in my knowledge was filled in amazingly. It was almost like whole new horizons opening up. It turned out that I not only had quite a few relatives in Barrow who I knew little about, but in Scotland as well – in both Glasgow and Inverness. This Scottish connection was particularly interesting at that moment, because it so happened that our present Sadler's Wells tour would be taking us north of the border to play in Glasgow itself, and further north in Aberdeen – which was within striking distance of Inverness.

The upshot of all this was that when we left Barrow, Uncle William not only gave us the relevant addresses in both places, but promised to write off to let these newly discovered relatives of mine know about the 'possibility' of our turning up on their doorsteps.

Since the most northern of these two Scottish 'theatre' venues, Aberdeen, came first on our tour list, the relatives in Inverness – apparently my cousin Jenny and her family – would be the first ones we'd have the chance of calling in on. As this would only be possible on the Sunday at the end of our Aberdeen week, when we'd be making our way down to Glasgow, and it would involve a detour north of some seventy miles, I decided to ring Jenny from Aberdeen first to check that this would be OK.

Fortunately it was, in fact she seemed just as keen about the visit as we were. So after our last performance on the Saturday evening we set off into the darkness of the Scottish Highlands, where we parked up for the night somewhere out on the moors. This was the beauty of the Dormobile – any remote bit of empty ground anywhere could immediately become our home for the night.

We reached the beautiful town of Inverness around mid-afternoon on the Sunday, to be met at the door by Jenny, her three young daughters and husband, Jim Armstrong.

Fortunately, Jenny remembered me from when we were in our teens, and was able to fill in quite a few more of the blanks in my memory of the family in Barrow. She was apparently the daughter of my Aunt Bessie, my dad's sister, who I actually 'had' heard of; and Aunt Bessie had particularly looked forward to meeting me because she was the only 'Auntie' I had. Unfortunately, I was never destined to do so because Jenny told me she'd died only a little while before our visit.

However, I had now met my Cousin Jenny and three little nieces. Their father, Jim Armstrong, was a born and bred Scot who was apparently an engineer in charge of looking after a large part of the highland road network, including the Isle of Skye.

After spending a lovely afternoon with them all, Babs and I set off for Glasgow vowing to keep in touch from then on.

As the route we chose led us right along the shores of Loch Ness we decided to park up for the night on a convenient lay-by overlooking the shore, with a panoramic view right along the loch.

To our surprise, once parked up, we spotted an intriguing group of vehicles parked up on another lay-by a little way down the loch from where we were. One of these vehicles was a truck with a large, wartime-like searchlight mounted up on its roof, which was pointing out across the loch. These turned out to be an expedition led by Donald Campbell which was carrying out a search for the Loch Ness Monster. Consequently, once darkness fell and the searchlight was switched on, we sat up for most of that night watching the beam sweep endlessly backwards and forwards over the surface of the water, while several small boats out there with camera crews circled around, obviously hoping for a sighting. Whether they got one or not we never discovered at the time, but it made for a fascinating, though sleepless, night of watching and hoping.

The searchlight was finally switched off towards dawn, and we were able to catch up with a few hours sleep before setting off again for Glasgow.

Once in Glasgow, with this being such a large city, we again had the usual overnight parking problems. So after the show each night we ended up driving sway out to Queensferry on the banks of the River Forth estuary right near the massive Forth Railway Bridge, where we'd park up in a little wood near the river.

As well as being large, Glasgow was a fascinating city full of bustling life and energy, and with its docks and shipbuilding industry I felt almost at home there. This feeling was further added to by the solid blocks of red sandstone tenement buildings everywhere, because copies of these tenement buildings had been built in Barrow to become the homes of shipyard workers 'there' too; and in one of them both my father and Uncle William had been born.

Glasgow had other fine buildings as well, like the Kelvin Museum and Art Gallery which became a favourite haunt of ours from then on. It also had a good, clattering tramway system winding its way through the city centre, which could also rattle you away out to the shores of Loch Lomond in about half an hour. With the Dormobile, however, we never got to use it. And in any case, finding our way to the address Uncle William had given us was our first priority.

When we finally pulled up there to knock on their door, it turned out to be a neat little bungalow tucked away in a quiet residential area of the city.

We were warmly welcomed in immediately by an elderly couple by the name of Hosie. They had another elderly lady living with them who was introduced as Mary Halden, who was apparently a retired school teacher. In fact, I got the impression that they'd all been school teachers at one time, and that they were all related in some way to the Workman clan, though quite how I never worked out.

However, they'd all apparently met my dad, and remembered him as a young soldier who'd come to visit them all in Glasgow just around the end of the First World War. Apparently, during his army service, he'd had quite a bit to do with horses – something he'd never mentioned to me. And since horses in the First World War were chiefly used for hauling gun carriages, munitions and supplies, I could only assume that he had something to do with an artillery regiment

This was all a real eye-opener for me, because my dad had never talked much about his army service, and to hear these three elderly relatives talking about a side of his life I'd known so little about was a revelation; almost like getting to know him properly for the first time.

Babs and I filled them in about ourselves and our touring adventures with the Wells, especially our recent night spent watching the search for the monster on Loch Ness. This brought a surprising reaction from Mary Halden.

"Well 'I' know it's there!" she declared eagerly, "because I've seen it myself." She then went on to describe a coach trip she'd been on with about twenty of her teacher colleagues some years before. This trip had skirted the Loch on the road above it, which gives a lovely clear view of the Loch looking down onto it. At one point along the road, apparently, one of her teacher colleagues suddenly called out excitedly that she could see something under the water.

The driver immediately pulled up and they all crowded over to the windows on that side, where every one of them could see what they all described as a very large creature swimming along just below the surface. And this was no fleeting glimpse, apparently, as they watched it for several minutes before it finally disappeared into the depths with a great swirl of water. . .

What a pity Donald Campbell wasn't there to hear her account.

We were soon heading south again, back across the border into England, and after all this hectic searching-out my long lost family, life on the road settled clown again to its normal pace. I was able to pick up on my writing again, which usually consisted of my dressing room scribbles in note books during performances, followed by typing up the results back in the van whenever I had the time. All of this made for a pretty slow process, but at least it kept the story images, which were constantly rising in my head, flowing out onto the paper.

The particular writing task I was engaged in at that time was, in fact, to be my second 'full length' children's adventure novel. The first one, *Wallace Winkle's Journey*, written some time earlier, had been aimed at slightly younger readers, so had been considerably shorter than this latest masterpiece was intended to be.

The main characters and plot for this longer one had been rolling around in the back of my mind for quite a long time and, as I've mentioned before, I'd even given it a name, *I'll See You in Somewhere*, but had got little further than that. I'd decided, therefore, that this particular tour was the time to bring it all to life and finally get it down on paper.

Although the story had been inspired to some extent by my memories of the sleepy country village of Orton, where I was evacuated during the war, it was to be a much 'wider ranging' fantasy adventure. Its main characters were a discontented small boy, and the old worn out country bus which had rattled through his village twice a week for as long as he could remember. When he learns that the old bus is as fed up as he is, having just found out that it's about to be thrown on the scrap heap, they decide to run away together in search of a wonderful, mysterious valley which the bus has heard about on its travels. The story is a tale of their adventures and all the weird and crackpot characters they meet along the way.

Our tour this year ended up once again with a season of two or three weeks at the Shakespeare Memorial Theatre in Stratford-upon-Avon, which took us over the Christmas period and into the New Year.

SOME MAJOR EVENTS OF THE YEAR:
(1) Lionel Bart's musical *Oliver* staged.
(2) Walt Disney's *101 Dalmatians* and *Exodus* Screened.
(3) BBC Children's Hour ends.
(4) Failed invasion attempt of Cuba by the USA backed Cuban exiles.
    (The Bay of Pigs disaster.)
(5) Yuri Gagarin becomes the first man in Space,
(6) Mini Cabs introduced in London.

38

Orpheus on TV

1962 (36 years old in July)
On returning to London, Babs and I decided that after almost two years of living summer and winter in our pretty cramped Dormobile, the time had come to move back into more civilised accommodation. We therefore found a decent bed-sit in Caledonian Road where we could get back to something resembling a normal existence. As it turned out, after her wandering gipsy life, Babs decided that she liked being back on her London home ground so much, that we agreed she should get herself a job and stay on in the bed-sit more or less permanently. I, therefore, would do all future Dormobile touring on my own.

Our new landlords were a very pleasant Italian couple, and despite the fact that Pentonville Prison was only about two hundred yards down the road in one direction and Holloway Women's Prison only a little further away in the opposite direction, the Caledonian area was quite a decent place to live, and was also within reasonable walking distance of Sadler's Wells Theatre.

Our first tour of the year opened up with a week at the Opera House in Manchester, which was followed by another week of rehearsing and recording a fully staged studio version of our *Orpheus in The Underworld* at the Granada TV studios there. Another new experience for us all. (There's a *Sunday Times* photograph depicting this in the photographic sections of this book.)

In a way, the new touring arrangement with Babs and I turned out to be just as well, because this year, after the first tour around Britain, we learned that our company was booked to go off on an extended tour on the continent; which Babs couldn't have come on anyway.

When embarkation day finally arrived, we set sail, literally, for foreign parts on the Cross Channel Ferry, to rattle along the continental railway lines from then on, while as usual our huge furniture vans of scenery, props, costumes, etc., had gone on ahead by road to blaze the trail. This time, however, not to the traditional theatres in Britain, but to a whole string of the largest opera houses in Europe.

Our first of these venues was to be the big opera house in Brussels, called the Theatre De La Monnaie; named Monnaie, apparently, because it had been built on what had been the site of the old Belgian Mint. One of the first things that struck me about our appearance there was the sheer size of the place, especially the stage area, which was like a huge warehouse full of purpose-built scenery which could be wheeled about on castors like moveable buildings. I remember that the first time I went down from the dressing rooms and through the door to go on stage, it was like stepping into a huge dark void with no sense of direction. In fact, I had to stop for a few seconds and listen to where the sound of the orchestra was coming from, to work out where the devil the front of the stage was.

One of the other, somewhat less impressive realities we all discovered about the 'Monnaie', were the toilet facilities, especially for the men. While the women in the company seemed to have all the normal toilets one would expect; men it seemed, shouldn't need these. At first we just looked around for them somewhat baffled, but when we asked, they just pointed out what amounted to nothing more than a trough in the wall of the busy main corridor through the dressing room area, which we were apparently expected to use in full view of all the people walking past. Since 'flashing' in public would get you arrested in Britain we refused to go along with it, even if it 'was' quite normal practice in Belgium. At first they seemed a bit bewildered by this. However, they ended up accepting it and partitioned off a section of the ladies loo, allocating it to us.

Fortunately, our opening night went down very well with the Brussels' audience. Which didn't surprise us, but apparently caused the Monnaie's management to breathe a great sigh of relief. This was because, with Saddlers Wells not being too well known on the continental operatic scene, they hadn't quite known what to expect. In the event, however, they were even more delighted with our reception than we were.

As usual for me, Brussels was not just a new operatic experience, but also another wonderful place to explore in my spare time between rehearsals and run-throughs. As well as being a beautiful historic city with ancient buildings, it also had other attractions, like the botanical gardens, and the huge 'Atomium' set in a park just outside the city. The 'Atomium' is an enormous metal structure about a hundred feet high and built in the shape of an atom. It had a huge globe suspended in the centre representing the nucleus, and smaller globes spaced around it representing the orbiting electrons. Each of these electrons was linked up to the large central globe by its own tube, one of which had a stairway inside leading up to the large central globe, which was actually a restaurant.

On the day I turned up, there didn't seem to be many people about. So I climbed these stairs up through the tube to the central nucleus and found that apart from the girl who served me at the coffee bar, I had the whole of this weird, metal bubble of a place to myself, so I sat there on my own thinking: 'Well, there can't be many people on the planet at this moment who are enjoying a coffee and a sandwich while sitting in the nucleus of an atom.'

Another special day of exploration I managed to fit in while at Brussels, however, had nothing to do with the world of atoms or fantasy, but with the stark reality of past history. This came about when I discovered that the famous 'Battle of Waterloo' which had determined the whole future of Europe – had actually been fought only a few miles outside the city. Not only this, but that the entire widespread battlefield area was still there with all its famous landmarks; having been preserved as a memorial; with a museum, visitor centre, etc.

Once I'd learned about this it didn't take me long to find out where to pick up the special bus that trundled out there several times a day, and after about half an hour of bumping through the sometimes cobbled streets in the outskirts of the city into the flattish Belgian countryside, I was dropped off with all the other, mainly foreign, sightseers outside the visitor centre.

The centre itself was full of maps, drawings and photographs, plus displays of battlefield debris that had been dug up on the site over the years. They also had a small cinema showing an ancient film about the battle; which was so old that I half expected to see Charlie Chaplin popping up here and there.

Once outside, however, I took my map and headed for the most outstanding landmark in the area. This was a huge manmade hill, at least a hundred feet high, on top of which stood an enormous red statue of the 'British Lion'; apparently a symbolic representation of the major part Britain had played in Napoleon's downfall.

There was a long flight of stone steps leading up to the statue and the viewing platform around it; which gave a panoramic view over the whole of the battlefield area. The flat balustrade top was marked out with arrows pointing to where all the major, well-documented actions of the battle had taken place: The 'Menin Road', the 'Farmhouse', etc. Apparently some 60,000 men had died out there during the battle that day, which was a chilling thought, even though it 'had' rescued the whole of Europe from coming under the heel of a ruthless dictatorship.

Our performances at the Monnaie finally came to an end after what had been a very successful week, and we were off by train to our next operatic venue, Amsterdam, which was just across the border in Holland. I'd passed 'through' Holland twice before, of course, when I was in the army on my way to Trieste, and back again to be demobbed in Aldershot. However, I'd never seen much of it except for glimpses from railway carriage windows, so this was my chance to fill in some of the blanks.

The Amsterdam Opera House, was again a large international operatic venue, with a stage and facilities to match, making it a real enjoyment to perform in. Our repertoire and performances seemed to go down just as well with the audiences as they had in Brussels, so we looked all set for another successful week.

Since Amsterdam was a new, inviting city to explore in my free time I was soon finding my way around among the maze of canals and bridges for which it was famous. The one place that I'd set my mind on finding above all the others, however, having only recently read *The Diary of Anne Frank* – was the house where she'd spent her last days during the war, hiding with her family in a garret from the Germans. It was where she'd written her incredibly moving diary, before they'd all been betrayed to the Gestapo, and taken off to end there lives in a Nazi death camp.

Since the house where it had all happened was now being preserved as a memorial museum to the tragedy that had been played out there, it didn't take me long to find. It stood in a row of other typically tall Dutch terraced houses, all very similar in appearance and four or five storeys high.

At the time I got there, fortunately, there seemed to be only two or three other visitors. So when they let me in and I climbed the main stairs to the landing, where the secret door up to the attic lay hidden behind a wardrobe, I felt as if I had the place to myself. The famous wardrobe was still there, but had been moved to one side to reveal the small door. As I climbed the narrow stairway up to the attic, the atmosphere of the place was so intense that it was like walking into the pages of the book. Everything was there; the sparse furniture, the table where she'd probably sat day after day writing her diary, and the roof

323

window out of which she'd constantly watched the nearby clock tower as it chimed away the hours as they slowly passed, having all the time to be careful not to be seen by people outside, or heard moving about by the neighbours. Constantly knowing full well that 'nobody' in that world outside could be trusted, and that their survival depended upon keeping absolute secrecy about their presence.

I stayed as long as I could in that attic, feeling that in some way they were all still there. Especially when the clock in the tower chimed; as it did a couple of times while I was wandering the rooms, and I found myself listening to the very sound that they'd all listened to in secrecy for so long.

Eventually I had to make my escape down the stairway and out into the everyday world of the present. Feeling that I'd been through an unbelievably moving, but rewarding experience.

After this exceptional highlight, the only other explorations I did in Amsterdam included a boat trip around the wide harbour, which was claimed to be one of the largest in Europe, and an expedition with a group from our company, male and female, into the famous red light district. This was quite a unique experience and apparently a popular tourist attraction. What struck me particularly about it, as compared to what I'd seen in London's Soho while working on the back door of the Regent Palace Hotel, was the absence of any sense of criminality. There was no sign of pimps and 'minders' lurking about, in fact the couple of streets involved here looked just like any ordinary, brightly lit area of shops; the difference being, that here the only commodity on sale was sex, with the goods on display in each shop window being a girl in her own well appointed boudoir. The way of doing business seemed to be, that any man who fancied one of the girls simply tapped on her window. She would then look him over, and if she didn't like the look of him, she'd simply wave him away and he'd have to go off to try one of the others. If she accepted him, however, she'd wave him to the side door to come in. She'd then close the window curtains to turn her boudoir into a private love nest.

I learned later that the reason for this absence of criminality, was simply that the sex trade here was controlled entirely by the local authority. Each girl was registered and under the protection of the police. They also, apparently, had to undergo regular medical examinations to ensure their fitness for the job.

Our performances in Amsterdam finally came to an end after another successful week, and we were soon packing up for our next Sunday train journey, this time to Hamburg in Germany.

Since Hamburg was a city which had suffered quite a lot during the

324

war from our RAF bombers, I was a bit apprehensive about what sort of reception we'd get. As it turned out, however, we were just as well received there as in Belgium and Holland. The fifteen years that had elapsed since the war ended, it seemed, had not only seen the city very much rebuilt, but the old antagonism between us confined to the past.

The beautiful Hamburg Opera House was not only one of the major operatic centres in Germany, but also in Europe. In fact, we were told that the city regarded their Opera House as so important that the subsidy they paid to it each year was more than the 'whole' of the arts council grant for Great Britain. It was also a real pleasure to work in, and their reception of our, by their standards 'small' company, was exceptionally warm and friendly. On our first night we even found that a fresh flower had been placed on every single dressing room table.

With opera being such a major part of the city life in Hamburg, all of our performances played to pretty full houses, and the press gave us some exceptionally good write-ups. One of the remarks made about our performance of Wagner's *Tannhäuser* – especially the 'Pilgrim's Chorus' – was that they were astonished at the volume and quality of the vocal sound being made by a chorus that was only half the size of their own resident one. Adding, much to our delight, 'Obviously if these singers were in Germany they'd all be singing as principals' – which pleased us all no end, as it was exactly what 'we'd' been trying to get across to the management all along. Unfortunately, this 'also' fell on deaf ears.

The only exploration I remember doing in Hamburg was when I wandered around the harbour area looking at the ships. On this occasion I couldn't find a café for a snack, until I spotted a group of harbour workers going down a gangway onto a sort of barge. They were obviously going for a refreshment break, so I followed them down. The barge turned out to be a sort of workers' canteen, and as nobody seemed too bothered about my presence, apart from a few odd glances, I had a coffee and a snack sitting among them, feeling somewhat like a bit of a square peg. However, the coffee and sandwiches were good, so I settled for that.

I'd also learned that Hamburg had its own tourist attraction red light area, but having just seen the one in Amsterdam, I adopted a blasé attitude to these fleshpots and decided to give this one a miss – after all, it could hardly have topped the one in Amsterdam.

As our stay in Hamburg drew to a close following another highly successful series of performances, we once more packed our suitcases and set off for our next operatic venue, which turned out to be the German capital itself, Berlin.

Since the country at that time was split up into 'East' Germany, controlled by Russia, and 'West' Germany, controlled jointly by England, America and France, the city of Berlin itself, although under the joint control of all the allies, actually lay isolated like an island inside Russian controlled East Germany. This meant that to reach it from West Germany you had to either drive along a strictly controlled road corridor through Russian occupied territory, or 'fly' into Berlin's Tempelhof Airport. For some reason 'we' were flown in, while our scenery vans had to get there through the road corridor.

On this flight our pilot actually did a circular sweep over the Russian controlled zone, to give us a glimpse of the vast difference there was between the bleak, basic austerity of the communist controlled areas of the city, and the brightly lit affluent area under western control. So by the time we landed in this small island of democracy in a sea of communism, it was obvious that 'this' part of our operatic tour was set to be a pretty unique experience.

The airport itself, and the part of the city we now found ourselves in, looked just like any of the other cities we'd been to in Europe, with most of the wartime bomb damage having been cleared away, and new building development obvious everywhere. My only personal disappointment being that we weren't going to be performing in the famous 'Berlin State Opera House', which I'd been particularly looking forward to, but in some other big theatre which I'd never heard of. The reason for this being simply that the 'Berlin State' was actually over in the Russian controlled part of the city, so was a no-go area for us.

Once settled in, however, our performances were soon under way to good, appreciative audiences, just as in all our venues so far.

With Berlin being such a wonderful 'one off' challenge, I was soon out and about on my free-time explorations of the many intriguing destinations in our half of this divided city. The most obvious of these being the notorious wall itself. And since the most iconic image I'd seen of this in the newsreels was the Brandenburg Gate, I headed for this on my first free day. Being such an outstanding Berlin landmark this didn't take too long to find, and I was soon standing in front of the huge stone archway staring through the barbed wire and down the Unter den Linden, which stretched away into the communist world on the other side.

Although the Unter den Linden, with its famous Linden Trees lining both sides, still looked attractive, there was a strangely deserted look about it. There was no sign of traffic or people – with the exception of the odd armed East German policeman strolling about here and there.

Fairly close to the concrete, barbed wire-topped wall which stretched away in both directions from the gate, I noticed that there was a wooden viewing platform with steps. And as this had obviously been built for nosey people like myself, I climbed the steps and took my first close look into the communist world on the other side. The first thing I noticed was that on their side, all the ground within about a hundred yards of the wall had been completely cleared of buildings, trees, etc. This had pretty obviously been done to create a rough area of open ground, which anyone on their side trying to do a runner to the West would have to cross just to reach the wall, let alone climb over it.

Since there were, apparently, tall watch towers manned by armed border guards at regular intervals along its whole length – one of which I could actually see from the platform – you'd have to be pretty desperate to try it.

As I was determined to see as much of the wall as possible, I set off to walk along its length as far as I could in the relatively short time available. Fortunately, I found that even on our side of the wall quite a bit of open space seemed to have been left clear through what had once been streets, small parks and woodland. There were, however, a few stretches where some of the houses had been left in place much closer to the wall.

In fact, in one place the borderline actually passed down the centre of a street, with the houses on the western side being occupied by West Berliners, while the houses on the opposite side had been left derelict with all their windows and doors bricked up to form part of the wall. This was Bernauer Strasse, a notorious street where in the past many people had attempted to escape through the upper stories of the derelict houses. Sadly, at quite a few places along the pavement below, there were the faded remains of wreaths where quite a few people had lost their lives trying to jump from these upper floor windows.

Once through Bernauer Strasse I followed the wall through a more open area, which judging from the number of tree stumps had obviously been part of a wood. Halfway along this section I had my first encounter with our own border patrols when a Jeep pulled up alongside me. Inside were three military policemen, one British, one American and one French. They seemed a bit surprised to see me and asked who I was and where I was going. When I explained, they just wished me luck and drove off, leaving me to carry on with my explorations in my own way.

Here and there I came across one or two other viewing platforms, which helped to give me a clearer picture into the world on the other side of the wall, complete with its watch towers. A couple of times, when staring into the communist world from these platforms, I'd find myself being watched through binoculars by one of these guards up in his tower some fifty metres away inside Russian controlled territory. What they made of me I couldn't imagine, since their main purpose was to stop their 'own' people from escaping 'out' over the wall into Western Territory, not westerners like me from climbing 'in'.

Much as I was enjoying this unique ramble through 'no-man's-land', I eventually realised that time was running out. So I had to head off back into the city for the evening performance.

Later in the week, to my surprise and delight, the members of our company were offered the chance of a coach trip over into the communist zone. For some reason most of them didn't fancy the idea, but about twenty of us grabbed it with both hands.

This trip, it turned out, was organised occasionally by the Russians as a sort of propaganda exercise to demonstrate to us westerners just how wonderful a life could be had under their benevolent regime.

Since the only way through the wall for us westerners was via 'Checkpoint Charlie', we had to gather at the appointed time near the gate for the coach to come through and pick us up. When it arrived it turned out to be manned by a male driver and a rather buxom woman courier, who was obviously in charge, and also pretty obviously pregnant. She gave us a brief but enthusiastic run down of the places we were going to see, and off we drove through the two barriers of Checkpoint Charlie, the one on our side being manned by American Military Police, and the one on the communist side by Communist Military Police. The transition from the Berlin we'd just left, to the one we now found ourselves in, was pretty dramatic. To me it was like stepping back into the grey austerity days just after the war. To our enthusiastic 'mum to be', however, it was obviously a sort of new Utopia. Her praise of the large areas of dull, grey, uniform concrete housing-block developments, half finished road works, etc., knew no bounds. The pretty sparse traffic trundling about seemed to consist mainly of lorries and busses, often driven by women, plus the odd official looking car here and there. Anything resembling private cars seemed virtually non-existent. As a Russian propaganda exercise, this tour was proving something of a flop, to say the least – a fascinating flop, but still a flop.

The main focus of the trip seemed to be on wartime memorials, culminating in what was obviously the high point of the tour, the Russian Cemetery. This had a huge stone monument built at one end and was packed with the graves of many of the Russian soldiers who'd been killed in the battle for Berlin.

After this fairly extended tour of the austere communist world, it was a relief to drive back though Checkpoint Charlie into the brighter freedom of our own.

One other odd anomaly I discovered during my wanderings in Berlin, was that one of the main Russian memorials to the troops they'd lost in their war against Germany was actually located in the British controlled area of the city. Despite this, the Russians had a round the clock guard of honour on its steps, who had to come through the wall every day to mount it. Because these Russian troops were then on British controlled territory, however, the British authorities had obviously decided that they in turn needed to be kept an eye on. The outcome being that 'our side' mounted their own British guards on the Russian guards who were guarding the monument. Quite an unusual sight, to say the least.

After a successful week of performances, and a pretty special one of wandering for me, we finally packed our bags and boarded our aircraft at Tempelhof Airport heading for our next venue. This turned out to be another capital city, namely Vienna in Austria. Once again I found myself disappointed at the venue, which I'd hoped would be the famous 'Vienna State Opera House', but turned out to be another big theatre, the 'Theatre an der Wien'. Which, although a fine theatre, did not carry anything like the charisma of the 'Vienna State'. This was, however, for a different reason to that in Berlin, and was simply that the authorities did not think Sadler's Wells was a big enough company to draw the large opera going public to fill the 'State'.

In the event, however, the 'an der Wien' was packed to the doors for every performance, and the press write-ups slated the authorities for not booking us into the 'Vienna State'.

After Berlin, Vienna turned out to be a return to reality as far as my wanderings were concerned. A lovely city, with beautiful picturesque walks along the banks of the 'far from blue' Danube – apparently it's only supposed to look blue to those who are in love. If this is true then 'my' love life just then must have been somewhat lacking, as to me its flowing waters looked decidedly muddy.

After my recent eye-opening experiences in and around the communist world, however, Vienna, beautiful as it is, all seemed a bit bland. The one really interesting highlight for me being a wander through the magnificent Schoenbrunn Palace. This was especially so after I learned of its connection with Napoleon, and the 'Battle of Waterloo' site I'd explored only four weeks earlier near Brussels. Apparently, if Napoleon had been victorious at Waterloo, he had Schoenbrunn Palace earmarked as his future European headquarters.

One other enjoyable aspect of life in Vienna, I found, were the coffee houses I dropped into here and there. These invariably had some sort of musical ensemble pouring out a background of mainly Viennese music to the crowd of cheerful coffee drinking customers.

After yet another week of successful operatic performances, and my wanderings, our company were once more packing their bags and setting off to another destination. This time back across the border to Frankfurt in Germany.

Frankfurt turned out to be a lovely town on the banks of the River Maine, where we found ourselves playing to enthusiastic audiences in a slightly smaller, but flourishing opera house. As for my wanderings there, apart from enjoyable walks along the river, the outing I particularly remember was to their famous zoo. The reason being that they had a creature there which I'd never encountered in a zoo before – a gigantic walrus. This had a large pond to itself, and when it came flopping out onto the bank to stare straight into my face from only about five feet away, on the other side of a pretty low barrier wall, its huge body and two foot long tusks made it look like a cross between a stranded whale and a legless elephant.

Our next venue was to be Munich, famous for its great beer festival – which being a non-drinker didn't exactly turn me on – and infamous for its association with Adolf Hitler, the night of the long knives, and the rise of fascism.

However, all of this being long in the past, I found Munich itself to be an attractive city, with a world renowned opera house, and an interesting place to wander around.

My accommodation on this occasion was a small hotel near the station in the city centre, which I felt was very handy, as this was where I'd normally do most of my exploring. In the event, however, the most memorable – though far from enjoyable – of my wanderings while in Munich was not even in Munich itself, but away out in the country; namely the wartime extermination camp of Dachau. This had been left pretty well as it was found by the Allied troops, who'd liberated it near the end of the war, as a stark reminder of the atrocities committed by the Nazi regime. I spent a couple of pretty disturbing hours wandering around through the grim collection of buildings inside this barbed wire enclosed death camp which had been the last glimpse of the world for so many innocent victims.

All the gas chambers were still there, into which so many of them had been herded like cattle, on the pretence of them being shower rooms, so that they could be gassed in large numbers. There was also a small, grim, execution enclave near the fence where the odd one here and there had been dispatched more quickly with a bullet through the head.

From the moment I'd walked through its gates I couldn't help thinking all the time of Anne Frank and her diary in Amsterdam, as this was the sort of place where she, along with other members of her family, had ended her short life.

All in all, a pretty devastating experience to put myself through, but one which I felt 'must' be kept for all to see, and experience for themselves.

Once again our performances in their magnificent, world famous opera house were very well received by pretty full houses, so the week, operatically speaking, was another success.

We were now drawing fairly close to the end of our continental tour, with only Geneva in Switzerland left to go. So on the Sunday morning, after our final Saturday Munich performance, we boarded the train as usual and headed off for the Swiss border. By this time we were all growing a bit fed up with these long tiring train journeys between venues every Sunday, so a suggestion was put to the management that on any future continental trips 'flying' should be our mode of transport. Something which they fortunately agreed to.

I suppose it is because of this feeling of having had enough of endless travelling and living out of a suitcase in hotels week after week, that my only real memories of Geneva are of the beautiful lake with its famous high water spout, the large shoals of fish that could be seen darting about just under the harbour walls, and the fact that this was the place where I came face to face with my first ever pizza. Pizzas, at that time, were something I'd heard about briefly but had never tried, so when I spotted a notice board outside a small café singing the praises of 'their' particular make, I gave them a try. My disappointment at being served with what to me tasted like a slab of half-cooked pastry, smothered in little more than tomato sauce, put an end to my interest in pizzas from then on. They still taste like this to me now. A rather odd final memory of our continental tour; but one that probably made our train and boat journey back to England all the more welcome.

Once safely back on home ground in London again, one of my fellow 'Wells' singers, Bob Foster, asked me if I'd be willing to join him in doing a concert at his local church in Brixton. Bob was a big Canadian baritone who lived in Brixton with his English wife and two children. I'd always got on well with him, and in fact he'd joined me a couple of times in my explorations during our continental trip.

He'd apparently been asked by the vicar to do some solos with the

331

choir and organist at a concert, and had agreed, but decided that it might be better if he could get someone else to share in the solos with him, and also possibly do a duet.

Since this was something different, I decided it would be an interesting challenge, so also agreed.

We did a few run-throughs in the front room of his house in Brixton, so felt reasonably ready when the day of the concert arrived. The choir opened the proceedings with a selection of choral pieces which seemed to go down OK; without being exactly outstanding. When it came to the solo items, I had drawn the short straw, it seemed, and was on first. For some season it had been decided that I should sing 'The Holy City', and since it was one of my favourites I was quite looking forward to it. The organist gave forth with a few rousing, but rather vague cords, which I assumed were 'supposed' to be my introduction. And being somewhat mystified as to what key he was supposed to be playing in, while at the same time faced with the expectant faces of a largish congregation, I had little option but to launch into 'my' version of 'The Holy City'. Just what the organist was playing as accompaniment I hadn't a clue, but it certainly had little to do with what I was trying to sing. In the end I just left him to stumble around the keyboard on his own, and plodded on as best 1 could, trying to ignore the cacophony of bum notes he was hitting, stumbling through to the end – eventually.

When I sat down with Bob after the fiasco was over, he looked totally embarrassed and whispered apologies, saying:

"I don't know how the devil you kept going."

"Neither do I," I hissed, "but there can't have been many renderings of 'The Holy City', like that. I only wish I had a recording of it."

Fortunately, being forewarned, we got through our duet from *Samson*, without coming to a sticky end; as did Bob with his solo, so we both lived to tell the tale.

SOME MAJOR EVENTS OF THE YEAR:
(1) The spy trial of Admiralty Clerk, William Vassell.
(2) The Cuban Missile crisis. Russia backs down and withdraws missiles.
(3) Gilbert & Sullivan Operettas run out of copyright – from this date anyone is free to perform them.
(4) Coventry Cathedral finally consecrated.
(5) Films: James Bond film *Dr No* and *Lawrence of Arabia* screened.
(6) Fluoride introduced into drinking water. / The Thalidomide disaster.

332

39

The End of the Open Road

1963 (37 years old in July)

After spending the Christmas of 1962 and a snowbound first week of 1963, on my own in our freezing cold Dormobile at our usual Stratford-upon-Avon venue, I was more than glad to get back to London with Babs and the warmth of our cosy bed-sit in Caledonian Road.

By this time, however, we'd both decided that the time had come for us to start thinking of a proper home of our own. So we began reading the newspaper property advertisements and doing the rounds of estate agents. With London being such a vast place the possibilities seemed endless, so it didn't take us too long to come across a house away out at Leyton in East London which looked exactly right. The price seemed within our range, and with Leyton being within comfortable reach of Sadler's Wells, by both bus and tube, we plumped for that.

Raising a mortgage in those days, however, was certainly no easier than it is today. In fact, in some ways it was harder, because mortgage companies at that time would not take the 'wife's' earnings into consideration at all. Added to this was the fact that they regarded anybody working in the theatre as a somewhat risky investment. However, with the help of a good estate agent, and a lot of persistence overcoming the conditions the mortgage companies imposed, we finally managed to get one to help us to take our first step onto the property ladder. Something that we've been grateful for ever since.

Once having moved into our first 'real' home at 51 Malta Road,

Leyton – which after years of touring, bed-sits, and living in the Dormobile seemed like Buckingham Palace – we finally said goodbye to our trusty old Dormobile and sold it off.

Life at Sadler's Wells continued as before, but with me now having to get there by London bus from the end of our street. We were soon in full swing with our operatic repertoire for the year, which included such new things as Rossini's *Count Ory*, *The Rise & Fall of the City of Mahagonny*, and Mozart's *Magic Flute*.

At sometime during all this, I was asked by Tom Hammond of the Wells management if I'd like to sing at a big concert in the Commonwealth Institute in London together with another Wells singer, Patricia McCarry, an Irish soprano who had an exceptionally beautiful voice. Naturally I jumped at the chance, particularly as Tom Hammond; who'd been part of the leading musical management in the Carl Rosa Opera Company before they were taken over by Sadler's Wells, had always shown an interest in my singing, and was the one person there who I felt would have liked to push me up the ladder if he could. Unfortunately, however, with him being an 'outsider' as it were, despite his great operatic background and experience, he didn't have the authority to do so.

The concert turned out to be quite a big affair with artists from various other companies in London taking part, including a troop of dancers from the Royal Ballet, so Pat and I were really looking forward to it, especially as we'd never sang anything together as a duo before. The contribution that we were being asked to make, was to sing the whole of the beautiful 'Love Scene', between Rudolfo and Mimi from the first act of Puccini's *La Boheme*; wonderful music which suited both our voices perfectly.

In the event, the whole concert turned out to be a great success with the large enthusiastic audience. Pat and I being absolutely bowled over by the effect that our romantic love duet seemed to have had; especially on the elderly ladies. A group of these came over to us afterwards to express their appreciation, and one of the comments which sticks in my mind, because it was directed at me personally, came from an elderly lady who declared:

"You've got a wonderful voice young man, but I wouldn't want you living next door to me when you're practising."

A 'backhanded' sort of compliment, perhaps, but one which I understood, since my voice has never been regarded as 'small'.

After an early tour in England with the Wells, we were told that we were booked to go off on yet another tour of the continent. This time, however, two of our venues were to actually take us 'through' the iron curtain into communist Czechoslovakia – namely to Prague, the capital, and Bratislava, one of their other major cities.

Since these two cities were run according to the strict laws and restrictions of a totalitarian state, we'd apparently need to be forewarned about what we could do; and more importantly, what we should 'not' do, in order to stay on the right side of their laws.

To this end, an official from the foreign office turned up one day at one of our rehearsals to put us in the picture. The first thing he told us was that during our time in both of these cities we'd all be staying in state-run hotels – apparently the only kind of accommodation available to foreign visitors. These hotels would be staffed by 'good party members', whose job, as well as looking after our needs, was to watch, listen to, and report on everything we did. As well as this, all the hotel rooms would also be bugged, so we should be careful about our bedroom conversations.

As if all this wasn't enough cloak-and-dagger stuff, we were also warned to be wary, when out and about in town, of being approached by provocateurs trying to trap us into illegal activities; such as exchanging our British currency for their pretty worthless currency at temptingly high rates. This was apparently quite a major industry over there, because British currency was worth far more on their black market than the miserable official exchange rate set by their government. In fact their currency was of so little value outside Czechoslovakia that most other countries wouldn't accept it, and our consular official warned us not to have any left in our pockets when we left the country, as it would simply be waste paper.

All of this seemed a bit too far fetched to us at the time, so it was simply a case of 'wait and see'?

When the day for our departure arrived we found that, as promised, we'd be doing all our travelling this time by air.

The early venues for this tour turned out all to be in Germany, so we found ourselves singing to new audiences at different opera houses in places like Münster, Kassell, Stuttgart, etc.

At some time along the way, however, I found myself making a brief, personal, detour to Dusseldorf. The reason for this being that shortly before we left London I'd managed to contact an opera agency there by the name of Friedrich Paasch. They had given me the times and dates of their auditions and told me to drop in to one of these if I got the chance. I'd worked out that, since one of their regular audition sessions was held every Monday morning, if I gave the Wells aircraft flight a miss on the Sunday, 'I could make my way to Dusseldorf by train, spend the Sunday night somewhere, do the audition in the morning, then carry on by train to our next venue in time for the opening performance that evening.

Of course, all of this would require the permission of the Wells management, and fortunately, to my surprise, they gave this without too much bother, on the strict understanding that I must turn up in time for our first performance on the Monday evening.

According to plan, I set off on the Sunday morning for the railway station with my suitcase, much to the surprise of my fellow Wells singers who were all busily climbing into coaches for the airport. To my slight concern, on arriving at the station I discovered that my trip to Dusseldorf was going to be a bit more convoluted than I'd expected, but as I had all day before me I wasn't too bothered. After a couple of changes at stations on the way, however, with a wait here and there things were not looking too rosy. And by the time I tumbled out onto the platform at Dusseldorf they looked decidedly glum. It was now early evening, and I still had to find somewhere to sleep for the night in order to face up to the audition next morning.

After asking some taxi drivers on the rank outside the station, who to my astonishment could not recommend anywhere, I simply set off walking around the town centre with my suitcase to see if I could spot anything worth a shot. After a while I spotted a group of people walking into what looked like a small hotel, so I followed them in. Since the management seemed to assume that I was one of the party, they took no notice of me for a while until I explained that I wasn't, and was simply looking for somewhere for the night. While they were very sympathetic, they explained that they were booked out by the party I'd followed in so couldn't help. However, they did point me in the direction of a small place down a side street nearby, where I might find something that would do for the night. Fortunately, I did; and while it was certainly in no danger of being mistaken for the Savoy, it was at least a 'superior' sort of doss-house. So I booked in and slept like a log.

After finding a small café to have breakfast next morning, I set off to find Friedrich Paasch's office in Drakestrasse, carrying my suitcase in one hand and my music case in the other. Fortunately it wasn't too far to walk and within half an hour or so I was climbing the stairs into their audition rooms. To my surprise, I was one of about a dozen other singers waiting to do their stuff, both male and female, and of every sort of nationality, including at least one American.

As always at these auditions, and especially at this, my first foreign one, I was particularly keen to listen to what sort of standard I was up against. Fortunately, this was quite easy, because although the auditions were held in another room, they could quite clearly be heard from the waiting room. To my relief, as I listened to one after another of them, although there were one or two really good voices, male and female, giving their all in there, I soon came to the conclusion that I was hearing nothing that I need be afraid of – especially from the tenors.

When it eventually came to my turn, I went in with my music case to find myself confronted by three men, one of whom I 'assumed' must be Friedrich Paasch, plus a pianist seated at a large piano.

This being Germany I'd decided to give them the 'Prize Song' from Richard Wagner's *Die Meistersinger* – which was one of my favourite party pieces anyway. When I announced this a few eyebrows were raised, as always, since this is something which very few tenors would attempt, especially not at an audition. Within a few bars of my opening up, however, I knew I'd made a good choice, because glances were exchanged by the adjudicators and one of them got up and walked out to come back with another man who I realised must 'really' be Friedrich Paasch himself.

When the 'Prize Song' ended, he expressed his approval, and asked if I'd got anything else they could hear. So sticking to the 'dramatic' tenor repertoire which they obviously approved of, I sang another of my favourites, 'Celeste Aida' from Verdi's *Aida*.

This also obviously went down very well, and after a few more questions about myself and my singing, they all declared that they felt sure that they'd be able to get me work in continental opera houses, of which there were 'many' in Germany itself.

When asked for more details of how this would happen, Friedrich Paasch explained that the system in Germany was that I would need to come over to Germany and spend about three months touring around the various opera houses doing auditions which they would arrange for me, and out of this they felt sure engagements would definitely come.

Although all of this was very encouraging, the idea of having to spend three months away in Germany was something of a problem. And when they also explained that all of this would have to be done at my own expense, the whole idea went straight out of the window. I now had a home and mortgage to support, so from a financial position alone it would have to remain an impossible dream.

After this encouraging, but disappointing experience, I managed to catch the train in time to join up again with the rest of the company at our next venue in Germany.

Shortly after this we finally crossed the Iron Curtain border, to begin our very first performances in the land of communism. After our

p

brief trip through the Iron Curtain in Berlin the previous year, the sudden decent into an almost wartime austerity came as no real surprise. If anything, however, the drabness of the streets seemed somehow worse than in East Berlin. What shops there were seemed to have little on display. In fact, most of their windows were filled with nothing but notice boards carrying long lists of the names of the young students who'd recently passed their exams to qualify as good communist party members.

The state run hotel we found ourselves in was The Slovan, which was located right near the Wenceslas Square; which to my surprise I found was named after the 'Good King Wenceslas' I'd sung about at Christmas as an eleven year old around the front doors in Barrow. In fact, the square was actually dominated by a huge statue of this benevolent old monarch. It was also, some years later, to become the scene of an iconic confrontation between a Russian tank and a young Czech protester during the Czech counter-revolution, which led eventually to the downfall of communist rule there.

As for the Hotel Slovan itself, after all the warnings given out by our man from the Foreign Office, the first thing we did after dumping our suitcases in our rooms, had been to go eagerly hunting secret microphones in every nook and cranny. To our astonishment we discovered that all his warnings turned out to be absolutely true. Microphones were found hidden away in light shades, behind pictures, wardrobes, etc., in such a pathetically inept way that to us they just seemed like a joke; so that's exactly how we treated them. Whenever we were in the rooms, especially after being out around the town, we lost no time in slagging off their oppressive, totalitarian regime in loud clear voices, which must have set the earphones of the listeners in the basement ringing like the devil.

The old city of Prague itself turned out to be an attractive, intriguing city to wander in, so I was soon off everywhere and anywhere. One of my first jaunts took me over the large river the city was set on, and across the lovely old ornamental main bridge, beyond which towered a large medieval castle brooding away on top of a high hill. Old castles had always fascinated me so I was soon plodding up the steep approach road and into its large stone-flagged courtyard. Most of the rooms seemed to be open to the public and I wandered up and down its stone stairways trying to guess at something of its history. Fortunately, I came across the odd information board here and there, some of which were printed out in English, so I managed to glean 'something' of what had gone on there in the past. One of the most famous incidents in its history seemed to be what they referred to as

338

'The Defenestration', Since I already knew that 'fenestration' referred to windows, I guessed that 'defenestration' must be something to do with throwing things out of them. This, I found was true; the only surprise being 'what' had been thrown out. This turned out to have been the whole of the ruling town council of the time. Apparently, the townspeople had revolted against these oppressive rulers, stormed the castle and pitched them all headfirst out of the top windows down onto the cobbled courtyard below. Somewhat drastic, but certainly effective.

Down in the city centre I came across what had once been a very fine art gallery.

Unfortunately, however, when 'I' wandered around its large rooms I found that most of the walls were bare, with only a few of their art works left; all of the others having been plundered during the war so I was told; and up to that time not yet recovered.

The only shops worth going in, as far as I was concerned, were the state run establishments, which were strictly for foreign visitors and not available to the Czech people. The reason being, apparently, that in this way all the foreign currency coming into the country would end up in the Government's own coffers. As far as I could see, the most attractive things on sale in these shops were the beautiful Bohemian glassware and china ornaments. So I earmarked these straight away as being just the thing to use up any surplus Czech currency I might have left when we finally set off back through the Iron Curtain.

During all my wanderings in Prague I'd never once been approached by any of the local 'agent provocateur' we'd been warned about so direly by our man from the foreign office. This seemed a bit odd to me because several of our company definitely had been. When I mentioned this to one of these, a member of the orchestra, his surprising answer was:

"It could be that coat you always wear," he suggested. "They probably think you're one of their lot."

Although this had never occurred to me before, it dawned on me that he could be right. Because I 'had' noticed just how many of the locals seemed to be wearing a similar kind of blue, nylon mac to mine, but had just put it down to them having the same good 'taste' as myself. The idea that it might have been singling me out as a 'good party member' was quite a thought.

My Prague wanderings finally came to an end when our week in this lovely old capital was over, and we moved on to Bratislava. This turned out to be a lot smaller and more mundane a place than Prague. With old trams rattling along the streets, driven mainly by women as far as I could see. And as there seemed to be very little in the way of old buildings, or historic places of interest, this didn't bode well for any of my spare time wanderings. It was though, like Prague, set on a river, with passenger ferries coming and going, which in themselves were quite something to watch. This was because they weren't conventional boats, but 'hydroplanes' which sped along the top of the water on huge skis. This meant that as they slowed down to come onto the landing stage they'd simply sink down onto their hulls to off-load their passengers. Then, as they pulled away again and built up speed, they'd rise up once more to skim along the surface on their skis. This all made for a constantly fascinating free show every time they arrived or departed.

The only other thing that stands out about this week in Bratislava, was that we all received an invitation from the 'Young Communist's Group' to visit their club. Since this sounded quite intriguing, about a dozen of us decided to give it a go. In the event, however, this turned out to be nothing more than a pathetic propaganda exercise, during which they tried to convince us how much 'better' life was under their 'benevolent' communist regime, than it was in the West. Even though there were about thirty or so of their members present, most of these kept very carefully away from us, leaving all the talking and fraternising to the two or three pretty obvious 'official' leaders. Needless to say, we treated these as a bit of a joke. And since there were no refreshments on offer, made our exits as soon as we decently could.

At the end of this week in Bratislava, we flew out of Czechoslovakia on a Russian Ilyushin Jet, which was the noisiest plane we'd flown in so far, and back to the normality of Western Germany. However, our operatic performances had gone down very well with the Czech audiences, and all in all it had been an unusual, and very enjoyable couple of weeks. I also had two nice pottery vases tucked away in my luggage from one of the state shops – the beautiful Bohemian glassware proving too expensive for the meagre amount of Czech currency I had left.

The rest of our continental tour passed off successfully, as always. And almost before we knew it, we found ourselves packing our suitcases for the flight home.

SOME MAJOR EVENTS OF THE YEAR:
(1) The 'Great Train Robbery' – £2.5 million from the London-Glasgow express.
(2) Kim Philby exposed as the third member of the Burgess-Maclean spy ring.

(3) Beatles rise to international fame.

(4) President Kennedy assassinated in Dallas by Lee Harvey Oswald.

(5) Beeching Report suggests closing half of all rail stations, and one third of all track. This man was the biggest vandal ever to inflict deliberate damage on the British Rail Transport System. But whereas all the 'other' vandals got jailed or fined, he received honours from the Government, and was awarded a peerage from the Queen.

(6) British TSR2 supersonic bomber developed.

(7) Anti-matter discovered.

(8) Valentina Tereshkova becomes the first woman in space.

(9) Films: *Cleopatra* and *Billy Liar* screened. Rachel Carson's book, *Silent Spring*, published – one of the first major warnings on environmental pollution.

40

Back Home to Normality

1964 (35 years old in July)
Once settled in at Sadler's Wells again, we soon found ourselves pitched into polishing up our repertoire for the rest of the season, as well as adding one or two different operas to our list.

The most memorable and unusual of these additional pieces being Stravinsky's, *The Rake's Progress*, also turned out to be the most musically challenging operatic work we'd ever had to tackle. Based on a famous painting by William Hogarth depicting the degradation and poverty of life in London slums in the eighteen hundreds, its weird jerky cross-rhythms like 7/8 time 5/4 time, etc., took a lot of practice to get right after the easy rhythms like 3/4 time, 6/8 time, etc., which we were used to. However, once we'd got tuned in to it, and saw how effectively its jerky rhythms fitted the gin-soaked degradation and debauchery of those times, it became one of our favourites.

The 'Rake' was definitely 'not' a role I'd care to sing myself – my sights being firmly set on the romantic, dramatic roles of Italian and German opera – but its dramatic effect was pretty powerful, and the tenor brought in to sing the role, 'Alexander Young', was exactly right for the part, and both sang and acted it beautifully.

An unexpected bonus with *The Rake*, however, turned out to be that as well as singing the opera in the theatre, we were also booked to do a special recording of it, with Stravinsky himself – then in his early eighties – conducting it. On the day of the recording, we found that the preliminary rehearsal was to be conducted by Stravinsky's youngish American musical assistant. While the rather elderly Stravinsky would turn up later to conduct the actual recording – which was, of course, to be the great selling point of the record.

When the great man eventually arrived, he took his place on the rostrum, raised his baton and gave the down beat to be met with a spirited rendering by us of 'Happy Birthday to You', because it so happened that the day of the recording just happened to be Stravinsky's birthday, and this little surprise had been set up by his musical assistant. The look of absolute bewilderment on Stravinsky's face as he rapped the music stand with the baton, wondering what the devil we were doing to his music, slowly turned into a smile as it dawned on him what we were singing.

At around this time one of our music staff-conductors, Gordon Kember, approached me and told me that he was involved in staging a production of Richard Straus's *Ariadne auf Naxos* for some amateur company in London. As he was also involved in 'casting' for the production he asked if I'd be interested in singing the role of Bachus in this; as apparently I had just the type of dramatic tenor voice required for the part. Even though it wasn't an opera I was familiar with, I readily agreed, as it would be an interesting challenge. Not having a score to learn the part from, he loaned me his own, which was apparently a presentation copy he'd received during his studying days in Germany. Unfortunately, however, he was soon transferred over to the 'other' Wells Company; and as 'I' was soon off out on tour with our own side of the company, I lost touch with him altogether and the production never happened.

The sad part of all this being that I still had his score. And with me being busy touring around myself, it somehow got lost among my own scores and forgotten about. The result being that I still have that copy of *Ariadne auf Naxos* among my own scores today, and would love to see it returned to him, or his family, if I only knew where.

The rest of the year was taken up with our touring around England and Scotland, mainly to venues we'd played before, but with one or two new ones thrown in, to make things a bit more of a challenge.

SOME MAJOR EVENTS OF THE YEAR:
(1) Labour won the general election (with only a 4 majority).
(2) Cyprus; fighting breaks out between Greeks and Turks.
(3) BBC opens a second TV channel – BBC2. The Windmill Theatre – a famous London wartime venue – closes. Topless dresses worn in London.
(4) Films *My Fair Lady*, *Mary Poppins* and *Zorba The Greek* screened.

343

(5) Pirate ship 'Radio Caroline' starts broadcasting from outside British territorial waters.
(6) Cassius Clay becomes world heavyweight boxing champion by beating Sonny Liston.
(7) Britain's rocket, Blue Streak, successfully launched.
(8) The discovery of Quasars (quasi stellar objects).

41

My Brush with a Famous Diva

1965 (36 years old in July)
At some time early in this year someone at the Wells suggested that I
should contact Eva Turner, the great international operatic soprano
celebrity of the nineteen-thirties; and still, apparently, an influential
name in the operatic world of London. This was in the belief that she
might be interested enough in my voice to give me the boost in the
direction that I needed.

Upon deciding that this was at least worth a shot I eventually rang
her number, and her secretary arranged a time for me to go along and
meet her. I duly turned up at her address, somewhere in Bayswater as
far as I remember. The secretary had already explained that 'Madame
Turner' was an extremely busy woman, who was in fact preparing to
fly off to Canada the very next day on a three months' teaching/lecturing
engagement; something she apparently did regularly. She would,
therefore, only be able to spare me about fifteen minutes. I was then
ushered in to meet the great lady to find that this legendary icon of the
operatic world was rather short and stocky with a lovely beaming
smile. She didn't want to hear me sing any of the songs and arias I'd
brought, just scales and arpeggios. So off she went, rattling away on
the piano, with me letting rip up and down the scales fit to wake up all
of Bayswater. She seemed rather surprised and pleased with what she
was hearing, and kept making encouraging comments here and there.
Occasionally she would join in to demonstrate how 'she' would do it,
revealing that she still had a clear strong voice even though she was
getting on a bit in years. On and on she went, bursting with energy like
a dynamo. The fifteen minutes was soon passed and by the time she

345

decided to call a halt the best part of an hour had elapsed; leaving me feeling as if I'd been put through the wringer, while she was as fresh as a daisy.

Her verdict on my singing was that while there was work to be done, she was enthusiastic enough about my operatic prospects to insist that I should contact her secretary in three months' time, when she'd returned from Canada, in order that we could start some serious coaching. Unfortunately I never did, simply because of the old financial problems of trying to earn a living, with a home and a mortgage to keep viable. By the time the three month deadline was reached, I'd already decided that the prospect of 'yet another' period of scraping money together to invest in my singing career was something we couldn't face. We'd already been doing that for the best part of fifteen years, and the gloss had gone off it somewhat. And in any case, my writing was now keeping my 'creative' instincts more and more fulfilled, so I settled for that.

As well as doing our usual 'operatic' touring around the country, this year the Sadler's Wells management had also decided to add something quite different to our repertoire. This was Verdi's great 'Requiem Mass', which was usually performed in concert halls and churches. In our case, however, we did two performances; one at the Sadler's Wells Theatre, and the second in the beautiful Ely Cathedral.

Ely itself turned out to be a fascinating small town set away up on the fens of Cambridgeshire. Built on raised ground it stood out above the flat fens like an island which could be seen for miles around. In fact, in the past when the Fens were largely wet swampland, it actually 'was' an island for much of the time.

Since the 'Requiem' is such a huge work to perform, both sides of our company, orchestras and choruses, had to be combined into one to do it justice. This in itself made these a totally new experience, especially the performance in the huge, packed nave of Ely Cathedral with its magnificent echoing acoustics. The trumpet solos blasting out from away up in the stone arches, and the thundering drum beats of the largest bass drum I'd ever seen – specially hired for the occasion, apparently – created one of the most memorable musical effects that I can ever remember.

SOME MAJOR EVENTS OF THE YEAR:
(1) Sir Winston Churchill died aged 91.
(2) Rhodesia, under Ian Smith, declares unilateral independence.
(3) The first communications satellite, 'Early Bird', launched.
   The Post Office Tower, London's tallest building to date, opened.

(4) Films: *The Sound of Music, Dr Zhivago* and *The Spy Who Came in From the Cold* screened.

(5) BP discovers gas in the North Sea.

(6) The first ever space walk, by Russian astronaut Alexei Leonov.

42

A Long Overdue Goodbye

1966 (36 years old in July)
This year I finally decided to say cheerio to Sadler's Wells and move on; something I felt I should have done long before.

Like quite a few other talented, but frustrated, singers who I'd seen come and go during my time at the Wells, I'd finally had enough of seeing far less talented singers than myself being brought into the company on principal contracts, while I was being almost totally ignored.

Sounds like 'sour grapes' doesn't it? However, I have a great many recordings of my singing on CDs and tapes; operatic arias, Italian and German songs, English, Irish & Scottish ballads, etc., which I'd be happy to put forward as proof that it isn't.

As I've stated earlier in this autobiography, I did receive quite bit of encouragement from various members of the music staff, including conductors, plus at least one member of the management, for which I'll always be grateful. Unfortunately, their opinions had counted for little against the narrow, class conscious views of the untalented man at the top. So, like all those other talented, but unappreciated singers I'd seen come and go, all I could do was move on and earn a living from my singing elsewhere.

My contract with the Wells ended on the 11th of June, and there I was, an operatic tenor on the open market with no immediate idea of what was to happen next. However, as this was a situation I was quite familiar with from my George Mitchell and club days, I was not too daunted by it.

Fortunately, I was contacted almost immediately by a man called

Vere Laurie and asked if I'd like to sing the leading role of Pinkerton in Puccini's *Madame Butterfly*; which he was staging at the open air theatre in London's Holland Park. Vere Laurie, I discovered, was of Irish decent, and held a Papal Peerage. He was one of those well off, slightly eccentric, but extremely likable characters who one comes across in the world of the performing arts. He was absolutely devoted to opera and spent most of his time, and a fair amount of money, putting on these operatic performances in London every year.

How he'd got hold of my name I'm not sure, but it was probably from someone at Sadler's Wells – most likely Tom Hammond, who'd been one of the leading figures in the Carl Rosa Opera Company before it was taken over by Sadler's Wells, and who'd always taken a particular interest in my singing, even getting me several singing engagements outside of the Wells during my time there.

Having never sung in an open air theatre before this was to be a new experience for me, but I did have a week's rehearsal to get the feel of it. I actually started off rehearsing the role in Vere Laurie's ground floor apartment in Bayswater, but soon moved on to Holland Park with the rest of the cast; or rather 'casts', as there were to be two full casts who would each sing the performances on alternate evenings.

The Holland Park theatre turned out to be set in a circular open air amphitheatre, with the stage and dressing rooms on one side, facing a large upward sloping seating area on the other.

The rehearsals went well and I was really looking forward to singing my first full-bloodied operatic role since *Maid Marian* in Dundee. When I turned up for the opening performance, however, it was to find there was a crisis on. It appeared that the Butterfly in our cast, who I'd done all my rehearsing with, had gone down with a throat infection and that I would therefore have to sing the role with the other one, whom I'd never sung a note with. In theory this should have been no real problem, in practice, however, it looked like being something of a nightmare, because each Butterfly had her own individual way of singing and acting the role, or even simply moving about the stage.

Since my new Butterfly was just as apprehensive as I was about the situation, I told her to simply do her normal performance and leave me to try and fit in as best I could. So when I made my first entrance at the start of the big duet scene, I hadn't a clue what to expect. In the event, it was pretty much a case of her flitting about the stage like a real butterfly, and me trying to go along with everything she did and be in the right place at the right time. Fortunately, our actual singing together worked OK and our scenes went down well with the pretty full house audience.

Since my original Butterfly never recovered in time to rejoin us, I ended up doing all my performances with the second one. This was fine for me, but I felt sorry for her as she was now faced with the task of having to sing the role of Butterfly every single night without a break.

Although the Holland Park open air theatre was a beautiful setting to sing in, I quickly discovered that singing in the open air definitely had its drawbacks. One of these being that Holland Park just happened to be under the flight path of aircraft from Heathrow Airport; so huge Jumbos, Tristars, etc., were thundering over every few minutes with a noise that virtually blotted out all our musical accompaniment. The effect of this being that although we kept on singing through the noise, it was bit like miming in a thunderstorm, and by the time we could hear the music again it was interesting to find just how far we'd wandered off from Puccini's intentions – and even more interesting to see how quickly we could waffle our way back into step with them.

Fortunately, the audiences seemed to accept all this in good spirit as part of the open air experience. The same thing applied with the occasional high pitched squawking of the family of peacocks who'd set up home around the amphitheatre, and seemed compelled to join in with us here and there, adding quite a few telling notes that Puccini had never thought of.

All in all though, it was an enjoyable experience, and at least I was singing one of the plum, principal roles in opera for a change.

Another interesting, though 'none singing' job was put my way when someone at the Wells rang to ask me if I'd like to earn a few bob doing 'extra' work at the BBC Television studios. It seemed that they were putting on a TV performance of Benjamin Britain's *Billy Budd*, and needed experienced 'extras' to swell the numbers in some of the scenes. The fact that it was 'none singing' didn't bother me a bit, because although Benjamin Britain's operas were wonderful dramatic musical works, his tenor roles had never appealed to me as ones I'd like to sing myself. Anyway, the fee was very good, so I accepted.

Our first rehearsals on *Billy Budd* took place in a large hall away out on the Mile End Road in the East End of London, where I arrived to find all the cast assembled, including Peter Glossop – a very fine baritone from the Wells. Benjamin Britain was also there with his tenor partner Peter Pears, and was strolling about keeping an eye on the proceedings. For me, with no particular role responsibility, it was all just an easy, enjoyable time acting my socks off with all the other extras as rough and ready sailors from the days of Admiral Nelson. This became even more enjoyable when we finally moved over to the

350

BBC Television Centre in Shepherds Bush to find ourselves manning the decks on what was almost a full-sized wooden man of war from the battle of Trafalgar. This had been built on the floor of the main studio there and was so realistic that being on board it was almost like being back facing the Spanish Armada.

Resisting the temptation to join in with the singing I found a bit difficult at times, especially during the actual TV broadcast, as this was the first time I'd ever been engaged purely as an actor. But at least being paid for 'not' wearing my voice out made a change, so I learned to live with it.

Shortly after *Billy Budd*, I was offered the chance by the Helen Jennings agency of a three week engagement over in Southern Ireland at the Wexford Opera Festival. This, apparently, was a special event put on every year in which they engaged well established international professionals to sing the leads, and other up and coming professionals to sing all the supporting roles. As this meant a chance to sing in a new venue with an international cast, even if I would only be singing supporting roles, I took up the offer. At the very least it would be three weeks' well paid work.

Our first rehearsals were to be held at practice studios just off the Marylebone Road in central London; which I'd never been to before. I turned up to find several other supporting-role singers already there with a pianist, and as others arrived, it turned out that there were eight of us altogether going over from London; two sopranos, two altos, two tenors and two baritones, so I wouldn't be lacking for company.

The two operas Wexford were putting on this year were *Lucrezia Borgia* by Donizetti, and *Fra Diavolo* by Auber, neither of which I knew anything about, so it was all going to be breaking new ground for me, and I suspect for all the others.

At the first rehearsal, the pianist/répétiteur, handed out scores for the individual parts we'd each been allocated, and we spent the next couple of hours note-bashing, and getting to know the plots of the two unfamiliar operas lying in wait on the other side of the Irish Sea.

We did two or three of these rehearsals before being finally handed our train and boat tickets, given the addresses of our various accommodations in Wexford, and left to make our own individual ways over to the land of the Shamrock.

After a windy trip across the somewhat lumpy Irish Sea from the port of Fishguard in Wales to Rosslare in Southern Ireland, followed by a short train ride on my first Irish train, I finally arrived in the little old town of Wexford. Slightly hilly, with narrow winding streets, the whole town looked, and felt, different from anywhere I'd been before.

There was an attractively 'laid back' atmosphere about the place, as if it was just rolling along at its own pace, unconcerned about what was going on in the outside world.

The landlady of the narrow three-storey terraced house, where I found myself staying, was a kindly soul. She was also, I soon found, living somewhat in the past and obviously seemed to think that Ireland's 'troubles' with England had only ended about a couple of months ago, instead of actually before she was born.

However, as she also seemed totally oblivious of the fact that 'I' was a member of that guilty English race, I was quite happy to listen to her goings on about her pet subject and we got on well.

Rehearsals for the two operas began almost immediately in the smallish Festival Theatre with our first rehearsal being a 'Sitzprobe'; where all the singers simply sit on the stage in front of the orchestra and sing through the music, with the leading singers usually sitting at the front of the stage and the supporting singers behind.

As the principal singers started off the proceedings, we got to hear all our leading internationals for the first time. This was a real treat, as they all turned out to have excellent voices; especially the tenor, who was an Italian with a really full, ringing top register – for me just how 'real' operatic tenors should sound. There was also a good American soprano, an equally gifted English soprano, who I'd never heard of before, a fine bass, two Italian buffo baritones to play the lighter character roles, and a Mezzo Soprano. All in all, a pretty exciting line up.

As the rehearsal progressed, we supporting singers were simply required to add our parts as they turned up in the score. When it came to my turn to get involved I let forth full voice, determined to show our internationals that they weren't the only ones who could sing. The result couldn't have pleased me more, because most of them immediately turned their heads in surprise to see who the singer was – something they hadn't done for anyone else. Small comfort, I know, but under the circumstances a worthwhile confirmation of my vocal abilities.

Although our rehearsals went on pretty intensely throughout these first two weeks, they still left me enough spare time to go off on my usual jaunts exploring any new town I arrived in – as well as the countryside around it. In the case of Wexford these included the river bank and bridge area, where according to my landlady various battles with the British had taken place during the 'troubles', so I was also doing my homework to keep her happy.

One unique feature of the town itself, I found, was the lack of anything that could be called a pub. Instead there seemed to be tiny drinking bars dotted here and there, which seemed to be little more than the front rooms of people's houses.

Not being a drinker myself their stocks of Guinness were quite safe from me. Nevertheless, I did have a brief wander into the odd one occasionally to see what they were all about. The scene that met me in all of them seemed to be pretty much the same; a jolly semi-inebriated atmosphere with men crowded up against a bar counter doing their best to support the Irish Brewers by quaffing a pretty fair share of their output. From what I could see Guinness, at least, were certainly in no danger of going out of business.

Apart from these casual 'drop-ins' during my wanderings, I had the chance of seeing one of these bars in action closer to home. This was because the house next door to where I was staying actually had one in their front room. Although my room was up on the third floor it overlooked the front street, so I dozed off to sleep most nights with the faint sound of distant revelry in my ears. There were, though, a few nights that were a bit more entertaining. On one of these I was woken up in the early hours by the revving of car engines, running feet and officious voices shouting out orders. On staggering bleary-eyed to the window I could see three police cars parked up below, with policemen banging on the door of the bar next door, while others were running down the street and disappearing round a nearby corner into the back street. Shortly afterwards, men were being rounded up and bundled into the police cars amid a lot of inebriated protestations. Eventually, the cars disappeared and peace descended again as if the whole thing had never happened.

Next morning the landlady never mentioned this at all, so I eventually brought the subject up.

"Oh! That," she muttered dismissively. "That's always goin' on. Some people 'ad drink all night if they could. But don't you worry, the garda (police) sort them out alright."

I couldn't argue with that as I'd seen them in action for myself.

"But why were some of them running around into the back street?" I persisted.

"Ah! Well," she replied, "they were off to catch all the crafty devils who try to escape over the wall at the back. They never make it though. The garda are on to their tricks, don't you worry."

Another free entertainment provided by the bar next door happened a few days later when I was awoken just around midnight by noises in the street below and red lights flashing around my bedroom walls. Once again I stumbled out of bed to the window and this time I found a large fire engine below with firemen milling around noisily and dragging a hosepipe into the bar. I couldn't see any smoke or flames, but obviously 'some sort' of emergency was under way so I watched all these goings on for a while. But since whatever it was obviously seemed to be under control I eventually crawled into bed and went back to sleep.

About seven o-clock in the morning, however, I was awoken again by the sound of happy voices below, and to my astonishment, when I looked out I could see that the fire engine was still there. So were all the firemen who were now stumbling merrily out of the bar and trying, somewhat unsteadily, to climb back onto the fire engine. Fortunately, they all eventually managed it and off they roared back to the fire station to recuperate and sober up after a long hard night of 'fire fighting' in the bar.

After two weeks of quite comprehensive rehearsals our first night finally arrived, and people from far and wide descended on Wexford to completely fill our auditorium every night. Many of these had come down by train on special excursions from Dublin, so every night we had a brand new audience, most of them from the Irish Capital. In typical Irish fashion these trains simply offloaded their passengers at the station, then sat there waiting to take them all back to Dublin after the performance.

This last bit wasn't quite so straightforward as it sounds, because although the theatre had closed when the performance ended, the bars hadn't, and most of the opera lovers simply transferred their attentions from absorbing beautiful music, to swallowing tasty Guinness. The result of this being that the train driver and his guard would have to tour round all the bars until midnight trying to get them back onto the train so they could head home for Dublin.

Unfortunately, this wonderful three week adventure in 'Never Never Land' eventually came to an end, and it was back across the Irish Sea to London reality.

Once back home in Malta Road, I decided that I'd have to pick up again on my club work up in the northern clubs just to earn a decent living. I'd already been contacted a couple of times by an agent in Sheffield by the name of Stan Farrell, who was keen to offer me club work on a regular basis, virtually guaranteeing me at least four bookings a week: Friday and Saturday evenings, plus Sunday noon and night.

These were to be at pretty good fees which would make it worth my while to drive up north every Friday, and back to London after every Sunday night venue, providing I possessed a car that is, which at the time I didn't.

354

Fortunately, my sister Jackie and husband John knew of a local car sales room which had a second-hand Vauxhall Velox for sale, which they thought might do the job. So Babs and I paid them a visit, and having looked the car over I decided that it would – particularly as it only cost £90.

So there I was, ready for a new assault on the northern clubland; only this time firing on all six cylinders – even if they were only second hand.

There was one other little thing that had to be sorted out before I dived back into the club world again, and this was my name. The problem this time being one of perception. My real aim was 'still' to remain a classical singer, of course, but no singer would have been taken seriously in this field if it became known that they were also singing in the clubs. The answer was simply a different professional name for each. So I told Stan Farrell to book me into the clubs as Alan Morris – a name that he himself suggested. So from then on I had three names: My bank manager knew me as Alan Workman, the classical world as Alan Morrell and clubland as Alan Morris. A bit complicated at times, but since my bank agreed to accept cheques into, and out of, my account in all three names, it worked out OK.

SOME MAJOR EVENTS OF THE YEAR:

(1) Labour party returned to power in the general election.

(2) Harold Wilson meets Ian Smith on HMS *Tiger* in Rhodesia crisis.

(3) Billy Graham opened his evangelical crusade in London.

(4) England win the world cup at Wembley, beating Germany 4-2.

(5) Film *Khartoum* screened.

(6) Nuclear submarine HMS *Resolution* launched in Barrow-in-Furness.

(7) Both the Severn Road Bridge and The Tay Road Bridge (Britain's longest) built.

(8) Fossil bacteria 3,000 years old found in rocks.

(9) US unmanned space craft 'Surveyor 1' makes a soft landing on the Moon.

43

One Foot Either Side of the Fence

1967 (37 years old in July)
Under Stan Farrell's agency my club work soon expanded tremendously. Apart from the North Yorkshire area, I found myself being booked for clubs throughout the Midlands and Lancashire, as well as whole weeks up in the Newcastle and Sunderland area, and away down in the coal mining valleys of South Wales. These bookings also included the social clubs of quite a few famous football clubs like Manchester City, Wolverhampton, West Bromwich, Sheffield United and Mansfield Town.

During these engagements I found myself sharing the bill quite regularly with other artists such as Marti Caine, Paul Shane, Little and Large, Norman Collier, Paul Daniels, Duggie Brown, etc., all of whom were just little known club acts at the time, but who later became big names on TV.

As well as my increasing load of club work, I was still managing to accept offers from the other side of the fence. One that particularly stands out was from a London agent asking me if I'd like a trip down to a place called Three Crosses, near Swansea in South Wales, to sing in a performance of Dvorak's *Stabat Mater*. Since this was the first time I'd ever been asked to sing in oratorio I hesitated, especially as oratorio had never particularly appealed to me as something I'd like to sing. However, when I learned that the *Stabat Mater* would only take up the first half of the concert, with the second half being devoted to operatic arias, I jumped at this chance of a new challenge.

As South Wales was much too far to drive on the day of the concert, especially as I'd need to be there on call for an afternoon rehearsal, I decided that I'd have to do most of the journey the day before, and book in for the night at my old theatrical digs in Bristol, leaving me a relatively easy run to Three Crosses in the morning.

Once this was fixed, it was then a matter of buying myself a vocal score of the *Stabat Mater* and getting down to learning it. Since I knew no oratorio singers who I could rehearse it with, it was simply a case of practising my own part and hoping for the best. Fortunately, I knew a very good Canadian lady pianist in Swiss Cottage who I'd worked with on things before, so I rang her and booked a few rehearsal sessions.

I duly drove from London to Bristol on the eve of the concert and spent the night at my old digs before motoring on to Swansea the next morning, keeping my fingers crossed about what lay ahead of me. It wasn't until I pulled up outside the hall in Three Crosses, however, to see the musicians with their instruments, and the male voice choir all streaming in through the main entrance, that the enormity of my situation really hit me. Here was I about to sing a performance of a work in public, that not only involved solos, but duets, ensembles etc with the other soloists and the choir, and I'd never sung a note of it with other singers before. My main thought at that moment was: 'God. . ! What the devil have I let myself in for!'

However, there was nothing I could do about it now, so I put a brave face on it and entered the hall to meet my three fellow soloists. From their introductory chatter I quickly gathered that they were all pretty experienced oratorio singers; a couple of them even being quite well known names. None of this did anything to ease my apprehension, and as the rehearsal began, my fingers were well and truly crossed.

To my great relief, however, when it came to my first vocal contribution, I found things going far better than I could reasonably have expected. My voice flowed quite well, and fortunately the benefit of all the rehearsals I'd done with my Canadian pianist kicked in and came to my rescue.

I received an extra boost to my confidence later in the rehearsal when during a break I found myself chatting with Mike Ripon, one of my fellow soloists, and admitted my lack of oratorio experience and earlier misgivings.

"Well, don't you worry about that," he replied in surprise. "With 'your' voice you can't fail." Coming from a very fine bass-baritone singer like him, with lots of oratorio experience, this was praise indeed, and just the encouragement I needed.

Later on I received another boost, this time unsolicited, from one of the male voice choir, who after listening to one of my operatic arias came up to shake my hand.

q

"Where have they been keeping you?" he declared. "Why haven't we heard of you before?"

Needless to say, after all this encouragement from fellow singers, the rehearsal became a much less daunting experience, so I finally relaxed and began to enjoy it; especially the operatic items, which included among other things my version of the tenor aria 'Salve Demure Casta e Pure' from *Faust*, and the 'Quartet' from *Rigoletto* for all of us.

The performance in the evening also went down well to a very receptive audience, so I set off to drive back to London afterwards feeling extremely relieved that I'd just about 'got away with' my first ever oratorio performance, but vowing 'never' to put myself in that position again.

After this brief, but refreshing step onto the classical scene, it was a case of straight back up north to catch up on my club engagements again. I didn't have time to catch up on many of these, however, before another unexpected chance to step back over the fence came my way. I received a phone call from Raymond Gubbay Promotions in London, whom I'd never heard of, asking me if I'd like to do a series of operetta concerts with Marion Studholme. Since Marion Studholme was at that time a well known principal soprano at Covent Garden Opera, whom I definitely 'had' heard of, having seen her perform there several times, I could hardly believe it. Also, how Raymond Gubbay Promotions had got hold of my name I'd no idea, but it seemed that 'someone' must be looking after my interests, so I jumped at the chance.

Rehearsals started soon afterwards, and I discovered that there were to be four of us involved in these Saturday evening concerts: Marion Studholme, the star name around whom the concerts were built, myself as the tenor, a baritone named Robert Bateman, and our pianist John Parry, who not only played our accompaniments but did a couple of solo piano pieces as well.

All four of us got along well right from the start. Marion Studholme was smallish, attractive and friendly, with the absolutely beautiful voice I already knew from my visits to Covent Garden. Robert Bateman proved to have an excellent lyric baritone voice and a very good stage personality, while John parry was a brilliant pianist and répétiteur, so all boded well for the concerts.

The programme that had been worked out for us couldn't have suited me better. I found myself billed to sing some of my favourite operetta pieces, which among other things included the tenor solos, 'Girls Were Made to Love and Kiss' from *Paganini*; 'You are my Hearts Delight', and the beautiful love duet with Marion, 'Love What Has Given You This Magic Power', both from Lehar's *Land of Smiles*.

The first of these Saturday Evening concerts turned out to be down south at the Congress Theatre in Eastbourne, which I was familiar with from my Sadler's Wells Days. This was followed on successive Saturdays by two more southern venues: the Palace Pier Theatre in Brighton, and the concert hall in Camberley (newspaper cutting included – in which the reporter mistakenly refers to me as a baritone), and finally ending with a trip north to a concert hall in Northampton.

All in all the concerts were a great success with appreciative audiences everywhere. For me particularly they were like a breath of fresh air, because to be singing the kind of beautiful romantic music that I'd always wanted to sing, in the company of such a superb soprano as Marion, was almost like a dream come true.

After Northampton, it was back to earth again with my club bookings. Once again, however, these were interrupted fairly soon when I got a call from Vere Laurie asking me if I'd like to sing the tenor lead in another of his Holland Park opera productions. This time it was to be 'Rudolfo' in Puccini's '*La Bohème*', one of the great tenor roles in all of opera, so how could I refuse. I managed to juggle my club dates around once more to fit it in, and was off to tread the boards again on the other side of the fence.

Since most of the *La Boheme* cast were also engaged elsewhere, just as I was, the initial rehearsals had to be fitted in here and there whenever we could. However, we all finally got together in Holland Park for a week of full rehearsals just before the opening night was due. As quite a few of the *Boheme* cast turned out to be those I'd sung with in *Madame Butterfly* the previous year, we were all pretty familiar with each other so things went well.

We opened to a pretty full auditorium on July 11th, and here I was again, singing another of my favourite tenor roles for the first time. Unfortunately, we soon discovered that the Holland Park Peacocks were just as keen to join in as ever; especially in the beautiful first act scene between Rudolfo and Mimi, where they meet for the first time and Rudolfo sings, 'Your Tiny Hand is Frozen', followed by Mimi's reply of, 'They Call Me Mimi', rounding off with the beautiful, impassioned love duet, 'Lovely Maid in the Moonlight'. However, once the Mimi and I got into full flow, we were so carried away by the beautiful music, especially on the full voice top 'C's' that the peacocks didn't stand a chance and gave up, leaving us to bring this wonderful love scene to its magical end as it should be.

This wonderful week of sheer pleasure, singing the music I'd always wanted to sing, finally came to an end unfortunately, and I found myself back touring around the clubs singing to different, but equally appreciative and discerning audiences. What particularly pleased me about the clubland scene, and made it all worth while, was that apart from the fact that it was giving Babs and I a good living, I was still able to sing all the things I'd always wanted to. Tenor songs and great classical arias were what the miners, steel workers and others wanted to hear me sing. In fact, at some of my regular club venues; especially around the Lancashire area, they'd have had me singing operatic arias all evening. This was great as far as I was concerned, but it did occasionally make for pretty hard work. I remember one club in Wigan where they had me singing, 'Di Quella Pira' from Verdi's *Il Trovatore* over and over again. With this being a real 'full voice belter' of an aria, with massive top C's, I really earned my money that night.

Later on in the year I was invited to do a further tour of 'Operetta Nights' concerts with Marion Studholme, Robert Bateman and John Parry. This time taking in such places as: Kings Hall, Derby, Warrington Concert Hall, and the Grand Theatre, Wolverhampton, among other places. Fortunately repeating the success of our previous tour, much to my delight.

SOME MAJOR EVENTS OF THE YEAR:

(1) Breath tests for motorists introduced.

(2) 'Scientology' leader, Ron Hubbard (headquarters at East Grinstead) refused entry to Britain.

(3) Che Guevara (revolutionary) killed fighting in Bolivia.

(4) *Forsyte Saga* shown on the BBC / Films *Camelot, Bonne and Clyde*, Walt Disney's *Jungle Book* screened. / First British Colour TV broadcast (625 lines).

(5) Donald Campbell killed on Coniston Lake / Torrey Canyon disaster off Land's End / Liner Queen Mary's last voyage / Liner *Queen Elizabeth II* launched.

(6) The first ever heart transplant operation performed by Christian Barnard in Cape Town.

(7) Russia's Venera 4 satellite makes a soft landing on Venus. 98" Newtonian telescope (the largest in Europe) installed at Hurstmonceux.

44

A New Home Up North

1968 (38 years old in July)
Despite the fact that I was still being offered the occasional booking in the classical field, I eventually decided, somewhat reluctantly, not to accept these bookings any more. The reason being simply, that as I was now earning most of my living from the clubs up north and elsewhere, continuing to live in London made no sense at all. Also, even though I always enjoyed the actual 'singing' on the classical platforms, I was by now growing somewhat disenchanted with the way of life that went with it. Trying to balance the extra work of rehearsing for these classical concerts, with all my club work, was proving to be a bit of a strain. And since the chances of 'earning a living' in the English concert world on its own were too few and far between to make this viable, I finally gave it up.

The logical outcome of this, therefore, was simply to sell up and move to where a good living with my singing was to be had for the taking. To this end my club trips up north each week also became house hunting expeditions. After a few unpromising viewings around the Sheffield area, we eventually stumbled across a very attractive detached bungalow just outside Doncaster. This was not only much more modern than our old London house, but a lot roomier, had lovely gardens, and was actually on the market for quite a bit less than we could expect for our London one. It was also empty and immediately available.

Babs fell in love with it at first sight, so we made an offer for it which was accepted. Our mortgage company was quite happy to swap the mortgage on our London house for this one virtually overnight, and that was it.

We had no difficulty in selling our old London House, so within a few weeks the new one was ours, and we found ourselves heading up the motorway behind the removal van to move in.

As 'Sod's Law' would have it, however, this moving day just 'happened' to fall on the day before I was due to start a week's tour in the miner's clubs away down in South Wales. So after unloading all the furniture, I had to grab a short night's sleep before heading all the way down to the Welsh valleys, leaving Babs behind to sort out the furniture as best she could.

The Welsh trip was, as usual, pretty hectic, but by now I was quite used to driving up and down the Welsh valleys seeking out clubs in places like Tony Pandy – the birthplace of the great heavyweight boxer Tommy Fan, who'd once fought Joe Louis for the world title, Merthyr Tydfil, and umpteen other mining communities with less pronounceable names.

One of these names which is particularly etched on my mind from the past, was the village of Aberfan. I arrived there when the town was still in mourning over the great tragedy that had happened there. This was when a whole school full of children had died under a huge black avalanche of spoil waste from the pit tip which had collapsed due to heavy rain and flowed down a steep hillside, completely engulfing the school and all the children in it. At the time of my visit to Aberfan, the black trail of pit spoil still formed a great scar down the hillside to the demolished school on the opposite side of the valley to where the club was.

As an offshoot of my regular club work this year I was also offered a tour by Mecca of their cabaret and holiday-camp circuit. This ranged from cabarets in Northern England to holiday camps on the South Coast, finally ending up at a big club in London. During the couple of weeks that this lasted I covered well over a thousand miles in the car; and although it was a new experience and I seemed to go down well, it only served to confirm my initial feelings that cabaret was not my scene, and was something I'd 'definitely' not be repeating.

I was also offered a week's work singing a concert in the Planet Room at Blackpool Tower. On this occasion I shared the bill with a very good soprano, and it was our job to entertain the huge hall of dancers during the half hour or so of intermission; another new singing experience which wasn't 'quite' my scene, although it certainly made a change from my regular club work.

During all this pretty hectic club work all over the country, I'd still managed, in my spare moments, to continue scribbling away at my children's writing, and had by this time built up quite a pile of manuscripts. These included collections of illustrated nonsense poems and comedy short stories, as well as several full length adventure novels, some straight, and others full of oddball, irascible characters. Two of these full length novels eventually found their way into published book form. In addition I've also written a pretty comprehensive manual on 'Voice Production for Singers'; something, which after my own experiences with some of the dodgy teachers I'd encountered along the way, I felt both 'compelled' and well qualified to write. And now, of course, there's this autobiography – which looks in danger of ending up longer than *The Encyclopaedia Britannica*.

A full list of all my writing is included at the end of the book.

As Christmas loomed this year we found ourselves threatened with a snowy whiteout. I'd already had to wallow through Snake Pass and over the snowbound Pennines on a couple of occasions to clubs in the Manchester and Wigan area. However, my trusty 16 Hundred E Cortina had good tyres and plenty of power so I'd always managed to make it OK.

For my Christmas Day venue this year I'd been booked to sing at the Potter's Club away down at Stoke-on-Trent, in the Potteries – the 'Black Country' as it was once named, due to the whole area being constantly shrouded under clouds of black smoke belching out from the hundreds of pottery kilns dotting the landscape everywhere. Although this Stoke trip meant a longer drive than simply crossing the Pennines, it was comparatively flat, so with no Snake Pass to negotiate it looked like being a bit easier.

As it turned out, however, my agent had also booked a young girl singer from the Doncaster area to share the bill with me, and he asked me if I'd take her and her husband down with me, as they didn't fancy driving through the snow themselves.

'Why not?' I thought. 'At least they'll be company for the trip.'

When I picked them up, though, I was somewhat surprised to see that the young girl singer has pretty heavily pregnant. My thoughts from that moment were not so much on getting to the venue in time, or on the snow we were sloshing through, but on the clock; were we going to make it there and back in time before a new addition to the human race put in its appearance. The fact that it was Christmas Day hadn't escaped my notice, and while it might have been all very well for Mary to give birth to Jesus in a stable on this day, the thought of the same thing happening in the back seat of my car on a dark, snowbound motorway was a bit more daunting.

However, in the event, fortunately it never happened, we got to the club on time, the girl sang beautifully (hopefully the baby could hear it), I managed my spots OK and the long sloshing journey back north through the snow passed off without any major incident. However, it came as quite a relief when I finally managed to drop them off at their door, and set off home to a warm, and a much needed, night's sleep wondering just how close a call it had been.

SOME MAJOR EVENTS OF THE YEAR:

(1) Martin Luther King assassinated at Memphis, Tennessee.
Senator Robert Kennedy shot at Los Angeles by Arab, Sirhan Sirhan.

(2) London Bridge sold to a US Oil Company for £2.4 million – re-erected over the Colorado River – apparently they thought they were buying Tower Bridge because they thought 'that' was London Bridge. However, they accepted their mistake in good grace, and the bridge became a big attraction over there.

(3) Films: *Oliver*, *Chitty Chitty Bang Bang*, and *The Charge of the Light Brigade* screened.

(4) The end of steam trains on British Railways.

(5) The two-tier postal service introduced.

(6) Britain's first heart transplant patient, Frederick West, survived for 46 days.

(7) Cambridge astronomers, led by Sir Martin Ryle, discover Pulsars.

(8) US Apollo 8 orbits the Moon with three astronauts aboard.

45

1969 (39 years old in July)
At some time early in this year I was asked if I'd like to enter the annual, 'Clubland Artist of the Year' contest, which this year was being held at the Ollerton Miners' Club in Nottinghamshire. For some reason I'd never thought of entering this contest before. However, as I'd now been specifically asked, and having sung at the Ollerton Miners' Club on a couple of occasions in the past, I decided to give it a try. At least it would be something different.

The 'Ollerton Miners', was a huge, modern club with good 'acoustics', which had always made it a pleasure to sing in, so in a way I was quite looking forward to it. And since there were to be quite a number of well known club acts taking part in the contest, we'd each only be required to do a fairly short spot – which suited me fine, as it would not only make for an easy night, but also give me a chance to listen to all of the other acts, some of whom I'd never come across before.

When the night arrived; being probably their biggest night of the year, it proved to be a really bustling, exciting affair. The big concert hall was absolutely packed to the doors, with not only their own members, but visitors from clubs for miles around. All in all, a great atmosphere to be involved in.

As my allocation amounted to only three songs, I decided to enjoy myself with three of my own favourites, ending with 'Nessun Dorma' – at that time always a show stopper. These all seemed to go down well, so having made my contribution I just sat down to enjoy the rest of what was a very good show. To my astonishment, when the judges came to deliver their verdict at the end, I could hardly believe it to hear my clubland name (Alan Morris) being pronounced as the winner. So there I was, having come along really as a matter of obligation, now holding the title of 'Clubland Artist of the Year'. Not only that, but with the added bonus of a cash prize that went along with it, which was quite a bit more than I'd have got for a normal performance.

Shortly after the Ollerton Miners' contest I was off to do one of my regular full weeks up in the Newcastle area, staying in my usual digs on the seafront at Sunderland, which were a regular refuge for visiting club artistes like myself. At this time Marti Caine and her husband were staying there too, which was great as I'd shared club concerts with her several times in the past and we'd always got on well together.

On this occasion it turned out that they were having trouble with their car, which was a large, somewhat rickety old Ford, and were desperately looking for something a bit more reliable. They took a real shine to my gleaming gold Ford 1600 E Cortina, and would like to have had something similar. Unfortunately, however, because they couldn't afford to buy a new car, this too would have to be secondhand. Not only that, but the dealer would also have to take their old banger in part exchange.

With their dodgy old Ford being so much on the sick list, I offered to run them around some of the Sunderland area car dealers to see if they could come up with something. Unfortunately, despite quite a wide ranging search, we couldn't find a single dealer anywhere prepared to accept their worn out old Ford at any price. So all they could do was get their somewhat 'less' than pride and joy bodged-up enough to rattle through the rest of Marti's club bookings as best they could. . . What a contrast to her TV stardom yet to come.

After this, my club work continued on as busily as ever, and even though it was not exactly what I'd set out to do, it was still enjoyable to be singing to very appreciative audiences, and it 'was', after all, giving Babs and I a very good living.

Later on, however, I did keep in touch with the operatic scene, by singing leading operatic roles for an amateur operatic society down in West Sussex. This was the Bel Canto Operatic Company in Crawley, whose performances were of a very high standard, and often had professional principals from London singing their leading roles. The way 'I' became involved with them was simply through my brother Colin. He'd lived in London with me during my singing study days before moving down to settle in that area, and with him being almost as keen an opera lover as I was, he'd become a member of the Bel Canto Company. This led eventually to them asking me if I'd sing some leading tenor roles for them; which of course I said I would. These roles were, 'Fenton' in Nicolai's opera *The Merry Wives of*

Windsor, and the title role in Gounod's *Faust*. Both of these were performed at the beautiful, modern 'Hawth Theatre' in Crawley.

As it turned out, being asked to sing the *Faust* role was oddly significant, because it dawned on me afterwards just how much of a coincidence *Faust* had been in my singing career. It had been the very first opera performance I'd ever seen; in Shrewsbury when I was doing my Army National Service. It was also the first opera I'd ever been involved in; when I agreed to help out as chorus/come Faust understudy while studying singing in London; and, as it happened, was now to end up as the 'last' operatic leading role I ever sang.

I did, however, continue singing, and sang in several operatic concerts with the Bel Canto, which gave me my last, enjoyable trips to the other side of the fence, plus many charity concerts at retirement homes, weddings and funerals. In fact, at one time I was being asked to sing at so many funerals that I began to think I'd soon be the only one left on the planet.

Although my voice is still in good shape, any singing I do now is purely for pleasure, with most of my creative activity now being directed towards my writing. This includes many children's illustrated stories, full length adventure novels, etc.

I have included the following verse here, because I feel it illustrates perfectly the basic ingredients I aim for when writing my stories for children. Namely, mystery, excitement, and adventure:

I actually wrote this piece of verse when I wanted to include the Scottish melody, 'Dark Island', in a selection of songs and arias I was recording to CD. Being unable to find any lyrics for it, however, my only solution was to write some myself, which I did. So in a way this piece of verse inadvertently brought my two creative ambitions, namely singing and writing, together.

DARK ISLAND
(Scottish melody)
Lyrics by **Alan Workman**

Dark was the Island, and wild was the sea.
When in days of my childhood
I roamed there so free.

O'er black rocks and green heather
all sparkling with dew,
down the deep water valleys
with streams rushing through.

I still see them as clear as in those days gone by.
The hills and bare mountains
reaching up for the sky.

The dark mystic forest, we'd wander inside.
Where Giants, and Fairies,
and Goblins may hide.

The wind-whispered voices, we'd hear from below,
As we scrambled the screes
to the ledges of snow.

What were the words saying? We never could find.
But I still hear them now
at the edge of my mind.

Oh! Dark was the Island, and wild was the sea,
When in days of my childhood
I roamed there so free.

I must wander again through its magical air,
To hear those far voices,
and learn, if I dare.

Are those Giants, and Fairies,
And Goblins still there?

'Why have I written my biography?'

Firstly, because being an instinctive writer for as long as I can remember, as well as a singer, getting my own life story down on paper was simply a natural extension of the life I have followed.

Secondly, I've written it in the hope that it may give others the encouragement to develop their own natural talents, whatever these may be, and whatever social or educational backgrounds they come from, just as I have.

To reiterate my motto from the beginning of the book:
Your birthright is *YOU!*
Your creativity, *your* intelligence,
your energy are *YOU!*
What you *make* of that birthright
is entirely up to *YOU!*

368

A FULL LIST OF ALL
ALAN WORKMAN'S WRITING

Children's Stories

(1) *I'LL SEE YOU IN SOMEWHERE* (A full-length fantasy/comedy adventure. 42,000 words.)

(2) *THE ADVENTURES OF TAGBAD & GUMBLE* (Eight comedy short stories. Fully illustrated. 36,000 words.)

(3) *TAGBAD & GUMBLE, AND THE GREAT DR DRACON MYSTERY* (Full length mystery/comedy adventure about these two – A follow on from their short stories. 67,000 words.).

(4) *WALLACE WINKLE'S JOURNEY* (A fantasy/comedy adventure story. Fully illustrated. 16,500 words.) Published.

(5) *THE QUEST OF RAHL* (A full-length science/fantasy adventure. 52,000 words.)

(6) *THE FLIGHT OF THE WINDBAG* (A full-length fantasy/comedy adventure. 36,000 words.)

(7) *THE FIRESTONES OF GAVA* (A full-length fantasy adventure 42,000 words,) Published.

(8) *POTTY PEOPLE* (19 fully illustrated comedy/nonsense poems. 30 pages.)

(9) *THE POTHERBS* (Six comedy/adventure stories Average length 3,300 words.)

(10) *HAGGIS & HAGGERTY* (Comedy/fantasy adventure story (illustrated). 14,000 words.)

(11) *THE LORBS OF OCCUL FOREST* (Fantasy, mystery story. 55,000 words.)

Other Work

„(12) *THE SINGER'S MANUAL OF NATURAL VOICE PRODUCTION* (An instructional course based on many years of experience as a professional opera singer. 26,000 words). I have CD samples as proof of my credentials for writing this course.

(13) *SINGING MY WAY TO SOMEWHERE LAND* (From Shipyard Apprentice to Opera Singer)